An approach to political philosophy: Locke in contexts brings together Professor Tully's most important and innovative statements on Locke in a treatment of the latter's thought that is at once contextual and critical. The essays have been rewritten and expanded for this volume, and each seeks to understand a theme of Locke's political philosophy by interpreting it in light of the complex contexts of early modern European political thought and practice. These historical studies are then used in a variety of ways to gain critical perspectives on the assumptions underlying current debates in political philosophy and the history of political thought. The themes treated include government, toleration, discipline, property, aboriginal rights, individualism, power, labour, self-ownership, community, progress, liberty, participation, and revolution.

JAMES TULLY is Professor of Philosophy and Political Science at McGill University. His many publications on political philosophy and the history of ideas include *A discourse on property: John Locke and his adversaries* (Cambridge, 1980) and, as editor, *Meaning and context: Quentin Skinner and his critics* (Polity, 1988) and Pufendorf, *On the duty of man and citizen* (Cambridge, 1991).

IDEAS IN CONTEXT

AN APPROACH TO POLITICAL PHILOSOPHY: LOCKE IN CONTEXTS

IDEAS IN CONTEXT

Edited by Quentin Skinner (General Editor), Lorraine Daston, Richard Rorty, J.B. Schneewind and Wolf Lepenies

The books in this series will discuss the emergence of intellectual traditions and of related new disciplines. The procedures, aims and vocabularies that were generated will be set in the context of the alternatives available within the contemporary frameworks of ideas and institutions. Through detailed studies of the evolution of such traditions, and their modification by different audiences, it is hoped that a new picture will form of the development of ideas in their concrete contexts. By this means, artificial distinctions between the history of philosophy, of the various sciences, of society and politics, and of literature, may be seen to dissolve.

For a list of titles in this series, please see end of book.

Ideas in Context is published with the support of the Exxon Education Foundation.

AN APPROACH TO POLITICAL PHILOSOPHY: LOCKE IN CONTEXTS

JAMES TULLY

Professor of Philosophy and Political Science
McGill University

CAMBRIDGE
UNIVERSITY PRESS

Published by the Press Syndicate of the University of Cambridge
The Pitt Building, Trumpington Street, Cambridge CB2 1RP
40 West 20th Street, New York, NY 10011-4211, USA
10 Stamford Road, Oakleigh, Victoria 3166, Australia

First published 1993

Printed in Great Britain at the University Press, Cambridge

A catalogue record for this book is available from the British Library

Library of Congress cataloguing in publication data
Tully, James, 1946–
An approach to political philosophy. Locke in contexts / James Tully.
p.   cm. – (Ideas in context)
Includes bibliographical references and index.
ISBN 0 521 43060 7 – ISBN 0 521 43638 9 (pbk.)
1. Locke, John, 1932–1704 – Contributions in political science.
I. Title.   II. Series
JC 153.L87T837 1993
320′.01 – dc20   92-16688   CIP

ISBN 0 521 430607 hardback
ISBN 0 521 43638 9 paperback

VN

for Richard

Contents

ix

Contents

Acknowledgements

The essays in this collection were written between 1979 and 1990. They have been rewritten and expanded for the purposes of this collection.

I am indebted to invaluable discussions with many colleagues and students, including Richard Ashcraft, Peta Bowden, Natalie Brender, James Burns, Monique Deveaux, John Dunn, Mark Goldie, Ed Hundert, Guy Laforest, Michael Morgan, David Norton, John Pocock, Darius Rejali, Gopal Sreenivasan, Charles Taylor, Bruce Trigger, Yasuo Tsuji, Richard Tuck, Brian Walker and Daniel Weinstock. I would also like to thank Quentin Skinner, as editor and critical reader, Richard Fisher and Jeremy Mynott of Cambridge University Press for their unfailing support and encouragement, and the anonymous reviewer for her or his helpful comments. Adam Jones has my gratitude for flawless word processing and checking the manuscript, as does McGill University for financial assistance and a superb intellectual setting.

I am grateful to the editors and publishers for permission to reprint the following chapters:

Chapter 1, parts I and II were first printed in *The Cambridge history of political thought: 1450–1700*, ed. James Burns with the assistance of Mark Goldie, Cambridge University Press, 1990.

Chapter 2 was first presented to the conference on The intellectual legacy of C. B. Macpherson, University of Toronto, 27–28 October 1989, and printed in Joseph H. Carens, ed., *Democracy and possessive individualism: the intellectual legacy of C. B. Macpherson*, State University of New York, Stony Brook, 1992.

Chapter 3 was first printed in *Theories of property: Aristotle to the present*, ed. Anthony Parel and Thomas Flanagan, The Calgary Institute for the Humanities, Wilfrid Laurier University Press, 1979.

Chapter 4, part I was first printed in *The Locke newsletter* 13 (1982) and part II in *Annals of Scholarship* 7, 3 (1990).

Chapter 5, parts I–II were first presented to the Conference on the tercentenary of the publication of the *Two treatises* and *An essay concerning human understanding*, Christ Church, Oxford University, 5–7 September 1990.

Chapter 6 was first printed in *Conscience and casuistry in early modern Europe*, E. Leites, Cambridge University Press, 1988.

Chapter 7 was first printed in *Annals of scholarship* 5, 3, 1988.

Chapter 8 was first presented to the symposium on Progress, the Royal Society of Canada, Université Laval, Québec, 1–3 June 1989, and printed in *Transactions of the Royal Society of Canada*, 1989.

Chapter 9, part I was first printed in *Conceptions of liberty in political philosophy*, ed. John Gray and Z. A. Pelczynski, Athlone Press, London, 1984, and part II in *The Garland encyclopedia of ethics*, ed. Lawrence Becker, Garland Press, New York, 1992.

Chapter 10 was first presented at the Symposium on John Locke: 300 years after, American Philosophical Association annual meeting, Boston, 28–30 December 1990, and printed in *The Journal of philosophy* 87, 10, 1990.

Introduction

The work of the philosopher consists in assembling reminders for
a particular purpose.[1]

I have sought to develop an approach to political philosophy that
throws light on the problems of the present age through contextual
studies of the history of modern political thought. I have drawn
inspiration from Wittgenstein, Sir Isaiah Berlin, the Cambridge
school of John Dunn, John Pocock, Quentin Skinner, and Richard
Tuck, Michel Foucault's histories of the present, and the work of
Charles Taylor. My approach is thus a contribution to the broad and
pluralistic movement to re-examine the relationships between political philosophy and its history that these authors and others set in
motion in the post-war era. It is therefore an honour to have these
essays published in the *Ideas in context* series, which exemplifies this
European and American movement and whose first publication,
Philsophy in history (1984), is one of the best statements of its main
themes.

All the essays are concerned first with understanding the political
philosophy of John Locke in a historically sensitive manner by
interpreting his writings in light of the discursive and practical
contexts in which they were written, published and read. The
appropriate contexts are various and overlapping, for authors such as
Locke and his adversaries were doing many things in writing a text,
and so it is necessary to approach the same text from many different
contexts to understand it. They range from specific debates and
events in England to European political movements and intellectual
traditions. By this somewhat meticulous underlabouring I hope to

[1] Ludwig Wittgenstein, *Philosophical investigations*, tr. G. E. M. Anscombe (Oxford: Basil
Blackwell, 1988), section 127.

I

furnish a better understanding of the complexity of both Locke's
political thought and its place in early modern political thought.
Second, I seek to bring out the critical significance or interest of the
interpretation for a late twentieth century reader. Critical significance too is various: questioning a conventional interpretation or
offering an interpretation of a disputed stretch of text, comparing
Locke's arguments to his contemporaries to show his conventionality
or originality, tracing the roles of his arguments in the formation of
the labyrinth of modern political thought, drawing either a contrast
or a comparison to a conventional assumption of later or current
political philosophy in order to call it into question, and so on – a
variety of exercises in placing specific aspects of the present in a
different, less familiar and more critical light. I have tried to meet the
criteria of historians of political thought and political philosophers,
and to show by example that both disciplines can be enriched by an
approach that combines the two.[2]

   Locke's political philosophy is particularly suitable for this type of
study, as John Dunn's pioneering work demonstrates, because it
addresses many of the central themes of seventeenth century political
reflection and it plays a multiplicity of roles in later political thought
in Europe and North America, especially in twentieth century
varieties of liberalism. A reinterpretation of Locke is thus not only a
reinterpretation of one strand of liberalism but also of the ways many
liberals and their critics understand the formation of modernity and
postmodernity, both of which are standardly defined in relation to
interpretations of Locke's philosophy. John Dunn, Michel Foucault,
John Pocock, Quentin Skinner, and Charles Taylor, for example,
have challenged the conventional understanding of Locke and
liberalism and, in so doing, altered our views of modernity. Thus, to
take up these penetrating challenges and investigate Locke's philosophy critically in the context of the current debates, often as a way of
testing the interpretations that set the terms of the debates, is to
contribute to a better understanding of Locke and the varieties of
liberalism, and, in so doing, of one aspect of our tangled identities as
moderns.

---

[2] See James Tully, 'Wittgenstein and political philosophy', *Political theory* 17, 2 (May 1989),
172–204, and the methodological writings of Quentin Skinner, to which I am greatly
indebted, in *Meaning and context: Quentin Skinner and his critics*, ed. James Tully (Cambridge:
Polity Press, 1988).

The essays, written over the last decade, have been rewritten and arranged thematically. Chapter 1 provides an overview of Locke's political philosophy, aspects of which are then taken up in more detail in the following chapters. At the centre of the *Two treaties of government* is – not surprisingly but often overlooked – a philosophy of *government*. The relation of governance between governors and free citizens is conceptualized, not as sovereign and subjects, as in the absolutist traditions, but rather as a game of conditional and mutual subjection in which each governs the other by subjecting the other to the rule of law. In the final chapter I suggest that this agonistic picture of government is his most distinctive and enduring contribution to modern political thought. Elsewhere I have argued that Locke and republican writers are closer, but not identical, in their views in this regard, and in their common opposition to the passive subjection characteristic of absolutism, than the conventional distinction be-tween juristic and civic humanist traditions leads one to believe.[3] Written, rewritten and published in the context of the struggles in England in the 1680s, the *Two treatises* is also seen by Locke to address a European-wide set of problems and to draw upon European political theories.

The development of Locke's defence of religious toleration and pluralism in *A letter concerning toleration* is the subject of the second section of chapter 1. It is an integral part of his political philosophy and light can be thrown on contentious aspects of the *Two treatises* by reading the two together. For instance, the specific groups of people in England (and France) who Locke believed had their rights and property violated, and so had the right to resist, were not capitalist landowners but oppressed religious minorities. A survey of Locke's historically important views on the arts of government, or applied political economy, rounds off the chapter.

The following four chapters deal with various features of Locke's theory of property. Chapter 2 surveys scholarship on property in the seventeenth and eighteenth centuries since the publication of C. B. Macpherson's *The political theory of possessive individualism* (1962) and reassesses this classic study in light of recent scholarship and the

---

[3] James Tully, 'Placing the *Two treatises*', in *Political discourse in early modern Britain: Essays in honour of John Pocock*, ed. Nicholas Philipson and Quentin Skinner (Cambridge: Cambridge University Press, 1993).

political problems of the late twentieth century that have given rise to it. This scholarship suggests that the theoretical development of concepts of rights-bearing individuals and the uses to which these concepts were put in political struggles from Grotius to Wollstone-craft were more multifaceted, and more widely challenged by alternative conceptions of agency, than Macpherson assumed. Chapter 3, the oldest in the collection, lays out the natural rights to the means of preservation that provide the frequently ignored framework of Locke's theory of property, thereby summarizing one of the themes of my book *A discourse on property: John Locke and his adversaries* (1980). I discuss a number of constructive criticisms of *A discourse on property* in chapter 4 and point out where I have corrected my original arguments and where they can be defended. Two recent studies, while disagreeing in some details, have independently substantiated the main lines of my interpretation, especially the importance of the right to the means of preservation and the role of the workmanship model: Richard Ashcraft, *Locke's Two treatises of government* (1987), and Gopal Sreenivasan, *The Lockean limits to private property* (forthcoming).

Chapter 5 illustrates the methodological point of how a change in context can alter and enhance one's understanding of the layers of meaning and significance of a text. I discuss the roles Locke's theory of property played in the justification of English settlement in America and the dispossession of the Amerindian First Nations of their property and sovereignty. This context not only clarifies a number of contentious passages in chapter 5 of the *Two treatises*; it also shows how some of the premises of Locke's argument functioned, and continue to function uncritically in theories and legal arguments that follow from Locke, to legitimate this monumental injustice.

Chapters 6 to 8 investigate aspects of Locke's influential views on the malleability of human thought and behaviour, the extent to which they are shaped by custom, education and practice, and the implications of these views for moral and political reform. Chapter 6, written in response to Michel Foucault's *Discipline and punish* (1977), is an attempt to place Locke's philosophical views on and practical proposals for the reform of human thought and behaviour in a broad European context. In his response to this essay John Dunn points out that there is an unresolved tension between the malleable conception of human agency in Locke's works that I discuss in this chapter and the conception of the human agent as having rights over his or her body, action and beliefs in the *Two treatises* and *A letter concerning toleration*, somewhat akin to Foucault's distinction between disciplinary and juridical systems of power, knowledge and subjectivity.[4] For it does not follow from the premise that humans are tractable that governments have a right to mould them as they please or that they will not rightfully resist. Indeed, Locke's philosophy of government is based on the two opposite assumptions. Furthermore, in the Introduction to John Locke, *A letter concerning toleration* (1983), I argue that the theory and practice of rights deriving from Locke has functioned as one of the most powerful bulwarks against the manipulation of humans by governments and other institutions in the modern world.

Chapter 7 takes up this tension in the course of a survey of ways in which a right in one's ability to labour has been conceptualized over the last 300 years. My main concern is to broaden the horizons of the current debate over self-ownership (of one's abilities) by recollecting the diversity of ways in which rights in abilities have been conceptualized and of the conceptions of agency and work relations that are implied by each. The survey shows that the conception of a rights-bearing subject in the *Two treatises* places limits on the way in which a government or, later, a capitalist, ought to treat citizens or workers. This tension, then, seems to be a permanent feature of liberalism and capitalism, held in counterpoise by the continual exercise of rights against abuses of power. Chapter 8, written to mark the two-hundredth anniversary of the French Revolution, places Locke's conception of reform, and the cognate concept of progress, in the broader perspective of views of progress, reform and scepticism from the seventeenth century to the present.

Locke's writings on liberty are analysed in the last two chapters. Section I of chapter 9 presents my first interpretation of Locke on political liberty, which I wrote from the perspective of the *Two treatises*. The main objective is to explicate his natural law based concept of political liberty relative to other early modern political traditions and to current conceptions of freedom. As I worked on chapter 6 I came to see that Locke altered his views on natural law and moral liberty throughout his moral, psychological, and theological writings. The second section is an attempt to present a synopsis of these views. Chapter 10 was written for the three-hundredth

---

[4] John Dunn, 'Bright enough for all our purposes: John Locke's conception of a civilised society', *Notes and records of the Royal Society of London* 43 (1989), 133–53.

anniversary of the publication of the *Two treatises* and in the wake of the revolutions in Eastern Europe. Here I argue that Locke's vision of the political freedom of citizens in relation to their government, introduced in chapter 1, is superior in a number of respects to many of its seventeenth century and current rivals.

One theme that runs through the collection is a critical attitude to Locke and liberalism. Liberals tend not to take history or their critics seriously enough and critics tend to reject the whole liberal tradition, or a historically unrecognizable caricature of it, on the basis of one criticism. There is, however, a third way. It is possible to use historical studies of the formation of modern political thought to gain a deeper understanding of, and critical perspectives on, the problems raised by both liberals and their critics. These essays are a tribute to this critical attitude and the many scholars who contribute to it, including Sir Isaiah Berlin, who opened up and demonstrated the potential of this way of relecting on the present, and especially John Dunn, John Pocock, Quentin Skinner, and Charles Taylor, whose works are exemplars.

A philosophy of limited government

CHAPTER I

An introduction to Locke's political philosophy

The political thought of John Locke (1632–1704) consists in work on and solutions to four problems that every major European political thinker faced in the seventeenth century. These are: the theoretical nature of government and political power, the relation of religion to politics, the practical art of governing, and the types of knowledge involved in religion and in political theory and practice. I discuss the first three problems in this chapter and the fourth in chapter 6. Of course his political thought and activity were provoked by and contributed to specific conflicts in England.[1] However, neither these events nor the ways of thinking about them were unique to England. Like Locke, Grotius and Pufendorf experienced civil war, religious dissension and exile; Spinoza and Bayle suffered religious persecution; Colbert and deWitt invigilated mercantile systems; and they all shared a body of political concepts. Both the political, religious, and economic difficulties and the way in which these were thought to render political practice problematic were European-wide phenomena.

The difficulties that occasioned the four problems of government were of four kinds: the religious and civil wars of the sixteenth and seventeenth centuries; the administrative–productive consolidation of modern European states as effective governing units; the formation of a balance of power and trade system of military–commercial rivalry among states; and the European imperial struggle over the conquest, domination and exploitation of non-European populations

---

[1] See Julian Franklin, *John Locke and the theory of sovereignty* (Cambridge: Cambridge University Press, 1978); Mark Goldie, 'The roots of true whiggism: 1688–1694', *History of Political Thought* I, 2 (1980), 195–236, and 'The revolution of 1689 and the structure of political argument', *Bulletin of Research in the Humanities* 83 (1980), 473–564; Richard Ashcraft, *Revolutionary politics and Locke's Two treatises of government* (Princeton: Princeton University Press, 1986), and *Locke's Two treatises of government* (London: Unwin Hyman, 1987).

and resources. These difficulties helped to sustain, and were partly sustained by, a general epistemological or 'legitimation' crisis which involved sceptical attacks on traditional bodies of knowledge and attempts to reconstruct the foundations of religious, political, and scientific knowledge, from Montaigne and Descartes to Leibniz and Locke. Political thinkers adapted and radically transformed conceptual tools that had been fashioned over the previous 500 years to characterize these difficulties as problems and to advance solutions to them.[2]

Locke's political thought is one of the most important responses to this European predicament. He worked over the traditions of the earlier period and the innovations of the seventeenth century to construct solutions to the immediate problems; and these in turn, to a remarkable extent, became foundational for the Enlightenment. It is the work, to be sure, of a political actor deeply engaged in local struggles and of a political theorist thinking within the available conceptual systems, and so must be studied in the light of both. However, insofar as it is Locke's own political thought, it is neither simply that which is embodied in action, and so condemned to speak only of it; nor is it that which only reproduces an ideology or repeats a tradition. On the contrary, it is what cannot be reduced to either: the activity of standing back to a degree from environing political practice and inherited ways of thinking, criticizing aspects of both, and working out distinctive resolutions.

GOVERNMENT AND POLITICAL POWER

The first problem is, what is government – its origin, extent and end? It is classically posed in the *Two treatises of government*, as the subtitle announces. Locke worked on this issue from the *Two tracts on government*, 1660–1661, to the *Two treatises*, 1681–89, moving from a solution of absolutism and unconditional obedience to one of king in parliament, popular sovereignty and the collective and individual right of resistance. The question is not about the nature of the state as a form of power over and above rulers and ruled, although he was familiar with this *raison d'état* way of conceptualizing early modern

---

[2] See Theodore Rabb, *The struggle for stability in early modern Europe* (Oxford: Oxford University Press, 1975).

politics and sought to undermine it (1.93, 2.163).[3] Rather, it is about 'government' in the seventeenth century sense of the problematic and unstable relations of power and subjection between governors and governed.

According to the first three introductory sections of the *Second treatise*, the problem of government is taken to be a problem about political power. This is not so much a question of what political power is; section three succinctly summarizes the early modern consensus on this (see below). Rather, government is composed of three relations of power: federative (international relations), executive, and legislative (including the judiciary) (2.143–8). The controversy is over the origin, extent and limits of these forms of power and how they differ from other relations of governance: of husbands over wives and fathers over children (domestic power), of masters over servants (economic power), of masters over slaves (despotic power), and of commanders over soldiers (military power) (2.2). All the classic texts of the seventeenth century analyse political power in this relational way, none more systematically than Samuel Pufendorf's *The law of nature and nations* (1668), which Locke recommends as the best of its kind.[4] Thus, the foremost problem of politics is, Locke reflects late in life, 'the original of societies and the rise and extent of political power'.[5]

What, in turn, rendered political power problematic? For Locke, as for his contemporaries, the religious and civil wars that accompanied the consolidation and formation of early modern states as exclusive, or at least hegemonic, ensembles of domination were struggles for political power.[6] This crisis in both the ability to govern and in the way of governing threw into question the nature and location of political power. The theoretical question around which the whole seventeenth-century debate revolves is thus the question of 'sovereignty', or, as Locke more crisply puts it, 'who should have it' (political power)? The great conflicts in practice, in the age of

[3] John Locke, *Two treatises of government*, ed. Peter Laslett (Cambridge: Cambridge University Press, 1970). The numbers in brackets refer to the treatise (first or second), section, and, where necessary, lines within the section. For example, (2.25.1–5) is *Second treatise*, section 25, lines 1–5, and (2.25–8) is *Second treatise*, sections 25 to 28.
[4] Locke, *Some thoughts concerning reading and study for a gentleman*, 1703, in *The educational writings of John Locke*, ed. James Axtell (Cambridge: Cambridge University Press, 1968), 397–404, 400.
[5] Locke, *Some thoughts*, 400.
[6] See Richard Dunn, *The age of religious wars 1559–1715* (New York: W. W. Norton, 1979).

'agrarian and urban rebellions' and of 'revolutionary civil wars',[7] were over this very problem of political power that was contested in political theory (1.106):

the great Question which in all Ages has disturbed Mankind, and brought on them the greatest part of those Mischiefs which have ruin'd cities, depopulated Countries, and disordered the Peace of the World, has been, Not whether there be Power in the World, nor whence it came, but who should have it.

Unless both the historico-causal question of which arrangements of political power do and which do not dissolve into civil wars, and the moral–jurisprudential question of who has and who has not the 'right' to political power can be answered satisfactorily, Locke continues, Europe will remain in 'endless contention and disorder'. The *Two treatises* is an answer to both these questions and it is the most radical answer that had yet been given: each individual does have and should have political power.

This European problem of continual conflicts over political power was also, of course, the overriding issue of English political thought and action from 1640 to 1690.[8] During the planning for an insurrection in 1681–3 Locke wrote the *Two treatises* as a populist resolution of the problem: for the people to reappropriate their political power through a revolution and to 'continue the Legislative in themselves or erect a new Form, or under the old form place it in new hands, as they think good' (2.243). In 1689 he published an expanded version of the *Two treatises* to recommend that King William could 'make good his title' to power only if it were grounded 'in the consent of the People', thus acknowledging their sovereignty, by means of a constitutional convention.[9] However, because it is written in the juridical language of European political discourse and addressed to a problem common to European politics, the *Two treatises* is a contribution to both the English conflict and the European crisis. In addition to difficulties of power which were

[7] See Perez Zagorin, *Rebels and rulers 1500–1600*, 2 vols (Cambridge: Cambridge University Press, 1982).

[8] See Caroline Weston and J. R. Greenberg, *Subjects and sovereigns: the grand controversy over legal sovereignty in Stuart England* (Cambridge: Cambridge University Press, 1981); and Franklin, *John Locke*.

[9] *Two treatises*, Preface, line 6, p. 155. He recommends a constitutional convention in a letter to Edward Clark, 29 January/8 February, *The correspondence of John Locke*, ed. E. S. de Beer (Oxford: Clarendon Press, 1978), 8 vols, III, 1102 (p. 545).

similar to other European states, even the English conflict itself was part of the wider European context. A major aim of the 1681–3 agitations, as Locke saw it, was to stop England from becoming aligned with and subordinate to France. William of Orange conquered England in 1688 in order to draw it into a European war against France, the Nine Years' War, and the *Two treatises* grants him 'federative' or war-fighting power, unchecked by Parliament (2.147). Indeed, this war is Locke's main concern in 1689.[10]

The form of problematization in which this issue was posed and diverse solutions advanced is the 'juridical' representation of politics. This is neither an ideology nor a tradition but a historically constructed complex of juridic *practices*: that is, ways of thinking and writing about politics and ways of acting politically (of governing, being governed, and contesting government) that have been assembled in Europe since the twelfth century. These legal and political practices developed around the extension of both the concepts and rule of law. The practices of governing conduct by universal rights and duties, law and sovereignty (as opposed to, say, prejuridical trial by battle, feudal particularity, or later governance by economic compulsion and non-juridic discipline) had become so central by the seventeenth century that Locke could write that moral, political, theological, and legal thought and action rest on the indubitable assumption (and practice) that man is an animal *'subject to law'*.[11] Locke and his contemporaries were of course aware that the juridicalization of European political thought and action was a more or less continuous process from the formation of legal institutions and bodies of knowledge in the eleventh and twelfth centuries.[12] Nonetheless, the specific context in which Locke explicitly places the *Two treatises* is the practical contests and theoretical debates over political power of his generation and of the previous sixty years.[13] This context thus comprises the struggles between King, Parliament and people in England (1640–90) and the theoretical discussion from the publica-

---

[10] Bodleian, MS Locke e. 18, fos 1–4, printed in James Farr and C. Roberts, 'John Locke and the Glorious Revolution: a rediscovered document', *The Historical Journal* 28, 2 (1985), 385–98.

[11] John Locke, *An essay concerning human understanding*, ed. Peter Nidditch (Oxford: Oxford University Press, 1976), 3.11.16.

[12] See Harold Berman, *Law and revolution: The formation of the Western legal tradition* (Cambridge, MA: Harvard University Press, 1983).   [13] Locke, *Some thoughts*, 400.

tion of Hugo Grotius' *The laws of war and peace* (1625) to the *Two treatises* (1690).[14]

Locke's solution to the problem of government and political power comprises five steps: i. the definition of political power, ii. the origin of political power, iii. the rule of right in accordance with which it is exercised, iv. the conditional entrusting of political power to government by the consent of the people, and v. the way the three parts of political power are exercised by government and limited by law and revolution. These five features make up a classic theory of individual popular sovereignty, succinctly summarized in section 171 of chapter 15. Each one, except the first, is unique to Locke in certain specific respects. I would like to survey these features in a way that brings out both what is conventional and what is distinctively Locke's own thought, as well as the practical and theoretical difficulties that provoked his innovations. Accordingly, I attempt to do this by comparing the similarities and dissimilarities of his five steps to the tangled and contested conventional steps of the European juridical discourse in which he wrote, concentrating primarily on the 60 year context.

i

Political power is defined as a tripartite right: to make laws both to preserve and to regulate the lives, activities and possessions of subjects (legislative power); to use the force of the community to execute these laws with penalties of death and lesser penalties (executive power); and to wage wars to preserve the community, including colonies and subjects abroad, against other states (federative power). The end of political power is the 'public good' (2.3, 2.131, 2.135, 2.171). This potent idea of the powers of government is closely tied to the actual claims and practices of the early modern mercantile states, with which Locke, as member of the Board of Trade, was professionally

---

[14] Hugo Grotius, *On the laws of war and peace* (1625), ed. J. Barbeyrac (London: 1738). For the importance of Grotius in setting out a common set of concepts see Richard Tuck, *Natural rights theories: their origin and development* (Cambridge: Cambridge University Press, 1979), 58–173, and 'The "modern" theory of natural law', in *The languages of political theory in early modern Europe*, ed. Anthony Pagden (Cambridge: Cambridge University Press, 1987), 99–122.

familiar. It would have been seen as a commonplace by his contemporaries.[15]

ii

Second, to determine who should have political power, Locke, like other juridic theorists, reduces it to an 'original' or 'natural' form of power from which the present tripartite power, and the author's preferred location, extent, and limit, can be historically and logically derived and justified.[16] The objective of this second step is to answer the question, who naturally or originally possesses political power? Locke's answer is that political power is a natural property of individuals. That is, 'the *Execution* of the Law of Nature is in that State [of nature], put into every man's hands, whereby every one has a right to punish the transgressors of that Law to such a degree, as may hinder its Violation' (2.7, *cf*: 2.8). It follows from this premise of political individualism that people are naturally self-governing, because they are capable of exercising political power themselves; naturally free, because they are not naturally subject to the will of another; and, third, naturally equal, because they equally possess and have the duty and right to exercise political power.[17] Therefore, prior to and independent of the establishment of institutionalized forms of government, people are able to govern themselves; and, second, the power of institutionalized forms of government is derived from the original powers of the individual members of the political society (2.87–9, 2.127–131, 2.171).

Locke says, 'I doubt not but this will seem a very strange Doctrine to some Men' (2.9, *cf*: 2.13). His premise of political individualism *is* strange: it is one of the major conceptual innovations in early modern political thought. To see this let us contrast it with the two

---

[15] See Lawrence Harper, *The English navigation laws: a seventeenth-century experiment in social engineering* (New York: Columbia University Press, 1939), 9–18; Charles H. Wilson, *England's apprenticeship 1603–1763* (London: Longmans, Green and Co., 1965), 236: Samuel Pufendorf, *On the law of nature and nations* (1672), ed. Jean Barbeyrac, tr. Basil Kennett (London, 1729), 7.4.1–7 and notes.

[16] For the development of this juridic way of thinking see Berman, *Law and revolution*, 271–95: Quentin Skinner, *The foundations of modern political thought* (Cambridge: Cambridge University Press, 1978), 2 vols, II, 113–88; Brian Tierney, *Religion, law and the growth of political thought* (Cambridge: Cambridge University Press, 1982).

[17] *Two treatises* 2.4, 2.7. *cf*: 2.5–6, 2.8–15, 2.22, 2.87, 2.90–1, 2.123, 2.171.

conventional ways of conceptualizing the origin of political power available to him and with reference to which Locke situates the *Two treatises*: the traditions of 'natural subjection' and 'natural freedom'.

The *Two treatises* is written in response to the defence of natural subjection and refutation of natural freedom put forward by Sir Robert Filmer (1588–1653) in his *Patriarcha* and other political writings, written between 1628 and 1652 to justify unconditional obedience to absolute monarchy.[18] These were republished in 1680 to justify obedience to the Stuart monarchy during the unsuccessful attempt to exclude the future James II from ascending to the throne. The popularity of Filmer's arguments in justifying absolutism and non-resistance can be judged by the fact that the two classic theories of revolution to come out of this period – Algernon Sidney's *Discourses concerning government* and Locke's *Two treatises* – both contain a refutation of Filmer.[19] In addition, the moderate whig theory of James Tyrrell, *Patriarcha non monarcha*, which was probably written in collaboration with Locke, also is an attack on Filmer's writings.[20] In 1684 Edmund Bohun published a defence of Filmer and a year later he brought out a new edition of Filmer's works.[21]

The thesis of natural subjection is that political power resides naturally and originally in the monarch to whom lesser political bodies and all citizens are naturally subject. Since this relation of subjection is unlimited and natural no resistance to it is justified. In Filmer's type of natural subjection, the political relation is patriarchal: the political power that monarchs naturally exercise over their subjects is identical to the unlimited and arbitrary power patriarchs exercise naturally over their wives, children, slaves, and private property.[22] This kind of patriarchal or 'Adamite' natural subjection theory of non-resistance had always been popular among

---

[18] See Robert Filmer, *Patriarcha and other political writings*, ed. Peter Laslett (Oxford: Basil Blackwell, 1949). For the relation of Locke to Filmer, see Peter Laslett, 'Introduction', Locke, *Two treatises*, 67–78; Gordon Schochet, *Patriarchalism in political thought* (Oxford: Basil Blackwell, 1974); James Daly, *Sir Robert Filmer and English political thought* (Toronto: University of Toronto Press, 1979).

[19] Algernon Sidney, *Discourses concerning government*, in *The works of Algernon Sidney* (London: 1772). For the relation of Locke to Sidney see Ashcraft, *Revolutionary politics*.

[20] James Tyrrell, *Patriarcha non-monarcha: the patriarch unmonarch'd* (London: 1681). For the relation of Locke to Tyrrell see J. W. Gough, 'James Tyrrell, whig historian and friend of John Locke', *The Historical Journal* 19, 3 (1976), 581–610; Ashcraft, *Revolutionary politics*.

[21] Edmund Bohun, *A defence of Sir Robert Filmer* (London: 1684). See Mark Goldie, 'Edmund Bohun and *jus gentium* in the revolution debate', *The Historical Journal* 20 (1977), 569–86.

[22] Filmer, *Patriarcha*, 57–63, 188; *Two treatises* 1.1, 1.9.

Protestant absolutists and among the Anglican clergy in the 1670s and 1680s.[23] It also had a widespread intuitive appeal in an age when familial relations were taken by most husbands to be patriarchal, absolute, and natural.[24] Locke attacked patriarchalism as early as 1669.[25] The two other prevailing types of natural subjection theories are divine right and *de facto* theories.[26] In all natural subjection theories the people neither possess nor exercise, nor consent to the exercise of political power.

In opposition to natural subjection is the larger and more complex tradition of natural freedom. This tradition includes all theories which posit that the people are naturally free in the sense of not being subject to the will of another. It follows that political subjection must be based on some kind of convention: consent, contract, trust, or agreement. Locke places the *Two treatises* in this tradition (1.3–6, 1.15, 2.4, 2.95). In setting out to attack this whole tradition Filmer characterizes it as consisting in the following propositions:

Mankind is naturally endowed with freedom from all subjection; Mankind is at liberty to choose what form of government it pleases; The power which any man has over another was at first by human right bestowed according to the discretion of the human multitude; Therefore, Kings are made subjects to the censures and deprivations of their subjects.

This account of political power, he argues, is 'the main foundation of popular sedition' because it supports the practical conclusion 'that the multitude have the power to punish or deprive the prince if he transgresses the laws of the kingdom'.[27] This whole tradition, according to Filmer, must be repudiated if the rebellions of the early modern period are to end.

Filmer is well aware that this is an old tradition with its roots in Roman Law and the renaissance of juridical political theory in the twelfth century. He is also aware that not only theories of limited government and the right to resist constituted authority had been built on its premises; the most prestigious theories of absolutism in the seventeenth century also came out of the natural freedom tradition: those of William Barclay, Hugo Grotius, Thomas

---

[23] *Two treatises*, preface, 50–1, 1.3, 2.112.   [24] See Schochet, *Patriarchalism*.
[25] Bodleian, MS. Locke c. 29, fos. 7–9, reprinted in Maurice Cranston, *John Locke: a biography* (London: Longmans, Green and Co., 1968), 131–3.
[26] Locke seeks to refute these at *Two treatises* 1.4–5, 2.175–96.
[27] Filmer, *Patriarcha*, 53–4, 68.

Hobbes,[28] and, after Filmer's death, Samuel Pufendorf, Richard Cumberland and the unpublished *Two tracts* of the young Locke.[29] Although the absolutist theories of natural freedom hold that the people completely alienate their natural freedom to the king, they always leave an exception where, in extraordinary circumstances, the people may withdraw their consent and defend themselves against a murderous tyrant.[30] This exception in even the most absolutist theories opens the way to justify resistance, as in fact Locke confirmed by using Barclay's absolutist theory in precisely this way (2.232-9). Accordingly, Filmer launched an attack on the whole tradition.[31] Many agreed with him, especially after the failed radical whig uprising and the Rye House Plot of 1681-3. The major tenets of natural freedom were condemned at Oxford and Locke's fellow revolutionary Algernon Sidney was executed for holding them.[32]

In writing the *Two treatises* Locke's task is not only to refute Filmer's natural subjection theory but also to rework the tradition of natural freedom in a form that both answers Filmer's criticisms and justifies constitutional government and revolution against the predominant natural freedom theories of absolutism. The first move Locke takes in refashioning the premises of natural freedom is, as we have seen, to place political power in the hands of individuals. Natural freedom theorists were willing to grant that individuals naturally have a right to defend themselves and their possessions from attack, even to kill the attacker if necessary. This right of defence of self and possessions, however, was never described as political power. Second, political power was said to come into being when the people agreed to establish institutionalized government. It is granted to the people by God or, according to Grotius, it 'immediately arises' at the moment of constitution of government.[33] Third, political power inheres in the

---

[28] Filmer, *Patriarcha*, 55, 73-4, 251-60, 279-313.

[29] For Locke's early absolutism see *Two tracts on government*, ed. Philip Abrams (Cambridge: Cambridge University Press, 1967).   [30] Filmer, *Patriarcha*, 54.

[31] Filmer was particularly prescient in seeing that Grotius' mitigated absolutism could be exploited to justify resistance to monarchs. It was used in this way in England from 1640 to 1690. See Filmer, *Patriarcha*, 66-73, 268-73. For the radical use of Grotius, see Tuck, *Natural rights theories*, 143-73; and Goldie, 'The revolution of 1689', 512. A good example of Grotian radicalism is Charles Blount, *The proceedings of the present parliament* (London: 1689). The relevant sections in Grotius' *De jure belli* are 1.4.7-14.

[32] *The Judgement and Decree of the University of Oxford . . . July 21, 1683*. Sidney was of course condemned as well for his alleged part in the Rye House Plot to kill the King and in the failed rebellion with which Locke was also involved. For the charge of treason for writing in favour of natural freedom see Sidney, *The arraignment, trial and condemnation* 1683 in *The works*, 4-5.

[33] Grotius, *On the laws*, 1.4.2, 1.

people as a corporate body, not individually. Fourth, the people as a whole never exercises political power. Rather, the people consents either to delegate (in limited constitutional theories) or to alienate (in absolute theories) its political power to one or more representative body that naturally represents the people: King, parliament, or both (in theories of mixed sovereignty). Finally, in the case of legitimate resistance to tyranny, the people, either individually, or as a body acting through their natural representative body, exercise their natural right to defend themselves or their community from attack. That is, the rebellions of the early modern period were not conceptualized as political activity but as individual or corporate acts of self defense against attack.[34]

Therefore, political power is conceptualized as the property of a constituted political body or ruler in the natural freedom tradition prior to Locke. Although the people is or are naturally free, this natural freedom is non-political. Politically, the individual is naturally subject to the community and the community to its natural representative bodies, with respect to the exercise of political power. This is true even for the most radical theorists such as George Buchanan, George Lawson, Richard Overton, and Algernon Sidney.[35] For example, in George Lawson's theory of mixed monarchy, when king and parliament deadlock political power devolves back not to the people but to their natural representatives: the original forty courts of the forty counties (i.e. to the local gentry).[36] No one was willing to grant that the people either individually or collectively had the capacity to exercise political power themselves. In positing individual popular sovereignty Locke thus repudiates 500 years of elite political holism and reconceptualizes the origins of political power in a radically populist way. And this in turn is ground work, as

---

[34] For Locke's innovation relative to the earlier Ockhamism of Jacques Almain, see James Burns, 'Jus gladii and jurisdictio: Jacques Almain and John Locke', *The Historical Journal* 26, 2 (183), 369–74.

[35] George Buchanan, *De jure regni apud Scotas*, in *Opera omni* (Edinburgh: 1715), 2 vols., I, 3–4, 38; George Lawson, *Politica sacra et civilis* (London: 1660), 45, 68; Richard Overton, *An appeale from the degenerative representative body* (London: 1647); Algernon Sidney, *Discourses*, 3.36–37, 3.45 (pp. 457–64, 501–2). The pamphlets of the Exclusion Crisis and 1689 also conform to these conventions (see below, note 86).

[36] George Lawson, *An examination of Mr Hobbes, his Leviathan* (London: 1657) 15. I therefore disagree with Franklin's claim that Lawson anticipated Locke's theory of resistance in this respect, in *John Locke and the theory of sovereignty*, and agree with Laslett, *Two treatises*, 2.211 note.

we shall see, for reconceptualizing rebellion as a political activity of the people.

There are three qualifications to this claim. In *De jure praedae commentarius* (1604) Grotius argued that the state's power to punish is derived from its individual members. However, he did not publish this manuscript and he abandoned the argument in *On the laws of war and peace* (1625). Hobbes also derived the power to punish from individuals in *Leviathan*, chapter 28 (the reaction to it shows how unconventional it was). It is, however, a power of self-defence only; not a jurisdictional power to judge any controversy over right, to execute the judgement, and to impose sanctions, as in Locke's theory. Although Pufendorf, in *On the law of nature and nations*, states that heads of families are 'self-governing' in the state of nature, he denies that they possess the powers of punishment and legislation, and stipulates that sovereignty is not derived from their natural power of self-defence (7.3.1–2).[37]

Turning now to the original nature of political power, Locke argues that it is the duty and right of each individual to settle 'controversies of Right'. This comprises three capabilities of governing oneself and others: to judge by means of 'trial' or 'appeal' if any person has transgressed the rule of right (natural law); to execute the judgement by means of punishment of the guilty party; and to seek reparations for the injured party (2.7–12). The three powers of present governments developed historically, and can be logically derived from this original form of political power. The distinction between the 'state of nature' and 'political society' is thus that in the former each individual is judge and executioner of the (natural) law, whereas in the latter the right to judge is voluntarily and conditionally entrusted to a common legislature and judiciary and the right to execute is entrusted to an executive (prince or monarch) (2.87, 2.88–93, 2.131). Hence, political societies are constituted by *representative* governing institutions and natural societies by direct, non-institutional practices of self-government (2.87):

Those who are united into one Body, and have a common establish'd Law and Judicature to appeal to, with authority to decide Controversies between them, and punish Offenders, are in *Civil Society* one with another: but those who have no such common Appeal, I mean on Earth, are still in the state of

[37] See James Tully, 'Introduction', Samuel Pufendorf, *On the duty of man and citizen* (Cambridge: Cambridge University Press, 1991), xxix–xxxv.

Nature, each being, where there is no other, Judge for himself, and Executioner; which is, as I have before shew'd it, the perfect *State of Nature*.

What evidence could Locke advance for his view of the nature of political power prior to the placing of political power in monarchies, representative bodies and, *pace* Lawson, prior to the establishment of the forty courts of the forty counties? Locke's account of the individual and self-governing origins of political power would have been seen as historically plausible by his audience, even though it was 'strange' and subversively populist. The reason is that it is a fairly accurate redescription of the *accusatory* system of justice by which Europeans governed themselves until the legal revolution of the twelfth and thirteenth centuries; until, that is, the inquisitorial system of justice and the juridical institutions of government expropriated political power. The accusatory system was supplanted by institutionalized and fiscalized forms of juridical government roughly during the reign of Henry II and it was officially banned throughout Europe at the fourth Lateran Council of 1215.

Locke's account conforms well to what we know of this 'natural' jurisprudence.[38] Accusations of transgressions were made by private individuals, not public officials, and not only by the injured party. The court of appeal was *ad hoc* in Locke's sense that it had no paid, permanent officials. The accusor who brought the charge swore an oath to the truth of his charge. Other members of the community, compurgators, supported the accusor's oath and others could come in on the side of the accused. Second, if this was thought to be insufficient a trial by ordeal of some kind would take place, on the assumption that God would make the correct judgement visible through the outcome of the ordeal. The most important technique for Locke is the third one: a 'trial by battle' or combat, understood as an 'appeal to Heaven', again on the assumption that God would judge through the battle's outcome. This is of course precisely the language Locke uses to describe revolution and no one could miss his point that a revolution consists in people taking back their original political power and exercising it in the 'natural' or accusatory way. Finally, the whole community had a hand in executing the punishment. This overwhelmingly took the form of reparation by means of payment of

---

[38] George Rightmore, *The law of England at the Norman Conquest* (Akron, Ohio: University of Ohio Press, 1932); Stephen Kuttner, 'The revival of jurisprudence', *Renaissance and renewal in the twelfth century*, ed. R. L. Benson and G. Constable (Cambridge, MA: Harvard University Press, 1982); Berman, *Law and revolution*, 49–83, 434–58.

goods or services of the guilty to the injured party, as Locke claims, and the majority of disputes in the century prior to the system's abolition were, as Locke argues, about property.[39]

Thus, Locke presents a picture of man as a natural political animal that is neither Aristotelian nor republican because, according to Locke, self-government exists prior to and independent of the formation of states.[40] Why should Locke conceptualize political power in this way? First, at the tactical level, he required a theory that would justify revolt by individuals against the oppression of religious Dissent (see part II). After the failure to gain toleration through parliament the Dissenters had to initiate revolt themselves. They had no support from the Anglican local gentry so could not appeal to any constituted body, as Lawson had done. Second, Locke had to justify armed resistance in support of an oppressed minority by those not immediately affected (since Dissent made up barely 10 per cent of the population). His conception of political power serves these tactical needs well and the conventional self-defence theories do not. In addition, the intense historical debate on the origins of parliament and monarchy made the pre-thirteenth century accusatory system available to Locke.[41]

At a more general level, the representation and explanation of rebellions in the seventeenth century were constrained by the vocabulary of self-defence by isolated individuals or representative bodies against direct attacks. This conceptual scheme became increasingly implausible as the great contests of the century unfolded, especially the English Revolution where people not directly attacked joined in, the people judged and executed their king, and they set up a new form of government. Locke's conceptual revolution enables him to represent these struggles more accurately and, for the first time in European thought, as revolutions involving the exercise of political power by the people. His involvement in the organization of revolution in 1681–83, and for the Monmouth Rebellion of 1685,

---

[39] *Two treatises* 2.7–4, 2.36–9, 2.50–1, and below. For the centrality of property disputes at the end of the accusatory age see Robert C. Palmer, 'The origins of property in England', *Law and History* 3, 1 (1985), 1–50; and 'The economic and cultural impact of the origins of property 1180–1220', *Law and History* 3, 2 (1985), 375–96; Janet Coleman, '*Dominium* in thirteenth and fourteenth-century political thought and its seventeenth-century heirs: John of Paris and John Locke', *Political Studies* 33 (1985) 73–100.

[40] Locke presents anthropological evidence for his thesis, based on Amerindian political organization, at 2.14, 2.106–12. For this context see chapter 5 below.

[41] For the historical debate see Ashcraft, *Revolutionary politics*, 181–228.

must have helped him to see that the people in fact make political judgements and act upon them. It should be remembered as well that many features of the accusationary system were incorporated into English judicial, parliamentary, and common law institutions, whereas the inquisitorial system supplanted it almost entirely on the continent.[42]

Locke presents two arguments on the basis of accepted practice for his premise of political individualism. In circumstances where individuals cannot appeal immediately to the law they are said to have the right to defend themselves and their possessions from attack by the use of force (2.18). This alleged natural principle of justice was traditionally used to justify resistance to tyranny. However, for it to work for Locke the act of self-defence would have to entail the exercise of jurisdictional power, and this is what writers such as Pufendorf were also to show self-defence did not involve.[43] Also, Locke argues, governments punish aliens. Since aliens do not consent, governments must exercise some natural power of judgement and execution (2.9). Again, even if this alleged right is accepted, it does not follow that it is a power originally possessed by individuals. (And, if it were accepted, then aliens could punish unjust governments, which is not widely accepted.)

iii

The third step is the explication of the rule of right in accordance with which political power is exercised, justified and limited. For Locke this is the law of nature, which enjoins the preservation of mankind. The law of nature is the means of translating the end of government into natural rights and duties of preservation. As we have seen in his definition of political power, the end of government is the 'public good'. The public good is the preservation of society and, as far as this is compatible with the preservation of the whole, the preservation of each member (2.134). The public good and natural law perform three functions: the standard by which controversies are adjudicated in the state of nature; the guide for legislation and executive action in

---

[42] See James Bradley Thayer, *A preliminary treatise at the Common law* (Boston: 1898), 37–56; E. N. Williams, *The ancien régime in Europe* (Middlesex: Penguin, 1983), 485–96. For example, Locke conceptualizes parliament in an historically accurate way as an adjudicating body (2.89).   [43] Pufendorf, *On the law of nature*, 7.8.7, and note 37 above.

political society; and the rule by which people judge their government.[44]

Within the natural freedom tradition a major division is between those who, like Hobbes and the humanists, hold that outside the state individuals are not law-governed, and so not moral; and those who, like Grotius and Locke, hold that people are governed by natural law. All share the basic assumption of juridical political thought from John of Salisbury to Hegel that the law is constitutive and hence the constitution of human society. In virtue of being subject to law in a law-governed community, people are social, moral, and rational beings (2.11). The difference is that the former identify the reign of law, and thereby civilization, with the establishment of juridical states whereas the latter envisage obedience to the law, and so moral life, in pre- and non-state natural societies (2.128).[45]

Filmer's first criticism of natural freedom is that any state of nature, even Grotius', must be a Hobbesian state of lawlessness in practice, due to the conflict of judgements, and thus a condition of license, not freedom.[46] Locke himself believed this in the *Two tracts* but changed his mind in the *Essays on the law of nature* (1661-2). By arguing in the *Two treatises* that the state of nature has a natural law enforced by the accusatory system he responded to Filmer and showed that natural freedom is not a Hobbesian 'absence of restraint' (or 'negative liberty') but the traditional juridical form of freedom as actions within the bounds of and subject to law (2.22, 2.57). He differs from the whole tradition, as we have seen, by characterizing these individualistically self-governing natural communities as ones in which individuals exercise the political powers of judgement and execution of natural law with respect to others. In the framework of Grotius and Pufendorf that dominated seventeenth century thought, each individual simply *obeys* the two precepts of natural law: the duty

---

[44] *Two treatises* 2.4, 7, 22, 134-5, 149, 171. For Locke's theory of natural law see Wolfgang von Leyden, 'Introduction', John Locke, *Essays on the law of nature* (Oxford: Clarendon Press, 1970); E. W. Urdang and F. Oakley, 'Locke, natural law, and God', *Natural law forum* 11 (1966), 92-109; John Colman, *John Locke's moral philosophy* (Edinburgh: Edinburgh University Press, 1983); David Wootton, 'John Locke: Socinian or natural law theorist?', *The religious and the secular from Hobbes to Mill*, ed. J. Crimmins (London: Routledge, 1989); James Tully, *A discourse on property: John Locke and his adversaries* (Cambridge: Cambridge University Press, 1980), 35-43; and chapters 6 and 9 below.

[45] For the 'humanist' counter-thesis that outside of an institutionalized political and legal order people are without law and morality, see Cicero, *De inventione* (Cambridge, MA: Harvard University Press, 1949) 1.2 (p. 4); and Machiavelli, *The discourses* (Middlesex: Penguin, 1978) 1.2 (p. 107).   [46] Filmer, *Patriarcha*, 264, 273-4, 285-6.

to abstain from that which belongs to another, and the right to preserve oneself by acquiring sustenance and to defend oneself and one's own from invasion by force, including killing.[47]

It follows from the constitutive role of natural law that individuals who transgress natural law, in civil or natural society, by using '*Force without Right*' or manifesting a 'declared design' to do so, place themselves outside of moral or human society, and thereby in a 'state of war' (2.16, *cf*: 2.8, 2.11, 2.19). If they refuse the appeal of law and adjudication, or if there is no time for an appeal, then 'the want of such an appeal gives a man the Right of War' against the defiant lawbreaker (2.19–20, 2.10–11). It is important to see the careful structure of this argument because the right of war he lays out in chapter 3 is the foundation of the right to take up arms against a monarch or legislature who transgresses natural law, as he immediately points out (2.17, 2.20–1). The right of war is thus a juridical decision by arms: the right to judge and proceed against a recalcitrant transgressor by force of arms is 'an appeal to heaven' (2.20–1). As Locke interprets the biblical account of Jephthah leading his people to battle against the Ammonites, 'then Prosecuting [judging], and relying on his *appeal* [to Heaven], he leads out his Army to Battle' (2.21). This means of enforcing the law of nature continues 'until the aggressor offers Peace, and desires reconciliation' on just terms (2.20).

Locke supports the right of war first with reference to the (alleged) natural right to kill an attacker or a thief (2.19, 2.176). Since this is too weak to justify the exercise of the right of war in the defence of the attacked by those not directly involved, he appeals to a right of all mankind to prosecute a common murderer (2.11). (The reason why this generalized right is taken to be a right of war, and not just of defence, is that a state of war is defined as any situation involving the transgression of natural law.) Since this precedent in turn is too weak to support activating a right of war in response to any violation of natural law (where other appeals have been exhausted) he argues that any design to violate natural freedom, to use force without right, threatens 'to take away every thing else', including preservation, and so is like a direct attack (2.17). By these means Locke stretches the traditional justifications of defence to the generalized right of proceeding against natural lawbreakers. Following George Buchanan he conceptualizes this as warfare, and war in turn, not as

---

[47] Grotius, *De jure belli*, 2.2.8, 2.3.16.

an act of self-defence, but as a juridical contest of decision by arms.[48] Since tyranny and usurpation can now be defined in the terms of any violation of natural law, as the use of power beyond right and of power without right respectively (2.197, 2.199), he broadens the base for justified revolt and redescribes it as a juridico-political activity of war.[49]

The reworking of conventional legal arguments for resistance is complemented by an innovation in the content of natural law. As a result of the wars of religion, the sceptical attack on the claims of warring Christian churches, and the development of mercantile and state-building policies, most seventeenth-century political thinkers agreed that the basic role of the state is to *preserve* and 'strengthen' society and its members, not to uphold the 'true' religion, unless it could be shown to be useful in bringing about preservation.[50] Accordingly, the basic concept of natural law that was said to guide and legitimate legislation was the law of self-preservation. This received its classical formulation in Grotius' formula of a natural duty and right of self-preservation and dominated the political thought of the century.[51] Locke's innovation here is to argue that the fundamental natural law is not self-preservation but *'the preservation of Mankind'* (2.135). It is this change which explains and grounds the distinctive set of natural duties and rights he is able to develop and which provides further support for a broader account of government activity and revolution.[52]

The preservation of mankind is broken into two natural duties: the traditional natural law duty to preserve oneself and, when one's preservation is not sacrificed, a new, positive and other-regarding duty to preserve the rest of mankind (2.6). Two natural rights to preserve oneself and others follow from the natural duties (2.7). Thus, when people accuse and adjudicate controversies involving others in the natural accusatory system they are exercising their natural rights and duties to preserve others. Hence, as we shall see, these rights and duties provide the justification for the wider population coming to the

---

[48] Buchanan, *De jure regni*, 38.
[49] Jean LeClerc makes this point in his review of the *Two treatises* in *Bibliotheque universelle*, xix, 591.
[50] Marc Raef, *The well-ordered police state* (New Haven: Yale University Press, 1983), 11–43; and chapter 6 below.
[51] Tuck, *Natural rights theories*, 58–82, and 'The "modern" theory of natural law'.
[52] For a more detailed account of Locke's natural rights and duties, see Tully, *A discourse on property*, 53–156, and chapters 2–5 below.

revolutionary aid of an oppressed minority; exactly the form of action Locke needed to legitimate and which could not be justified in the Grotian framework of self-preservation.[53] These in turn correlate with the traditional negative duty to abstain from that which belongs to another (2.6).

Further, two different kinds of power are employed in the exercise of each of these natural rights and duties: the power to preserve one's life and the life of others by punishing natural lawbreakers (political power) and the power to preserve oneself and others from starvation (labour power or productive power) (2.129–30). Locke discusses the natural rights and duties of labour power in chapter 5. If humans have the duty and right to preserve themselves and others from starvation, then they must have the right to 'Meat and Drink, and such other things, as Nature affords for their Subsistence' (2.25). Therefore, the world must belong to 'Mankind in common' in the sense that each has a natural claim to the means necessary for 'Support and Comfort' (2.26). This modifies the popular seventeenth-century premise in the natural freedom tradition that the world belongs to no one but is open to the appropriation of each.[54]

Filmer's second criticism is that each act of appropriation would require the consent of all and so everyone would starve waiting for universal consent.[55] Locke's famous reply is that consent is not required in the early stages of history (2.28). The exercise of one's labour power as a *person* on what is given to mankind in common bestows on the labourer a right to the product insofar as it is used for the preservation of self and others and as long as 'enough, and as good [is] left in common for others' (2.27, 2.31).[56] Thus, labour power is the means of individuating the common into individual possessions to be used for preservation (2.25–6, 2.28–9). Labour power also creates

---

[53] Thus, the *Two treatises* overcomes the conceptual difficulty the Levellers had in justifying revolutionary assistance from their Grotian premise of self-preservation (Tuck, *Natural rights theories*, 150).

[54] Grotius, *On the laws*, 2.2.1–2; Pufendorf, *On the law of nature*, 4.4.2. Istvan Hart and M. Ignatieff, 'Needs and justice in the *Wealth of nations*', in *Wealth and virtue* (Cambridge: Cambridge University Press, 1983), 1–44 at 35, deny that Locke departs from the convention of a negative community. If this were so then the right to the means of preservation would be idle, but it is not. In addition to chapter 3 below, see Richard Ashcraft, *Locke's Two treatises of government* (London: Unwin Hyman, 1987), 81–97; and Gopal Sreenivasan, 'The limits of Lockean rights in property' (Oxford: B. Phil thesis, 1989), chapter 2.   [55] Filmer, *Patriarcha*, 273.

[56] For Locke's concept of the person, see John Yolton, *Locke and the compass of human understanding* (Cambridge: Cambridge University Press, 1970), 181–97.

products of value, insofar as they are useful, and the whole chapter underscores the productivity and importance of labour (2.40–4).[57]

In the state of nature the exercise of labour power and possession are *regulated* by political power in accordance with the 'enough and as good' proviso and the natural law enjoining use for preservation. A person who abuses possessions acquired by his own labour, or who appropriates more than one can use without spoiling, takes 'more than his share, and [it] belongs to others' (2.31). He thereby 'offended against the common law of Nature, and was liable to be punished; he invaded his neighbor's share, for he had *no Right, farther than his Use*' (2.37). Natural property rights are, accordingly, use rights set within a larger framework of rights and duties to preserve the community (mankind) and regulated by everyone through the accusatory system.

Increase in population, the introduction of money, development of agricultural arts, the extensive appropriation of land, the division of labour and the emergence of commercial activity all lead to interminable disputes and quarrels over property rights (2.36–7, 2.40, 2.44, 2.45, 2.48). The accusatory system is ill-suited for this situation and so the resulting instability provides one of the major causes of the historical transition from the pre-state accusatory systems to the agreements to establish the first forms of institutionalized and territorial forms of government (monarchies) and formal legal codes to regulate property (2.45, 2.30, 2.50).[58] I return to his transition argument below. The important points here are, first, that Locke has argued that it is a natural function of political power to regulate both labour and possessions for the sake of preservation, or the public good. This provides the justification for the extensive regulation and disciplining of the labouring population in the mercantile systems of the early modern states, when this power is delegated to government, as Locke recommends in his *Report to the Board of Trade* (1697). On the other hand, this framework of natural law rights and duties of preservation and to the product of one's labour places a limit on property legislation, the transgression of which justifies revolt. Once government has determined a system of 'property' – by which he means a right to some thing such that it

[57] See Ashcraft, *Locke's Two treatises*, 81–150.
[58] For the Exclusion Crisis context of these arguments see Ashcraft, *Revolutionary politics*, 181–228.

cannot be taken without the consent of the proprietor or the consent of his representatives (2.140, 2.190) – a transgression of these rights constitutes a violation of natural law and hence a ground for legitimate revolt, just as in the state of nature (2.119, 2.130). A further question is whether these arguments for appropriation without consent and punishment for abuse of land were used, or were intended to be used, to justify the dispossession of Amerindians of their property and the imposition of European forms of property (see chapter 5 below).

iv

The fourth step in the juridical problematic is the way in which political power is placed in the hands of monarchs and/or representative bodies. It is a historical, logical and normative question concerning the rights and conditions under which the great centralizing monarchies or the representative institutions of early modern Europe exercised political power. In the natural freedom tradition two general genealogies were proposed. The first and dominant explanation, which Locke adopted in the *Two tracts*, is that the people as a corporate whole, and usually acting through their representative body, consent to *alienate* completely political power to the monarch and to renounce the right of self-defence. The monarch is sovereign, above the law and therefore absolute. The monarch is said to be bound by natural law but, since the people have renounced their right to defend themselves, only god can punish the ruler's transgressions. Most absolutists mitigate this doctrine of non-resistance in cases where the monarch alienates his kingdom or sets about destroying his subjects. Then, as William Barclay puts it, and Locke quotes with approval, the people may defend itself (without injuring the king), usually through its representative body. Or, as Grotius and Pufendorf concede, an individual may defend himself against direct attack by a murderous tyrant.

The main argument for alienation in its pure or mitigated form is that if sovereignty is shared by monarch and parliament (or estates), or if the people do not renounce their (or its) right to judge when it is a situation of self-defence, then, given human partiality, this will lead to disagreement, dissension, tumults, and so to civil war. The idea that political power is shared by parliament and monarch was castigated as a throwback to the strife-ridden feudal past and an impediment to centralization and modernization under absolute monarchy.[59] The second argument, famously advanced by Rousseau against the *Two treatises*, is that unless alienation is complete no sovereign is formed and people remain in a quasi state of nature.[60] Locke used both of these arguments in the *Two tracts*.

The second genealogy is that the people, as a whole, consent or contract to conditionally entrust political power to the monarch or to monarch and parliament (in mixed monarchy theories), or to parliament (in parliamentary sovereignty).[61] When the ruler abuses the trust it is broken and power devolves back to the people. Then, the people may defend themselves either through parliament or, if it is a mixed monarchy, through a natural representative body such as Lawson's forty courts of the forty counties. As we have seen no one was willing to say that dissolution of the trust returned the exercise of political power to the people either individually or collectively.

In the *Two treatises* Locke adopts the trust theory of the relation between government and governors and adapts it to his individual account of political power. There are three reasons why he accepted the trust hypothesis. First, according to the alienation hypothesis, the sovereign is by definition outside of political society, since he is not subject to law, and thus absolutism is not a form of political society (2.90). Further, since the people resign their right to judge and punish him for violations of natural law, it is worse than the inconveniences of the state of nature since they have no right to protect themselves against his violence. Hence it would be irrational to consent to alienate: 'to think that men are so foolish that they take care to avoid what Mischiefs may be done them by *Pole-Cats* or *Foxes* [in the state of nature], but are content, nay think it safety, to be devoured by *Lions* [in absolute monarchy]' (2.93). This is clearly directed against *any* natural freedom theory of alienation, whether Grotius, Hobbes, Pufendorf, or Locke himself in the *Two tracts*. Not only is it irrational. Since it involves transferring absolute power over one's life to another, it presupposes that individuals have the right to dispose of their own life. Locke points out to his Christian audience that only god has such a right (2.23, 2.135, 2.149, 2.171, 2.222). Even if

[59] See Pufendorf, *On the law of nature*, 7.5.12–15, 7.8.7; Filmer, *Patriarcha*, 88; and J. H. Sheenan, *The origins of the modern European state: 1450–1725* (London: Hutchinson, 1974).
[60] Jean-Jacques Rousseau, *Du contrat social*, ed. R. Grimsley (Oxford: Clarendon Press, 1972) 1.6 (p. 115).   [61] See Franklin, *John Locke and the theory of sovereignty*.

absolutism enjoys universal consent it is a form of 'despotical power' and 'slavery' that violates the natural law to preserve life by exercising unlimited power over subjects (2.172). By claiming absolute power over another, a monarch 'does thereby *put himself into a state of war*' (2.17). Therefore there is no normative foundation for absolutism, or for the analogous practice of a right to consent to enslavement. The point here again is that man's natural condition is not one of license but of liberty constituted by natural law, and this precludes absolute freedom and so absolute subjection.[62]

His second reason for rejecting the alienation theory is that governments tend over time to tyranny. As states develop, rulers gain the wealth and power to cultivate interests different from and contrary to the people. In addition, they become open to ideological manipulation by religious elites, who use their influence to have their religious beliefs imposed by political means. The resulting tyranny causes civil war. Hence the alienation theory, like any absolute theory, is part of the problem rather than a solution (2.106–112, 2.94, 2.208–10).

The third and major reason for the change is that Locke came to believe that the alienation theory is implausible: post-Reformation, and especially post-English civil war individuals as a matter of fact do not alienate their natural political power. He abandoned the alienation theory in his 1667 *Essay concerning toleration*.[63] In the face of the imposition of the Clarendon Code in 1661–2 – legislation to compel conformity to Anglican forms of worship and punish Presbyterians, Baptists, Quakers, Independents, and Catholics – thousands of religious Dissenters refused to conform, disobeyed the law and suffered draconian persecution. The *Essay concerning toleration* is a justification of this passive resistance based on the premise that individuals neither do nor ought to alienate their right to judge and to disobey laws they believe to be unjust. By 1675, as we see in part II,

---

[62] *Two Treatises* 2.22–3 and Laslett's note to section 24. For the theories that posited unlimited liberty in order to justify unlimited subjection to absolutism and to slavery on the basis of consent see Tuck, *Natural rights theories*, 52–4. Locke's justification of slavery is that if a person has committed an act that deserves death (a felon or a captive in war) he may be enslaved rather than killed, since he has forfeited his life. For the use of this kind of justification to legitimate the indenture and enslavement of labourers see Abbot E. Smith, *Colonists in bondage: white servitude and convict labor in America, 1607–1776* (Chapel Hill: University of North Carolina Press, 1974). See Wayne Glauser, 'Three approaches to Locke and the slave trade', *Journal of the history of ideas* 51, 2 (April–June 1990), 199–216.

[63] John Locke, *An essay concerning toleration* (1667), Bodleian, MS. Locke c. 28, fos. 21–32, in John Locke, *Scritti editi e inediti sulla tolleranza*, ed. Carlo Viano (Turin: Taylor, 1961).

Locke had gone further towards the *Two treatises*, arguing that individuals never alienate their right to enforce the rule of right against their governors by force of arms. The English experience thus provided an impetus to reinterpret the whole civil war experience of early modern Europe as the practical repudiation of the alienation hypothesis, or any hypothesis that posits depoliticized individual subjects. Alienation and natural subjection theories are thus out of touch with practical reality. As he classically and presciently puts it in the *Two treatises*, popular revolution is a permanent feature of modern politics, irrespective of the official ideology (2.224):

> For when the *People* are made *miserable*, and find themselves *exposed to the ill usage of Arbitrary Power*, cry up their Governors, as much as you will for sons of *Jupiter*, let them be Sacred and Divine, descended or authoriz'd from Heaven, give them out for whom or what you please, the same will happen. *The People generally ill treated*, and contrary to right, will be ready upon any occasion to ease themselves of a burden that sits heavy upon them. They will wish and seek for the opportunity, which, in the change, weakness, and accidents of humane affairs, seldom delays long to offer it self.

Let us turn now to the complex practice of *trust*, compromising the relations between governed and governors which constitute political society.[64] Individuals consent to entrust the two natural powers they exercise themselves in the state of nature to make up a government. First, labour power, the power '*of doing whatsoever he thought fit for the Preservation of himself*, and the rest of Mankind' each individual '*gives up* to be regulated by Laws made by the Society, so far forth as the preservation of himself, and the rest of that society shall require' (2.129). That is, property and labour are now regulated by the two policy objectives of collective and individual preservation, with the individual being subordinated to the preservation of the collectivity (public good) when these two great rationales of government conflict: '*the first and fundamental natural Law*, which is to govern even the Legislative it self , is *the preservation of the society*, and (as far as will consist with the publick good) of every person in it' (2.134). This, as Locke notes, confines the liberty each had by natural law (2.130–1). Second, political power, the power of punishing, each individual

---

[64] For Locke's hypothesis that government rests on the conditional trust of the governed see John Dunn, *The political thought of John Locke* (Cambridge: Cambridge University Press, 1969), 120–48, 165–87; 'The concept of "trust" in the politics of John Locke', in *Philosophy in history*, ed. R. Rorty, J. Schneewind, Q. Skinner (Cambridge: Cambridge University Press, 1984); *John Locke* (Oxford: Oxford University Press, 1985) 34–55.

'wholly *gives up*' to be used to make and to enforce laws, with each individual's assistance if necessary (2.130).

The transfer of powers involves three parts. Individuals consent with each other to give up their powers to form a political 'society' of which each becomes a member. Only explicit consent, 'by positive Engagement, and express Promise and Compact', makes one a member or subject and constitutes a political society, and binds each to the determination of the majority until either his citizenship is revoked or the society is dissolved (2.95–9, 2.120–2). Thus, although Locke is a natural political individualist, he is a conventional political holist because consent makes a person a subject of a community that embodies political power and acts in accordance with the majority. The majority then constitutes the society into a constitutional form of government by placing the legislative power – the power to make laws – in specific hands. If this legislative power, as well as executive power, remains in the majority then it is a 'perfect' democracy; if in the hands of a few, oligarchy; and so on (2.132). The legislative power is the 'supreme power' in any commonwealth because it is the power to make laws and this comes from the members' natural power to judge controversies: 'And this *puts Men* out of a state of Nature *into* that of a Commonwealth, by setting up a Judge on Earth, with authority to determine all the Controversies, and redress the Injuries, that may happen to any member of the Commonwealth: which Judge is the legislative, or magistrates appointed by it' (1.89, 2.212). Finally, the legislative entrusts the 'natural force' of the community to the executive (and, *eo ipso*, the federative) to enforce the laws and protect society, members and colonies by means of war and diplomacy (2.144–8).

Locke sees two objections to his thesis that lawful government is based upon explicit consent, involving the delegation of political power, and binding each member to the majority: there are no historical instances of it and that now people are born into, and thus naturally subject to, a government (2.100). In response to the former objection he assembles historical and anthropological evidence to illustrate that free men have commonly set rulers over themselves (2.101–2). In these examples Locke is concerned to falsify both the natural subjection thesis and the equally popular *de facto* thesis that lawful government can be founded in successful conquest. This aim is spliced rather awkwardly into the first section of the Second treatise, perhaps in response to the widespread use of *de facto* arguments to justify William's rule in 1688–9, and taken up in chapter 16. The constant danger that provoked Locke's attack on conquest theories was the widespread fear, from the early 1670s on to the end of the Nine Years' War, of a French invasion. The 'noise of War, which makes so great a part of the History of Mankind', has caused many to mistake 'the force of Arms, for the consent of the people; and reckon Conquest as one of the Originals of Government' (2.175).[65]

The latter objection is no more plausible. History furnishes many examples of people leaving their government and founding new commonwealths by consent, which would be impossible if subjection were natural. Further, present governments themselves do not assume that subjection follows from birth, but from consent and they in fact demand express consent (2.113–18). Recent scholarship on the origins of institutionalized forms of political power and citizenship in Europe, whether in the Communes, free cities, principalities, or English commonwealth, has stressed the widespread practice of consent and oath-giving.[66] Explicit oaths of allegiance to the present form of church and state were precisely the form the central issue of obedience and resistance took from 1660 to 1690.[67] In 1689 Locke insisted on explicit oaths renouncing *Jure Divinio* doctrine (because it entailed continued allegiance to James II) and *de facto* doctrine (because it did not base allegiance on the *justice* of William's invasion and it would equally legitimate a successful French counter-conquest).[68]

The most difficult question Filmer puts to the consent thesis is one of motivation. Why should anyone ever consent to give up their natural freedom and self-government for subjection to others? As Locke rephrases it (2.123):[69]

---

[65] For *de facto* arguments in 1689 see Goldie, 'The revolution of 1689', 508–18; Farr and Roberts, 'John Locke and the glorious revolution', 385–98; and Locke's comments on William Sherlock, *The case of allegiance due to sovereigne powers* (1691), in Bodleian, MS Locke c. 28, f. 96.

[66] Berman, *Law and revolution*, 359–403; Gerhard Oestreich, *Neostoicism and the early modern state* (Cambridge: Cambridge University Press, 1982), 135–55, 166–87.

[67] See John Locke, *A letter from a person of quality*, 1675, in *The works of John Locke* (London: Thomas Tegg, 1823), 10 vols, x.

[68] Farr and Roberts, 'John Locke and the glorious revolution', 395–8.

[69] Filmer, *Patriarcha*, 286: 'the original freedom of mankind being supposed, every man is at liberty to be of what kingdom he please, and so every petty company hath a right to make a kingdom by itself; and not only every city, but every village, and every family, nay, and every particular man, a liberty to choose himself to be his own King if he please; and he were a madman that being by nature free, would choose any man but himself to be his own governor'.

If man in the state of Nature be so free as has been said; if he be absolute Lord of his own Person and Possessions, equal to the greatest, and subject to no Body, why will he part with his Freedom? Why will he give up this Empire, and subject himself to the Dominion and Controul of any other Power?

Locke answers that there are three disadvantages of the natural or accusatory system that caused people to abjure it: the lack of established, settled or known law, the lack of a known and indifferent judge, and a want of power to execute a judgement (2.124–6). Natural law can be known and settled, but, because people are always partial in their own cases, they will not admit to a law that applies against them. The second difficulty also turns on the jurisprudential axiom that individuals are biased judges in their own case due to 'interest' or 'partiality'. As a result, 'Passion and Revenge is very apt to carry them too far, and with too much heat, in their own Cases; as well as negligence, and unconcernedness, to make them too remiss, in other mens.' Even the third turns on partiality since he argues that people will not enforce a sentence when the guilty party resists and makes punishment 'dangerous, and frequently destructive'.[70]

He argues in chapter 5 that these disadvantages do not cause serious problems until the pressure of population growth on available land, the increase of and division into towns and villages, the development of agriculture and technology, and the introduction of forms of money conjoin to cause disputes over property which destabilize the natural regime. He also speculates that these developments, especially money, enhanced the sense of self and thus served to enlarge, if not create, the self-interest that undermines the accusatory system (2.37, 2.107–8, 2.111). Thus, confusion and disorder eventually follow from a way of life in which men are 'Judges in their own cases', because 'Self-love will make men partial to themselves and their Friends' and 'Passion and Revenge will carry them too far in punishing others' (2.13). At this conjunction in human history the greatest transformation in the way of governing occurs – from self-government to institutionalized government. Locke immediately remarks that it is absurd to assume (as he had in the *Two tracts*) that people would consent to absolute monarchy at this point as a remedy to their problems. Since the problem is human partiality where each

---

[70] Cf: 2.13, 2.136. These remain the conventional arguments against self-government: see David Miller, *Anarchism* (London: J. M. Dent and Son, 1984), 169–83.

is judge, what kind of a remedy is absolute monarchy 'where one Man commanding a multitude, has the Liberty to be Judge in his own Case, and may do to all his Subjects whatever he pleases, without the least liberty to any one to question or controle those who Execute his Pleasure'? (2.13). Rather, Locke advances a more plausible history of the formation of states.

While still self-governing, people were used to entrusting their authority to a single ruler to lead them in time of war, although they retained the right, exercised in *ad hoc* councils, to declare war and peace. Only later did they turn to this custom of delegated authority to settle internal disputes (2.108, 2.110, 2.112) (as in the itinerant justices sent out from the King's court from 1166 onward). Thus, institutionalized forms of government evolved out of the practice of external war, hence explaining the initial plausibility of conquest theories. However, delegation of power in wartime and later in internal disputes was based on consent and a somewhat naive trust in the application of the original form of government, 'which from their infancy they had all been accustomed to'; the patriarchal family (2.107). Filmer is thus right in saying that the first forms of civil government are monarchies, patterned on the patriarchal family, but wrong in construing this as natural rather than a contextually rational and conventional response to the breakdown of an earlier way of life.[71]

The initial trust was naive because people had no experience of the abuse of power and so of the need for explicit limitations, even though they understood it to be limited like paternal care of children (2.107). As central authority developed, the monarch, through luxury and ambition, stretched his prerogative 'to oppress the People', and developed interests separate from them (2.111, 2.163). They then realized that it is necessary to limit monarchy by placing the legislative power 'in collective bodies of men, call them Senate, Parliament, or what you please' (2.94). Men examined more carefully 'the *Original* and Rights of *Government*', and set up legislative bodies 'to *restrain the Exorbitances*, and *prevent the Abuses*' of princely power, thus ushering in the present age of disputes about privilege and contests between kings and people about government (2.111). Not only did this attempt at separating and balancing power not succeed in constraining the abuse of power (2.107), as proponents of

---

[71] See Ashcraft, *Revolutionary politics*, 181–227 for similar arguments in the Exclusion literature.

mixed monarchy falsely claim, but princes have been further emboldened in the present age by arguments from custom and new ideologies of divine right promulgated by religious elites to advance their own interests (2.94, 2.112). Locke's reconceptualization of the trust between governed and governors is thus designed to provide a solution to the problems of civil wars caused by the failure of the first attempt of representative institutions to curb the power given to princes and by the seventeenth-century resurgence of absolutism.

v

The fifth and most important step in juridical political thought is the twofold question: how is political power exercised by governors and what prevents the abuse of power? The answer to the first question for Locke is that political power is to be exercised in accordance with the trust. This comprises: laws should be made and executed in accordance with the common good or natural law (the natural rights and duties of preservation); governors themselves should be subject to the laws they make; and the laws and legal rights should not be changed without the consent of the majority through their represen-tatives.[72] The first and fundamental criterion follows from the nature of political power itself because it is bound by this end in the state of nature (2.171). The second makes it clear that there is no sovereign in Locke's theory of government: both governed and governors are mutually subject to the law (1.93).

In response to the second question, in *A letter from a person of quality* (1675), Locke rejected his earlier view that fear of divine punishment would constrain rulers from abusing power (see part II below). He also rejected the prevalent absolutist view that removal of grounds for legitimate contestation of the exercise of political power will remove the cause of oppression (2.224). Locke is also sceptical of the view that parliaments and mixed monarchies are sufficient means to check the abuse of power. Parliaments and elected bodies are themselves susceptible to corruption, as the history of republics illustrates (2.201, 2.221-3, 2.138, 2.149). Unchecked and frequent popular assemblies are untrustworthy, imprudent, and prone to abuse (2.156). Further-more, even in mixed monarchies, monarchs are able to override the limitations placed on them by parliaments (2.107, 2.111-12, 2.163).

---

[72] 2.94. 2.135, 2.140. The executive may act against civil law if it is in the public good, 2.160.

Locke prefers the customary English system of king in parliament. The king checks the tendency of parliament to corruption (the weakness of republics and democracies), by convoking and dissolving parliaments as the need arises, and by exercising powers of disallowance. The parliament in turn checks the king's tendency to rule in favour of special interests, the weakness of absolute monarchies (2.151–167). This system is the best because it is adaptable to the contingencies of politics, it has proven itself in practice, and the English people are accustomed to it (2.160, 2.165, 2.223).[73] Even with this system of conjoint sovereignty of king in parliament, however, the problem remains of how the king and parliament are to be constrained to their respective and mutually limiting roles.

Locke's solution to this problem, and so to the early modern crisis of government, is that the people themselves must govern their governors. They must judge when and if their governors act contrary to the trust and, when necessary, execute their judgement by a revolution and the establishment of new governors or a new form of government.

Locke's concept of trust captures this reciprocal practice of government. The people entrust their political power to their governors or trustees and consent to subjection as long as it is exercised in accordance with the trust. Reciprocally, the governors are under an obligation to the people to exercise power accordingly. Hence (2.149),

the Legislative being only a Fiduciary Power to act for certain ends, there remains still *in the People a Supreme Power* to remove or *alter the Legislative*, when they find the *Legislative* act contrary to the trust reposed in them. For all *Power given with trust* for the attaining an *end*, being limited by that end, whenever that *end* is manifestly neglected, or opposed, the *trust* must necessarily be *forfeited*, and the Power devolve into the hands of those that gave it, who may place it anew where they shall think best for their safety and security.

How does this work in practice? In a system where the executive is separate from the legislative, the legislative, being the superior power, governs the executive, which may be 'at pleasure changed and displaced' by the legislative (2.152). If the legislative fails or it abuses the trust in other ways, then, as we have seen, power devolves to the

---

[73] These arguments are probably directed at his republican contemporaries such as Algernon Sidney, Henry Neville, and William Moyle, as well as at absolutists.

people. In England, the monarch has a share in the legislative, and so is not subordinate to it, and thus cannot be removed by the legislative. These sections (149–52) end fifty years of insoluble debate over the location of sovereignty in mixed monarchy. The legislative cannot effectively act against an executive which ignores its protestations without undermining the mixed nature of the constitution. If a legislature exercises the authority to judge and remove an executive then this establishes parliamentary sovereignty and thus undermines the mixed sovereignty of king in parliament. If, on the other hand, a legislature allows an executive to rule without limitation, then this concedes absolute sovereignty in the executive, and so undermines mixed or conjoint sovereignty again.[74] This was the dilemma of the Civil War and again in 1681, when Locke wrote the *Two treatises*: Charles II dissolved the third Exclusion Parliament and signalled his intention to rule without it. It was also the situation again in 1687–8 when Locke rewrote and published the *Two treatises*: James II ruled against the consent of parliament.[75] Consequently, to preserve the conjoint sovereignty of king in parliament, in a system where there is no constitutional court of appeal, it is necessary to appeal to an independent body to adjudicate the dispute: namely, the people (2.218, 2.222).

There are two means by which this may be done. Subjects may appeal to the legislative, not only to judge controversies among themselves, but also controversies between them and their government (unlike absolutism) (2.93–4, 2.207). Parliament was established, according to Locke, to judge this sort of appeal. However, when religious Dissenters made appeals throughout the Restoration against the transgression of their civil and political rights and the confiscation of their property, their appeals were castigated as 'sedition' and 'faction' (2.209), 2.218). When this means is blocked the trust is broken and the people turn to the second means of redress: revolution as the means of executing the law of nature (2.221–2, 2.202, 2.204).

In chapter 19 Locke distinguishes between the dissolution of government and the dissolution of political society, states that virtually the only way political society is dissolved is by foreign

[74] This dilemma is exposed by Filmer in his criticism of Philip Hunton's theory of mixed monarchy in *Patriarcha*, 295.

[75] See Franklin, *John Locke and the theory of Sovereignty*, for these two contexts and the earlier Civil War debates on mixed monarchy.

conquest, and goes on to analyze cases in which government, but not political society, is dissolved by various breaches of trust (2.211). In this situation, the unjust rulers have dissolved the government, the people are no longer subject to the governors who have broken the trust, so they 'may constitute to themselves a new legislative, as they think best, being in full liberty to resist the force' of the illegitimate governors (2.212). In these cases the unjust rulers (legislators or executive) are in a state of war with the people because they have acted contrary to right or used force without right, just like any individual lawbreaker in the state of nature.[76] Although Locke states that 'Every one is at the disposure of his own will' (2.212), in the first instance after dissolution of government, the people must be bound together as a corporate body, governed by majority rule, in virtue of their initial consent to join political society (2.96). This dissolution of the bond between the people and their governors should not affect the independent and logically prior bond among citizens to form a political community. This is indeed how Locke puts it at sections 242 and 243, where he says that 'the Body of the *People*' should be the judge or umpire. Here, Locke probably has in mind a representative constituent assembly, as he and many Whigs recommended for the Convention Parliament in 1689.[77] Since the 'dissolution of government' entails only the dissolution of the bond between the people and the unjust ruler who has violated the constitution, the constitution and legal structure of political society remain intact. The representative constituent assembly has, by definition, the authority to amend or restore the constitution, but it remains in force throughout the process, as in 1689.

Locke then turns to the more extreme situation where 'the Prince, or whoever they be in the Administration, decline that way of Determination', by the majority (2.242). Who then has the right to judge when the trust is broken and dissolution has occurred? Locke's unequivocally radical answer is that each individual man has this right: '*every Man* is *Judge* for himself' (2.241). Not only may any man (or woman?) make this judgement, he may make it on the basis of a *single* violation of right, on the judgement that his ancestors had been wronged by conquest (thinking of a French invasion), or even if no

---

[76] 2.222, 2.232 state the general argument, whereas 2.212–19 take up the specifics of 1681 and 1688.

[77] See letter to Clark, note 9 above; Goldie, 'The roots of true whiggism'; and chapter 2, part I, below.

transgression has been committed but the individual discerns a
tyrannical tendency or design.[78]

Who has the right to execute this judgement by taking up arms to
punish the government? Again Locke replies that each individual has
this right.[79] As we have seen this follows from the premises since the
revolution is the people governing lawbreakers as they do naturally
when other forms of appeal have failed. Then, the majority of the
people again have full constituent authority to change office-holders,
re-establish the old form of government, to set up a new form, or to set
up direct democracy – 'to continue the legislative in themselves'
(2.243). To drive home his point that revolution is the exercise of
natural political power by the people he calls it exactly what the right
of war is called: an 'appeal to Heaven'. Here, because there is no
common judge on earth, the only recourse is a decision by arms. 'And
where the Body of the people, or any single Man, is deprived of their
Right, or is under the exercise of a power without right, and have an
appeal on earth, there they have a liberty to appeal to Heaven,
whenever they judge the cause of sufficient moment' (2.168, following
2.21). The elaborate account of the state of nature is thus stage setting
for the introduction of revolution as the natural and legitimate way
the people govern rulers who abuse their power.

Locke attempts to make this doctrine appear acceptable by making
William Barclay's respectable natural freedom theory of absolutism
appear more populist than it is. George Buchanan had argued that a
king who becomes a tyrant dissolves the constitutive pact between
king and people, forfeits his rights, and so may be proceeded against
by means of a judicial act of war by the body of the people or an
individual, just as in the case of a common criminal.[80] In his reply
William Barclay countered that an inferior can never punish a
superior so neither an individual nor the people as a whole can
punish, attack or prosecute their king. However, as we have seen,
Barclay does concede that if a king becomes an *intolerable* tyrant the
people as a whole, and not an individual, may defend itself as long as
it does not attack the king.[81] Although Grotius repudiated
Buchanan's theory as well he did go on to assert against Barclay that
the people, individually or collectively, could defend themselves by

[78] 2.21, 2.168, 2.203, 2.210, 2.220, 2.240.
[79] 2.222, 2.224, 2.228, 2.231–2, 2.235, 2.239, 2.242.
[80] Buchanan, *De jure regni*, 38. Cf: *Two treatises* 2.19.
[81] Barclay, *De regno*, 3.8, cited in *Two treatises* 2.232–3.

force of arms against an intolerable tyrant who attacked them directly.[82] In this exceptional case the people exercise their natural right to defend themselves. This is justified because the reason people originally established government is self-preservation. Pufendorf repeated this mitigated absolutism, explicitly making the point against Barclay that the duty not to punish a superior does not apply because resistance is an act of defence, not of jurisdiction.[83] This line of argument, as we have seen, was used and abused – as Filmer predicted – to justify resistance throughout the century.

In his commentary on Barclay Locke reverses this trend. Instead of saying that resistence is a non-judicial act of defence he is able to show that even Barclay admits that when a king destroys his people or alienates his own kingdom he ceases to be a king. He thereby 'divests himself of his Crown and Dignity, and returns to the state of a private Man, and the people become free and superior'; he 'sets the people free, and leaves them at their own disposal.'[84] Although Barclay is thinking of extraordinary circumstances he concedes that a king can lose his superiority and thus, as Locke immediately concludes, the rule that an inferior cannot punish a superior does not apply and so the people may prosecute him (as Buchanan originally argued) (2.239). With his very different account of the natural political power of the people and his more extensive concept of tyranny firmly in place, Locke is able to exploit this opening and make it appear that his radical doctrine is not far out of line with the very same absolutists Filmer had criticized for opening the door to resistance (2.239 cf. 1.67):

only that he [Barclay] has omitted the principle from which his Doctrine flows; and that is, the breach of trust, in not preserving the Form of Government agreed on, and not intending the end of Government itself, which is the publick good and preservation of Property. When a King has dethron'd himself, and put himself in a state of War his People what shall hinder them from prosecuting him who is no King, as they would any other Man, who has put himself into a state of War with them.

Despite Locke's exercise in feigned respectability, his theory of resistance is one of the most original accounts in early modern political thought and the first to conceive the rebellions as political contests involving ordinary people seizing political power and

---

[82] Grotius, *On the laws*, 1.4.7, 1.4.10–11 (referring to Barclay).
[83] Pufendorf, *On the law of nature*, 7.8.7.   [84] Barclay, *De regno*, 3.16; *Two treatises* 2.237–8.

reforming government. We can measure how unconventional it is by noting two contemporary responses to its publication in 1690. First, Locke's whig friend James Tyrrell repudiated it in *Bibliotheca politica*, arguing that political power does not revert to the people but to representative bodies or 'great councils'.[85] In *The fundamental constitution of the English government* (1690) William Atwood stated the major objection to Locke's account:[86]

> others [Locke] are too loose in their notions, and suppose the dissolution of this contract [James II vacancy] to be a mere [i.e. pure] commonwealth, or absolute anarchy, wherein everybody has an equal share in the government, not only landed men, and others with whom the balance of power has rested by the constitution, but copy-holders, servants, and the very faeces Romuli which would not only make a quiet election impractical but bring in a deplorable confusion.

Atwood's objection is that Locke's theory would entail that the Convention Parliament would not only be a constituent assembly, a conclusion he and other moderate whigs wished to avoid by denying that the government had been dissolved, but also that it would have to represent the majority of all the adult male population. He believes that such a popular election of delegates to the assembly would be impractical and chaotic; and in fact no election occurred. However, Locke does not stipulate how a legitimate constituent assembly is to be selected. There is no reason why the consent of the people, which Locke lays down as essential to William's legitimacy in the *Preface*, could not be given by a ratification of the assembly's proposals in a referendum, irrespective of the manner in which the assembly was constituted.

Locke's theory appears to be the most implausible solution of all.

---

[85] James Tyrrell, *Bibliotheca politica* (London: 1727) 12, 643.

[86] William Atwood, *The fundamental constitution* 1690, 100. See Franklin, 105. Four pamphlets of the Glorious Revolution are similar to the *Two treatises* on this point of dissolution. As a result of James II's breach of trust government dissolved, political power devolved to the people who had the right to reconstitute government. [John Wildman] *Some remarks upon government* in *State Tracts* I, 149–62; [Wildman] *A letter to a friend* in *Somers tracts* x, 195–6; [John Humfrey] *Good advice before it be too late* in *Somers Tracts* x, 198–202; [Edward Stephens] *Important questions of state* in *State Tracts* I, 167–75. Nonetheless, Humfrey seems typical in construing the people as a natural community and stating that the people have the right to place political power in new hands, not to exercise it themselves as Locke explicitly states in 2.243, lines 17–19. For these writers and the movement of radical Whigs of which they were a part see Goldie, 'The roots of true whiggism'. For a discussion of the pamphlets of the revolutionary period 1681–3 when the *Two treatises* was composed, especially John Ferguson *A just and modest vindication* 1681, see Ashcraft, *Revolutionary politics*, and Goldie, 'The structure of revolution'.

Hobbes had argued that civil war is caused by each individual claiming the right to judge the law in accordance with their subjective standard of conscience or 'private judgement'.[87] In the *Two tracts* Locke argued that in a system of popular sovereignty members would withdraw their consent and revolt whenever a law conflicted with their private interest, claiming that it contravened the public good.[88] Grotius launched a blistering attack on the theory of mutual subjection of king and people, where the people (parliament) obey if the king does not abuse his trust and the king becomes dependent on the people if he does abuse it. It would lead to confusion and disputes because king and people would judge and act differently; 'which disorders,' he concludes, 'no Nation (as I know of) ever yet thought to introduce'. Although this is directed at Buchanan's mutual pact theory, it is the kind of criticism that could be levelled at any theory which gives a right of judgement to the people or their representatives.[89]

Filmer too had made the 'anarchy' of individual judgements the centrepiece of his attack on the natural freedom tradition, citing the authority of Aristotle that 'the multitude are ill judges in their own cases'. As he roundly concludes in his criticism of Philip Hunton's defence of mixed monarchy, *A treatise of monarchy*: 'every man is brought, by this doctrine of our authors, to be his own judge. And I also appeal to the consciences of all mankind, whether the end of this be not utter confusion and anarchy.'[90] This argument was repeated throughout the Restoration by defenders of absolutism and mixed monarchy and it has remained the mainstay of conservative criticism of popular sovereignty. Locke cannot deny that people are biased in their judgements or claim that they will impartially judge in accordance with the common good. He uses the assumption of partiality to explain the breakdown of the accusatory system and of the tendency of absolutism to tyranny (2.13, 2.124–6). Therefore he must answer his conservative critics on their own ground, by showing that partiality does not entail confusion and anarchy. A sign that Locke may have seen his answer as the most controversial and unconventional aspect of the *Two treatises* is that he presents it in two separate places in the text (2.203–10, 2.224–30).

---

[87] Thomas Hobbes, *Leviathan* (Oxford: Basil Blackwell, 1957) 2.29 (p. 211).
[88] John Locke, *Two tracts on government*, 120–1, 137, 226.
[89] Grotius, *On the laws* 1.3.9.   [90] Filmer, *Patriarcha*, 296–7.

Here is the question (which is clearly in response to Filmer) (2.203):[91]

May the *Commands* then *of a Prince* be opposed? May he be resisted as often as anyone shall find himself aggrieved, and but imagine he has not Right done him? this will unhinge and overturn all Polities, and instead of Government and Order leave nothing but Anarchy and Confusion.

He presents six reasons why this will not lead to 'anarchy'. First, as we have seen, people revolt when oppressed irrespective of the type of government. A government that establishes the exercise of popular sovereignty by means of appeals to courts and parliament when people find themselves aggrieved is more likely to avoid revolution than one where juridical contestation of government is forbidden (2.224). Second, just because people are partial, they will be motivated to revolt only if the oppression touches them directly (2.208). Third, again due to partiality, they will not in fact revolt on slight occasions but only when oppression spreads to the majority or, when it affects a minority but appears to threaten all. This is so because they will calculate that it is not in their interest to revolt unless they expect to win, and this requires a majority (2.209, 2.230). (This is the sobering lesson Locke learned when the Whigs refused to support the revolution in support of the minority Dissenters in 1681–3). Fourth, people will revolt only when they are sincerely persuaded in their conscience that their cause is just because they fear divine punishment for unjust rebellion (2.21, 2.209). Fifth, people are in general habituated to the *status quo* and custom causes them to be content with its minor abuses.[92] Sixth, even when there is a revolution people usually return to the old forms of government to which they are accustomed, as English history shows (2.223, 2.225, 2.230, 2.210). In sum, Locke plays the conservative trump card of partiality and habit against his conservative opponents, showing that these causal factors make popular sovereignty more stable than absolutism. The radical right of revolt is restrained in practice by the conservative motive of self-interest and the force of habit.

In section 230 Locke asks himself the central question of seventeenth century politics: whether rulers' oppression or people's disobedience gives rise to civil war? He says that he will leave it to 'impartial

---

[91] This question is also posed by Buchanan, *De jure regni*, 145–6; and Sidney, *Discourses*, 1.24 (pp. 185–215).   [92] 2.225, 2.137, 2.158, 2.229–30.

History to determine'. One thing he means by this, I think, is whichever answer one accepts his theory is the only viable solution. However, since the question is preceded by a rehearsal of conservative motivation of the people, there is little doubt that Locke's answer is what the whole text is designed to prove: that the people react to oppression initiated primarily by princes, but also by legislatures. If so, then '*this Doctrine* of a Power in the People of providing for their safety a-new by a new Legislative, when their legislators have acted contrary to their trust, by invading their Property, is *the best fence against Rebellion*, and the probablest means to hinder it' (2.226). The reason is that rebellion means opposition to law and thus rulers are the most likely to rebel because they have the temptation and the means, as well as the encouragement of interested elites, close at hand. Showing them that the people both will revolt and have justice on their side brings the rulers' interest and duty in line with the public good: 'the properest way to prevent the evil [rebellion], is to shew them the danger and injustice of it, who are under the greatest temptation to run into it' (2.226).

However, Locke does not believe that the mere threat of revolution and the public recognition of its rightness are sufficient to guarantee good government. He grows impatient in these late sections with persuading his conservative audience that popular sovereignty is the most orderly form of government. It is, for him, enough to show that it does not lead to anarchy and confusion. Revolution is not the worst thing in politics; oppression is.[93] The only guarantee against oppression is not a doctrine but the practice of revolution itself. He argues that *no* form of government guarantees freedom and rights because every form can be abused (2.209). Only the activity of self-governing rebellion grounds freedom (2.226–9). Those who say popular sovereignty lays a foundation for civil war are, after all, right, but wrong to conclude that it is not to be allowed because it disrupts the peace of the world. It disrupts only the unjust peace of state oppression, violence, illegality and robbery (2.228):

But if they, who say it *lays a foundation for Rebellion*, mean that it may occasion Civil Wars, or Intestine Broils, to tell the People they are absolved from Obedience, when illegal attempts are made upon their Liberties or Properties, and may oppose the unlawful violence of those, who were their Magistrates, when they invade their Properties contrary to the trust put in

---

[93] 2.92, 2.111, 2.152, 2.158, 2.163, 2.210, 2.224–30.

them; and that therefore this Doctrine is not to be allowed, being so destructive to the Peace of the World. They may as well say upon the same ground, that Honest Men may not oppose Robbers or Pirates, because this may occasion disorder or bloodshed.

The justice of resistance to oppression: this is the theme of the *Two treatises*. As strange as it sounds, this is also the solution to civil wars. If Locke is correct about the causal constraints on popular revolts, then they occur only when the people are in fact oppressed. Hence the cause of civil wars must be the abuse of power by governors, who, being partial, cultivate oppression when it is possible and in their interest to do so. If, however, they know that the people have a right to revolt and will in fact revolt when oppressed, then either their interest in avoiding civil war will outweigh their interest in oppression or it will not (2.226). If it does, then oppression has been 'fenced', government normatively and causally 'limited' and civil war avoided. If, on the other hand, the right and threat do not deter abuse of power then there is nothing that can be done short of revolt, which is both just and necessary.

TOLERATION

The second problem faced by Locke and his contemporaries is the nature of religion and the relation between religion and politics, ecclesiastical and political power, in post-Reformation Europe. The wars that swept Europe were not only struggles for power; they were also religious conflicts. Religion had become, Locke argued in 1660,[94]

a perpetual foundation of war and contention [:] all those flames that have made such havoc and desolation in Europe, and have not been quenched but with the blood of so many millions, have been at first kindled with coals from the alter.

Twenty-five years later, still grappling with this problem, he said, 'I esteem it above all things necessary to distinguish exactly the Business of Civil Government from that of Religion, and to settle the just bounds that lie between the one and the other' (*LT* 26).[95] Without this there would be no end to the controversies.

Like the *Two treatises*, Locke's solution, *A letter concerning toleration*,

---

[94] Locke, *Two tracts*, 160–1.
[95] John Locke, *A letter concerning toleration*, ed. James Tully (Indianapolis: Hackett Publishing Co., 1983). *LT* hereafter.

has both an English and European context. It was written in 1685 in support of the Dissenters' struggle for religious and civil liberty in England, and translated and published by William Popple for that purpose in 1689. Locke wrote it in exile in Holland to his friend Phillip von Limborch with whom he discussed the whole Reformation experience. Also, it was written immediately after not only the failed Monmouth Rebellion for toleration in England, but also after the Revocation of the Edict of Nantes and the persecution of Huguenots. Published at Gouda in Latin, 1689, it became a classic in the European struggle for toleration. The way in which the question is posed sets it within a recognizably European problematic, the terms of which were set by the generation of Grotius and Lipsius, and it is addressed to the European-wide crisis of 150 years of wars of religion.

As early as the *Two tracts* Locke began to explore the religious causes of war. He argued that Christian leaders had inculcated two erroneous beliefs in both princes and the laity: that there is only one true way to heaven; and that it is a Christian duty to uphold and to spread the true way by force and compulsion and to suppress heresy. Both rulers and the people consequently believe themselves to have an overriding duty and an interest (fear of hell and hope of heaven) to use the force of arms to solve religious disputes. Given the multiplicity of Christian faiths, each of which considers itself orthodox and the others heterodox, this alignment of duty and motivation leads to persecution by government and religious revolts by the people.

The clergy of *all* sects, in turn, have propagated these two false beliefs in order to use either the rulers (prince or parliament) or the populace to gain access to political power, thus achieving what they want: power, dominion, property and the persecution of opponents.[96] When they succeed they use the state to persecute their competitors and potential challengers by means of jail, burning and hanging, and to confiscate and/or distribute property of various kinds and in various ways: appropriation of lands, fines, religious taxes, rights to vote and to hold public office, allocation of civil and ecclesiastical offices at the parish and natural level, transportation, and so on.[97] In

---

[96] Locke, *Two tracts*, 158, 160–2, 169–70, 211.

[97] Cf: *LT* 23–6. For persecution during the Restoration, see Edward Calamy, *The non-conformists memorial, being an account of the ministers who were ejected or silenced after the Restoration* (London: 1802), 2 vols.; G. R. Cragg, *Puritanism in the period of the great persecution* (Cambridge: Cambridge University Press, 1957); Michael Watts, *The Dissenters from the Reformation to the French Revolution* (Oxford: Clarendon Press, 1978).

using political power in this way religious elites thus provide those who serve the elites' purposes by taking up arms with an additional and temporal interest in performing their (erroneous) religious duty. Political power is thus used not to preserve property but to transfer it.

Hence, civil wars are waged in the name of religious 'reform' and religion serves as a 'vizor' or ideology which masks the struggle of competing elites for access to, and use of political power.[98] By showing the relation of ideological legitimation between religion and contests for political power Locke brings his analysis of the religious problem in line with his claim in the *Two treatises* that the central struggle in early modern Europe is over political power.

The two true Christian beliefs are the antithesis of the widely propagated false beliefs: that god tolerates each man to worship him in the way he sincerely believes to be right (over and above a few plain and simple essentials: the existence of Christ, heaven and hell and the core Christian ethics); and that Christianity should be upheld and spread by love and persuasion only, not by force and compulsion.[99] Locke held that these are the two true Christian beliefs as early as 1659, in opposition to the prevailing endless contention over 'indifferent' things: forms of worship not expressly stated in the Bible yet taken by one church or another to be enforceable and necessary to salvation.[100] These two theses about the nature of Christianity had been articulated by Hugo Grotius early in the century and they were frequently discussed by English protestants.[101] Locke's epistemological justification of the first is that nothing more than the essentials can be known with certainty, and of the second that the kind of belief necessary for salvation cannot be compelled, but must be voluntary.[102]

On the basis of this analysis Locke advanced two radically different solutions. One, like Grotius' solution, is for absolutism and the imposition of religious uniformity, in the *Two tracts*, and the other for popular sovereignty and religious toleration, in *A letter concerning toleration*. A brief account of the former and of its failure will show how

[98] Locke, *Two tracts*, 160, 169–70.   [99] Locke, *Two tracts*, 161.
[100] Locke to S. H. (Henry Stubbe) mid-September 1659, *The correspondence*, 1, 75 (109–12).
[101] Hugo Grotius, *De veritate religionis Christianae*.
[102] Locke worked on these epistemological arguments in *An essay concerning toleration* (1667), *Draft A of An essay concerning human understanding* (1671), ed. Peter Nidditch (Sheffield: University of Sheffield, 1980); *A third letter for toleration . . .* (1692). See Carlo A. Viano, *John Locke, dal razionalismo all'illuminismo* (Turin: Taylor, 1961).

he moved to the latter and provide a better understanding of its main features, as well as throwing light on the *Two treatises*. Both solutions turn on removing the cause and justification of the wars of religion – that it is the duty of the state and people to uphold the true religion – and on replacing this with preservation, or the 'public good', as the duty of government.

The *Two tracts* is Locke's proposal for the political and religious form of the Restoration settlement of 1660–2. He argues – against a proposal for toleration based on individual conscience advanced by Edward Bagshawe – that as long as the two false beliefs continue to be widely held, a policy of religious toleration would be used by religious groups to build up strength and, eventually, to precipitate another civil war in the attempt to gain political power.[103] The call for toleration thus masks the underlying will to power of a clerical elite bent on domination, as he repeats even in *A letter concerning toleration* (32–3, 43). His solution is for everyone to alienate irrevocably their natural power, including over indifferent things, to an absolute monarch, Charles II. Without this total alienation no sovereignty would be formed. As we have seen, Locke repudiates this type of alienation theory of sovereignty in the *Two treatises*. Indeed, the *Two treatises* often reads as a direct refutation of the *Two tracts*.

Given total alienation, the monarch would then impose whatever forms of worship he judged necessary for peace, order and the public good, using solely customary and prudential considerations as his guide. The magistrate does not have the duty to impose the true religion, convert his subjects or suppress heresy. Religious activity is assessed and governed in accordance with the political criterion of the 'public good'.[104] Locke then suggests that if the Dissenters (Baptists, Presbyterians, Quakers and Independents) were peaceful, the monarch could tolerate them in the form of a Declaration of Indulgence (as Charles II in fact wished).[105] 'Indulgence' would permit Dissenters to practice their religion on the pragmatic condition that it did not disrupt public order, not on the ground of right as in the case of toleration. Dissenters could not be tolerated on the grounds of individual conscience, as Bagshawe proposed, because this would

---

[103] Edward Bagshawe, *The great question concerning things indifferent in religious worship* (London: 1660); *The second part of the great question . . .* (London: 1661). See Abrams, 'Introduction', John Locke, *Two tracts.*   [104] Locke, *Two tracts*, 119, 124–6, 149–50, 169–70, 229–32.
[105] Locke, *Two tracts*, 170. See Charles II, *Letter and declaration from Breda*, 1660.

limit the monarch's sovereignty and reintroduce a religious criterion into politics.[106]

The greatest threat to peace according to Locke comes not from the Dissenters but from the Church of England. The monarch must be absolute in order to be free of the national church or they will use the state to impose religious uniformity and gain power: [they] know not how to set bounds to their restless spirit if persecution not hang over their heads.'[107] Throughout his writings, Locke consistently attacks the Anglican Church as the greatest threat to peace and calls for its disestablishment.[108] Finally, as a consequence of alienation, a subject is always obligated to obey any law and not to question it, even if it prescribes forms of worship the subject believes to be unacceptable to god. This will not compromise a person's faith because faith is a matter of inner belief – judgement or conscience – whereas obedience to the law need only be a matter of will or outer behaviour. With this crucial Protestant distinction between inner conscience and faith and outer will and obedience, Locke could argue, like all English uniformists, that conformity and obedience are compatible with liberty of conscience.[109]

Locke never published this proposal and it would have failed if he had, because Charles II was not as absolute as Locke envisaged. He was dependent on Parliament and it was dominated by an Anglican church–gentry alliance whose aim was the imposition of religious uniformity, the extirpation of Dissent and the control of public life. Their justification for this policy was the need for a common and public religious life and the identification of religious Dissent with divisiveness, sedition and civil war, as Locke notes in the *Two treatises* and *A letter concerning toleration*. Even the moderate Anglicans or 'latitudinarians', with whom Locke is sometimes erroneously grouped, opposed toleration and worked for comprehension within the established church. Charles II fought for indulgence of Dissent and English Catholics, but the Anglican–gentry alliance was powerful enough to enact the Clarendon Code, a set of repressive laws designed to stamp out Dissent. These laws were enforced and augmented during the Restoration, sending thousands of Dissenters

---

[106] Locke, *Two tracts*, 121, 137, 154.   [107] Locke, *Two tracts*, 169.
[108] See Mark Goldie, 'John Locke and Anglican royalism', *Political studies*, 31 (1983), 581–610; Ashcraft, *Revolutionary politics*, 39–128.
[109] Locke, *Two tracts*, 220–40.

into poverty, death, jail, or transportation. Charles II used his prerogative to attempt to suspend some of these laws and to grant Indulgence to non-Anglicans, against the wishes of Parliament.

Rather than causing Dissenters to conform to Anglicanism, the Clarendon Code had the opposite effect. The Dissenters refused to comply, continued to practice their religion, disobeyed the law and suffered imprisonment and martyrdom throughout the 1660s and 1670s. The Code created a permanent underclass – oppressed and denied the freedom to practice their religion, to assemble in private or public, and to hold any public or military office – who struggled for toleration until the Act of Toleration in 1689. The Act was only a partial remedy and they were treated as second-class citizens until well into the nineteenth century. By that time the Anglican–Dissent division had become the major political cleavage in English society. From 1667 onward Locke wrote in support of this minority's struggle for toleration in the twofold sense of religious and civil liberty.

Locke first changed his views and began to defend toleration in *An essay concerning toleration* (1667). He prepared this manuscript for Anthony Ashley Cooper (soon to be the first Earl of Shaftesbury), the leader of the struggle for toleration and Locke's employer and closest friend until his death in 1683. The battle for toleration comprises three phases: by royal prerogative 1667–73; by parliamentary legislation 1674–81, and by revolution 1681–3, 1685, and 1688–9. The 1667 manuscript was used to persuade Charles II to support the concerted but unsuccessful effort of the dissenting congregations to gain an Indulgence by royal prerogative and to block new legislation to repress Dissent, especially the use of bounty hunting informers and transportation to the colonies in permanent servitude as punishment. First, Locke revised his views on belief and action in the light of the Dissenters' refusal to conform from 1662 to 1667. Also, he had travelled to the Duchy of Cleves in 1666 and saw that toleration could work in practice if it were based on the two true Christian beliefs.[110] Now, Locke argues if a person sincerely believes that an article of faith is true and a form of worship is acceptable to god, and thus necessary to salvation, he evidentially will profess and act accordingly. Hence, the judgement and will are not separate.[111] Rather, as he later put it in the *Essay concerning human understanding*, the 'judgement determines

[110] Locke to Robert Boyle, 12/22 December 1665, in *The correspondence*, 1.175 (227–9).
[111] Locke, *An essay concerning toleration*, 1667, in Viano, *John Locke, scritti*.

the will', and so religious liberty must include liberty of practice as well as belief.[112]

Second, god judges people on the sincerity, not the truth of their beliefs, and thus if a person sincerely believes that something is necessary and not indifferent, it is necessary for salvation. This ushers in Locke's radically subjective definition of religion, which is fully articulated later in *A letter concerning toleration*: 'that homage I pay to that God I adore in a way I judge acceptable to him'. Consequently, to profess or act contrary to one's religious beliefs, even if the magistrate so orders, is now the paramount sin of hypocrisy and it would lead to eternal damnation. This doctrine reverses the *Two tracts*. Duty and interest (salvation) are now aligned with disobedience to the imposition of religious uniformity, thereby justifying the Dissenters' widespread resistance to conformity. It also expresses for the first time *the* Lockean belief about the modern, post-Reformation individual: that the civic person is constituted by moral sovereignty over one's core beliefs and practice that cannot be alienated. He also introduces the argument that the kind of sincere belief necessary for salvation cannot be acquired by force and compulsion but only by argument and persuasion. The use of coercion in religion thus creates either enemies (as with the non-conforming Dissenters) or hypocrites (as with those who outwardly complied). In *A letter concerning toleration*, and in the three following *Letters* in its defence against the attack by Jonas Proast, the claim that sincere belief cannot be induced by coercion is singled out as the main justification of toleration and of the separation of churches, as purely voluntary societies, from state power.

The magistrate's role continues to be to uphold the public good. However, he now does not have sovereignty over his subjects' indifferent beliefs and he knows that the imposition of uniformity will in fact be resisted. Thus, a policy of uniformity will in fact be resisted. Thus, a policy of uniformity causes civil unrest – it is not a response to unrest, as the Anglicans argued – and toleration is the pragmatic means to civil peace. Given this analysis, he reiterates that *any* attempt to impose uniformity under the guise of unity or conversion is a stratagem to gain power and domination. Enforced uniformity, he continues, unites all the competing sects into one hostile opposition, whereas toleration would remove the cause of hostility, create trust

---

[112] Locke, *An essay concerning human understanding*, 2.21.48.

and tend to cause the proliferation of sects, thereby dividing and weakening further any potential threat to peace and security. The uniformists argued the other way round: Dissenters instigate civil unrest, hoping to reverse the Restoration and regain power, and the uniformists' legislation is designed to curb their ambitions and restore peace.[113]

The practical problem with this solution is: what interest do rulers have in toleration even if they accept that it brings about the public good? Locke stipulates that although Dissenters have a religious duty to disobey bad laws they also have a civil duty to suffer the punishment, since they must show that they are bound by the public good. This theory of passive resistance permits him to separate the defence of Dissent from defence of sedition, thereby undermining his opponents' identification of the two. As a result, rulers need not fear rebellion and, on the other side, as Locke is well aware, they have a lot to gain in temporal rewards from imposition. To outweigh this kind of utility calculation Locke introduces a providential argument at the end of the manuscript. God punishes with eternal damnation any ruler who abuses his power by supporting the dissimulation and domination involved in the imposition of religious uniformity. Fear of divine punishment also restrains individual subjects from sedition. Thus, belief in this providential apparatus is as necessary to good government as it is to good individual conduct: it outweighs the temporal rewards of imposing uniformity. Although he later abandons the belief that providentialism is sufficient to restrain rulers, the doctrine is an essential feature of his ethics and it is the explanation of why he believes atheists should not be tolerated (LT 51).

In 1672 Charles II introduced a Declaration of Indulgence which suspended the penal laws against Dissent. The Anglican–gentry alliance in Parliament attacked it on the grounds that it undermined mixed monarchy, the rule of law, and the constitution. Shaftesbury defended it as a legitimate exercise of royal prerogative. This long struggle for toleration through absolutism, and against Parliament and its constitutionalist justification of uniformity is expressed in Locke's treatment of prerogative in the *Two treatises*. He says that the monarch may act in his discretion not only 'beyond the law' but

---

[113] For uniformists' views, see Samuel Parker, *A discourse of ecclesiastical polity* (London: 1670); Edward Stillingfleet, *The mischief of separation* (London: 1680); *The unreasonableness of separation* (London: 1681). Locke and Tyrrell replied to Stillingfleet: Bodleian, MS. Locke c. 34.

'against the law' if this is in accordance with the public good.[114] It also leaves an opening for Lord Monmouth to introduce toleration by prerogative if the revolutions of 1681–3 or 1685 had been successful.

When Charles II withdrew his Indulgence one year later, abandoned his thirteen-year alliance with Dissent, and began to go along with the uniformists in Parliament, the Anglican–gentry alliance became monarchist and Shaftesbury and Locke turned against Charles II and absolutism. They began to build the 'radical' whig movement that would struggle for toleration first through Parliament (1675–81), then, when this did not work, through the failed revolt of 1681–3, the unsuccessful Monmouth Rebellion of 1685, and the partially successful Glorious Revolution of 1689. The transition to the combination of popular sovereignty and toleration as a right that Locke presents in *A letter concerning toleration* is first sketched in *A letter from a person of quality to his friend in the country* (1675).[115] It is a defence of Shaftesbury's opposition to an oath of allegiance, to an oath of non-alteration of the present form of church and state, and to the introduction of a standing army. Locke saw this proposed legislation as the culmination of the Church of England's drive for power: to make the monarchy absolute and *jure divino*, yet subordinate to the national church: 'to set the mitre above the crown'.[116] The monarchy had thus reached the stage mentioned in the *Two treatises* where it is open to the flattery and manipulation of the clergy (2.112, 2.209–10).[117] Since until then parliament had been manipulated in the same way, and since they failed to rally behind Shaftesbury when Charles II dissolved the three toleration (or Exclusion) parliaments in 1679–81, it is not surprising that Locke never entertained the solution of parliamentary sovereignty but moved directly to popular sovereignty.

Locke states in the 1675 *Letter* that what distinguishes limited from arbitrary monarchs is that they have not only the fear of divine punishment hanging over their heads but also 'the fear of human resistance to restrain them'.[118] Thus, a government has a sufficient motive to rule in accordance with the public good only if it fears

---

[114] 2.160, 2.164. See Weston and Greenberg, *Subjects and sovereigns*, 171–5 for Shaftesbury's defence of prerogative.

[115] In *Works*, x. It is not known for certain that Locke is the author.

[116] Locke, *Works*, x, 232.

[117] Cf: Andrew Marvell, *An account of the growth of popery and arbitrary government in England* (London: 1677).   [118] Locke, *Works*, x, 222.

armed revolt. On the other hand, the people revolt only when the government genuinely abuses the public good because they fear that the revolt will be crushed unless they have the majority on their side. If this is true, then an oath of allegiance to the present form of government, rather than the public good, undermines good government because it gives the subject who should revolt a motive not to revolt: fear of divine punishment for breaking his oath. Locke argues that a standing army is also an instrument of oppression for an analogous reason. If government governs in accordance with the public good only in virtue of fear of popular revolt, then the threat of popular revolt must be credible. But, a standing army puts this balance of power and interests in disequilibrium, because the standing army can crush rebellion and so it undermines the restraint on oppression.

Locke concludes that when people are oppressed, as with the Dissenters, they will resist, not only passively (as in *An essay concerning toleration*), but actively, by the force of arms, and they do so 'justly and rightly'.[119] Understandably, Locke left for France when this pamphlet was published and did not return until 1679. The pamphlet enunciates Shaftesbury's strategy: to work for toleration through parliament with the background threat of revolt if this was blocked. It was only after Charles II dissolved three toleration parliaments and parliamentarians 'trimmed' in 1681 that Shaftesbury and Locke turned to revolution and Locke wrote the corresponding sections of the *Two treatises*. Accordingly, Locke moved from the 1675 thesis that a credible threat of revolt is sufficient to protect liberty to his mature thesis that, as we have seen, only the actual practice of revolution is sufficient to free a people from oppression. We can also see why the right to revolt had to be lodged in the hands of individuals if the Dissenters were to liberate themselves. Most of them, after all, had experience of revolution and government from the 1640s and 1650s. The Rye House Plot was not carried through, the Monmouth rebellion of 1685 failed, and the repression was so vicious that Dissent did not surface as a political force for almost a century, except for a tiny group around Locke in 1689 lobbying, again unsuccessfully, for the radical, religious, and civil liberty of *A letter concerning toleration*. Algernon Sidney and Lord Russell were executed in 1683 and over

---

[119] Locke, *Works*, x, 222.

100 dissenters were publicly hanged following the Monmouth Rebellion.

Locke fled from England to the United Provinces in 1683 and did not return until the successful invasion of England by William in 1688. *A letter concerning toleration* was written while he was living in political exile in Holland during the winter of 1685. The text opens with the claim that toleration is the fundamental Christian virtue and duty, and he goes on later to describe it as a right. He presents three reasons why government is not concerned with the care of souls: individuals *cannot* alienate sovereignty over their speculative and practical religious beliefs necessary for salvation; outward force, political power, cannot induce the kind of sincere belief required for salvation, only persuasion can; and even if coercion could induce belief, there is no certainty that the religion of any particular government is the true religion (*LT* 26–8). One major cause of the religious wars is holding religious beliefs with more certainty than is warranted. The criteria of reasonable belief worked out in *An essay concerning human understanding* are designed to solve this problem.[120] The 'principal Consideration' he favours is the combination of the first two reasons: coercion cannot induce sincere belief and god judges on the basis of one's sincerity. These are used to justify toleration, the thesis that a church is a purely voluntary organization, and the separation of church and state. That is, they free 'men from all dominion over one another in matters of religion' by separating coercion and religious belief, introducing his two true beliefs, and thereby removing the cause of religious wars (*LT* 38).

Nonetheless, religion, like everything else in civil society, must be assessed and governed in accordance with the public good (*LT* 39). Therefore, toleration is not an absolute or sovereign right. For example, it would be the duty of government to proscribe the religious practice of sacrificing animals if the population needed the food (*LT* 42). Atheism is disallowed because fear of god is a necessary motive to cause people to keep their promises and contracts, and these are necessary in turn for social order. Religions which teach that promises are not to be kept with heretics are not to be tolerated. This would exclude some millenarian protestants and those English Catholics who retained a political allegiance to the pope. Further, any church that does not teach the duty of toleration would not be

---

[120] Locke, *An essay concerning human understanding*, 1.1.2–3, 4.15.4, discussed in chapter 6 below.

tolerated (*LT* 49.5). This would appear to eliminate the Church of England.[121]

What prevents a magistrate from arguing that a policy of outward religious uniformity is necessary, not to save souls or because it is true, but because public order requires a shared public life; that the atomism of religious diversity is deeply divisive and 'inclinable to Factions, Tumults, and Civil Wars'?[122] Locke had argued this way in 1660 and many pragmatic defenders of uniformity or comprehension did the same. Locke's first answer is to argue that, as a matter of fact, religious diversity does not cause political divisiveness nor civil unrest. Conventicles are not 'nurseries of factions and seditions' as the opponents of Dissent claim and therefore cannot be repressed on prudential grounds. European history shows that quite the opposite is true (*LT* 55):

> It is not the diversity of Opinions (which cannot be avoided) but the refusal of Toleration to those that are of different Opinion, (which might have been granted) that has produced all the Bustles and Wars, that have been in the Christian World, upon account of Religion.

If we ask why the imposition of uniformity has continued in the face of its failure to bring peace, Locke gives the predictable answer that the alleged purpose of the public good is entirely spurious. Rather, the real reason is the greed and desire for domination of the clergy and their ability to manipulate rulers and people (*LT* 55.*cf*: 24–5, 33, 35, 43, 50):

> The Heads and Leaders of the Church, moved by Avarice and insatiable desire of Dominion, making use of the immoderate Ambition of Magistrates, and the credulous Superstition of the giddy Multitude, have incensed and animated them against those that dissent from themselves.

This analysis is repeated throughout *A letter concerning toleration* and his account of the abuse of political power in the *Two treatises* traces it to the same religious roots (2.209–10, 2.112, 2.239). Remember also that Filmer's theory is singled out because it is used by the Church of England to legitimate uniformity. The *Two treatises* and *A letter concerning toleration* are two complementary analyses of civil war, or, as

---

[121] See the replies by Jonas Proast, *The argument of the letter concerning toleration briefly considered and answered* (London: 1690); Thomas Long, *The letter for toleration decipher'd* (London: 1689); Harry Bracken, 'Toleration theories: Bayle, Jurieu, Locke', *Mind and language* (Dordrecht: Foris Publications, 1983), 86–96.

[122] LT 54. Stillingfleet makes this form of argument in *The mischief of separation.*

Locke would have it, of religious domination of civil society through the state and justified popular resistance to it.

Locke is concerned not only with domination by the Church of England but also by the Catholic Church. The secret Treaty of Dover of 1671 between Charles II and Louis XIII caused the fear that the monarch might introduce Catholicism. Second, Shaftesbury's aim in the three dissolved parliaments of 1679–81 and the two rebellions was to try to exclude James II, a known Catholic, from coming to the throne and introducing Catholicism, as well as to replace him with Lord Monmouth, who would introduce toleration. Third, Locke feared that the Anglican clergy would convert to Catholicism if it served their interest in staying in power (*LT* 37–8). Fourth, he feared a Catholic invasion after the Glorious Revolution. The practical problem with Filmer's theory of non-resistance was that it left the people powerless against any of these possibilities.

Locke goes on to elucidate what specifically the clergy seek to gain by their 'Temporal Dominion' thereby illuminating another important feature of the *Two treatises* (*LT* 35). He says that 'they deprive them [Dissenters] of their estates, maim them with corporal Punishments, starve and torment them in noisom Prisons, and in the end even take away their lives' (*LT* 24). Yet, on Locke's account, nothing should be transacted in religion, 'relating to the possession of Civil and Worldly Goods', or civil rights (*LT* 30, *cf:* 31–3, 39, 43). Further, those who favour intolerance really mean that they 'are ready upon any occasion to seise the government, and possess the Estates and Fortunes of their Fellow-Subjects' (*LT* 50). Dissenters, by the imposition of uniformity, are 'stript of the Goods, which they have got by their honest Industry' (*LT* 55). Yet, the preservation of property in the sense of lives, liberties and estates earned by industry is the reason why people enter civil government in both *A letter concerning toleration* and the *Two treatises* (*LT* 47–8; *Two treatises* 2.123). The violation of this trust is also the form of oppression Locke is specifically concerned to condemn.[123] *A letter concerning toleration* thereby illuminates the property that the *Two treatises* is written to defend. It is not the private property of the bourgeoisie, but the properties – the possessions and legal, political, and religious rights – of an oppressed minority who, in the course of time, became the backbone of English

---

[123] *LT* 48–9; *Two treatises* 2.209, 2.222.

working class radicalism and took up Locke as their philosopher.[124] Revolution, property, and toleration are all of a piece for Locke.

If the strategy of religious uniformity is as Locke suggests, then we should not expect religious elites to pay any heed to his argument that it is the cause of civil unrest. Rather, we should expect them to defend their use of political power: the hinge on which their domination turns. This was indeed the response. Jonas Proast, the Chaplain of All Souls, Oxford, defended the use of force to bring Dissenters to consider the true religion in his three assaults on *A letter concerning toleration* and on Locke's two following letters. Proast argued that although coercion should not be used directly to induce religious belief, it can be used indirectly to bring people to examine religion, as, for example, public education is enforced. Further, it would be a dereliction of duty for the government to provide no public support for religion. Another Anglican attacked the *Letter* as the work of a Jesuit disguised as an atheist whose aim was to bring about chaos and ruin so Catholicism could regain hegemony.[125] In addition, the *Essay concerning human understanding* (used as a text in Dissenter academies), as well as the *Reasonableness of christianity*, were seen to threaten the established Church, and they were attacked by leading Anglicans and defended by several Dissenters.[126] The Toleration Act of 27 May, 1689 shows how far outside of reasonable opinion was Locke's call for toleration of anyone who believed in any god and for the end of coercion in religion. The Act denied freedom of worship to unorthodox Dissenters (those who denied the Trinity) and Roman Catholics, and granted it, as a revocable exemption from earlier legislation, to Protestant Trinitarian Dissenters who took the oath of allegiance and obtained a licence to meet, but it denied them access to public office.

Locke was well aware that just showing that the public good is disrupted by policies of uniformity and best served by toleration would have no positive effect on the ruling elite. As in the *Two treatises* he reports that the rulers will simply claim that those who protest and dissent from the policy will be said to be the cause of unrest, and their protestations used to justify further repression (*LT* 52–5; *Two treatises* 2.218). His practical solution to the problem is to argue in the same way as in the *Two treatises* that individuals must exercise their popular

---

[124] Max Beer, *A history of British socialism* (London: The National Labour Press, 1921), 101.
[125] Thomas Long, *The letter for toleration decipher'd*, 1689.
[126] John Yolton, *John Locke and the way of ideas* (Oxford: Clarendon Press, 1956), 26–72.

sovereignty and judge for themselves whether any law concerning religious practice is in the public good. If the magistrate enjoins anything 'that appears unlawful to the Conscience of the private individual' and it is also judged to be 'directed to the publick Good', then 'a private person is to abstain from the Action that he judges unlawful [according to his conscience]; and he is to undergo the Punishment' (*LT* 48). A person has the right to disobey a just law if it conflicts with his conscience, provided he recognizes his political obligation to the public good by suffering the punishment.

The case Locke is of course primarily concerned with is when the law appears not only unlawful to the conscience but also contrary to the public good. If, for example, 'the People, or any Party amongst them, should be compell'd to embrace a strange Religion, and join in the Worship and Ceremonies of another Church', they would be under no obligation to suffer punishment for disobedience (*LT* 48). What if the magistrate continues to believe it is for the public good and the subjects believe the contrary? Locke answers with the same revolutionary doctrine as in the *Two treatises* (*LT* 49):

Who shall be the Judge between them? I answer, God alone. For there is no judge upon earth between the Supreme Magistrate and the People.

And he leaves no doubt as to what this means: 'There are two sorts of Contests amongst men: the one managed by Law, the other by Force: and these are of that nature, that where the one ends, the other always begins.'

Therefore, as in the *Two treatises*, people are justified in turning to revolution when they are stripped of their properties and their religion (*LT* 55):

What else can be expected, but that these men, growing weary of the Evils under which they labour, should in the end think it lawful for them to resist Force with Force, and to defend their natural Rights (which are not forfeitable on account of Religion) with Arms as well as they can.

Civil wars will continue as long as the 'Principle of Persecution for Religion' continues to prevail. The attempt to impose uniformity by coercion is not only the justification of revolt but also its cause. The reason is that oppression naturally causes people to struggle to cast it off (*LT* 52):

Believe me, the Stirs that are made, proceed not from any peculiar temper of this or that Church or Religious Society; but from the common Disposition of all Mankind who when they groan under any heavy Burthen, endeavour naturally to shake off the Yoke that galls their Neck.

Revolution is necessary to establish and protect toleration. Churches would be required to preach toleration as the basis of their freedom, to teach that 'Liberty of Conscience is every man's natural Right', and that no body should be compelled by law or force in religion (*LT* 51). This would undermine the link between religious and political power that legitimates religious domination and, hence, 'This one thing would take away all ground of Complaints and Tumults upon account of Conscience.' Unlike a National Church, which causes turmoil, a plurality of equally treated congregations would be, according to Locke, the best guard and support of public peace. Knowing they can do no better than mutual toleration, the churches 'will watch one another, that nothing may be innovated or changed in the Form of the Government' (*LT* 53). Again, his point seems to be that the only solid foundation for civil and religious liberties is the readiness to govern those who violate them by means of popular political rebellion. Popular religious sovereignty, like popular political sovereignty, is the solution to the problem of government.

THE ART OF GOVERNMENT

The third problem is to develop a practical 'art of government', as Locke calls it, appropriate to the conditions of early modern state building.[127] This practice comprises internal administration, 'the art of conducting men right in society', and international relations, 'supporting a community amongst its neighbours'.[128] Locke's solution to this problem is as important and influential as his other two, and would have been accorded as much space by contemporary and Enlightenment commentators.

The aim of the early modern art of governing is, as we have seen, the preservation of society and its members. This comprises the negative role of maintaining law and order and the positive role of increasing the productive capacities, maintaining the welfare of subjects, and of co-ordinating these to bring about the 'riches and

---

[127] Locke, *Some thoughts*, 400.
[128] Locke, draft letter to the Countess of Peterborough, 1697, in *Educational writings*, ed. Axtell, 392–6, 396.

power' of the community.[129] In this mercantile strategy, Locke points out, the wealth and strength of the nation is assessed relative to other European states in a zero sum situation of commercial and military rivalry.[130] This balance of power and trade system of independent and sovereign states, each with the right to wage war to preserve itself, was officially recognized in the Treaty of Westphalia in 1648. The commercial and military struggle was among European states, but it was over the conquest, colonization and exploitation of the non-European world. This required the co-ordination of the four following jurisdictions: the administration of the colonial system and slave trade to the advantage of the mother country; the regulation of national and international trade; the reform of labouring activities and welfare and population measures; and the maintenance of a global military and diplomatic complex capable of protecting and extending the mercantile system. The art of governing this welfare–warfare system was called, from Montchretien's treatise of 1615 to Locke's contemporaries, Sir William Petty and Sir Dudley North, political economy or political arithmetic.[131]

Locke was at the centre of this activity as secretary to Shaftesbury, with his extensive colonial holdings, and as a member of two Boards of Trade: 1673–4 and 1696–1700. The Board was an inquisitorial body responsible for the invigilation of the following areas of the mercantile complex: national and international trade, manufacturing, the employment of the poor, commercial exploitation and administration of the colonies, and the navy. The Board reported to the king or the Privy Council, not parliament.[132] Locke's experience on the Board surely partially accounts for his broad construal of prerogative in the *Two treatises*. In the *Two treatises* Locke outlines the mercantile strategy (2.42):[133]

This shews, how much numbers of men are to be preferred to largenesse of dominions, and that the increase of lands [*sic?* hands. *cf*: 1.iv.33] and the right

[129] Bodleian, MS. Locke c. 30, fos. 18–19, partly printed in Richard Cox, *Locke on war and peace* (Oxford: Clarendon Press, 1960), 175–6.
[130] Locke, *Some considerations of the consequences of lowering the interest and raising the value of money*, *Works*, v, 13.
[131] See Eli Heckscher, *Mercantilism*, tr. M. Shapiro (London: Allan and Unwin, 1955, 2nd edn).
[132] See Hubert Smith, *The Board of Trade* (London: Putnam, 1928); E. E. Rich, 'The first Earl of Shaftesbury's colonial policy', *Transactions of the Royal Historical Society*, 5th series, 7 (1957), 47–60; Peter Laslett, 'John Locke, the great recoinage, and the origins of the Board of Trade', in *John Locke: problems and perspectives*, ed. John Yolton (Cambridge: Cambridge University Press, 1969).   [133] See chapter 5 below.

imploying of them is the great art of government. And that Prince who shall be so wise and godlike as by established laws of liberty to secure protection and incouragement to the honest industry of mankind against the oppression of power and narrowness of Party will quickly be too hard for his neighbours.

He promises more 'bye and bye' but does no more in the *Two treatises* than lay out the general framework for governing the actions of each individual for the sake of preservation. Nonetheless, his writings on the art of government are extensive: *The constitution of Carolina* (1668), *Some considerations of the consequences of the lowering of interest and raising the value of money* (1692), *Further considerations* (1695), and *The Report of the Board of Trade on the reform of the Poor Law* (1697). In addition, *Some thoughts concerning education* (1693) and *On the conduct of the understanding* (1706) are also concerned with the art of government in the broad seventeenth-century sense of governing and reforming the mental and physical conduct of others.[134]

   The Report of the Board of Trade is Locke's proposal to reform the system of about 200 workhouses or poorhouses 'for setting on work and employing the poor of this kingdom, and making them useful to the publick and thereby easing others of that burthen'.[135] Throughout the Restoration the number of poor increased and, consequently, so did the parish poor relief and the level of concern about an ungovernable population of poor and vagabonds. Locke's proposal was one among many put forward during the Restoration. Charles Davenant calculated the cost of the system to each parish and Gregory King estimated that over half the population were dependent in some way on poor relief.[136] Both were members of the Board of Trade and their works helped to establish political statistics or economy: the administration and reflexive monitoring of the labouring population considered as a resource utilizable in policies to increase riches and power.[137]

   For Locke in *The report*, as for Davenant and others, it is a case of lazy 'drones' living off the labour of others (similar to his description

---

[134] Chapter 6 below takes up the following theme in more detail.
[135] Printed in H. R. Fox Bourne, *The life of John Locke* (London: 1876), 2 vols., II, 377–91. Since it is short, I have dispensed with the page references in my summary below.
[136] Gregory King, *Natural and political observations* (London: 1696); Charles Davenant, *An essay on the probable means of making a people gainers in the balance of trade* (London: 1699); *An essay upon ways and means* (London: 1695).
[137] See Peter Buck, 'Seventeenth-century political arithmetic: civil strife and vital statistics', *Isis*, 68 (1977), 67–84; Edgar Furniss, *The position of the laborer in a system of nationalism* (New York: A. M. Kelley, 1965).

of the Anglican clergy). The cause of the growth of the poor is 'relaxation of discipline and corruption of manners'. The solution is to use the workhouses in three ways to correct and reform the inmates by instilling habits of 'virtue and industry' through a system of severe corporal punishments and simple, but useful and repetitive work. First, the system should be used as houses of correction for able-bodied men caught begging, to 'amend' their habits 'by the discipline of the place'. These men would then serve the needs of state by being pressed into three years' 'strict discipline' in the Royal Navy or put to work in the parish. Those over fifty, the maimed, and women would remain in the houses of correction, and engage in productive labour as the local parish requires. Locke's main target group, however, consists of the children of all those on poor relief. The poorhouses in this case function as working schools for male and female children, thus freeing the mother and father for work and removing the basis for their claim for relief. Children would attend from three to fourteen, learning basic skills and the rudiments of Christianity. Through a regimen of work and punishment they would be 'from infancy inured to work, which is of no small consequence to the making of them sober and industrious all their lives'. Unlike his friend Thomas Firmin who was running workhouses on a profit basis, Locke did not expect them to be entirely self-supporting. His aim was rather to habituate the young to a life of industry and discipline. From fourteen to twenty-three they were to be placed in the service of local parishioners to learn a trade, and the local proprietors were to be forced to train them. The system would be operated by storekeepers, guardians, and overseers caught up in a network of legal and financial rewards and punishments.

The proposal became a Bill but it was not enacted as a national policy. Nonetheless, it was utilized in Bristol and it served as a highly praised model for discipline of the labouring classes, organization of child labour, factory discipline, and reform schools right up to the Webbs.[138] The editors of the 1793 London edition enthused that 'Mr Locke' appears (viii):

to be convinced that rewards and punishments, and the mixing habits of industry with principles of religious duties, were the best and surest means of effecting that reformation on the manners of the people, which in those days was judged essential to the strength and safety of the nation.

[138] Sidney and Beatrice Webb, *English local government, English Poor Law history: Part 1: the old Poor Law* (London: Longmans, Green and Co., 1927), 102–20.

Moreover, Locke points out that the lack of the means of subsistence for the poor is a major cause of rebellions.[139] Since access to the means of subsistence is a natural right and the fundamental duty of government, these subsistence revolts are obviously legitimate. The solution to this problem is Locke's proposal for the reform of the national workhouse system, for it provides subsistence work for the able-bodied poor and relief for the disabled. In so doing, it conforms to the theory of the *Two treatises*: it operationalizes the natural right to the means of preservation and the duty to preserve oneself; and it implements the natural duty to preserve others by compelling the local landlords to support their workhouse and hire its inmates as servants.[140] Although Locke's proposal is severe and disruptive of the traditional familial bonds and habits of the poor, it should be assessed relative to the actual functioning of the workhouse system. The system was not reformed and by the mid-eighteenth century Jonas Hanway estimated that 80 per cent of the children died in workhouses.[141]

The proposal, and the austere regimen he put forward to reform the gentry to industry and virtue in *Some thoughts concerning education*, is part of the European-wide proliferation of 'neo-stoic' techniques of disciplining the population recently discussed by a number of historians.[142] The individual labourer is considered as a resource who, on the one hand, needs to be cared for, and, on the other, can be reformed by repetition and practice to be a productive and utile part of a strategy to increase the strength of the nation *vis-à-vis* other states. Political economy as social science developed in conjunction with these techniques and employed the new kinds of probabilistic reasoning and knowledge which are classically presented in Locke's *Essay concerning human understanding*. What is not stressed enough in recent work in this area, and is particularly clear in Locke's case, is the overall integration of these policies into the 'strengthening' of the state for military and commercial rivalry. This overriding concern is evident as well in Locke's analysis of the revolution settlement of

---

[139] Locke, *Some considerations*, *Works*, v, 71.
[140] Locke's rights and duties of preservation are very close to the seventeenth-century legal rights and duties of subsistence that the Poor Law embodied. See 39 Eliz. c.3; 43 Eliz. c.2; 1 James c.17, 3; 14 Char. II c.12, 4–14, c.18, c.21.
[141] John Hutchins, *Jonas Hanway, 1712–1786* (London: S.P.C.K., 1940), 50–71.
[142] Michel Foucault, *Discipline and punish: the birth of the prison*, tr. A. Sheridan (New York: Pantheon, 1977); Marc Raeff, *The well-ordered police state*, Gerhard Oestreich, *Neostoicism*.

1689. He underlines the need to settle differences and to unite with King William in a Protestant alliance against France.[143]

At the centre of Locke's analysis is the premise that the individual is, as he famously states in *Some thoughts concerning education*, 'only as white paper or wax, to be moulded and fashioned as one pleases'.[144] He cleared the way for this by attacking the competing view that the individual is born with innate ideas or dispositions (either to good or to evil). The only restraint on the moulding of individuals is that each has an innate 'concern' or 'uneasiness' to avoid punishment (pain) and to seek reward (pleasure, or diminution of pain). Therefore, one can be led to engage in mental or physical behaviour by the use of punishments and rewards and, by the continual repetition and practice of the behaviour, the individual becomes accustomed and habituated to it, eventually finding pleasure in it.[145] The three techniques of punishments and rewards for forming virtuous habits are: the use of praise and blame of teachers or peers as rewards and punishments in the educational system of *Some thoughts concerning education*; the use of the punishments and rewards of the workhouse system; and the use of fear of hell and hope of heaven to instill basic Christian virtues, in the *Reasonableness of Christianity*. Locke argues that these techniques have always been used by elites to inculcate ideas and dispositions, which they then claimed were innate. This is especially true of the clergy who have used these techniques to instill their false beliefs about Christianity and so legitimate their domination and cause the 150 years of war.[146] It is now possible to use these techniques to break down the old habits of thought and behaviour that have caused such havoc in Europe and mould new ones of toleration, industriousness, and military preparedness.[147] That is, the application of these disciplinary techniques in churches, workhouses and educational institutions would render individuals 'subject to law' and make them the fit bearers of the rights and duties laid out in the *Two treatises*.

These ideas, and his proposals for education and political economy built upon them, are written within the broad context of this modern or objectifying way of thinking about and governing subjects. Locke,

---

[143] Farr and Roberts, 'John Locke and the glorious revolution', 395–8.
[144] Locke, *Some thoughts*, 325.
[145] Locke, *An essay concerning human understanding*, 2.21.69–70.
[146] Locke, *An essay*, 1.3.27, 1.4.24.
[147] Locke, *Some thoughts*, Dedication, sections 1–3, 54, 64, 216.

especially in his idea of the malleability of the individual, took these ideas further than most, as his critics quickly pointed out. However, it should be remembered that for Locke, in his writings of the 1680s, reform and habituation by these techniques are limited by mankind's 'common disposition' to resist oppression; to fight against a yoke that galls one's neck. It follows from this that any reform ought to be enacted and administered in a way that not only preserves the population but also respects the rights of the person and human agency laid out in the *Two treatises* and *A letter*, or it would violate natural law and meet with justifiable resistance. Perhaps chapter 5 of the *Second treatise* is a model for this, for he writes that the management of labour must be in accordance with the 'laws of liberty' (42, quoted above). Nonetheless, it is unclear to what extent Locke was aware of the tension between his juristic political theory, which limits the degree and manner of control government can exercise over citizens, and some of his methods of reform, which treat the human subject as a malleable resource. Yet, even in *The report to the Board of Trade*, Locke shows that his proposal is in conformity with the old poor laws and that the local parishioners who support the workhouse are bound by their duties to the poor (see chapter 7 below).

For the eighteenth century, Locke's writings on the arts of government were at least as important as the *Two treatises* and *A letter concerning toleration*. As Marx noted, 'Locke became the philosopher *par excellence* of political economy, in England, France and Italy.'[148] On the basis of these diverse and inchoate theories and techniques of discipline and reform, the eighteenth century was to construct more meticulous and more totalizing practices of government and revolution than juridical thought and action allowed. Juridical practices and classical political philosophy, which had been sovereign from John of Salisbury to Locke, came to be challenged by these new ways of governing, involving the disciplines of applied social science and social theory.

[148] Karl Marx, *Capital*, tr. B. Fowkes (New York: Random House, 1977), I, 14, 513 note.

Property disputes

CHAPTER 2

After the Macpherson thesis[1]

INTRODUCTION

C. B. Macpherson's thesis of possessive individualism has played a role in contemporary political thought similar to the role of Max Weber's thesis of the Protestant ethic and the spirit of capitalism. Initially a challenge to the received wisdom, it soon became the reigning orthodoxy and then it was subjected to intense and sustained criticism. The problems with the thesis that this scrutiny brought to light were sufficient to cause many scholars of early modern English political thought to become sceptical of it, and many of its supporters argue, as Gordon Schochet has recently done, that Macpherson was right for the wrong reasons.[2] Accordingly, scholarship has moved in two directions. First, the research concerned with the relations between early modern political thought and capitalist relations of production has become considerably more technical, both historically and analytically, than Macpherson's original argument.[3] Second, scholars have moved on to study different questions. The thesis of possessive individualism now stands partly aside from and

---

[1] A paper delivered at the conference on *The intellectual legacy of C. B. Macpherson*, University of Toronto, 27–8 October 1989.

[2] 'Macpherson was almost right – but not at all for the right reasons'. Gordon Schochet, 'Radical politics and Ashcraft's treatise on Locke', *The Journal of the History of Ideas* 50, 3 (July–Sept. 1989), 491–510, 508. See also Neal Wood, *John Locke and agrarian capitalism* (Berkeley: University of California Press, 1986). He argues that capitalism in England arose in the agrarian section and he abandons Macpherson's model of a possessive market society (which had the virtue of being testable) for the description of capitalism growing and evolving out of seeds in the seventeenth century.

[3] See: Alan Ryan, *Property* (Minneapolis: University of Minnesota Press, 1987); Andrew Reeve, *Property* (Atlantic Highlands: Humanities Press, 1986); Jeremy Waldron, *The right to private property* (Oxford: Clarendon Press, 1989); James Grunebaum, *Private ownership* (London: Routledge and Kegan Paul, 1987); Gopal Sreenivasan, 'The limits of private rights in property', Oxford B.Phil. thesis, 1988; Stephen Buckle, *The natural history of property* (Oxford: Basil Blackwell, 1990).

tangential to the central concerns and debates in this area. Nonetheless, like the Weber thesis, it has not only had a substantive influence on how we think of the history of the present but it also continues to be an important object of comparison and contrast when we reflect critically on early modern political thought and our relationship to it. If we think of its role, therefore, as a constant provocation to critical research and reflection on the history of the present, rather than as a dogma whose worth is measured by the number of adherents, then it is one of the most challenging and successful hypotheses to be advanced in the history of European political thought over the last thirty years.

My aim in this chapter is to review the major criticisms which caused some scholars to dissent from the possessive individualism thesis, and to present an overview of current research in the field. I do this in the following steps. First, I review the political problem of the post-war period Macpherson sought to illuminate by means of his thesis. Then, I lay out the various parts of the thesis and briefly summarize those criticisms brought against the thesis which themselves have managed to survive critical scrutiny. In the following section, I turn to current work in the field: first to the flowering of specialized studies of early modern English political thought and then to three lines of research that occupy the ground once held by the Macpherson thesis.[4] These are the work on republicanism or civic humanism initiated by John Pocock, on the 'arts of government' begun by Michel Foucault, and on juristic political thought and institutions by Richard Tuck and Istvan Hont. This work shows us that early modern English political thought is more complex and addressed to a wider range of political problems than the thesis of possessive individualism led us to believe. We now have a richer and more nuanced account of the variety of ways Europeans reflected on the emergence of markets and how they sought to explain, challenge and justify them. In addition, this scholarship has opened up a form of reflection on the seventeenth century which is not determined by the question of the rise of capitalism, yet which was in fact recommended by Macpherson as a line of research twenty-seven years ago.

---

[4] There is also a large body of feminist and ecological scholarship which I do not discuss because it does not challenge the Macpherson thesis as directly as the other three, and it is discussed in the other papers of the conference.

THE 'TWENTIETH-CENTURY DILEMMA' AND A NEW PROBLEM

As Macpherson saw it in 1962, liberal-democratic political theory faced a dilemma: it was impossible in the twentieth century to generate a valid theory of political obligation for societies that are both liberal-democratic and market societies.[5] For there to be a valid theory of obligation for such societies two conditions have to be met: 1. the members of the society must 'see themselves, or [be] capable of seeing themselves, as equal in some respect more fundamental than all the respects in which they are unequal' (272); and 2. there must be 'a cohesion of self-interests, among all those who have a voice in choosing the government, sufficient to offset the centrifugal forces of a possessive market society' (273). In the 'heyday of the market society', from the seventeenth to the mid-nineteenth centuries, the equality condition was met by the apparent equality of subordination to the laws of the market and the cohesion of interests condition was met by the restriction of political power to a cohesive possessing class. The emergence of class-conscious industrial work-forces with the franchise in the later nineteenth century undermined both the belief in the equal subordination to the market and the cohesion of interests, and thereby rendered invalid the liberal theory of obligation that had been based on these conditions.

Since modern societies are still market societies, he continued, the assumptions of possessive individualism continue to be factually accurate. That is (275):

The individual in market society *is* human as proprietor of his own person. However much he may wish it to be otherwise, his humanity does depend on his freedom from any but self-interested contractual relations with others. His society does consist of a series of market relations.

This premise is, as he puts it, 'factually accurate' yet 'morally offensive'. So, the dilemma is: 'Either we reject possessive individualist assumptions, in which case our theory is unrealistic, or we retain them, in which case we cannot get a valid theory of obligation' (275). Thus, we can see that what he hoped to do in advancing the thesis of possessive individualism was to show that, with the emergence of industrial working classes, liberal theory could not provide 'a valid

---

[5] C. B. Macpherson, *The political theory of possessive individualism* (Oxford: Oxford University Press, 1962). All page references in brackets are to this edition.

theory of political obligation to a liberal democratic state in a possessive market society' (275).

As we might expect, he goes on to entertain one practical route out of the dilemma; namely, to abandon the actual relations of a possessive market society while retaining liberal political institutions. This, by definition, would solve the problem of cohesion since the centrifugal forces were said to be caused by market relations. Nonetheless, he goes on to claim that this socialist alternative would not solve the problem of equality. This is surprising since in his later works an equality of non-possessive, productive and expressive individualism is advanced on a democratic-socialist base. Instead, this early text takes a completely unexpected turn in the last pages.

He says that the question of whether or not we need to change the actual possessive market relations is now of 'second importance' because there has been an additional change in modern societies. This is the introduction of atomic warfare. Now, the destruction of every individual on the planet is a real possibility and this has 'created a new equality of insecurity among individuals' (276). This new Hobbesian equality of insecurity itself provides the basis for a new theory of obligation, not to a nation-state, but to a 'wider political authority'. The possibility of global destruction has caused the problems of possessive individualism to shrink and they now can 'be brought to manageable proportions' (277). Thus,

the self-interested individual, whatever his possessions, and whatever his attachments to a possessive market society, can see that the relations of the market society must yield to the overriding requirement that, in [Richard] Overton's words, which now acquire a new significance, 'human society, cohabitation or being, . . . above earthly things must be maintained'.

Overcoming existing market relations – the transition to socialism – is accordingly not the first priority. Rather, the task of liberal-democratic political theory is to develop a theory of obligation to 'a wider political authority' based on the equality of insecurity brought about by the change in the technology of warfare, and then to investigate how market relations are connected to the primarily political–military framework. Once this has been ascertained, one could ask how far market relations, as well as military relations, 'must yield' within a theory of obligation based on humanity's interest in security rather than in acquisition. Such a theory, which he saw as amending Hobbes 'more clearly than he was by Locke', would require careful attention to the changes wrought by the new mode of warfare (277).

This challenge to set aside the transition to socialism debate and to face the new problem posed by atomic weapons straight-on was rarely taken up by his followers or his critics. They continued to let the problematic of capitalism versus socialism set the terms of their reflection on seventeenth century political thought. Indeed, one of the ironies of contemporary political thought is that Macpherson's best critic, John Dunn, was one of the few to take up precisely this issue of political obligation in the nuclear age.[6] However, after a period of sustained testing of the thesis of possessive individualism from within the conventions of the contemporary problematic of socialism versus capitalism, political theorists have freed themselves from this problematic, which has tended to dominate our scholarship since the war and which has been held in place by the division of the world into capitalist and socialist states. These scholars have shifted their attention to the political and military dimensions of early modern political thought and action. This research has thus begun to furnish us with histories of the foundations of our contemporary political–military predicament and, thereby, to put us in a position to take up the question Macpherson recommended to us twenty-seven years ago.

THESIS AND CRITICISMS

'I'll teach you differences.'
(Kent, *King Lear*, I.4.88–9)

Macpherson summarized the thesis of possessive individualism as follows:[7]

(1) Man, the individual, is seen as absolute natural proprietor of his own capacities, owing nothing to society for them. Man's essence is freedom to use his capacities in search of satisfactions. This freedom is limited properly only by some principle of utility or utilitarian natural law which forbids harming

---

[6] John Dunn, 'Political obligations and political possibilities', in *Political obligation in its historical context* (Cambridge: Cambridge University Press, 1980), 241–301, and 'The future of political philosophy in the West', in *Rethinking modern political theory* (Cambridge: Cambridge University Press, 1985), 171–90.

[7] C. B. Macpherson, 'The deceptive task of political theory', in *Democratic theory* (Oxford: Oxford University Press, 1975 [1973]) 195–207, 199. Compare *The political theory of possessive individualism*, 3.

others. Freedom therefore is restricted to, and comes to be identified with, domination over things, not domination over men. The clearest form of domination over things is the relation of ownership or possession. Freedom is therefore possession. Everyone is free, for everyone possesses at least his own capacities. (2) Society is seen, not (as it had been) as a system of relations of domination and subordination between men and classes held together by reciprocal rights and duties, but as a lot of free equal individuals related to each other through their possessions, that is, related as owners of their own capacities and of what they have produced and accumulated by the use of their capacities. The relation of exchange (the market relation) is seen as the fundamental relation of society. Finally (3) political society is seen as a rational device for the protection of property, including capacities; even life and liberty are considered as possessions, rather than as social rights with correlative duties.

He claimed that this conception of 'man'[8] as 'an infinitely desirous consumer of utilities', of society as a set of market relations, and of government as a mechanism to protect the property each individual has in his person, capacity to labour and contracts can be found in the writings of Thomas Hobbes, the Levellers, James Harrington, John Locke, David Hume, Edmund Burke, Jeremy Bentham, and James Mill.[9] These authors developed this shared set of beliefs in response to and as the legitimation of a 'possessive market society', which Macpherson carefully defined by means of a model and claimed that it emerged in England by the 1640s. This ideology replaced an earlier 'traditional' view that was neither possessive nor individualist. Finally, the shared beliefs of these writers make up a single tradition of political thought called 'English liberalism' or 'English utilitarian liberalism'.

The major criticisms of this thesis up to 1981 were summarized by David Miller in a well-known article in *Political studies* in 1982.[10] Miller concluded his summary by saying, 'It is not easy, on the basis of these critical observations, to develop an ideological model of

---

[8] Macpherson uses 'man' throughout all editions. I have followed this in presenting his views. See the comments in Carole Pateman and T. Brennan, 'Mere auxiliaries to the commonwealth: women and the origins of liberalism', *Political Studies* 27, 2 (1979), 183–200 on the absence of gender analysis in Macpherson's thesis.

[9] Political thought from Hobbes to Locke is treated in *The political theory of possessive individualism*. For Hume, see 'The economic penetration of political theory: some hypotheses', *The Journal of the History of Ideas* 39 (1978), 101–18. For Burke, see *Burke* (Oxford: Oxford University Press, 1980). For Bentham and Mill, see *The life and times of liberal democracy* (Oxford: Oxford University Press, 1977). And, further, *Property: mainstream and critical positions* (Toronto: University of Toronto Press, 1978).

[10] David Miller, 'The Macpherson version', *Political Studies* 30, 1 (1982), 120–7.

comparable power to Macpherson's which can then be applied to each of our subjects [i.e., authors]' (125). This is certainly true. Not only did the critics show that these authors, with the important exception of Bentham, were not endorsing unlimited acquisition of property in a capitalist society, but also that each of the authors was addressing slightly different problems within a variety of political vocabularies or languages. Where Macpherson saw one continuous tradition over two centuries his critics have seen a motley or plurality of political problems and responses, and also a variety of different uses of similar concepts. The emphasis has been on *difference*, not sameness, as it has been throughout the human sciences in recent years. Having disaggregated Macpherson's synthesis and shown the diversity of political thought and action of the early modern period it causes us to overlook, no one has attempted to erect a new synthesis which would, after all, as a new form of reflection, simply obscure again the diversity and ambiguity of use of early modern political thought we have so painstakingly sought to recover.

However, to build a bridge to the three lines of research I wish to discuss, let us recall some of the common threads of criticism Miller mentioned in 1982 (125). From Hobbes to Locke unlimited consumption was not considered rational or morally permissible. By the late eighteenth century Europeans may have been faced by the possibility of a society given over to unlimited consumption, but this does not seem to be a concern of writers in the earlier period. When property rights were defended, this was against attacks from absolute monarchs or 'degenerative' representative bodies. These rights were limited by government and correlated with obligations to the destitute. The word 'property' had a broader reference than today: it included personal rights, especially religious and civil liberties. Although no one argued against commerce, manufacturing or agricultural improvement *per se*, no one had a vision of a full-scale commercial or capitalist society. Macpherson's model of a 'possessive market society' misrepresents the political economy in the texts as well as what we know of the English 'economy' in the seventeenth century. Moreover, the thesis of possessive individualism misidentifies the primary problems these theorists were addressing. They were not concerned with justifying unlimited accumulation in a market society but with more basic political problems of political order, preservation, state-building, obedience and liberty in a situation of insecurity brought on by a century of civil wars, religious wars, the Thirty

Years' War, and the European wars of the latter half of the seventeenth century.

Initially, of course, these criticisms were advanced within the framework presupposed by the thesis of possessive individualism: that is, that these texts were responses to problems thrown up by the emergence of capitalist relations. In general, the criticisms were simply that the authors were not endorsing market relations as fully as Macpherson claimed or that England was not as far along the road to capitalism as he claimed. However, the cumulative effect of these criticisms was to call into question the background picture which both Macpherson and his critics shared. It now looked as if we imposed a form of representation on the period and that our debates within it simply reinforced this framework and so caused us to misunderstand the texts. As Wittgenstein famously described this type of philosophical problem, 'A *picture* held us captive. And we could not get outside it, for it lay in our language and language seemed to repeat it to us inexorably.'[11] It was within this period of scepticism in the late 1970s about the appropriateness of the background picture of the period held by Macpherson and his critics that new lines of research were initiated. The works in this period by Quentin Skinner on Hobbes, Richard Tuck on Hobbes and the Levellers, John Pocock on Harrington, John Dunn and Mark Goldie on Locke, and Keith Tribe on economic discourse all criticize and set aside the central questions of Macpherson and his critics.[12] They took up the *political* problems that the earlier critics had identified as central to the theorists of the period. At the same time, Michel Foucault published his study of early modern forms of power, bodies of knowledge, and types of subjectivity. Carole Pateman began to

[11] Ludwig Wittgenstein, *Philosophical investigations*, tr. G. E. M. Anscombe (Oxford: Basil Blackwell, 1988), r. 115.
[12] Quentin Skinner, 'The ideological context of Hobbes's political thought', *Historical Journal* 9 (1966), 286–317, and 'Conquest and consent: Thomas Hobbes and the engagement controversy', in *The interregnum*, ed. G. E. Aylmer (London: Macmillan, 1974), 79–98, and 'The limits of historical explanation', *Philosophy* 41 (1966), 199–215. John Pocock, ed., *The political works of James Harrington* (Cambridge: Cambridge University Press, 1977), and *The Machiavellian moment* (Princeton: Princeton University Press, 1975). Richard Tuck, *Natural rights theories, their origins and development* (Cambridge: Cambridge University Press, 1979). John Dunn, *The political thought of John Locke* (Cambridge: Cambridge University Press, 1969). Mark Goldie, 'The roots of true whiggism: 1688–1694', *History of political thought* 1, 2 (1980), 195–236. Keith Tribe, *Land, labour, and economic discourse* (London: Routledge and Kegan Paul, 1978). See the overview in John Pocock, 'The varieties of whiggism from exclusion to reform', in *Virtue, commerce, and history* (Cambridge: Cambridge University Press, 1985), 215–311.

probe gender relations in early modern English political thought and Carolyn Merchant presented a provocative study of attitudes to ecology and women in seventeenth-century political thought.[13] There is of course no doubt that Macpherson welcomed this plurality of approaches, even though it both displaced and disaggregated the synthetic picture on which his thesis rested. Let us now survey this literature using the thesis of possessive individualism as an object of comparison in order to draw three contrasts.

THE IMPORTANCE OF POLITICAL POWER

One common feature of current work on seventeenth century English and European thought has been the claim that the central problem of the period is the nature of political (not economic) power.[14] How had the representative bodies and absolute monarchies acquired political power? How do the people, individually and collectively, stand in relation to it as subjects or citizens? How can it be exercised without causing civil war? What is the 'true original, extent, and end of civil government'? As Locke put it in the *Two treatises* (1.106):[15]

> The great question which in all ages has disturbed mankind, and brought on them the greatest part of those mischiefs which have ruined cities, depopulated countries, and disordered the peace of the world, has been, not whether there be power in the world, nor whence it came, but who should have it.

One way in which this problem was conceptualized was to think of the people as individuals who have rights over their powers to defend themselves and to preserve themselves, and then to conceptualize the relation between governors and governed as the 'delegation' or 'alienation' of these powers to the ruler under certain conditions. It is within this context of explaining the nature of political power that the concept of man possessing rights over his person and capacities was used by a number of juristic political philosophers.[16] Macpherson

---

[13] Michel Foucault, *Surveiller et punir* (Paris: Editions Gallimard, 1975). Carole Pateman and T. Brennan, 'Mere auxiliaries to the commonwealth' (n. 7). Carolyn Merchant, *The death of nature: women, ecology and the scientific revolution* (San Francisco: Harper and Row, 1981).

[14] I have discussed the theme of this section more fully in John Locke, *A letter concerning toleration*, ed. James Tully (Indianapolis: Hackett Publishing Co., 1983), 1–17; and chapters 1 and 8.

[15] John Locke, *Two treatises of government*, ed. Peter Laslett (Cambridge: Cambridge University Press, 1962), first treatise, section 106 (1.106).

[16] For the historical background to this juristic way of thinking about political power, see Quentin Skinner, *The foundations of modern political thought*, 2 vols. (Cambridge: Cambridge University Press, 1978), II, 113–349; and Richard Tuck, *Natural rights theories*.

famously underscored the importance of a concept of self-proprietorship in Hobbes, the Levellers, and Locke, but he set this in the
economic context of a possessive market society. Let us examine the
contrast.

The first and basic premise of possessive individualism, from which
the thesis takes its name, is that man is proprietor of his own person
and capacities. This is taken by Macpherson to be an economic
conception of the self: a concept of an individual who possesses rights
of ownership over his person and capacities that he exercises through
contractual relations on a market free of the authoritative allocation
of work and in which the capacity to labour is alienated for a period of
time in exchange for a wage. The psychological motive which moves
the possessive individual is an infinite desire to consume, acquire or
seek to satisfy utilities.[17]

The first part of this concept, that of jural self-possession or
self-ownership, is neither necessary nor sufficient to liberalism. In
contemporary liberalism, for example, John Rawls, in the most
influential liberal theory of the post-war period, holds that a person
has a contingent relation to his or her own abilities, as the mere
repository of them, and that one's abilities are the 'common assets' of
the community.[18] (I return to this repository conception below.)
Jeremy Bentham as well thought it was 'nonsense upon stilts' to speak
of persons having rights over themselves and he chastised the drafters
of the *Declaration of the rights of man and citizen* for introducing this
language.[19] Conversely, Jerry Cohen has argued in a number of
recent articles that socialists should accept the basic political premise
of 'self-ownership' – that individuals have rights over their persons
and capacities – and then show that 'partial egalitarian' conclusions
can be drawn from it.[20] In this he echoes, as Richard Ashcraft and
Christopher Lasch have shown, early nineteenth-century English
and American radicals who argued that the best way to defeat the
claims of capital was to defend the rights of labour over their person
and capacities.[21]

---

[17] Quotation 6 above. Compare *The political theory of possessive individualism*, 53–61.
[18] John Rawls, *A theory of justice* (Oxford: Oxford University Press, 1971), 179.
[19] See Jeremy Waldron, *Nonsense upon stilts* (London: Methuen and Co., 1987), 19–77.
[20] G. A. Cohen, 'Socialist equality and capitalist freedom', in Jon Elster, ed., *Work, markets, and social justice* (Oxford: Oxford University Press, 1986).
[21] Christopher Lasch, 'The sociology of liberty in recent historical writing', *Seminar on republicanism* (University of Rochester, 1988; unpublished). Richard Ashcraft, 'A Victorian working class view of liberalism and the moral life', *Conference on liberalism and the moral life* (City University of New York, April 1988).

My preliminary point here is that a similar concept can be used in various and indeed contradictory ways in different political contexts. How then was the concept of self-proprietorship used in the seventeenth century?

It is certainly true that it plays a central role in the writings of some of the Levellers and in Locke's *Two treatises of government* as Macpherson claimed. However, its conventional and long-standing Roman law use was not economic. To say that a man was master or proprietor of himself was to define him in opposition to a slave, who was by definition under the will of his master. It thus had the double register of signalling one was master of oneself in the sense of being able to govern oneself ethically, in the neo-stoic texts, and of exercising some form of jurisdiction over the self free from the control of others. This was taken in two directions. In the absolutist tradition, if 'men' have rights of ownership over themselves, then, since rights are alienable, they are able to alienate these rights completely to another. It is thus possible to argue that individuals alienate their selves completely to an absolute monarch, without limitation, and thus stand to the sovereign as slave to master. We see Rousseau arguing against this theory in the *Contrat social*.[22] The second way in which this strong theory of self-ownership was used was to justify the slave trade, on the assumption that blacks freely alienated their rights over themselves in a contractual relation with European slave traders.

These 'alienation' theorists were opposed by what are called 'delegation' theorists. They wished to defend a limited form of constitutional monarchy and thus interpreted self-ownership in a slightly different way. Although an individual has rights over the self and its capacities, in contrast to a slave, these rights are limited and some are inalienable, so one could never contract into complete subjection to a sovereign nor be without a right to defend oneself if attacked by a tyrant. (This is the context in which the notion of an 'inalienable right' is first used.)[23] As Keith Thomas pointed out, the difficulties the Levellers had with extending the franchise to servants were not with wage labour, as Macpherson assumed, but, rather, with servants being under the will of another and so not their own masters.[24]

[22] Jean-Jacques Rousseau, *Du contrat social*, ed. R. Grimsley (Oxford: Oxford University Press, 1974) I, iv.

[23] See Tuck, *Natural rights theories* 52–4, 101–42; and James Tully, *A discourse on property* (Cambridge: Cambridge University Press, 1980), 104–16.

[24] Keith Thomas, 'The levellers and the franchise', in *The interregnum*, ed. G. E. Aylmer.

The primary use of the concept of rights over the self in the seventeenth century is in the constitution of government and the relation of subjection to it. The framework in which this is discussed by both Hobbes and Locke is laid down by Hugo Grotius in *The laws of war and peace* (1625). Grotius wrote in the wake of seventy years of religious wars, and in the midst of a wave of civil wars and the Thirty Years' War. This catastrophe led to a widespread sceptical crisis which began in the 'rule of faith' controversy and spread to the moral and natural sciences. Grotius was faced with constructing a political theory for a Europe that had a plurality of religions and no unifying political authority above the individual states.[25] He argued that despite their religious and moral differences all Europeans desire self-preservation. States established for this purpose alone, and not for enforcing higher order religious beliefs, would secure the obedience of all subjects and bring peace. He put this basic agreement on the principle of self-preservation in the terms of self-ownership (*suum*): each man has a natural right to defend himself from attack and a natural right to preserve himself by acquiring things necessary for subsistence. A natural duty to abstain from that which belongs to another correlates with the two rights. This constitutes the *suum*: that which is properly one's own. Governments are established by alienating the rights of self-defence to the sovereign and by agreeing to the regulation of the right of preserving oneself in the interest of peace and order.

This is a juridical concept of self-ownership. However, the concept is moral, political and military, not economic. It is not concerned with the alienation of labour power but with political power (the power of self-defence). The individual as well as the state are concerned with preservation not consumption. Labour power appears here as the means to preserve oneself, not something that facilitates utility satisfaction, and it is regulated by government for

---

[25] See Richard Popkin, *The history of scepticism from Erasmus to Spinoza* (Berkeley: University of California, 1979) for the sceptical crisis. For Grotius in this context, see Richard Tuck, 'The modern theory of natural law', in A. Padgen, ed., *The languages of political theory in early modern Europe* (Cambridge: Cambridge University Press, 1987) 99–123; and his *Philosophy and Government 1572–1651* (Cambridge: Cambridge University Press, forthcoming); and James Tully, 'Introduction' to Samuel Pufendorf, *On the duty of man and citizen*, ed. J. Tully (Cambridge: Cambridge University Press, 1991).

the sake of preservation. This Grotian framework plays a powerful role in English political thought throughout the century.[26]

Hobbes was concerned with the same problems as Grotius: how to build a strong state that subjects would obey in the face of civil war caused by religious diversity. What Macpherson saw as economic competition among self-interested consumers in Hobbes' state of war is now seen as competition for power to protect oneself in the English Civil War.[27] Hobbes does not strengthen Grotius' concept of self-possession nor does he put it to economic uses. He reduces it to an impracticable right to preserve oneself which is alienated to a sovereign in all cases except when one's life is directly threatened. The sovereign regulates labour and trade in order to preserve the population and to strengthen the state in relation to other European states.[28]

The Levellers use a concept of self-ownership, not to legitimate market exchanges, but, rather, to justify the right to resist constituted authority (first the King and then Parliament) in the terms of a natural right to self-defence. The proprietorship model is used in this way by the Parliamentary side throughout the Civil War and later in the Exclusion Crisis and the Glorious Revolution.[29]

Turning now to Locke, it is clear that he wrote within this general Grotian framework, although, of course, he made a number of important innovations within it. In Locke's theory individuals are said to have the right to defend themselves and others, and the right to acquire things necessary for preservation by means of labour. These two rights correlate with duties to others. The power one has to defend oneself and others is the origin of political power. This is conditionally delegated to governors when political society is established. If government abuses this power it devolves back to the people

---

[26] Richard Tuck, *Natural rights theories*, 58–174; Knud Haakonseen, 'Hugo Grotius and the history of political thought', *Political Theory*, 13 (1985) 239–65; Stephen Buckle, *The natural history of property*.

[27] David Johnston, *The rhetoric of Leviathan* (Princeton: Princeton University Press, 1986); Deborah Baumgold, *Hobbes's political theory* (Cambridge: Cambridge University Press, 1987); Richard Tuck, *Hobbes* (Oxford: Oxford University Press, 1989); S. A. Lloyd, *Mind over matter: Hobbes's political philosophy* (Cambridge: Cambridge University Press, 1990).

[28] Thomas Hobbes, *Leviathan*, ed. C. B. Macpherson (Middlesex: Penguin, 1968), 261–74, 294–302, 728.

[29] Richard Tuck, *Natural rights theories*, 143–56; Julian Franklin, *John Locke and the theory of sovereignty* (Cambridge: Cambridge University Press, 1978); David Wootton, ed., *Divine right and democracy* (Middlesex: Penguin, 1986), 22–58.

individually who exercise it in an armed struggle to defend themselves against their governors. Further, the right everyone has to preserve oneself by labour is given up to be regulated and limited by government for the sake of preservation. Gopal Sreenivasan has argued persuasively that this limit is never transcended.[30]

As the work of Richard Ashcraft, Julian Franklin, and Mark Goldie shows, Locke wrote this to justify armed resistance by a group of radical Whigs against Charles II and his policy of religious uniformity. Locke certainly argued that the government infringement of property constituted a justification for revolt, but by 'property' he meant the civil and religious rights of Dissenters and their possessions, which were confiscated during the great persecutions of the Restoration. Here governments were exercising a wider range of political power than the people had conditionally entrusted to them and so were treating political subjects as if they were slaves, as in the alienation theory, rather than as persons with a range of inalienable rights over their person, capacities, and possessions.[31]

Max Weber once wrote that you could take the conceptual scheme developed by Marx to explain the historical appropriation and alienation of labour power from workers to the capitalist class and apply it just as well to the historical appropriation and alienation of political power from the people and local lords (the 'private bearers of executive power') to the institutionalized concentration of political power in the modern world. 'The whole process is a complete parallel to the development of the capitalist enterprise through gradual expropriation of the independent producers.'[32] The irony of this statement is, as I have sought to suggest, that the conceptual scheme was first developed to explain political power and state formation and then, from Smith to Marx, transferred to labour power. In *The political theory of possessive individualism* Macpherson took for granted

[30] John Locke, *Two treatises*, sections 7, 129, 130. This framework of Locke's theory was brought out by Franklin, *John Locke*, Tuck, *Natural rights theories*, and Tully, *A discourse on property*, in the late 1970s and 1980. It has been enriched, improved, and corrected by Richard Ashcraft in *Revolutionary politics and Locke's Two treatises of government* (Princeton: Princeton University Press, 1986), and *Locke's Two treatises of government* (London: Unwin Hyman, 1987). The study of Locke on property by Gopal Sreenivasan, 'The limits of private rights in property' surveys the major studies of Locke on property from Macpherson to Jeremy Waldron and finds Locke's concept of property to be essentially 'limited'.

[31] I set this out in detail in chapter 7 below.

[32] Max Weber, 'Politics as a vocation', *From Max Weber*, ed., Gerth and Mills (New York: Oxford University Press, 1978), 79–129, 82.

the application of this conceptual scheme to labour power and projected it back onto the texts of Hobbes, the Levellers and Locke. In so doing he overlooked what is central to these texts: the analysis of political power. Second, this scheme, which presupposes that labour power is alienated or delegated to a capitalist class, caused him to misinterpret the role of labour power as well, as Keith Tribe pointed out. The problem is not how labour power is exchanged with a master (which is not seen as problematic at all). Rather, as we saw above, the problem of labour power is how it is given over to be 'regulated' by government for the sake of preservation.[33]

MERCANTILISM AND THE UTILIZABLE INDIVIDUAL

The second contrast I wish to draw is between Macpherson's argument that seventeenth-century England was a possessive market society which theorists from Hobbes to Locke wrote to legitimate, and the current view that seventeenth-century political economy is better understood as a 'mercantile system' (to use Adam Smith's phrase).[34] On this view, labour power, property relations, and trade are regulated by political power, or government, in order to preserve and 'strengthen' the state. The state in turn is considered to be locked in a zero sum, balance of power system of military and commercial rivalry with other European states over the conquest, colonization and exploitation of the non-European world. In order to strengthen the state and increase its wealth it was considered necessary to promote, regulate and coordinate the productive activities of the population by means of law. The 'improvement' of the productivity of labour required not only legal and administrative regulation, but also the development of knowledge of the 'history of trades', of demography, of the conditions of work, and thus the beginnings of political economy, statistics, comparative political science, and demographics. Labourers, in order to be trained to work or to fight, have to be cared for in their health, manners, and education, and directed to productive labour, which is integrated into the mercantile strategies of the 'welfare–warfare' state (to use Lawrence Stone's apt phrase).[35]

[33] Keith Tribe, *Land, labour, and economic discourse*, 51, and chapter 1 above.
[34] I have discussed the theme of this section more fully in chapters 6 and 7 below.
[35] Eli Heckscher, *Mercantilism*, tr. M. Shapiro, 2nd edn, 2 vols. (London: Allen and Unwin, 1955); Lawrence A. Harper, *The English navigation laws* (New York: Columbia University Press, 1939); John Coleman, ed., *Revisions in mercantilism* (London: Methuen, 1969).

As we have seen, labour power is conceptualized as a means to preservation and it is regulated by political power to this end in both the state of nature and political society. Both Hobbes and Locke picture labouring activity as regulated and 'limited' by the government.[36] The key term they use to describe and legitimate this political economy is 'improvement' and they contrast this ethos of European improvement with Amerindian hunting and gathering society, not with feudalism. Indeed, the emphasis on labour, cultivation, and improvement is the standard justification of the dispossession of Amerindians.[37]

Moreover, the way in which the labouring individual is conceptualized in the political economy literature from Montchrétien to William Petty is very different from the concept of an individual with rights over his person and capacities in the *Two treatises*. The individual is taken to be a mere repository of productive capacities that could be trained into mechanical abilities by the repetition of simple operations. This concept of the utilizable self is given expression in Locke's immensely influential *An essay concerning human understanding* and applied in his 1697 *Report to the Board of Trade* on the reform of the workhouse system.

At the centre of his analysis is the premise that an individual is 'only as white paper or wax to be moulded and fashioned as one pleases'.[38] Since each individual desires to avoid pain or punishment and to seek reward or pleasure, they can be led to engage in mental or physical behaviour by the application of punishments and rewards. As a result of the continual repetition and practice of any complex behaviour, suitably broken down into operational parts, the individual becomes accustomed and habituated to it, eventually finding pleasure in it.[39] One system of rewards and punishments that Locke lays out to apply in order to reform the 'relaxation of discipline and the corruption of manners', to uproot the vice of idleness, and to implant the virtue of industry is the use of bodily rewards and punishments in the workhouse system. His proposal for reform of the national system of

---

[36] Hobbes, *Leviathan*, 297–8, 367–8; Locke, *Two treatises*, sections 3, 31, 37, 38, 42, 50, 120, 130.
[37] Hobbes, *Leviathan* 301–2; Locke, *Two treatises* 2, sections 30, 41, 42, 43. William Cronon, *Changes in the land* (New York: Hill and Wang, 1983); and chapter 5 below.
[38] John Locke, *The educational writings*, ed. James Axtell (Cambridge: Cambridge University Press, 1968) 325.
[39] John Locke, *An essay concerning human understanding*, ed. Peter Nidditch (Oxford: Oxford University Press, 1975), 2.21.69–70.

workhouses was praised as a model for reforming and habituating children and adults to labour right up to the Webbs. As his 1793 editors remarked,[40]

> Mr Locke appears to be convinced that rewards and punishments, and the mixing of habits of industry with principles of religious duties, were the surest means of effecting that reformation of the manners of the people, which, in those days, was judged essential to the strength and safety of the nation.

This malleable individual was also said to have an overriding interest in or love of self, as Macpherson correctly noted. However, this self-referring motivation, whether Augustinian, Epicurean or neo-stoic in inspiration, was not taken to be an interest in the satisfaction or maximization of market or economic utilities. Rather, it was believed to be an interest in avoiding punishment and gaining reward. The typical forms of punishment were eternal damnation, violent death, starvation, or, amongst republicans, dishonour, and the typical rewards were salvation, preservation, power, honour, and reputation.

Michel Foucault studied the dispersion of techniques of discipline and habituation in the workhouses, schools, armies and administrative institutions. In his lectures on *raîson d'état* he argued that these techniques and types of rationality were linked to state-building and later to the formation of an array of 'arts of government' of individuals and populations. He concluded (with, perhaps, a reference to the Macpherson thesis):[41]

> The main characteristic of our modern rationality . . . is neither the constitution of the state . . . nor the rise of bourgeois individualism. I won't even say that it is a constant effort to integrate individuals into the political totality. I think that the main characteristic of our political rationality is the fact that this integration of the individuals in a community or in a totality results from a constant correlation between an increasing individualization and the reinforcement of this totality.

William McNeill's study of military discipline and the rise of a permanent military–commercial complex, Marc Raeff's study of the

---

[40] John Locke, *A report to the Board of Trade* (London: 1793 [1697]), preface.
[41] Michel Foucault, 'The political technology of individuals', in *Technologies of the self*, ed. Luther Martin *et alios* (Amherst: University of Massachusetts Press, 1988), 145–63, 161–2. See also 'Governmentality', *Theoretical practice* (Summer 1979), 5–21; 'Politics and reason', in *Michel Foucault: politics, philosophy, culture*, ed. Lawrence Kritzman (New York: Routledge, 1988), 57–86.

'well ordered state' in Germany and Russia, and Michael Ignatieff's study of eighteenth-century England all followed in the early eighties. Neal Wood discussed Locke's analysis of techniques of habituation. And Sidney Pollard has shown how the experimentation on child labour in the workhouse system laid the basis for factory discipline and scientific management.[42]

One of the necessary features of Macpherson's possessive market society is 'no authoritative allocation of work'.[43] This more recent work shows that seventeenth-century theory and practice failed to approximate this condition. Quite the opposite. In Locke's plan for the workhouse system the majority of the labouring population remains under the jurisdiction of the workhouse authorities from age three to fifty-five. Whether successive Boards of Trade recommended more or less regulation, or whether their policies aimed at constituting individuals or collectivities of various kinds, they understood these as tactics within an overall strategy of regulation and reform.[44]

The rediscovery of the concept of the individual as a passive repository of abilities, open to manipulation and use, in political economy and proposals for labour reform renders problematic our understanding of the genesis of capitalist wage labour. With the separation of the workers from the means of production, the owner (the capitalist) came to control the production process. It is clear from Dugald Stewart and Adam Smith on that the capitalist inherited the concept of the worker as a repository of abilities.[45] But this is incompatible with the labourer having any kind of rights or proprietorship over his person and capacities, as he does in the *Two treatises*. The labourer in the capitalist wage contract must totally alienate the rights he has over his capacities in the workplace. Therefore, the wage-relationship under capitalism must consist in the

---

[42] William McNeill, *The pursuit of power* (Chicago: University of Chicago Press, 1982), 117–44; Marc Raeff, *The well-ordered police state* (New Haven: Yale University Press, 1983); Michael Ignatieff, *A just measure of pain* (New York: Pantheon, 1978); Neal Wood, *The politics of Locke's philosophy* (Berkeley: University of California Press, 1983); Sidney Pollard, *The genesis of scientific management* (Cambridge, MA: Harvard University Press, 1965). See also Paul Slack, *Poverty and policy in Tudor and Stuart England* (London: Longman, 1988), and the interesting discussion in Charles Taylor, *Sources of the self* (Cambridge, MA: Harvard University Press, 1989), part 3.

[43] C. B. Macpherson, *The political theory of possessive individualism*, 53.

[44] See the reform proposals in F. M. Eden, *The state of the poor*, 3 volumes (London: 1797).

[45] Dugald Stewart, *Lectures on political economy*, in *The collected works* ed. W. Hamilton (1855), VIII, 318; Adam Smith, *An inquiry into the nature and causes of the wealth of nations*, ed. R. H. Campbell (Oxford: Clarendon Press, 1976) II, v.i.f.50, 781–2. See chapter 7 below.

junction of the 'alienation' conception of rights associated with absolutism and slavery, which I mentioned earlier, and the conception of the labourer as a repository of capacities.[46]

The concept of the individual as proprietor and master of his own labour in the non-absolutist tradition in which Locke wrote is incompatible with wage labour under capitalism, since the labourer could not alienate his sovereignty over his abilities. Rather, he sells a complete 'service' to a master, as in the pre-capitalist putting-out system.[47] This explains, therefore, how both civic humanists and Lockean jurists, from Adam Ferguson to Henri Storch, could use the concept of sovereignty or rights over one's abilities to combat – rather than to justify – the degradation of labour in the capitalist division of labour (see chapter 7 below).

COMMERCIAL SOCIETY AND THE SELF-INTERESTED INDIVIDUAL

Perhaps the biggest challenge to the political theory of possessive individualism has come from historians working on 'civic humanist' or republican forms of political thought. John Pocock's monumental reconstruction of republicanism or civic humanism is at the centre of this enterprise. He first challenged Macpherson's interpretation of Harrington.[48] Pocock argued that *Oceana* is a contribution to a tradition of republican political thought running from the Italian Renaissance to the late eighteenth century. In this tradition property is conceptualized differently from the juristic tradition we have been considering. Landed property provides the independence necessary for citizenship and citizenship consists in developing and exercising civic virtue through political participation in service – especially military service – to the public good. In this manner one comes to develop what is of utmost value, a civic personality. Accordingly, the

---

[46] Compare Marx's definition of capitalist wage labour: Karl Marx, *Capital*, I, tr. Ben Fowkes (New York: Vintage Books, 1977), 480.

[47] John Locke, *Two treatises of government*, section 85.

[48] John Pocock, *The political works of James Harrington*, 43–76 (n. 11). Pocock's republican studies include: *The Machiavellian moment* (1975) and *Virtue, commerce, and history* (1985; see especially, 'Authority and property: the question of liberal origins', 51–73, and 'The mobility of property and the rise of eighteenth-century sociology', 103–25). For criticisms of Pocock's work, see Ian Shapiro, *Political criticism* (Berkeley: University of California Press, 1990), 166–206.

distribution of property is of primary importance; it determines the form of government and the access to public office. In attempting to explain Harrington's theory in the terms of the possessive market model Macpherson overlooked this distinctive form of political analysis.

Pocock's work is part of a larger project to recover republican modes of political thought and action across Europe, from the sixteenth century to the French and American revolutions, by scholars such as Nanneral Keohane, Haitsma-Mulier, Richard Tuck, Gordon Wood, Carol Blum and Quentin Skinner.[49] These authors have underlined not only the importance of republican language in the early modern period, in contradistinction to the juristic language of Hobbes and Locke, but also the variety of political uses to which it was put. This thus complements the way historians of juristic political thought have brought to light the contradictory ideological uses of the terms of possessive individualism, which Macpherson assumed were used solely to legitimate the rise of capitalism. In addition, these scholars have sought to probe how juristic and republican thinkers responded to the development of the analysis of politics in the terms of interests and reasons of states, which I mentioned in the previous section.[50]

Historians influenced by the 'Pocockian Moment' have turned their attention to eighteenth-century English, Scottish, French and German political economy. The upshot of this work has been to suggest that Hobbes, Locke and possessive individualism are largely *irrelevant* to the ways in which market societies – capitalism – were reflected on, criticized and legitimated.[51] The reflection on capitalism occurred in the eighteenth century in a discussion centred on the concept of a 'commercial society' and in terms different from and

---

[49] Gordon Wood, *The creation of the American republic* (Chapel Hill: University of North Carolina Press, 1969); Nanneral Keohane, *Philosophy and the State in France* (Princeton: Princeton University Press, 1980); Eco Haitsma-Mulier, *The myth of Venice and Dutch republican thought* (Assen: van Gorcum, 1980); Carol Blum, *Rousseau and the republic of virtue* (Chicago: University of Chicago Press, 1986); Richard Tuck, *Philosophy and the state*, 1992; Quentin Skinner, *The foundations of modern political thought: I, The Renaissance*, and 'The idea of negative liberty: historical and philosophical perspectives', in *Philosophy in history*, ed. Richard Rorty (Cambridge: Cambridge University Press, 1984), 193–225.

[50] See Anthony Pagden, ed., *The languages of political theory in early modern Europe*, (Cambridge: Cambridge University Press, 1987).

[51] See Istvan Hont and Michael Ignatief, eds., *Wealth and virtue* (Cambridge: Cambridge University Press, 1983); especially, John Dunn, 'From applied theology to social analysis: the break between John Locke and the Scottish Enlightenment' 119–35.

often opposed to those of Hobbes and Locke. Consequently, it is this complex and distinctive eighteenth-century vocabulary that was gradually woven into the day-to-day practices of capitalism and came to be partly constitutive of it. Let me try to summarize some of the features of this third challenge to possessive individualism.

First, with the establishment of the Bank of England in 1696 and the introduction of public credit and debt (to finance foreign wars), a new kind of moveable, non-landed property appeared. It was conceptualized in the republican language of a 'monied interest', the 'corruption' of public life and the loss of citizen virtue. The language of republicanism continued to be central to both the criticism and legitimation of market relations in the eighteenth century, challenging and even displacing juristic modes of analysis.

The transition to a distinctively 'commercial society' was complemented in England – and all of Europe according to Theodore Robb – with a widely shared perception of political stability and steady economic growth. The earlier conventional stance that politics is the art of basic state-formation and preservation in conditions of insecurity was now taken as solved. Theorists could thus turn to the question of sustained economic growth, the causes of the wealth of nations, and even to the regulative idea – at the end of the century – of a consumer society. In this context the modern notion of progress began to be applied, calling into question the variety of concepts of a 'limit' in seventeenth-century republicanism, neo-stoicism, natural law, and political economy.[52]

One of the dominant questions of eighteenth-century Scottish and English political thought is, What is the explanation of the apparently self-sustaining growth of commercial societies? The first response was to argue that Europe had progressed through four historical stages of society, each individuated by its unique mode of production, from hunting and gathering to its present 'commercial' or 'civilized' stage. Locke's history of property in the *Two treatises* was interpreted in this scheme and his Scottish commentators, from Gershom Carmichael on, redescribed the natural law tradition of Grotius, Pufendorf and Locke in these new terms.[53]

---

[52] See chapter 7 below.

[53] See James Moore, 'Locke and the Scottish Jurists', *Conference for the study of political thought* (Washington, 1980, unpublished); James Moore and Michael Silverthorne, 'Gershom Carmichael and the natural jurisprudence tradition in eighteenth-century Scotland', in *Wealth and virtue*, ed. Hont and Ignatieff, 73–88 (n. 50); Istvan Hont, 'The language of sociability and commerce', *The languages of political theory*, ed. A. Pagden, 253–77; and chapter 5 below.

The most striking feature of a commercial society was taken to be the self-sustaining character of its basic institutions. Writers as diverse as Mandeville, Hume, Smith, Ferguson, Condercet, and Sieyès attributed this characteristic to the 'division of labour' and 'specialization'. In virtue of being caught up in the practices of division of labour in economic, political, and military life, individuals were constrained to behave in ways which – willy-nilly and unintentionally – led to the overall improvement and growth of these societies. In addition, individuals constrained to act in this way would gradually become 'polished', 'disciplined', 'civilized', and 'pacific'. If behaviour within the causal constraints of divisions of labour within commercial society explained the growth of European society, then the regulation and governance of every area of life in the seventeenth century could be seen as unnecessary. Mandeville can be read as advancing precisely this observation.[54]

As a result, the kind of regulation in detail typical of seventeenth-century reform was criticized and repudiated. It was associated with enlightened absolutism in France, from Richelieu and Colbert to Linguet and Louis XVI, and with the mercantile system in England. Smith, Condorcet, Bentham, and Sieyès all argued that modern commercial societies with representative political institutions and the division of labour were far too complex to know and to govern in this way. Indeed, they argued that the attempt to exercise this type of control failed and stifled improvement. Rather, progress and the wealth of nations are the unplanned consequences of leaving individuals more or less alone to pursue their enlightened self-interest in divisions of labour in commercial society. They disagreed over how much coordination and invigilation were required of the autonomous 'processes' in which humankind found itself constrained to work and live, but they all agreed on the existence and permanence of the processes themselves.

As we can see in hindsight, these later thinkers simply took for granted the organized forms of thought (the scientific disciplines) and the political, economic, and technical institutions the seventeenth-century theorists and state-builders had constructed. These appeared now to be quasi-autonomous and tending in a progressive direction without an overall director. The political act which symbolized this transition from early modern to modern thought was the execution of

---

[54] Bernard Mandeville, *The fable of the bees*, 2 vols. (London, 1727).

Louis XVI. The absolute monarch, who stood above the law, was replaced by the republic, in which everyone was equally subject to the laws of politics, economics, science, and the division of labour, and moved forward by this very subjection.

Individuals caught up in the dependence relations of the market, which rewarded economically rational behaviour and punished irrational behaviour, would gradually become enlightened. Their selfish pursuit of unlimited wants would bring about the greatest good of the greatest number. As markets spread around the globe governments would become economically interdependent and war would no longer be in their interest. Citizens, experiencing the cost and destructiveness of war, and thinking only of their self-interest, would curb military spending and adventurism through a free press and representative government. Thus, as Kant was able to sum up this line of thought in *An idea for a universal history from a cosmopolitan point of view*, supposing humans to be devils, the unintended consequences of their unsocial sociability in commercial societies were leading them to material progress and international peace.[55]

Does the thesis of possessive individualism apply, therefore, to late-eighteenth-century Scottish political economy? First, it would have to be rewritten to take into account these features I have mentioned since these continue to be constitutive of our liberal political theory. Most important of these is the assumption that there is an independent economic realm in which work is allocated in accordance with the law of supply and demand. Therefore, the authoritative allocation of work by government is not required. Macpherson claimed that this feature was present in seventeenth-century theory and practice, whereas eighteenth-century theorists thought this was unique to their own era and present-day scholars tend to support this view. Further, if we think of liberalism as a practice of government in which we question if there is 'too much government' and test policy against its effects on the independent economy, then liberalism is a tradition which emerged in the eighteenth, not the seventeenth century.[56]

Second, these writers were ambivalent about the achievements of commercial society. The basis of their ambivalance, as Pocock has

---

[55] Immanuel Kant, *Idea for a universal history from a cosmopolitan point of view*, in *Kant selections*, ed. Lewis White Beck (New York: Macmillan, 1988), 413–27.
[56] Michel Foucault, *Resumé des cours 1970–1982* (Paris: Juliard, 1989), 114.

argued, was the charge, advanced by neo-Harrington republicans, that the division of labour, specialization, and dependency would lead to the loss of 'civic virtue', the disintegration of a manly and unified civic personality, and to a soft or 'effeminate' character. The apologists argued, not without hesitation and nostalgia, that commercial society brought about progress, civility, polish, sociability, and manners, thereby superseding the rude and militaristic eras of civic virtue that the republicans sought anachronistically to revive. Thus, the debate over early modern capitalism was conducted in distinct vocabularies different from those of Hobbes and Locke. Defenders and critics of commercial society also questioned and criticized class structure, the degree of political participation, the subordination of women, the degradation of the individual, and especially the rise of standing armies and interstate war.[57] Even writers such as Smith who endorsed commercial society did not justify unlimited accumulation. Private property was limited by the needs of the destitute on the one hand and by the needs of the modern state on the other.[58] Most of these writers were also aware of the sociological and historical conditions which gave rise to and sustained the self-interested and possessive individual. Moreover, to concentrate on the 'individualism' of these writings is, as Foucault has argued, to overlook the other side of the analysis: the attempt to explain and to govern the 'population' as a whole, which was seen as a distinct domain with its own regularities and requisite policies of regulation and administration.[59]

Finally, it is misleading to see this body of thought focused on nothing but a 'market society'. These writers saw commercial societies as divided; composed of an economic realm and a political–civil realm of representative institutions, a public sphere, and a range of civil and religious liberties, and a problematic military complex. As Habermas, Foucault, Fontana, Landes, and others have stressed, these divisions of 'man', 'woman', 'citizen', and 'soldier' were as

[57] For Enlightenment views of women, see Sylvana Tomaselli, 'The Enlightenment debate on women', *History Workshop Journal* (1985), 101–23; Joan Landes, *Women and the public sphere in the age of the French revolution* (Ithaca: Cornell University Press, 1988). For the critical response to war and war-preparation see F. H. Hinsley, *Power and the pursuit of peace* (Cambridge: Cambridge University Press, 2nd edn, 1985). Pocock has always stressed the ambivalance to commerce and specialization among eighteenth-century writers.

[58] Hont and Ignatieff, 'Needs and justice in the Wealth of Nations', in *Wealth and virtue*, 1–44 (n. 50).

[59] Michel Foucault, 'Governmentality'.

problematic for Hutcheson, Hume, Montesquieu, Voltaire, Rousseau, Sieyès, Kant, and Constant as they were later for Hegel and Marx, and for us today.[60]

As we saw in the introduction, Macpherson wished to preserve liberal political and civil institutions while altering the market relations which thwart our participation in and expansion of them. However, the original thesis of possessive individualism does not contain an analysis of the history of these institutions in English political thought or practice. He went on in his later writings to investigate aspects of civil and political society in English political thought, and to recommend research into military–economic relations. In so doing he was following in the footsteps of the great critical thinkers of the eighteenth and nineteenth centuries, yet also passing on to us his own distinctive contribution to this tradition which still forms the horizon of our political thought – even for those who wish to question and deconstruct the traditon itself. Macpherson's original and thought-provoking questioning within this 200-year tradition of critical reflection on the history of the present is his true intellectual legacy.

---

[60] See the *International conference on republican thought and practice*, organized by Bianca Fontana, Pasquale Pasquino, and François Furet, Cambridge and Paris, October–December, 1989. Jurgen Habermas, *Strukturwandel der Offtenlichkeit* (Neuwied: Luchterhand, 1962); Michel Foucault, *Survellier et punir*; Joan Landes, *Women and the public sphere*, John Pocock, 'Virtue, rights, and manner', in *Virtue, commerce, and history*, 37–51; Bianca Fontana, ed., *Constant's political writings* (Cambridge: Cambridge University Press, 1989), 1–42.

CHAPTER 3

The framework of natural rights in Locke's analysis of property

I

This chapter has two aims.[1] The first is to throw light on one aspect of the theory of property which John Locke intended to convey in the *Two treatises of government*. The second is to recommend a way in which we might come to understand political writing in past time.[2] The two aims come together in that my interpretation of Locke is an application of the way of approaching texts which I present and defend in the chapter. The relevance of the chapter for contemporary discussions of property is indirect and chiefly by way of contrast. Locke conceptualizes property in a manner different from our mutually exclusive concepts of private property and common property. He does not use the modern concept of private property, which, like its modern antithesis of common property, emerged in the eighteenth century. Understanding Locke's thought will help us to see the limits of the way in which we normally think about property.

It is now well known that Locke's immediate audience received his work predominantly with silence, and, when noted, with abuse.[3] The first point at which it became an important element in an English political movement was in the early nineteenth century. Locke was

---

[1] This chapter is a presentation of one theme in my book, *A discourse in property: Locke in the natural law tradition*, Cambridge University Press, 1979. I am indebted to the following scholars for discussions on some of the points covered in the chapter: John Dunn, Anndale Goggin, Edward Hundert, Greg Ostrander, Alan Ryan, John Shingler, Quentin Skinner, Charles Taylor, Keith Tribe, Richard Tuck, and John Yolton.
[2] The methodology is adapted in part from John Dunn and Quentin Skinner. Refer to note 17 for further readings.
[3] See M. P. Thompson, 'The reception of Locke's *Two treatises of government 1690–1705*', *Political Studies* 24, 2 (1976), 184–91; Mark Goldie, 'Edmund Bohun and *jus gentium* in the revolution debate', *The Historical Journal* 20, 3 (1977), 569–86; J. P. Kenyon, *Revolution principles: the politics of party 1689–1720* (Cambridge: Cambridge University Press, 1977); and John Dunn, 'The Politics of Locke in England and America', in J. W. Yolton, ed., *John Locke: problems and perspectives* (Cambridge: Cambridge University Press, 1969).

96

read as the father of modern socialism in England by the 'Lockean' socialists.[4] This was paralleled by a socialist reading of Locke in France by Etienne Cabet and in Germany by Karl Grün.[5] We can gauge the importance of this interpretation by Marx's attack on it when he began to move against the unscientific socialists in *The German ideology*.[6] The last socialist reading of Locke that I have been able to locate is an article by Charles Driver in 1928.[7] The second major wave of interpretation is the liberal one, which can be said to have been securely established in the 1930s.[8] This also marks the first appearance of the view that Locke's analysis is confused and superficial, a view which remains a constituent of present-day liberal readings.[9] The immensely influential works of Leo Strauss and Professor Macpherson gave rise to the third interpretation – that of the illiberal Locke. Locke is said to have defended and recommended 'possessive individualism' and unlimited accumulation, and to have freed ownership of social obligations.[10] A fourth interpretation, which now appears to be common, is that Locke leaves it up to governments to define property as they see fit.[11]

These four major interpretations rest on a common methodological premise. This is the central tenet of the Whig view of history: that twentieth-century political theories and institutions 'grew out of', or 'evolved from', or have their 'roots' in seventeenth-century theories

[4] Max Beer, *The history of British socialism* (London, 1921), 101–279; and A. Menger, *The right to the whole produce of labour*, tr. M. E. Tanner (London, 1899).

[5] Etienne Cabet, *Voyage en Icarie, roman philosophique et social* (Paris, 1842), 485; K. Grün, *Die soziale Bewegung in Frankreich und Belgien. Briefe und Studien* (Darmstadt, 1845), 261.

[6] Karl Marx and Friedrich Engels, *Collected works* (London: Lawrence and Wishart, 1976–), 50 volumes, V, 520–4.

[7] C. H. Driver, 'John Locke', in *The social and political ideas of some English thinkers of the Augustan age 1650–1750*, ed. F. J. C. Hearnshaw (London: G. G. Harrap, 1928), 69–97.

[8] P. Larkin, *Property in the 18th century with special reference to England and Locke* (Cork, 1930); J. L. Stocks, *John Locke* (Oxford: Oxford University Press, 1983); G. Sabine, *A history of political theory* (New York: Holt, 1937); and J. D. Mabbott, *The state and the citizen* (London, 1947).

[9] P. Laslett, ed., *Two treatises of government* (Cambridge: Cambridge University Press, 1970), 92–120.

[10] Leo Strauss, *Natural right and history* (Chicago: Chicago University Press, 1950), 202–52; C. B. Macpherson, *The political theory of possessive individualism* (Oxford: Oxford University Press, 1962).

[11] Hillel Steiner, 'The Natural Right to the Means of Production', *Philosophical Quarterly*, 27 (1975), 45; Gordon Schochet, *Patriarchalism in political thought* (Oxford: Basil Blackwell, 1975), 253; and Thomas Scanlon, 'Nozick on Rights, Liberty and Property'. *Philosophy and Public Affairs* 6, 1 (Autumn, 1976), 23. Professor Nozick's work, *Anarchy, state, and utopia* (Oxford: Basil Blackwell, 1974) represents a transition between these last two interpretations: beginning with an endorsement of the illiberal view, he goes on to acquiesce in the most recent orthodoxy (see p. 350, n. 9).

and institutions.[12] The normative use of metaphors of development, growth, and evolution, which informs most if not all of these studies, came under sustained attack in the late 1960s.

One line of attack was launched by the post-structuralists in France, especially Louis Althusser and Michel Foucault.[13] Evolutionary assumptions were shown to predispose us to look for our own set of problems, in primitive form, in past writers, thus imposing an alien interpretive framework on the text and so yielding an unavoidably circular argument.[14] This critique was carried forward in England by Maurice Dobb's pupil, Dr Keith Tribe, and, *inter alia*, applied to Locke scholarship.[15] He argued that to impose a primitive capitalist market as an explaining factor causes us to misunderstand the uniqueness of seventeenth-century economic structures and so to misinterpret Locke.

Another criticism came from the revival of interest in hermeneutics, especially by Hans-Georg Gadamer and Charles Taylor.[16] It was argued that to recover the meaning of a text it is necessary to situate it in its intersubjective matrix of conventions and assumptions, in light of which the text can be said to have meaning for the author and his or her audience. John Dunn and Quentin Skinner went on to link the sense of meaning involved in hermeneutics to the author's intention in writing, or what the author was doing in writing it.[17] Thus, the meaning exists for a subject but is equally dependent upon

---

[12] For example, Macpherson, *Possessive individualism*, and his *Democratic theory* (Oxford: Oxford University Press, 1975).

[13] Louis Althusser, *Pour Marx* (Paris, 1966); Michel Foucault, *L'Archéologie du savoir* (Paris: Editions Gallimard, 1969).

[14] Foucault, *L'Archéologie*, chapter 1.

[15] Keith Tribe, *Land, labour, and economic discourse*, (London: Routledge and Kegan Paul, 1978).

[16] Hans-Georg Gadamer, *Truth and method* (London, 1975); Charles Taylor, 'Interpretation and the sciences of man', *Review of Metaphysics* 25 (September 1971), 3–51; and see Alaisdair MacIntyre, 'Ideology, social science and revolution', *Comparative Politics* 5, 3 (April 1973), 321–42.

[17] John Dunn, 'The identity of the history of ideas', *Philosophy* (April 1968); 'Practising history and and social silence on realist assumptions', in *Action and interpretation: studies in the philosophy of the social sciences*, ed. C. Hookway and P. Pettit (Cambridge: Cambridge University Press, 1978); Quentin Skinner, 'Meaning and understanding in the history of ideas', *History and theory* 8, 1 (1969), 3–53; 'Conventions and the Understanding of speech acts', *Philosophical Quarterly* 21, 79 (April 1970), 113–38; ' "Social meaning" and the explanation of social action', in *Philosophical Quarterly* 21, 79 (April 1970), 113–38; ' "Social meaning" and the explanation of social action', in *Philosophy, Politics and Society*, 4th series, ed., P. Laslett, G. Runciman, and Quentin Skinner (Oxford: Basil Blackwell, 1972), 136–57; 'On performing and explaining linguistic actions', *Philosophical Quarterly* 21, 82 (January 1971), 1–21; 'Some problems in the analysis of political thought of action', *Political Theory* 2, 3 (August 1974), 277–303; 'Hermeneutics and the role of history', *New Literary History* 7 (1975–6), 209–32.

the intersubjective and conventional vocabulary available for its articulation. In *The political thought of John Locke* John Dunn showed that it is necessary to interpret Locke's writings in light of the normative theological vocabulary available to him and in terms of which his theory is written if his meaning is to be recovered.[18] Professors Hundert, Neale, and Pocock have all presented studies along these lines which throw into question the four major interpretations outlined above.[19]

The primary criticism of the methodology exemplified by the Whig historical approach rests on a distinction between explanation and understanding.[20] An agent can be said to have performed an action only if the description under which the action is defined and performed is available to him or her.[21] To redescribe and so explain a complex linguistic action, such as a text, in terms of an explaining factor unfamiliar to the author seems to provide an interpretation which he or she would not recognize. It would not be the meaning the author intended. What stands in need of interpretation – the meaning the text had for the author and immediate audience – is elided by redescribing it in terms of an explaining factor more familiar to us. Understanding, as opposed to explanation, turns on recovering the meaning the author intended to convey by reading the text in light of the available conventions and assumptions, and so of coming to understand it in those terms. This is what I attempt to do for one neglected but important aspect of Locke's writings on property.

II

The range of normative vocabulary available to Locke and in terms of which he articulates his theory is the language of seventeenth-

---

[18] John Dunn, *The political thought of John Locke* (Cambridge: Cambridge University Press, 1969).

[19] E. J. Hundert, 'The making of homo faber: John Locke between ideology and history', *Journal of the History of Ideas* 33, 1 (1972), 3–22; 'Market society and meaning in Locke's political philosophy', *Journal of the History of Philosophy*, 15 1 (January 1977), 33–44; R. S. Neale, 'the bourgeoisie historically, has played a most revolutionary part', in *Feudalism, capitalism and beyond*, ed. E. Kamenka and R. S. Neale (London: Edward Arnold, 1975), 84–101; J. G. A. Pocock, 'Early modern capitalism: the Augustan perception', ibid., 62–84; and see Alan Ryan, 'Locke and the dictatorship of the bourgeoisie', *Political Studies* 13, 2 (1965), 219–30.

[20] See George Henrich von Wright, *Explanation and understanding* (London: Routledge and Kegan Paul, 1971).

[21] See Alaisdair MacIntyre, 'A mistake about causality in social science', in *Philosophy, political and society*, 2nd series, ed., P. Laslett and W. G. Runciman (Oxford: Basil Blackwell, 1962).

century natural law and natural rights discourse. Thus interpretation should take place in light of other natural law writers whom he recommends or who can be seen, for historical and textual reasons, to be important in understanding Locke. This is essential in order to make explicit the conventions usually adopted in natural law discussions of property. It enables us to see which aspects of Locke's writings are conventional, in which he wishes to endorse or reassert prevailing norms and assumptions. It also provides a backdrop against which it is possible to gauge where Locke diverges from the norm and presents his audience with something new and different. Other natural law writers, therefore, function as objects of comparison which throw light on Locke's work in virtue of their similarities and dissimilarities.

In addition, this method permits the demarcation of intersubjective beliefs which the audience had no reason to doubt and thus could function as public criteria for justifying arguments.[22] I am of course aware that natural law was not the only discursive mode available and that an historical form of political argument was popular in England in the 1680s.[23] One of the merits of the approach I adopt is that it explains why Locke chose to write in natural law language rather than in the historical mode.[24]

It is also necessary to situate the *Two treatises* in the context of the range of social and political action Locke addresses in writing on property. We can scarcely understand Locke unless we recover the forms of political and social action which he intends to recommend or to repudiate at various points in his arguments. Therefore it is essential to outline this ideological context.

The leading issue to which Locke responds in the *Two treatises* is arbitrary and absolutist government. He mounts a blistering attack on its most popular defence: the political tracts of Sir Robert Filmer (1588–1652). In its place Locke reasserts a radical constitutionalist

---

[22] That problematic norms are standardly justified by an appeal to criteria which are public (enjoy a consensus) is, of course, one of the central lines of Wittgenstein's later work. See Ludwig Wittgenstein, *On certainty*, tr. G. E. M. Anscombe and G. H. von Wright (Oxford: Basil Blackwell, 1974); and John Richardson, *The grammar of justification* (Sussex: Sussex University Press, 1976).

[23] Quentin Skinner, 'History and ideology in the English Revolution', *The Historical Journal* 8, 2 (1965), 151–78; Kenyon, *Revolution principles*; J. G. A. Pocock, *The ancient constitution and the feudal law* (Cambridge: Cambridge University Press, 1957).

[24] See chapter 1 of my book, *A discourse on property: John Locke and his adversaries* (Cambridge: Cambridge University Press, 1980).

theory, or theory of popular sovereignty, and an individualist theory of resistance to arbitrary government.[25] Filmer's treatises, a Royalist defence of absolute monarchy, were written between 1638 and 1652, and originally published in 1648, 1652 and 1653. They were republished in 1679 and again in 1680. *Patriarcha*, the locus of Locke's attack, was published for the first time in the 1680 collection.[26] The occasion of their republication was the Exclusion Crisis (1679–81), engendered by the Whigs' attempt to exclude James, Duke of York, the son of King Charles II, from accession to the throne of England. The Tories pressed Filmer's writings into service as an ideological justification of James' promotion. The perceived threat on the basis of which the Whigs resisted the King was a combination of popery and arbitrary government. The Tory defence was based on Divine Right and passive obedience to hereditary succession, even if this entailed a Roman Catholic monarch.[27]

As a result of Mr Laslett's painstaking efforts to date the composition of the *Two treatises*, it is apparent that Locke began to move against Filmer in this context as early as his reading of the 1679 edition of Filmer's work in that year.[28] Thus, insofar as the Tories described and so legitimated court action in terms of Filmer's writings, Locke was necessarily attacking their position in attacking Filmer. This ideological point shows that Locke's refutation of Filmer is a positive Whig contribution to the Exclusion Crisis without being what Mr Laslett calls an 'Exclusion tract'.[29] The continuing appeal to Filmer during and after the Glorious Revolution of 1688 explains Locke's publication of the *Two treatises* in 1689.[30]

To refute Filmer and to provide an alternative theory in terms of natural law and natural rights, Locke had to answer the objections brought against natural law by Filmer in his tract entitled *Observations on Hugo Grotius' the laws of war and peace*. Locke's complete project would have seemed ridiculous to his audience unless he replied to

[25] See John Dunn, *Political thought of John Locke*. For a meticulous placing of Locke within the constitutionalist tradition see Quentin Skinner, *The foundations of modern political thought* (Cambridge: Cambridge University Press, 1979).
[26] P. Laslett, ed., *Patriarcha and other political works of Sir Robert Filmer* (Oxford: Basil Blackwell, 1949), 1–48.
[27] John Dunn, *The political thought of John Locke*, 43–58; P. Laslett, *Two treatises*, 45–67.
[28] P. Laslett, *Two treatises*, 60–7; John Dunn, *The political thought of John Locke*, 48.
[29] P. Laslett, *Two treatises*, 61.
[30] See M. P. Thompson, 'The reception of Locke's *Two treatises*'; and Mark Goldie, 'Edmund Bohun'.

Filmer's claim that there were inconsistencies in Grotius, inconsistencies which threw the whole natural law mode of political discourse into question. The contradictions which Filmer alleged to have found are in Grotius' treatment of property (*dominium*). Therefore, it was necessary for Locke to develop a theory of property which would answer Filmer's critique and so save natural law as a viable form of argument.

The constraints of the context thus make a theory of property the necessary precondition for Locke's main and explicit aim of overthrowing Filmer's modern theory of absolutism and of reasserting the older and more traditonal constitutionalist or consent theory of government.[31] However, the situation is even more complex than this. Hugo Grotius (1583–1645), the Dutch scholar, statesman, and jurist, in *The laws of war and peace* (1624), and Samuel Pufendorf (1632–92), the German jurist, historian and political theorist, in *The law of nature and nations* (1672), both use the normative vocabulary of natural law to present rationalist theories of absolutism.[32] In addition to saving natural law from Filmer's attack, Locke is faced with the task of using natural law vocabulary to construct a theory of property different from the compact theory which both Grotius and Pufendorf set up as a means of establishing their absolutist conclusions. Locke requires a theory which will yield, or be consistent with, a non-absolutist or limited theory of government, grounded in the consent of the people.[33]

III

In his criticism of Grotius, Filmer pounces on the apparent inconsistency that natural law is said to sanction common property in the state

---

[31] See the title page of the *Two treatises* and the first treatise, section 6 (1.6) where Locke states his intention to return to the older mode of political discourse.

[32] For an account of Grotius see Richard Tuck, *Natural rights theories. Their origin and development* (Cambridge: Cambridge University Press, 1981), an excellent study to which I am greatly indebted. For Pufendorf see Leonard Kreiger, *The politics of discretion: Pufendorf and the acceptance of natural law* (Chicago, 1965).

[33] For recent attempts to situate various aspects of Locke's political writings in this context see Karl Olivecrona, 'Appropriation in the state of nature: Locke on the origin of property', *Journal of the History of Ideas* 35, 2 (April–June 1974), 211–31; 'Locke's theory of appropriation', *The Philosophical Quarterly* 24, 96 (July 1974), 220–34; and Patrick Kelly, 'Locke and Filmer: Was Laslett so wrong after all?', *The Locke Newsletter* 8 (summer 1977), 77–91.

of nature and private property in political society. 'Grotius', writes Filmer, says

that by the law of nature all things were at first common, and yet teacheth, that after propriety was brought in, it was against the law of nature to use community. He does thereby not only make the law of nature changeable, which he saith God cannot do, but he also makes the law of nature contrary to itself.[34]

This problem in Grotius, of natural law endorsing both common and private property, is a result of the radical innovation Grotius introduces in the treatment of rights. In his early work, *De jure praedae* (1604), written at the age of twenty-one, he makes a decisive break with the Scholastic orthodoxy of the previous century. To see the full importance of Grotius' move, and of Locke's later repudiation of it, it is necessary to view it in light of the theory he rejects.

In the autumn of 1535 the Dominican theologian Francisco de Vitoria began his lectures in the University of Salamanca on the second part of Aquinas' *Summary of theology*, lectures which were to provide the theoretical suppoort for the Catholic counter-reformation. One of Vitoria's pupils, Domingo de Soto (1494–1560), published his *Ten books on law and justice*, based on Vitoria's lectures, and it ran to twenty-seven editions in the sixteenth century alone. This work was carried forward by the Jesuit Luis de Molina (1535–1600) and by another Jesuit, Francisco Suarez (1547–1617), in *The laws and God the lawgiver* (1612) and *The defence of the catholic and apostolic Faith* (1612). They sought to reestablish Aquinas' concept of natural law as the foundation of moral and political philosophy.[35] However, they were faced with the emergence and widespread use of the concept of subjective rights after Aquinas' death. A subjective right is a right which an individual is said to have or to possess, such as a right to education or to a material object. This is distinguished from the objective concept of right, when we say that such and such is right or is the right thing to do. Aquinas seems not to employ the subjective concept of right and its appearance is usually dated in the early fourteenth century.[36] During his student years at the University of

34 Robert Filmer, *Patriarcha and other political works*, ed. P. Laslett (Oxford: Basil Blackwell, 1949), 274.

35 For detailed studies of this school, see Richard Tuck, *Natural rights theories*, and Quentin Skinner, *The Foundations of modern political thought*, vol. 2.

36 Michel Villey, 'La genèse du droit subjectif chez Guillaume d'Occam', *Archives de philosophie du droit* 9 (1964), 97–127.

Paris in 1507–22, Vitoria had been exposed to the last advocates of an unlimited subjective rights theory associated with Jean Gerson (1363–1429). The task of Vitoria and his followers was to use the language of subjective rights, but to give political theory a more objective basis, and subjective rights a more limited purchase, by grounding both in natural law. Suarez' work is the culmination of this school of Vitorian neo-Thomists and it provides the best object of comparison for understanding Grotius.

Suarez develops his concept of a subjective right by considering two accepted meanings of justice (*iustitia*).[37] First, he writes that 'right' (*ius*) has the same meaning as 'that which is just' (*iustum*) and 'that which is equitable' (*aequum*). These are the two objects of justice. Thus 'right' will have two meanings corresponding to the two objects of justice. Justice in turn stands for (1) every moral virtue, since every moral virtue is, in some way, directed towards and brings about equity, and (2) a special moral virtue which renders to another that which is his due.[38] Thus a just man in the first or generic sense is just in all his relationships, whereas a man would be just in the latter or specific sense by acting justly in a specific sort of relationship.

Suarez writes that 'right' in the generic sense is what is fair and in harmony with reason, this being the general object of virtue in the abstract. 'Right' in the specific sense, the object of justice in the specific sense, refers to the equity which is due to each individual as a matter of justice.[39] Having distinguished 'right' from justice, and having identified it primarily with the object of justice in the specific sense, he redescribes 'right' in this objective sense in terms of two subjective rights. First he writes,

According to the latter and strict acceptation of right, this name is properly wont to be bestowed on a certain moral power which every man has, either over that which is rightfully his own or with respect to that which is due to him.

He defines 'right' in the strict sense above as that which is due to a person as a matter of justice, as opposed to justice, which is the

---

[37] Francisco Suarez, *De legibus ac Deo legislatore* (1612), in *Opera Omnia* (Paris: 1856–78), 28 vols. IV & V, sections 1.2.4–5 (hereafter referred to as *The law*). I have used the following translation whenever possible: F. Suarez, *Selections from the three works*, ed. G. L. Williams (Oxford: Clarendon Press, 1944).

[38] Suarez is applying Aristotle's two senses of 'justice': Aristotle, *Nicomachean ethics*, 1129a3–1134a16.

[39] Suarez notes his agreement with Aquinas, *Summa theologiae*, II, II, 57.1.

rendering of that which is due. Then he unpacks this formulation to show that it contains two traditional objects of justice: that which is rightfully one's own (*rem suam*) and that which is rightfully due a person (*ad rem sibi debitam*). The reason why the moral power which a man has with respect to these two objects (which are right) can itself be called 'right' in the subjective sense is that the moral power cannot but be right in the objective sense. That is, the moral power is objectively right because it is a moral power with respect to what is right by definition: one's own and one's due. Thus subjective right is derived from and limited by natural law, the standard of what is objectively right. The basis is laid for a subjective rights theory limited by natural law, the sort of theory Locke reasserts sixty years later.

Suarez goes on to distinguish between the moral power that one has with respect to that which is rightfully one's own and one's due:

For it is thus that the owner of a thing is said to have a right in that thing (*ius in re*) and the worker is said to have a right to his stipend (*ius ad stipendium*) by reason of which he is declared worthy of his hire. Indeed, this acceptation of the term is frequent, not only in law, but in Scripture; for the law distinguishes in this way between a right already established in a thing (*ius in re*), and a right to a thing (*ad rem*).

The right to a thing (*ius ad rem*) is a claim right to that which is due to a person as a matter of justice (e.g. a stipend) but which he does not yet possess. As Suarez redescribes it: 'a right to claim a thing which in some way pertains to him'. The right in a thing (*ius in re*) is a right in that which rightfully belongs to a person and which he does possess. In each case, the object belongs to him, but in different senses of 'to belong'.

To use Locke's terminology, in fulfilling his obligation the person who possesses a right to a thing 'comes to have' a 'right in' or a 'property in' the object.[40] Suarez' translation of right in the objective sense into two subjective rights allows a person to discuss the two objects of justice in terms of subjective rights.

A right to a thing (*ius ad rem*) and a right in a thing (*ius in re*) as defined by Suarez and Locke are conceptually linked in a way which can be illustrated by a modern example. The claim right to ride on public transportation is a right not to be excluded from riding and correlates, we may say, with a positive duty on the part of the

[40] Locke, *Two treatises*, second treatise, section 25 (2.25).

community to provide the necessary transportation. When an individual is exercising her or his claim right by using public transport they come to have a right in the use of the seat they occupy. This is now a right to exclude others from the use of the seat while it is occupied. The claim right is a right not to be excluded (to be included) and so may be called an inclusive right. The right in the use of the seat, which is necessary to complete, or make good, the claim right, is a right to exclude others, temporarily, from using it and so may be called an exclusive right.[41] The example illustrates the crucial logical point that a claim right of this sort requires some kind of exclusive right in what is claimed, and some criterion of 'coming to have', for it to be exercised.

Suarez' analysis of property (*dominium*) begins, as does Aquinas' and Locke's, with the premise that there is common ownership of all things (*communitas rerum*).[42] He argues against an Adamite theory similar to Filmer's and states that there is no original donation of private dominion, either from God directly to Adam or from natural law.[43] *Genesis* 1.28 is to be interpreted as giving mankind dominion in common. The original dominion in common is power to use the world and the inferior creatures:[44]

Nature has conferred upon all men in common dominion over all things, and consequently has given to every man a power to use those things; but nature has not so conferred private property with that domain.

This exposition is similar to Aquinas in its sharp distinction between dominion in common and any form of private or exclusive property (*proprietas*). Suarez continues by redescribing Aquinas' concept of dominion in common in terms of a natural, subjective claim right: 'for we have said that "right" is sometimes "law" while at times it means *dominium* or *quasi-dominium* over a thing; that is, a claim to its use'.[45] He makes it clear that this is an inclusive claim right to use that which belongs to all: 'a positive precept of natural law to the effect that no one should be prevented from making the necessary use of the common property'.[46]

Suarez' further analysis of the individuation of property takes place

---

[41] For a recent discussion of the concepts of inclusive and exclusive rights to which I am indebted, see C. B. Macpherson, *Democratic theory*, 120–42.
[42] Suarez, *The law*, 2.14.14; and Aquinas, *Summa theologiae* II, II, 66.
[43] Suarez, *The law*, 3.2.3.   [44] Suarez, *The law*, 2.14.16.   [45] Suarez, *The law*, 2.14.16.
[46] Suarez, *The law*, 2.14.17.

within this framework of the world belonging to all men in common. Once property has been distributed within a society in accordance with various criteria, some natural and some conventional, the natural claim right remains as the foundation for a positive theory of charity. Not only is Locke's theory similar, but his theory of charity develops from the same foundation. The striking feature of this sort of theory is that private and common property are interdependent rather than mutually exclusive concepts; private or exclusive property is necessary to individuate and so distribute common property.

Grotius' early work, *De jure praedae* (1604), presents a completely different picture. He informs his reader that *dominium* used to mean the common right to use common property. *Dominium* used to mean a kind of common possession different from *proprietas*. However, this is no longer the way in which the terms are to be used. *Dominium* means solely its Roman sense of exclusive possession. Use (*usus*) means only exclusive use:[47]

Accordingly, it must be understood that, during the earliest epoch of man's history, *dominium* and common possession (*communio*) were concepts whose significance was different from that now ascribed to them. For in the present age the term *dominium* connotes possession of something peculiarly one's own, that is to say, something belonging to a given party in such a way that it cannot be similarly possessed by any other party; whereas the expression 'common property' is applied to that which has been assigned to several parties, to be possessed by them in partnership, so to speak, and in mutual accord, to the exclusion of other parties. Owing to the poverty of human speech, however, it has become necessary to employ identical terms for concepts which are not identical. Consequently, because of a certain degree of similitude, and by analogy, the above mentioned expressions descriptive of our modern customs are applied to another right, which existed in earlier times. Thus, with reference to that earlier age, the term 'common' is nothing more nor less than the simple antonym of 'private' (*proprium*); and the word *dominium* denotes the power to make use rightfully of common property. This attribute the Scholastics chose to describe as a concept of fact but not of law. For the legal right now connoted by the term 'use' (*usus*) is of a private nature.

In his great work, *The laws of war and peace* (1624), Grotius continues and clarifies his break with the Thomist tradition. He defines 'right' (*ius*) in three ways.[48] First, 'right' in the objective sense signifies that

---

[47] Hugo Grotius, *De jure praedae*, Latin–English edition, ed., G. L. Williams (Oxford: Clarendon Press, 1950), 12.3.

[48] Hugo Grotius, *De jure belli ac pacis*, Latin–English edition, ed. F. W. Kelsey (Oxford: Clarendon Press, 1925), 1.1.3. (Hereafter referred to as *The laws*.)

which is just (*iustum*). The second, subjective sense is a 'moral faculty annexed to a person, enabling him to have or to do something justly'. He then collapses the concept of a subjective right into a right in that which one actually possesses, an exclusive right, thus eliding the concept of an inclusive claim right to one's due: 'lawyers call a faculty that right which a man has to his own, but we shall hereafter call it a right properly and strictly taken'. It is impossible to speak of Suarez' subjective right which redescribes ownership in common using Grotius' concept of a right. *Dominium* for Grotius is solely an exclusive right over one's possessions, the same kind of right as that which one has over one's liberty, children, and slaves.[49] Grotius' *dominium* is the same as Filmer's 'private domination'. Translated as 'property' in the English editions and abstracted from its regulative absolutism, it passes into legal theory in the eighteenth century in the works of Sir William Blackstone:[50]

the right of property, or that sole and despotic dominion which one man claims and exercises over the external things of the world, in total exclusion of the right of any other individual in the universe.

Thus when Grotius discusses the origin of property he uses *dominium* and *proprietas* interchangeably, since they both denote the same exclusive right.[51] The right which each man is said to have is not an inclusive claim right but rather an exclusive right to use the things which one happens to come to possess (*ius in res*). He uses Cicero's simile of the theatre to show that originally the world belongs to no one but is open for the first taking of anyone: 'although the theatre is common for anybody who comes, yet the place that everyone sits in is properly his own'.[52] On this model, if the theatre fills to capacity, the people excluded have no rights. Suarez' inclusive claim right, on the other hand, suggests that the theatre (world) belongs to everyone and those excluded have a claim right on the basis of which they may impose the duty on others of moving over and making room.

Putendorf, in *The laws of nature and nations* (1672), differs from Grotius in many respects, but he continues Grotius' fundamental revision in the concept of a subjective right: '*proprietas* or *dominium* is a right whereby the substance, as it were, of something belongs to a person in such a way that it does not belong in its entirety to another

[49] Grotius, *The laws*, 1.1.5.
[50] Sir William Blackstone, *Commentaries on the laws of England* (London: 1778, 8th edn), 2.1.1.
[51] Grotius, *The laws*, 2.2.1.   [52] Grotius, *The laws*, 2.2.2.

person in the same manner'.[53] Pufendorf draws the important conclusion that it is no longer conceptually possible to speak of community, of everyone owning the same object in the same manner, as a form of property. With Grotius' concept of dominium it is possible to speak of individual *dominium* and *dominium* in several, but not of *dominium* in common:[54]

> I say 'in the same manner' for nothing prevents, and, indeed, it very often happens, that the same thing belongs to different persons according to their different ways of holding it. Thus, over the same land a state has eminent, the owner direct, and the user useful *dominium*. It was also said 'in its entirety' for also several persons can possess the same thing in the same way of holding, but each one for his own share and not in its entirety.

For Pufendorf, as for Grotius, 'common' means that it belongs to no one and is open for the appropriation of anyone. For Suarez 'common' means that the object belongs to everyone and so must be individuated such that each realizes their claim.

III

Our passage to Locke is facilitated by the commentary on Grotius and Pufendorf by Jean Barbeyrac (1674–1744), a French legal theorist and historian. He annotated a Latin edition of Grotius' *The laws of war and peace* (1735) and annotated and translated into French Pufendorf's *The law of nature and nations* (1725). He corresponded with Locke, learned English in order to read the *Essay concerning human understanding*, and wrote a history of natural law political theory which situates Locke in the context described above.[55] As Mr Laslett writes of Barbeyrac, 'no man was in a generally better position than he to know about the relationship of his [Locke's] writings with the natural law jurists and with the whole tradition of social and political theory'.[56] Many of his notes on Pufendorf consist of references to the *Two treatises*, with unreserved enthusiasm for Locke's superiority. His note on Pufendorf's definition of *dominium* is precisely what one would expect from a person familiar with Grotius' and Pufendorf's collapse

---

[53] Samuel Pufendorf, *De jure naturae et gentium*, Latin–English edition, ed. C. H. Oldfather and W. A. Oldfather (Oxford: Clarendon Press, 1934), 4.4.2. (Hereafter referred to as *The law*).

[54] Pufendorf, *The law*, 4.4.2.

[55] Jean Barbeyrac, 'A Historical and Critical Account of the Science of Morality', in his annotated edition of Pufendorf's *De jure naturae et gentium* (1725).

[56] P. Laslett, *Two treatises*, 306n.

of the vocabulary of property into exclusive rights: 'our author [Pufendorf] gives us a notion of a particular kind of *dominium*, rather than of *dominium* in general'.[57] He refers his reader to Locke's refutation of Filmer for clarification.

Locke hammers out the foundation of his rights theory in the *First treatise*, in the course of his refutation of Filmer. When Filmer speaks of property or private dominion he means the same kind of exclusive right as we have seen in Grotius and Pufendorf. Locke paraphrases this concept of property and draws special attention to its unlimited and unlimitable nature:[58]

This *Fatherly Authority* then, or *Right of Fatherhood*, in our A__'s sence is a Divine unalterable Right of Sovereignty, where a Father or a Prince hath an Absolute, Arbitrary, Unlimited, and Unlimitable Power, over the Lives, Liberties, and Estates of his Children and Subjects; so that he may take or alienate their Estates, sell, castrate, or use their Persons as he pleases, they being all his slaves, and he Lord or Proprietor of every Thing, and his unbounded Will their Law (1.9).

Locke's aim in the *First treatise* is to overthrow this unlimited rights theory and to establish the framework for a limited rights theory bounded by natural law. He does this by arguing for a rival interpretation of scripture and by showing that his limited rights can be derived from natural law.

The scriptural text to which both Filmer and Locke appeal is *Genesis* 1.28:

The words of the Text are these; ' And God Blessed them, and God said unto them, be Fruitful and Multiply and Replenish the Earth and subdue it, and have Dominion over the Fish of the Sea, and over the Fowl of the Air, and over every living thing that moveth upon the Earth.' (1.23)

Filmer interprets this as granting to Adam '*Private Dominion* over the Earth, and all inferior or irrational Creatures' (1.23). Filmer calls this private dominion 'property' (1.23). Locke agrees that there is 'nothing to be granted to *Adam* here but Property' (1.24). However, property is not the same as private dominion according to Locke. He writes (1.24):

I shall shew . . . That by this grant God gave him not *Private Dominion* over

---

[57] Jean Barbeyrac, ed., Samuel Pufendorf, *The law of nature and nations*, tr. Basil Kennett (London: 1729), 4.4.2 n.

[58] All quotations from the *Two treatises of Government* are from P. Laslett's edition (Cambridge: Cambridge University Press, 1970). The first number in the bracket refers to the treatise, the second to the section.

the Inferior Creatures, but right in common with all mankind; so neither was he Monarch, upon the account of the Property here given him.

As Barbeyrac comments, property is 'right in common with all mankind . . . a right common to all'.[59]

Locke then gives a more extensive redescription of *Genesis* 1.28: 'Whatever God gave by the words of this Grant . . . it was not to Adam in particular, exclusive of all other men: whatever *Dominion* he had thereby, it was not a *Private Dominion*, but a *Dominion* in common with the rest of Mankind' (1.29). This is the first characterization of Filmer's private dominion as exclusive and particular, and he contrasts this with dominion in common. He argues for this conclusion and states that 'God in this Donation, gave the World to Mankind in common, and not to *Adam* in particular' (1.30).

He then repeats that this right in common is property (1.36, 39, 45–7). Dominion in common is then defined in terms of subjective rights: 'God gave his sons a Right to make use of a part of the Earth for the support of themselves and Families' (1.37). Locke's concept of property at this point is different from Filmer's in two respects. First, it is predicted of all men, not just of Adam. Second, it is a claim right to use the world for support, a right not to be excluded from such use. It says nothing yet about actual possession. Property is the same kind of inclusive claim right as we have seen in Suarez. As Locke reiterates, 'God . . . himself gave them all a Right, to make use of the Food and Rayment, and other Conveniences of Life, the Materials whereof he had so plentifully provided for them' (1.41). Locke's concept of property here is, as he points out, community translated into the language of rights: 'this Text is so far from proving *Adam* Sole Proprietor, that on the contrary, it is a confirmation of the original Community of all things amongst the Sons of Men' (1.40).

Having established that common property is consistent with Scripture and that it can be discussed in terms of a natural claim right to one's due, Locke goes on to show that this right can be derived from natural law. The fundamental law of nature for Locke is that mankind ought to be preserved.[60] He derives three natural rights

---

[59] Barbeyrac, ed., Pufendrof, *The law of nature and nations*, 4.4.3 n. 1.

[60] Locke, *Two treatises*, 1.86, 2.6, 2.7, 2.11, 2.16, 2.23, 2.60, 2.79, 2.129, 2.135, 2.138, 2.149, 2.155, 2.159, 2.168, 2.171 and 2.200. By making the preservation of mankind, rather than self-preservation, the foundation of his natural rights Locke is consciously writing in opposition to Hobbes. As he writes in his journal: 'An Hobbist, with his principle of self-preservation, whereof he him self is to be the judge, will not easily admit a great many plain duties of morality' (reprinted in Lord Peter King, *The life of John Locke*, London: 1830), I, 191.

from this, the third of which is the claim right to use the world for the
sake of preservation. He does this by enunciating the law of nature in
two ways: first, carrying the substantive 'preservation'; and second,
carrying the verb 'to preserve'.[61] In the first case he writes that '*the
fundamental law of Nature* [is] *the preservation of Mankind*' (2.135). This is
nothing but the continued subsistence of the human race and he gives
each man a right not to be denied it: 'Men, being once born, have a
right to their Preservation' (2.25).

In his second enunciation he writes that 'all the members of the
Society are to be *preserved*' (2.159). This is redescribed as a duty of all
men to preserve themselves and others (2.6). There will always be a
natural right in this case: 'they will always have a right to preserve
what they have not a power to part with', namely their lives (2.149).
He calls this the 'original right' (2.220), or '*the Right of Preserving all
Mankind*' (2.11).

These two natural rights, as Father Copleston notes, are unique.[62]
We normally think of the duties involved in a particular right as
correlative with it, although there are exceptions.[63] That is, if a person
has a right then others are said to have a correlative duty either to
abstain from (a negative duty) or to provide (a positive duty) the
object to which the right refers. A right to a piece of land correlates
with a negative duty on the part of others to abstain from the use of
that land unless the consent of the rightholder is given. A right to an
education correlates with the positive duty of others to provide
educational facilities. Locke's two natural rights have correlative
duties but, in addition, they are tied to other duties in a unique
manner.

We usually think of a right as a liberty, the exercise of which is at
the possessor's discretion. Locke's two natural rights, of preservation
and to preserve oneself and others, are not liberties. They are natural
rights directly resulting from, or entailed by, the natural duty to
preserve mankind. Their exercise is not at the rightholder's discretion; their exercise is the exercise of the natural law duty to preserve
mankind. It may seem redundant to say that each man has a claim

[61] Preservation: 1.86, 2.129, 2.135, 2.149, 2.159, 2.170, 2.182, 2.209. To preserve: 1.88, 2.6, 2.8,
2.11–16, 2.159, 2.220.
[62] F. Copleston, *A history of philosophy* (New York: Image Books, 1964), vol. v, part 1, 139.
[63] See H. L. A. Hart, 'Bentham on legal rights', in *Oxford essays in jurisprudence*, 2nd series, ed. A.
W. B. Simpson (Oxford: Clarendon Press, 1973), for the analysis of a legal right constituted
by duties in a manner similar to Locke's natural rights.

right to exercise his duty of ensuring preservation and of preserving mankind, but Locke's point is well taken. These perpetual duties could be blocked by, say, the unlimited rights of property in a society modelled on the theories of Grotius or Filmer. In these cases a person may require natural claim rights in order to override the conventional rights of property, to preserve himself and one's family and, if need be, others.

Locke illustrates his point by applying his third natural right in such a case. The third natural right is derived from the logically prior right to preservation. He writes that, 'Men, being once born, have a right to their Preservation, and consequently to Meat and Drink, and other such things, as Nature affords for their Subsistence' (2.25). That is, every man has the natural right to the means to preserve himself: 'He that is Master of himself, and his own life, has a right too to the means of preserving it' (2.172). This claim right is entailed by both the right to preservation and the right to preserve oneself and others (2.26). This third right is property; it is identical to the natural right which Locke derives from Scripture, as we have seen.

He explains how his natural rights would work in a society in which property is distributed in such a way that some are legally excluded from the means of preservation. His natural right, or property, gives the needy the moral justification to take what they need from the conventional property of others (1.42):

But we know that God hath not left one man so to the Mercy of another, that he may starve him if he please: God the Lord and Father of all, has given no one of his children such a Property, in his peculiar Portion of the things of this world, but that he has given his needy Brother a Right to the Surplusage of his Goods; so that it cannot be justly denied him, when his pressing Wants call for it.

The moral claim to the means of preservation overrules the purely legal description of such an act as theft. The man's need creates a title *in* the goods of another, thus individuating his natural right not to be excluded from the means of preservation: '*Charity* gives every man a Title to so much out of anothers Plenty, as will keep him from extream want, where he has no means to subsist otherwise' (1.42). This is similar to Aquinas' formulation.[64] Also, the proprietor cannot use the man's need to force him to work for his subsistence (1.42). This theory of charity is a repudiation of the negative theories of Grotius and

---

[64] Aquinas, *Summa theologiae*, II, II, 66.7.

Pufendorf and a reassertion of Thomist theory. It should be read as an illustration of how natural rights would work in a society not constituted in accordance with natural law. In the *Two treatises* Locke is primarily concerned with showing how property would be distributed in a society organized in accordance with natural law, such that the above circumstances would not occur (2.135).

v

Locke carries his framework of natural, inclusive claim rights forward to the *Second treatise*, where it functions as a premise. His famous chapter entitled 'Of Property' begins with a recapitulation of the argument we have traced in the *First Treatise*. Natural law teaches that each man has a claim right to the means of preservation, and this is logically equivalent to saying that the world belongs to all in common (2.25):

> Whether we consider natural *Reason*, which tells us, that Men, being once born, have a right to their Preservation, and consequently to Meat and Drink, and such other things, as Nature affords for their Subsistence: Or *Revelation*, which gives us an account of those Grants God made of the World to *Adam*, and to Noah, and his Sons, 'tis very clear, that God, as King *David* says . . . *has given the Earth to the Children of Men*, given it to Mankind in common.

As in Suarez, this inclusive concept of property necessarily leads to the problem of individuation or distribution. Locke writes, 'But this being supposed, it seems to some a very great difficulty, how any one should ever come to have a *Property* in any thing . . . I shall endeavour to shew, how Men might come to have a *property* in several parts of that which God gave to Mankind in common' (2.25). The 'great difficulty' is one which Filmer voiced in his criticism of Grotius: 'where there is community there is neither *meum* nor *tuum*'.[65] Filmer is correct only if 'community' means belonging to no one, as with Grotius. If 'community' means belonging to everyone in the same manner, as their due, then mine and thine are not only logically possible, but are logically necessary if each man's due is to be realized. Thus natural law can be seen to consistently sanction common property and private property in this special, interrelated sense.

A theory in which private property exists as the individuation or

---

[65] Filmer, *Patriarcha*, 264.

realization of common property constitutes a concept of property different from a theory in which private and common property are construed as mutually exclusive. One linguistic feature which Locke uses to tie his analysis together is to call the right involved in a claim right to something and a right in something 'property'. This wide use of the term 'property' was first noted by Barbeyrac:[66]

Mr Locke means by the word 'property' not only the right which one has to his goods and possessions, but even with respect to his actions, liberty, his life, his body; and, in a word, all sorts of right.

Locke goes on to show in chapter 5 of the *Second treatise* how common property can be individuated naturally and how the common property of a political community can be individuated conventionally, both in accordance with natural law.[67] In both cases the inclusive sense of property provides a framework within which the distribution takes place. It is not, as J. P. Day assumes, a 'justification of private property'.[68] 'Locke wants to explain', writes Professor Yolton, 'how particularisation of the common is possible'.[69] It is an attempt to work out the distribution of common property as defined and constituted by his natural rights framework.[70] This however is a complex story and falls outside the confines of the paper. I would like nonetheless to briefly outline one point: the way in which Locke's framework limits exclusive rights.

That each man has the claim right to use and to enjoy the good things of the world naturally limits the amount of things which any particular person can come to have a property in. It is noteworthy that Locke uses the locution 'a property in' to describe an individual, exclusive right which a person comes to have as a result of exercising his natural claim right in accordance with natural law. This locution, it seems to me, is simply his translation of the Latin *ius in re*.[71] If a man comes to have a property in things to the extent that it excludes others from the exercise of their claim right, then his surplus ceases to be his property. This is the major difference between Grotius and Locke. Grotius, like Professor Nozick, starts with the primitive concept of an

---

[66] Barbeyrac, 'A historical and critical account of the science of morality', in Pufendorf, *The Law of Nature and Nations*, ed. Barbeyrac, tr. Kennet (London, 1729), 4.

[67] See Locke, *Two treatises*, 2.117–120, 2.138.

[68] J. P. Day, 'Locke on property', *Philosophical Quarterly*, 16 (1966), 207.

[69] J. W. Yolton, *Locke and the compass of human understanding* (Cambridge: Cambridge University Press, 1970), 187.   [70] See Dunn, *The political thought of John Locke*, 67, n. 4.

[71] See especially *Two treatises*, 1.86, 1.87, 1.90, 1.92, 2.25, 2.173.

exclusive right and, if he is interested in limiting it in some way, he must introduce limits based on a different principle. By working with exclusive rights as rights in what the exercise of an inclusive right realizes, Locke has a theory in which exclusive rights are self-limiting.[72] The limits which Locke introduces are internal limits which follow from the nature of the original position – of the world belonging to all in the same manner and of man under the direction of natural law (2.4).

For example, the first limit derived from the original position is that a man is entitled to what he acquires by the labour of his person only 'where there is enough, and as good left in common for others' (2.27). If this criterion is fulfilled then Locke can answer his own question in the negative: 'Was it a Robbery thus to assume to himself what belonged to all in common?' (2.28). If the world belongs to no one, as with Grotius and Pufendorf, then the question of robbery cannot arise until after first occupancy. This would be the first appearance of the concept of belonging to, which is the logical precondition of robbery. As a consequence, robbery is defined with reference to the primitive concept of exclusive rights.[73] Locke's reassertion of the Thomist logical priority of the world belonging to all in common turns the concept of robbery around. The question for Locke is this: is an exclusive right an instance of robbery, given that the world belongs to all? For him, the primitive concept of belonging to is the inclusive one. An exclusive right is not robbery solely because, as a right in the means to realize the end for the sake of which the world exists, it is a common gift.[74]

The argument that I have attempted to recover would not seem untoward to Locke's audience. Each man possessed Locke's claim right in a legal form. The parish authorities had a duty, not merely to provide the local poor with welfare, but to provide them with the means by which they could make bread and so on, and so preserve themselves and their families.[75] Each man had the legal right and the legal duty to work.[76] Locke's argument 'makes sense' within the

[72] As he claims at *Two treatises*, 2.31.
[73] Professor Nozick argues in a manner similar to Grotius and, as a consequence, finds taxation and redistribution to be forms of robbery, defined with reference to a primitive concept of exclusive rights. Nozick, *Anarchy, state, and utopia*, 169–72, 265–8.
[74] See *Two treatises*, 2.28, 2.33, 2.37, 2.38, 2.46.
[75] See 'Act for the relief of the poor', 43 *Elizabeth*, c. 2 1601, 1.
[76] See Sir William Holdsworth, *A history of English law*, 3rd edition (London: 1922–6), 9 vols., IV, 375–85.

intersubjective assumption of the economy (if we may call it that) as a large household, as carefully reconstructed by Karl Polanyi and Keith Tribe.[77]

Appealing to a concept of natural law which enjoys widespread consensus, Locke alters it slightly in order to arrive at a concept of property, or exclusive right, within a framework of common property consistent with natural law, thus replying to Filmer's criticism. In so doing he establishes a rights theory which functions as a precondition for his major task of enunciating a theory of popular sovereignty.[78] The concern here, as I have attempted to show, is not with capitalist accumulation. That sort of debate, as Professor Pocock shows, emerges in the eighteenth century in quite different circumstances.[79]

---

[77] Karl Polyani, *The great transformation* (Boston: Beacon Press, 1944); Tribe, *Land, labour.*

[78] See how Locke's property as the natural right to the means to preserve oneself functions as the foundation for the right to resist arbitrary government at *Two treatises*, 2.149.

[79] John G. A. Pocock, 'The mobility of property and the rise of eighteenth-century sociology', in *Theories of property, Aristotle to the present*, eds, Anthony Parel and Thomas Flanagan (Waterloo, Ontario: Wilfred Laurier University Press, 1979), 141–66.

CHAPTER 4

Differences in the interpretation of Locke on property

I

In the last twenty-five years Locke's political thought has received more and better scholarly commentary than in any other period, with the possible exception of mid-eighteenth century Scotland. I am particularly pleased that my book, *A discourse on property: John Locke and his adversaries* (1980), is partly responsible for the continuation of one aspect of this renaissance in Locke studies; namely, careful analyses of his explanation of property. It was very kind of the editor of *The Locke newsletter*, Mr Roland Hall, to invite me in 1983 to respond to the papers by T. R. Baldwin and J. Waldron and I was most grateful for the opportunity to clarify some of my arguments in the light of their comments.[1]

Baldwin summarizes my account of Locke on property in land from the point at which good, unused land becomes scarce in the state of nature to the institution of political society and states clearly some difficulties he has with this. He then advances his own interpretation and insists – somewhat paradoxically – that it is both a version of the standard account and highly implausible.

His major difficulty consists in an apparent conflict between two theses; the first being my account, which I will now present, clarifying a few minor points in Baldwin's summary. Thesis Ia: When good, unused land becomes scarce in the state of nature the rule governing property in land – that everyone should have as much as he[2] can make use of, by applying his labour without consent – no longer obtains because the enough and as good proviso is not fulfilled (36).[3] Ib: Men

---

[1] Thomas Baldwin, 'Tully, Locke, and land', *The Locke Newsletter*, ed. Roland Hall, 13 (1982), 21–33; Jeremy Waldron, 'The turfs my servant has cut', *ibid.*, 9–20.

[2] I use exclusively male pronouns out of historical fidelity to the text, not out of moral choice.

[3] All references in brackets are to numbered sections of the *Second treatise*.

then institute or join political society, give up the exclusive rights in land they acquired under the old rule in order that their property be determined, regulated, and settled by majority consent, in conformity with natural law or the public good (omitted in Baldwin's summary), and government then protects this property. Although he mentions several passages which say or 'suggest' this (add. 129–30, 135, 138–40), Baldwin claims, when he paraphrases it, that it 'is weaker than Locke's actual claim' and this because it cannot do justice to, and conflicts with Locke's central claim, which I will call thesis II: political societies are instituted to preserve property. He believes I and II conflict because he assumes that if political societies are instituted to preserve property, then men must have property in land prior to entering into political society which is simply clarified and codified by positive law. He also assumes that the kind of property in land in the state of nature is private property. It seems to me that there is no conflict between I and II and that Baldwin runs into difficulty as a result of his two, common, but nonetheless mistaken, assumptions.

The first assumption – that governments are established to codify and protect pre-existing property in land – can be corrected briskly. Locke literally writes what I have put in Ib and what Baldwin dismisses as weaker than his actual claim; namely, that the property men have on entering political society and which government preserves is 'a right to the goods, which by the Law of the Community are theirs' (138). This must be the case since the person who enters 'submits to the Community those Possessions, which he has, or shall acquire' (120), and these are to be regulated by the public good, Locke repeatedly states, not by the old rule of property. Once we read II in the way Locke explains it then we can read 'determine', 'regulate' and so on straightforwardly and not translate them into 'clarify' as Baldwin does. *En passant*, I take this to be the standard account. As Dunn, *inter alios*, writes, on entering political society, what 'property *now* is, is what the legal rules specify'.[4] Although Scanlon, to whom Baldwin refers,[5] can speak for himself, I see nothing in the quotation about money creating a new kind of right; only that it enables people to enlarge their possessions. One page earlier he

---

[4] John Dunn, 'Consent in the political theory of John Locke', in *Life, liberty, and property: essays on Locke's political ideas*, ed. Gordon Schochet (Belmont, California: Wadsworth, 1972), 140.
[5] Thomas Scanlon, 'Nozick on rights, liberty, and property', *Philosophy and Public Affairs*, 6 (1976).

writes in a somewhat ambiguous way that the introduction of money and of government gives rise to new systems of property.

It is helpful to remember Locke's radical point in stating that the end of government is the preservation of property. He defines property in some thing as the right to it such that it cannot be taken without the proprietor's consent (193–4), or the consent of the majority, or their representatives (138–40). To say that government ought to preserve property is to claim that they, and especially the king, cannot infringe the citizens' life, liberty, or possessions without their, or the majority's, consent. This is an attack on the absolutist doctrine of Filmer, as well as most of the Royalists, that the sovereign rules by divine right, not by consent, and so can take any part of a man's property without his consent. Locke's 'property' is a right that holds against government as well as against fellow citizens, and this is true independent of the reference of the right (life, liberty, action, goods and so on) (139).

The second assumption which leads Baldwin into difficulty is that 'property' means private property in land. He uses 'property', 'exclusive rights in land', 'estate' and 'possessions' as synonyms for private property in land. Since Locke says nothing about private property in the state of nature, Baldwin imputes to him the implicit view that the tacit acceptance of money entails the tacit acceptance of private property; a view which he admits is highly implausible. Rather than accepting this implausible conclusion, it seems more sensible to question its enabling assumption, shared by liberals and Marxists, that Locke must be justifying private property and, rather, try taking him at his word when he says he means by property in something the right to it such that it cannot be taken without consent.

In my book I defined private property as the right to exclude others from some object (which is to say that it cannot be taken without consent) plus the right to use, abuse or not to use, and to alienate the object, and this without any binding social obligations. I defined it this way for two reasons: first, because this is the definition of private property, except with respect to the monarch, that Locke argues against, as advanced by Filmer and most theorists and defenders of absolutism; and, secondly, because this definition has actually been imputed to Locke by commentators such as Macpherson. Baldwin realizes that for Locke there is no property without binding social obligations and so agrees that Locke does not posit private property in this sense. Nonetheless, he still wishes to claim that private property exists in the state of nature, presumably in the sense of the right to exclude plus the right to use, abuse, or not to use and to alienate.

Locke's definition of property does not specify what degree of control one has over the object except that it cannot be taken without consent, and this is true of any right. This is why Locke's first commentator, Jean Barbeyrac, stated that Locke meant by 'property' any kind of right. I tried to show in my book how straightforward his argument is once it is read with this in mind. In the state of nature labour creates rights of usufruct in land: a cultivator may exclude others from his cultivated land only insofar as he continues to use it, and he may consume, barter or sell the fruits (32, 46–7). That is, his title is conditional upon labour or use (31, 34, 51). A person cannot abuse his land or its products, nor can he claim land he does not use, nor can he sell land (although he may be able to sell the improvement) (36–8). This conditional exclusive use-right in land falls so far short of the definition of private property above, as well as what most people standardly mean by private property, that I believe no one would want to call it private property, except for ideological purposes. Baldwin agrees with this but maintains that usufruct is transformed into private property with the tacit acceptance of money. However, all Locke says is that money permits people to trade their products for money, thus allowing them to avoid the spoilage limitation and so put more land under cultivation (46–9). People thus enlarged their possessions, but they are still conditional on use; there is no need to introduce a new kind of right – private property – to explain this (50). Since Locke says that people commonly incorporate into political societies without fixed property in land (38: 13–19), and since they incorporate after the introduction of money (45), I do not see how money could have introduced private property in land, which must involve at least fixed property in land (38).

I certainly agree with Baldwin that there would be some continuity between the possessions one held in the state of nature and those protected in political society, at least for the industrious and rational, and this because the legislators are bound by natural law to ensure property in the product of one's labour insofar as this is consistent with the public good (45). Perhaps we are thus closer in our views than it appears. However, the legislators must also take into account the legitimate claims of those without good land to use to the means of preservation, as opposed to the illegitimate claims of the quarrelsome and contentious who wish to live off the labour of others (34). I take it that the conflicting legitimate claims explain why even the industrious would be willing to give up some of their liberty of use for the other benefits of political society (130). Since the whole tenor of the argument is that property in land should be conditional on use and should not allow abuse, non-use or freedom from social obligations, I see no reason to assume that Locke's aim was to justify private property in land even in political society.

Finally, Baldwin suggests that if land reverts to common ownership, as I quoted Mackie,[6] then any establishment of exclusive rights by the majority involved would require universal consent. He is correct to say that there is an illicit inference from 'community ownership' (my phrase) to 'common ownership' (Mackie's phrase). I took Mackie to mean the common ownership of the community who form a political society and amongst whom there is the land scarcity problem, and thus I took this as equivalent to community ownership. Baldwin, I think, takes 'common ownership' to mean common ownership of mankind. Although the way I phrase it makes this reading plausible, I would like to close it by referring to the passages where Locke says political societies are formed one at a time as local land scarcity problems arise (38, 45). Such a group renounces any claim to use land outside their territory and agrees to be bound by majority consent within it. They would require universal consent only if the whole world experienced land scarcity at the same time, but this is not the case (45). It seems to follow that those without citizenship, refugees, can always make a claim to the means of preservation against any country if there is no free land available.

I turn now to Waldron's defence of Macpherson's view that Locke, in his use of the master–servant relation, was already working with capitalist categories and so, unwittingly, laid the ideological foundations for the emergence and legitimation of industrial capitalism. He accuses me of anachronism for *not* finding the capitalist and wage-labourer in Locke's state of nature and for finding instead the pre-capitalist master and handicraftsman. I should point out that although Waldron has a great deal to say about alienated labour I do not discuss it in my book. My point in explicating Locke's master–servant relation was to show that it is dissimilar to the modern,

---

[6] John L. Mackie, *Ethics: inventing right and wrong* (Middlesex: Penguin, 1977) 176, cited in Tully, *A discourse on property*, 165.

post-eighteenth century relation between capitalist and wage-labourer in a number of important respects.

The first argument Waldron mentions is that, since Locke defines the servant as a freeman, and a freeman as a person with freedom of choice, the servant is dissimilar to the wage-labourer who has no choice but to work for another because all available land has been appropriated. Rather than criticizing my analysis, which I believe requires revision, he moves on to attack my subsidiary point that if a man is driven into a relation by material necessity it cannot be a master–servant relation, which I support with section 42 of the *First treatise*. Whatever Locke meant by 'necessity' in section 77, which Waldron cites, he obviously thought that marriage and the decision to have children could be based on choice, so I cannot see how it bears on the point. He then suggests that the duty of charity in 1.42 could be met by the capitalist offering the propertyless labour employment. What Locke says here is that the 'needy Brother' has 'a Right to the Surplusage of his (the proprietor's) Goods', and this, it seems to me, has to be read and translated pretty anachronistically to come out as an offer of employment by a capitalist. The point about the sections 41–3, as I understand them, is that Locke denies legitimacy to a form of private dominion (property), in addition to a form of sovereignty, which puts men in a condition of material necessity by denying them access to the materials necessary for food, clothing, and conveniences (1.41). The absolutist form of private property attacked here by Locke was defended by Filmer, and by the whole mainstream of seventeenth-century absolutists, and this helps to illustrate the historically unsurprising similarity between absolutist and capitalist property relations.

The second argument of mine which Waldron attacks is that Locke does not have the concept of someone selling his undifferentiated labour power to be employed in the routine and piecemeal operations characteristic of the modern division of labour, both capitalist and communist. Rather, Locke's servant is pre-modern: he sells a complete service or task which he directs and performs with his knowledge and skill, characteristic of handicrafts, guilds, the putting-out system, farming, and all the examples of labour Locke mentions in chapter 5. I believe with Harry Braverman, Moses Finley, Michel Foucault, Keith Tribe, and others that it was not at least until the eighteenth century, when the material conditions were also present, that a worker was conceived to sell, not a skill and execution, but his labour power which could be integrated into a labour process. Further, I argued that since Locke does conceptualize the servant as performing a task or service, and the master as directing him to work but not in his work, then this model could not be used to legitimate the modern division of labour, since the engineer and manager now perform operations integral to Locke's servant. Oddly, Waldron says my point that it is logically impossible for an agent to alienate his labour is 'either false or unhelpful' and then he goes on to use it, as I did, to distinguish between the intentional activity of the labouring servant and the operational movements formed from the labour power of the wage-labourer.

Waldron advances only two reasons for obliterating this distinction and reading the modern concept of labour power into Locke's concept of a servant. First, he asks why Locke would bother to write 'for a certain time' and 'temporary power' in section 85 if a complete task is intended. My answer is that both phrases stress the independence and the contractual status of the servant, and this in contrast to the dependence and the natural status of the servant in Filmer's more orthodox account. I stress the context here again because recent work tends to support the hypothesis that Locke's intended audience was made up largely of people who were servants in this sense much of the time and who would have been more than happy to have property in land conditional on use.[7]

Second, Waldron claims that Locke does have a concept of alienated labour power, and this is the Jewish concept of selling oneself into drudgery in *Exodus* which Locke cites once. He believes that this concept 'could be applied to characterise the plight of the industrial proletariat' and, since Locke does not condemn it and since it is compatible with his concept of a servant, it seems to follow for Waldron that Locke unwittingly laid the ideological foundations for legitimating wage-labour under capitalism. To make only the most obvious point, Locke says that this is an example of men selling *themselves*, not a service, so it is in fact incompatible with the master–servant relation. I will leave the reader to judge where the anachronism lies.

I would like to thank Baldwin and Waldron for permitting me to

---

[7] Richard Ashcraft, 'Revolutionary politics and Locke's *Two treatises of government*: radicalism and Lockean political theory', *Political Theory* 8, 4 (November 1980), 429–87; Mark Goldie, 'The roots of true whiggism: 1688–94', *History of Political Thought* 1, 2 (June 1980), 195–236.

respond to their commentaries. I enjoyed reading and replying to both of them and I trust that the exchange has shed some further light on Locke on property.

II

The editors of *Annals of scholarship* have kindly asked me if I would like to reply to the comments on aspects of chapters 6 and 7 of my book, *A discourse on property*, by James R. Jacob in his article, 'Locke's *Two treatises* and the revolution of 1688–9: The state of the argument' (in *Annals of scholarship* 5, 3 [1988] 311–44). I am pleased to do so and thankful for the opportunity to clear up some of the misunderstanding in his comments and to point out our genuine disagreements, as well as the reasons for them, in hopes that this will contribute to the advancement of Locke scholarship.

I will restrict my comments to Jacob's criticisms of my work and will not discuss in detail his interpretation of other recent works on Locke. However, when the way he misunderstands my work also seems to inform his description of these other works I will point this out.

Allow me to say at the outset that *A discourse on property* is now almost ten years old. I have learned considerably more since then about Locke, seventeenth-century political philosophy, the issues involved in interpretation, and the complex relations between seventeenth-century political thought and action and our present political predicament. I have also learned from the scholarship of the last ten years. Accordingly, some of my views have changed. Some arguments I now believe to be mistaken, in others the emphasis is wrong, and there are whole areas I did not discuss which, I now see, throw considerable light on Locke's political philosophy. I have discussed these changes elsewhere in this volume. This constant activity of working on and changing one's understanding – of past thought and one's relation to it, and using this exercise as a way of freeing oneself from the customary and stultifying ways of thought in the present – is what the history of political philosophy is about. I thank Jacob for contributing to and encouraging me to continue in this activity.

Taking these changes into account, however, I still find that I cannot agree with everything Jacob says (although I think he disagrees with me more than I do with him). Some of his criticisms remain unconvincing, either because they are based on a misunderstanding of my argument or because it is difficult to square them with what Locke wrote.

Before I discuss these criticisms in detail I would like to mention the major reason why Jacob misinterprets parts of my chapters 6 and 7 (and of recent scholarship on Locke). He does not fully understand the context in which *A discourse on property*, as well as other recent Locke scholarship, was written. The article by Jacob, as well as the book Jacob endorses in it – *John Locke and agrarian capitalism* by Neal Wood – return to an older way of doing the history of political thought. The regulative question that governs this type of interpretation is: can the *Two treatises*, or any suitable text, be interpreted in such a way that it can be seen as a justification of capitalism? One of my aims in writing *A discourse of property* was to try to free us (or at least myself) from the tyranny of this question in governing our investigations of seventeenth-century political thought, thus enabling us to ask new questions and perhaps to gain a more fine-grained understanding of the historically specific set of questions to which the *Two treatises* is addressed. I thought that one way to do this was to show – in the course of my contextual investigation – that the arguments of the *Two treatises*, in a number of crucial respects, do not justify capitalism, as C. B. Macpherson carefully defined it in his classic study, *The political theory of possessive individualism*. I also suggested that if we take other definitions of capitalism it appears that not all of Locke's arguments are justifications of it, or even contributions to such a problematic.

One response to this is to redefine capitalism so broadly in biological metaphors of embryo and growth that almost any argument written in the seventeenth century can be read as a justification of it. This seems to be the procedure of Jacob (and Wood[8]), since he does not refer to Macpherson's specific definition of capitalism, to which I was explicitly contrasting Locke, nor propose an alternative. My response, on the other hand, was to try to present a perspicuous survey of this distinctive, seventeenth-century 'political-

---

[8] Wood, *John Locke and agrarian capitalism*, 92, writes: 'a fundamental shortcoming of Tully's analysis is a failure to perceive capitalism as an historical phenomenon, developing over the centuries from bare beginnings to a complex and mature stage . . . What we should be searching for in his [Locke's] ideas, among other things, is some discernible sign of those roots [of Classic British Capitalism] beginning to shoot . . . At best we can maintain that Locke's thought was in part expressive of certain basic social changes occurring in England, of a transition to the early stages of capitalism, and that he began to conceive of the social relations of production in a manner suggestive of an embryonic capitalist outlook'. I can't imagine a more accurate and complimentary description of my 'fundamental shortcoming'.

economy' – of this slightly different way of thinking about property. The aim here was not to translate the discourse into our familiar concepts of feudalism, capitalism, and socialism, but to use these as objects of contrast to highlight its unique aspects. This different way of thinking of property could then be used in turn, I hoped, to throw light on, and help to dislodge, the conventions which habitually constrain our political imagination in current thinking about property (Preface: x):

The mutually exclusive concepts of common and private property divide the modern world into two spheres. By coming to understand a way of thinking about rights in which our opposed concepts do not exist, we can begin to see what is contingent and what is necessary in our predicament.

In engaging in this type of study, I followed the lead of John Dunn, Michel Foucault, Edward Hundert, John Pocock, and Quentin Skinner, whose works were ceaselessly discussed by us as graduate students in those exciting years at Cambridge. They had all raised doubts about the 'rise of capitalism' as the governing framework for interpreting seventeenth-century political thought, and, as a consequence, had gone on to enrich our understanding of the complexity and the distinctiveness of the problems and ways of thinking about them in this period. The brilliant scholarship of Ashcraft, Franklin and Goldie, discussed by Jacob, has followed in this context, showing us the local questions Locke was struggling with and the political movement of Dissenters and radical Whigs in the context of which the *Two treatises* was written. This research enhances our comprehension of the *Two treatises* and the 1680s, exposing an abundance of false assumptions in the secondary literature and opening up new disagreements and lines of research.[9] Instead of discussing this 'state of the argument', Jacob goes on to assess it in the terms of his central concern: the justification of capitalism. In turning back the clock in this way and imposing this old framework on the recent scholarship, Jacob inadvertently occludes the new ways of investigating and understanding the *Two treatises* and 1680s it offers, including new, more pluralistic and less monolithic (either for or against capitalism) ways of thinking about our radical traditions (as both Ashcraft and Goldie suggest). If we must retain this old explanatory category, why not turn it right around, as Pocock has often recommended, and

---

[9] I have discussed where I agree and disagree with Ashcraft, Franklin, and Goldie in chapter 1 above.

assess the viability and the utility of the 'rise of capitalism' in the light of the new horizons opened up by the recent scholarship?

Turning now to Jacob's specific criticisms, he first discusses Locke's justification of enclosing unused land. On Jacob's interpretation, Locke justified enclosure because, even though it would deprive others of land, it would raise productivity and this would benefit the poor, since they could work on the enclosed lands of the rich (317). He rejects my interpretation of Locke that, as Jacob phrases it, 'the increased productivity of enclosed land allows the encloser to use so much less land to provide for his own comfortable subsistence that there is much more unenclosed land left over to provide for everybody else' (317). Yet, if we turn to the text, Locke nowhere says what Jacob imputes to him and he explicitly states the view I attributed to him (section 37: lines 11–22):

> . . . he who appropriates land to himself by his labour, does not lessen but increase the common stock of mankind. For the provisions serving to the support of humane life, produced by one acre of inclosed and cultivated land, are (to speak much within compasse) ten times more, than those, which are yielded by an acre of Land, of an equal richnesse, lyeing wast in common. And therefor he, that incloses Land has a greater plenty of the conveniencys of life from ten acres, than he could have from an hundred left to Nature, may truly be said, to give ninety acres to Mankind. For his labour now supplys him with provisions out of ten acres, which were but the product of an hundred lying in common.

I realize that if we approach the text with the prejudgement that Locke is justifying capitalism, and if we know that one of the standard justifications of capitalism is that the propertyless wage-labourer is better off working for the productive capitalist, then this passage must be explained away or translated into the standard justification. My point is not only that Locke is clearly not advancing this standard justification of capitalism, but also, before we translate the argument into our familiar terms, we might try to understand it in something closer to its own terms. He seems to be saying here that if property in land is made conditional on *use* (37: 35–41, 38: 5–8), then more land would be available for others. This is certainly a justification of possession of land for the sake of use and improvement. It is not, however, the standard justification of capitalist property in land, since the claim that more land is available contradicts the standard justification that no land is available (for the wage-labourer). Nor is it an argument about capitalist forms of property in land, since a capitalist right of property is held independent of whether the owner uses the land.

If we look at the context we see that the demand that property in land be conditional on use, and thus distributed more broadly, was a conventional, radical attack on large estates, advanced by Levellers and by the Dissenters and radical Whigs, in support of whom, according to Ashcraft and Goldie, Locke wrote the *Two treatises* (Jacob, 322–5). This movement lost out in the 1680s but their successors a century later formed the working-class opposition to capitalism and continued to see Locke as their spokesperson. It seems strange to me not to discriminate between this distinctive concept of property and standard justifications of capitalism, and so to elide the richness of our history.

If we look at this and other passages where Locke discusses enclosure and use, he does not discuss the contemporary Enclosure movement nor how much better off a wage-labourer would be working for a landlord than he would be working the land himself. Yet Jacob continually translates Locke's discussion into these terms. The capitalist landlord is not mentioned where one, on Jacob's reading, would expect it (section 43). Locke's discussion always involves the contrast of how much better off mankind is in a society in which land is used and improved (by agriculture and industry) as opposed to one where the land is not improved, in this sense, at all (a hunting and gathering society). This is pretty far from capitalism on anyone's account. The contrast is between European techniques of land improvement and Amerindian culture, as Locke explicitly states. His aim is to try to show the superiority of the former and, in this context, the argument about less land being used to produce more makes perfect sense. The context, therefore, is the legitimation of the dispossession of Amerindians, the destruction of their way of life, and the imposition of European agriculture and industry based on improvement.[10] Here is another aspect of the *Two treatises* that we can never hope to understand if we continue to try to force it into the time-honoured categories of our current discussions of wage-labour. Alternatively, once we do understand it we can see how parochial our current debates are, for both socialism and capitalism take the superiority of 'improvement' to Amerindian ways of using the land for granted. And, if we wish to think intelligently about the ecological

[10] See chapter 5 below.

destruction 400 years of 'improvement' has wrought, one way to begin is to study these early, specious justifications and the alternatives to them.

Second, Jacob mentions two features of property in land in the state of nature, according to Locke, which I discussed: property is conditional on use and land itself cannot be bought and sold. Jacob says that as long as the products of land can be sold for profits then this is 'using land as capital' (318). Again, it seemed to me worthwhile to distinguish between, and not to conflate, this usufructuary economy in Locke's state of nature and a capitalist economy in which there is a market in land and capitalists can own land for speculation (i.e. non-use).

Third, Jacob disagrees with my argument that 'government is required to constitute a new order of social relations' (318) that is, 'new' relative to gradual erosion of order caused by the introduction of money, increase of population and industry, and so on in the state of nature. He also challenges me to show that it is government's role to guarantee 'everyone's natural use right in land' (318); which he appears to believe to be equivalent to the 'government is required . . .' statement. Of course I cannot show this because Locke does not say this, nor do I (as the lack of quotation marks around it in Jacob's article clearly signals). My interpretation of chapter 5 is the opposite of this. The unregulated appropriation of land in accordance with the rule of property that every man has a right to as much as he can make use of after the introduction of money leads eventually to quarrels and disputes over title (sections 36, 51, 123; *A discourse on property* 151–4). Some rule other than unregulated 'use' (36: 33–40) or unregulated 'appropriating' (35: 11–13) must be agreed upon to insure everyone's background natural, inclusive rights. This rule is the regulation of property by a government based in the consent of the governed. Far from guaranteeing 'everyone's natural use right in land', Locke, in, for example, section 36: 33–40, argues that the rule on which it is based no longer holds. His solution, as I wrote, is 'to remove the rule that every man should have as much as he can make use of' (152).

Let me make three quick points about this transition to political society. There is no question that Locke gives governments the right to 'determine' and 'regulate' property, as Jacob concedes (319), for they could scarcely solve the disputes over property that caused people to establish them unless they had this power (sections 129, 130). Jacob then quotes Locke's passage on unequal possession. It is certainly true that Locke thought inequalities of land possession based on labour could be justified to some extent. But, it is also equally clear by the last sentence of this passage that these properties in land are regulated by law and 'determined by positive constitutions' (50: 15–16). That is, he is reiterating the mercantilist commonplace that political power regulates and preserves property (including land and labour) for the 'Publick Good' (section 3). This is incompatible with capitalism as defined by Macpherson and others.

The second point here is that Locke seems to be making an important remark about the ethos of 'improvement', which was shared by almost all Europeans. It is not that 'Enclosure' is good in itself, as Jacob falsely attributes to Ashcraft (327). Nor is it that enclosing land from common use for the sake of intensive improvement is good in itself, since this is what caused the disruption of the state of nature. Rather, enclosure and improvement, as regulated and directed by the government to build a nation strong enough to compete with other mercantile states is good – the 'public good' – and even 'god like' (42: 21–8).

Further, the right of government to determine property cannot be a justification of existing property relations, for, if there had been a revolution (as Locke planned), then the people – the majority – would have had the right to reconstitute legal relations as they thought good. Existing property relations would have been open to constitutional amendment. As recent scholarship has shown, this is a feature of the *Two treatises* that contemporary readers noted with horror. Franklin (105) quotes the appropriate passage from William Atwood, a moderate Whig, in *The fundamental constitution of the English government* (1690):

But as the men of form are too strict [on the composition of a convention parliament] others [i.e. such as Locke] are too loose in their notions, and suppose the consequence of a dissolution of this contract to be a mere [i.e. pure] commonwealth, or absolute anarchy, wherein every body has an equal share in the government, not only landed men, and others with whom the balance of the power has rested by the constitution, but copy-holders, servants, and the very *faeces Romuli*, which would not only make a quiet election impractical but bring in deplorable confusion. . . . all the people are restored to their original rights; and all the laws which fettered them are gone.

This feature helps to explain why the rich landowners, who are supposed to be the beneficiaries of Locke's political philosophy, either did not read the *Two treatises* or explicitly repudiated it.

Jacob's fourth and last claim is that there is 'nothing in Locke's thinking inconsistent with capitalism' in his treatment of the master–servant relation (319). I am happy to acknowledge that my analysis of the master–servant relation was mistaken in the way Wood has correctly pointed out. However, it does not follow from the servant being driven by necessity to work for another that the servant is in all respects a wage-labourer in capitalist relations of production. In *Rights in abilities* (chapter 7) I have sought to clarify a distinction I would like to retain between types of human agency in Locke's juridical, master–servant relation and in various capitalist organizations of work.

My second remark about the master–servant relation is that it is not only the necessity of starvation that is a legitimate form of coercion to labour, as in capitalism, but also coercion by the state. In his *Report to the board of trade* (1697), Locke lays it down in no uncertain terms that young children, the unemployed, and the 'idle' can be forced into the workhouse, and thus into the apprenticeship system, and then, later, into employment. Landowners in turn can be forced to pay for the local workhouse, to hire the 'inmates', and to pay them a certain wage. It scarcely needs to be said that this mercantilist regulation of labour and land to increase the wealth and power of the state is incompatible with a free market in labour (a necessary condition of capitalism for Macpherson).

What does require comment is how the regulation of labour and trade through the national workhouse system put into operation Locke's natural rights and duties of preservation in the *Two treatises*. I cannot see how, as Jacob claims, this 'confuses' Locke's 'utopianism' and 'governing the kingdom' (320). I think it shows how part of his political theory is related to this political practice as a member of the Board of Trade.[11] Perhaps we do not disagree so much on this issue. Assuredly we agree on the importance of the original and invaluable work by Hundert in this area, referred to by Jacob at the end of his article.

I hope that this reply will encourage the reader to consider the new scholarship on the *Two treatises* and the 1680s, the challenges it presents to our conventional interpretations, and the important areas

---

[11] I have discussed this and other issues mentioned above in chapters 5–7 below.

of research it opens up. At the centre of this interdisciplinary reappraisal[12] should be, it seems to me, Ashcraft's monumental work, *Revolutionary politics and Locke's two treatises of government*. Moreover, such an exercise should include two further contexts, in addition to the context of Dissent, revolution, toleration, and political economy in Restoration England. The first is the context of all Locke's writings and the tangled intellectual milieu in which they were written. (It is important to remember that Locke wrote chapter 5 independently of the *Two treatises* and then rather awkwardly spliced it into the text.)

The second context is even more important to mention because it is often ignored. It is the multifaceted context of the development of European political and moral philosophy from Grotius to Locke and the equally complex European political activities into which it was woven – of republican revolutions, struggles for toleration and confessional uniformity, early modern state building, inter-state warfare and commercial rivalry, European imperialism, and the 'reform' of work and leisure attitudes and behaviour of all segments of European society. For example, the radical Whigs had European-wide connections, as Ashcraft has shown, and their failed revolutions of 1682 and 1685 were against a Catholic and absolute monarch closely associated with France. The Dutch conquest of England in 1688 was undertaken to initiate the Nine Years' War against France, itself a tactic in the strategy of European Protestant rulers to roll back the overwhelming, seventeenth-century victories of counter-Reformation Catholicism and absolutism. (In 1590 one-half of Europe was officially Protestant; by 1650 only one-fifth remained Protestant.) It is important to remember that Locke himself placed the *Two treatises* and *A letter concerning toleration* in the context both of these European political conflicts and of the political philosophies from Grotius onward in which theorists articulated and debated them.

In the chapters of *A discourse on property* which Jacob and I have not discussed, I tried to show the importance of aspects of these two further contexts in understanding Locke's theory of property. My knowledge of both was rudimentary. In my more recent work I have tried to increase my grasp of these two contexts and to begin to show how they enrich and modify our understanding of Locke's political

[12] John Pocock has already begun this reappraisal. See, 'Recent scholarship on John Locke and the political thought in the late seventeenth-century', *Theoretische Geschiedenis* 11, 3 (1984), 251–61, and the relevant chapters of his *Virtue, commerce, and history* (Cambridge: Cambridge University Press, 1985).

philosophy and its place in European political thought and action. This is an area of research that needs much more work. By interpreting Locke's texts in the light of the motley of early modern European political thought and action of which they are a part we will be better able to understand them fully in their own right and the roles they played in the formation of that complex of thought and action we call the Enlightenment. Important studies for situating Locke's writing in these wider contexts, from which I have learned a great deal, are Neal Wood's *The politics of Locke's philosophy* (1983) and the many fine articles by Jacob.

In conclusion, I would like to thank the editors of *Annals of scholarship* and Jacob for this opportunity to discuss issues in the interpretation of Locke's *Two treatises* and to say something about how my views have evolved since *A discourse on property*. The key disagreement seems to be over the different questions we ask of the text. I would like provisionally to set aside this question about the rise and justification of capitalism because, as I have tried to show, it distorts and limits our understanding of seventeenth-century political thought. I prefer to bring to light other ways of thinking in the past and about the past, and I see some recent Locke scholarship going in this direction as well. Not only do these studies open up more discriminating vistas on early modern thought, but the understanding of the genealogies of modern political thought we gain from them can also be used to broaden our political horizons and to think differently in the present – to stray a little from our conventional political self-understandings (as both Skinner and the late Foucault, in different ways, have suggested).[13] Let's follow this line of thought for a moment, for this is not an easy task. (This final argument is not directed at Jacob's article.)

The principle in accordance with which much of academic political discussion is conventionally governed still seems to be the legitimacy or de-legitimacy of capitalism in contrast to socialism. This principle determining the form of much contemporary political thought is woven deeply into the language games in which we participate in the course of our training and studies, and in which our

---

[13] See Michel Foucault, *The use of pleasure*, tr. R. Hurley (New York: Pantheon Books, 1985), 8; and Quentin Skinner, 'A reply to my critics', *Meaning and context: Quentin Skinner and his critics*, ed. James Tully (London and New York: Polity Press and Princeton University Press, 1988), 284–88.

ways of thinking are formed and sustained. And this regime of political thought in the republic of letters is partly supported by and supports, not only the momentum of our studies and disputes about them, but also the division of the political world into capitalist and socialist states and the role these capitalism-versus-socialism debates play in further entrenching this post-1945 division and excluding alternatives. So, it is not surprising that our (acquired) disposition is to continue to think about and investigate past and present political thought in accordance with this firmly entrenched and familiar convention, which constitutes and orders our republic of letters even, it seems, in the face of the overthrow of Soviet forms of socialism in Eastern Europe. However, it is just as important to resist this regime in our thinking about some area of contemporary politics as it is in our thinking about the early modern period, and for the same reason: it distorts and constrains our understanding of some features of the present.

This is so because the political predicament we face is, to a significant extent, shared by capitalist and (post) socialist regimes. To continue to treat the differences between these two systems as the central question serves to buttress the whole and to exclude from discussion, not only alternative ways of organizing our political activities, but also what both systems have in common. The contemporary political problems of nuclear war, the consolidation of states into war-preparing complexes, ecological destruction, the starvation, torture, and repression of millions, the lack of participation and self-government, and enormous inequalities are all common to socialism and capitalism. To a considerable degree, they are the consequences of motley ways of thought and action (such as 'improvement'), constitutive of modernization, on which capitalism and socialism are both built and which they both reproduce. If we are to think at all clearly about our political problems, we are going to have to confront directly these shared practices which bring the problems about. We can scarcely do this by conceptualizing them in terms of the relative merits of capitalism and socialism, for this problem rests on, and takes for granted, these shared forms of thought and action and disagrees only about the form of relations of production. The form of relations of production is, to be sure, an important problem in its own right; although, even here, we need to stretch our political imagination by learning about past alternatives. But, this problem cannot in turn be used as a framework to understand, let alone to explain, the very practices of thought and action that provide the shared framework for it.[14]

On the other hand, the historical investigations that have set aside this problem as their organizing principle have helped to bring to light some of the practices that have become constitutive of (capitalist and socialist) modernity, and so of our identity as moderns – the foundations of modern political thought and action. They help us to see how these were constructed and conventionalized, and the alternative forms of political life they supplanted or marginalized. As a result, the studies of Ashcraft, Foucault, Merchant, Pocock, Skinner, and Taylor give us, I believe, a clearer survey of the formation of the practices in which we are participants and the possibilities for modifying them; for thinking and acting differently.[15]

[14] See John Dunn, 'The future of political philosophy in the West', *Rethinking modern political theory* (Cambridge: Cambridge University Press, 1985), 171–90.

[15] Michel Foucault, 'Omnes et singulation: towards a criticism of "political reason"', *The Tanner lectures on human value*, ed. S. M. McMurrin (Cambridge: Cambridge University Press, 1981), 225–54; Carolyn Merchant, *The death of nature* (New York: Harper and Row, 1983); John Pocock, 'Virtues, rights, and manner', *Virtue, commerce and history* (Cambridge: Cambridge University Press, 1985), 37–51; Quentin Skinner, 'The idea of negative liberty: philosophical and historical perspectives', *Philosophy in history*, ed. R. Rorty (Cambridge: Cambridge University Press, 1984), 193–224; and two articles to which I am particularly indebted, Charles Taylor, 'Overcoming epistemology', *After philosophy*, ed. K. Baynes (Cambridge, Mass.: MIT Press, 1987), 464–88, and 'Philosophy and its history', *Philosophy in history*, ed. R. Rorty, 17–31.

CHAPTER 5

Rediscovering America: the *Two treatises* and aboriginal rights

INTRODUCTION

Three hundred years after its publication the *Two treatises* continues to present one of the major political philosophies of the modern world. By this I mean it provides a set of concepts we standardly use to represent and reflect on contemporary politics. This arrangement of concepts is not the only form of reflection on modern politics, not our 'horizon' so to speak, but it is a familiar and customary one.

At the centre of Locke's political philosophy is a theory that accounts for much of its appeal. This is a delegation theory of popular sovereignty built out of two concepts: political society and property. First, political societies are said to be derived from the delegated political powers of the individual members. The members always retain the right to regain these powers when their governors act contrary to their trust, overthrow them by means of revolution, and set up new governors as they think good. Second, the productive powers of any political society are said to be derived from the labour power, the property, of the individual members. These powers also are, as Locke puts it, 'given up' in establishing political societies so they may be 'regulated' by government for the public good. Again, if labour power is regulated contrary to the trust the members have the right to overthrow their governors and set up new ones.

Many of the leading problems of the modern world, as well as the diverse solutions to them, can be and have been posed in the terms of this theory of popular sovereignty. Locke's concept of political society provides the foundation for questions of political legitimacy: What constitutes consent to delegate political power? How much power should be delegated and for what ends? What levels of participation and representation are appropriate? When is revolt justifiable? His concept of property provides the foundation for questions of economic justice: To what extent should labour power be regulated? Can it be organized without exploitation? What is a just distribution of the products of labour? These great questions of political and economic justice, from the Scottish enlightenment through Wollstonecraft, Marx, and Mill to Rawls and Dworkin, have been asked and answered to a remarkable degree within the problem space opened up by Locke's concepts of political society and property.[1]

In this chapter I do not wish to deny that these two concepts provide an appropriate and useful representation of many aspects of modern politics. Rather, I would like to argue that the concepts of political society and property are inappropriate to and misrepresent two specific political problems: the problems of aboriginal self-government and ecology. These two problems are closely related. The struggle of aboriginal peoples for recognition as self-governing first nations is not only a struggle to right an injustice that dates from the era of European expansion: the denial of their status as distinct political societies with title to their traditional lands. It is also a struggle to reclaim their traditional lands and to practise their customary forms of land-use. This has brought them into direct conflict with the modern forms of land-use that pose the greatest threat to the environment. Whether they are the Maori of New Zealand, the aboriginal peoples of the Amazon rain forests or the Haida of the Queen Charlotte Islands, the 250 million aboriginal peoples are at the forefront of the ecological movement. The ecologically benign forms of land use, attitudes to nature and property relations they seek to preserve seem to offer an alternative to the ecologically destructive forms of property and attitudes to nature that have gradually elbowed theirs aside over the last 400 years. I mean that aboriginal land use and property relations offer an alternative, not in the sense of a solution, but in the sense of a contrasting concept of property that is different enough from our own to give us the much needed critical distance from the basic assumptions that continue to inform our debates about property and ecology.[2]

The reason why Locke's concepts of political society and property

[1] See, for example, Ian Shapiro, 'Resources, capacities and ownership: The workmanship ideal and distributive justice', *Political Theory* 19, 1 (Feb. 1991), 47–73.

[2] For an introduction see Juliam Burger, *First peoples: a future for the indigenous world* (New York: Anchor Books, 1990).

are inadequate to represent these two problems clearly is that Locke constructed them in contrast to Amerindian forms of nationhood and property in such a way that they obscure and downgrade the distinctive features of Amerindian polity and property. Let me state this thesis in two parts. First, Locke defines political society in such a way that Amerindian government does not qualify as a legitimate form of political society. Rather, it is construed as a historically less developed form of European political organization located in the later stages of the 'state of nature' and thus not on a par with modern European political formations. Second, Locke defines property in such a way that Amerindian customary land use is not a legitimate type of property. Rather, it is construed as individual labour-based possession and assimilated to an earlier stage of European development in the state of nature, and thus not on equal footing with European property. Amerindian political formations and property are thereby subjected to the sovereignty of European concepts of politics and property. Furthermore, these concepts serve to justify the dispossession of Amerindians of their political organizations and territories, and to vindicate the superiority of European, and specifically English, forms of political society and property established in the new world. In using these concepts in this way Locke was intervening in one of the major political and ideological contests of the seventeenth century.

What were the long-term consequences? Locke's theory of political society and property was widely disseminated in the eighteenth century and woven into theories of progress, development, and statehood. Debates – between jurists and humanists, free traders and mercantilists, and capitalists and socialists – over the great questions of political and economic justice have thus tended, as we have seen, to work within this basic conceptual framework. Consequently, in interpreting the *Two treatises* there is a similar tendency to overlook the European–Amerindian context and to ask questions which take the concepts for granted.[3] Indeed, the very manner in which Locke

---

[3] There are notable exceptions to this tendency to ignore the American context. See Richard Ashcraft, 'Political theory and political reform: John Locke's essay on Virginia', *The Western Political Quarterly* 22, 4 (December 1969), 742–58; John Dunn, 'The politics of Locke in England and America in the eighteenth century', *John Locke: problems and perspectives*, ed. John Yolton, (Cambridge: Cambridge University Press, 1969), 45–80; Peter Laslett, 'John Locke, the great recoinage, and the origins of the board of trade: 1695–1698', *ibid.*, 137–65; Herman Lebovics, 'The uses of America in Locke's *Second Treatise of government*', *Journal of the history of ideas* 47 (1986), 567–81.

arranged these concepts causes a reader to overlook the way European concepts of political society and property are imposed over and subsume Amerindian nations and property (thus foreshadowing what was to occur to a large extent in practice in the following centuries). One misses the philosophical and ideological contest in the text between European and Amerindian sovereignty and property (for a reader sees only the result of the contest) and misunderstands some of the basic arguments of the text. Moreover, insofar as these concepts of political society and property continue to be taken for granted, aboriginal claims to self-government are misunderstood. And, the critical perspective on the ecological crisis that their systems of property and resource use could provide is correspondingly lost.

Accordingly, my aim in this chapter is to recover the context in which Locke presented the concepts of political society and property in contrast with Amerindian forms of government and property, and to show how this increases and alters our understanding of the *Two treatises*. By setting out a clear view of how these four concepts were arranged, I also hope to loosen their continuing hold on political thought today.[4] The chapter consists in four sections. The first two are on the role of the state of nature and the account of state formation in the *Two treatises* in the light of the Amerindian context. A brief section on the uses of Locke's arguments in the eighteenth century follows, and the conclusion brings the issue up to the present.

DISPOSSESSION: THE ROLE OF THE STATE OF NATURE

Locke had extensive knowledge of and interest in European contact with aboriginal peoples. A large number of books in his library are accounts of European exploration, colonization and of aboriginal peoples, especially Amerindians and their ways. As secretary to Lord Shaftesbury, secretary of the Lord Proprietors of Carolina (1668–71), secretary to the Council of Trade and Plantations (1673–4), and member of the Board of Trade (1696–1700), Locke was one of the six or eight men who closely invigilated and helped to shape the old colonial system during the Restoration. He invested in the slave-trading Royal Africa Company (1671) and the Company of Merchant Adventurers to trade with the Bahamas (1672), and he was

---

[4] For this type of approach see James Tully, ed., *Meaning and context: Quentin Skinner and his critics* (Princeton: Princeton University Press, 1988).

a Landgrave of the proprietary government of Carolina. His theoretical and policy-making writings on colonial affairs include the *Fundamental Constitutions of Carolina* (1669), Carolina's agrarian laws (1671–2), a reform proposal for Virginia (1696), memoranda and policy recommendations for the boards of trade, covering all the colonies, histories of European exploration and settlement, and manuscripts on a wide range of topics concerning government and property in America.[5]

In the *Two treatises* America is immediately identified as one example of the 'state of nature' and then classified as the earliest 'age' in a worldwide historical development. '[I]n the beginning all the World was *America*' Locke asserts in section 49.[6] America is 'still a Pattern of the first Ages in *Asia* and *Europe*' (108), and Amerindians and Europeans who make contact with them 'are perfectly in a State of Nature' (14, cf. 109).

The two basic elements of his theory of popular sovereignty in a state of nature are illustrated by examples of life in native America. First, the inhabitants exercise what has come to be called 'individual popular sovereignty' or 'individual self-government'. That is, 'the *Execution* of the Law of Nature is in that State, put into every Mans hands' (7). This individual and natural exercise of political power comprises the abilities to know and to interpret standards of right (natural laws), to judge controversies concerning oneself and others in accordance with these laws, and to execute such judgements by punishments proportionate to the transgression and appropriate for purposes of restraint and reparation (7–12, 136). Individuals are free to order their actions within the bounds of natural laws and are equal

[5] There is no collection of Locke's colonial writings nor even a bibliography of them. See John Locke, *The fundamental constitutions of Carolina, The works of John Locke*, 10 vols (Germany, Scientis Verlag Aalen, 1963) (a reprint of the 1823 edition), x. This volume also contains 'The whole history of navigation from its original to this time' (1704), 358–511, sometimes attributed to Locke. John Locke, 'Some chief grievances of the present constitution of Virginia . . .', Bodleian, Locke MS. e. 9. Bodleian, Locke MS. c. 30 is on colonial affairs. See also W. Noel Sainsbury, ed., *Calendar of state papers, colonial series, America and the West Indies*, 43 vols (London, 1862), esp. IX–XI, *Records in the British public record office relating to South Carolina 1663–1710*, 5 vols. (Cambridge: Cambridge University Press, 1928–47), Langdom Cheves, ed. *The Shaftesbury papers and other records relating to Carolina . . . to 1676, South Carolina historical society collections* 5 (London: 1897).

[6] All quotations from John Locke, *Two treatises of government*, ed. Peter Laslett (Cambridge: Cambridge University Press, 1970). Numbers in brackets refer to sections in the *Second treatise* unless preceded by a 1.

in the 'Power and Jurisdiction' to govern the actions of those who transgress these bounds (4,6). This system of individual self-government is illustrated with examples from America (9, 14, 107). Political society is then defined in explicit contrast to this natural mode of individual self-government: namely, where individuals have given their 'natural power' to the community and set up 'a common establish'd Law and Judicature to appeal to, with Authority to decide Controversies between them, and punish Offenders' (87).

The second aspect of life in America that is definitive of the state of nature is individual and exclusive rights over one's labour and its products. Everyone is free to exercise their labour in accordance with natural law for the sake of preservation and without the consent of others. Appropriation without consent is illustrated with examples of Amerindians acquiring fruit and venison (26), hunting deer (30), growing corn (48), and so on. Property in political society is then defined in explicit contrast to their natural mode of labour-based property: namely, where labour, appropriation and its products are regulated by government and positive laws (30, 38, 50, 129).

Two major conclusions follow from the premise that America is a state of nature. First, Locke claims in the *First treatise* that no one doubts that European planters have a right to wage war 'against the *Indians*, [and] to seek Reparation upon any injury received from them', and this without authorization from a constituted political authority (1.130, cf. 1.131). In this case, a European planter in the West Indies is exercising his right to execute the law of nature and seek reparations as explained in the *Second treatise*. Although Locke calls this a 'strange Doctrine' (9), there is one sense in which it is commonplace.

Within the long reflection on European contact with America from 1492 to 1690, a number of justifications were advanced for the assertion of European sovereignty over the new world. Papal grants, royal charters, symbolic acts, such as the planting of crosses, discovery and occupation, the right to trade, and the duty to spread Christianity to non-Christians were the most common. Objections were raised to each of these justifications by writers such as Francisco de Vitoria (1480–1552), Alonso de la Vera Cruz (1507–84), and Bartholomé de Las Casas (1484–1566).[7] After advancing a number of objections to

---

[7] For surveys of European justifications for sovereignty in America see Delia Opekokew, *The first nations: Indian government and the Canadian confederation* (Saskatoon: Federation of Saskatchewan Indians, 1980); Brian Slattery, *Ancestral lands, alien laws: judicial perspectives on*

the standard justifications, Vitoria concluded his long discussion with a justification of conquest he believed to be invulnerable. Since both Spaniards and Amerindians are in the state of nature, if the Spaniards conduct themselves in accordance with the law of nature, then they have the right to defend themselves against any wrong committed by the Amerindians 'and to avail themselves of the rights of war'.[8] The natural right of self-defence to proceed with force against the violators of natural law was adapted by Francisco Suarez (1548–1617), Hugo Grotius (1583–1645), and Samuel Pufendorf (1632–94). Locke's 'strange Doctrine', although it differs in some respects from the arguments of his predecessors, is a reassertion of this conventional justification of war and, as we have seen, Locke uses it in this context.

When a person violates natural law they lose their natural rights and they may be enslaved or killed (16–24). Scholars who work on this part of Locke's theory assume that it refers to black slavery.[9] Notwithstanding, it may also refer to Amerindian slavery. Of all the English colonies, Carolina had the largest slave trade. In 1663 eight proprietors were granted full title to the area that covers most of present-day North Carolina, all of South Carolina and almost all of Georgia. The proprietors established government and a system of property in order to recruit settlers to engage in agriculture, initially drawing surplus planters from Barbados. Lord Shaftesbury and Locke assumed leadership of the project in 1669. Their plan was to make a profit from land-rent and the trade of agricultural products. The colonists turned instead to the more lucrative fur and slave trade with the Amerindians, even though this was expressly forbidden in article 112 of the constitution. Agriculture failed, the settlers became

---

aboriginal title (Saskatoon: University of Saskatchewan Native law centre, 1983); Wilcomb E. Washburn, 'The moral and legal justifications for dispossessing the Indians', *Seventeenth-century America, essays in colonial history*, ed. James M. Smith (Chapel Hill: University of North Carolina, 1959), 15–32; Ruth Barnes Moynihan, 'The patent and the Indians: The problem of jurisdiction in 17th century New England', *American Indian culture and research* 2, 1 (1977) 8–18; Chester Eisenger, 'The Puritan justification for taking the land', *Essex Institute historical collections* 84 (1948) 131–43; Maureen Davies, 'Aspects of aboriginal rights in international law', *Aboriginal peoples and the law*, ed. Bradford Morse (Ottawa: Carleton University Press, 1985), 16–47; James Muldoon, *Popes, lawyers, and infidels* (Pennsylvania: University of Pennsylvania Press, 1979); L. C. Green and Olive P. Dickason, *The law of nations and the new world* (Calgary: The University of Alberta Press, 1988); Robert A. Williams jr, *The American Indian in Western legal thought: the discourse of conquest* (Oxford: Oxford University Press, 1991).

[8] Francisco de Vitoria, *De Indis et de jure belli relectiones*, Classics of International Law (Oxford: Clarendon Press, 1917), section II (p. 153e).

[9] This scholarship is reviewed in Wayne Glausser, 'Three approaches to Locke and the slave trade', *Journal of the History of Ideas* 51, 2 (April–June 1990), 199–216.

heavily indebted to the proprietors, little profit accrued to the proprietors and the trade with the coastal native nations, the Cusabos and Coosas, led to conflict. Locke introduced a temporary law in 1672 forbidding Amerindian slavery and offering the native peoples individual plots of land under proprietary government. The colonists ignored the law and, after the 1674 peace treaty with the powerful Westos nation against the Spanish to the south, they expanded their trade. The Lords Proprietor responded with an unsuccessful proposal to settle a new group of planters at Locke's island and with an attempt to control the Indian trade themselves, declaring a monopoly in 1677. By 1680 the fur trade and the sale of Indian slaves to the West Indies were the staples of Carolina's economy.[10]

When either slavery failed or all other means of dealing with the Amerindians proved ineffective, the practice in the colonies was to make war against the local tribes in a piecemeal fashion. For example, the colonists in Carolina revolted against the proprietors' monopoly on Indian trade, declared war on the Westos in 1679 and killed those they were unable to enslave. The usual justification for wars of this type was that the Indians had resisted the settlers in some way or stolen something, and so violated natural law, activating the settlers' right to defend themselves and avail themselves of the rights of war.[11]

Locke underscores in no uncertain terms the natural law right to punish theft and violence with death and he construes this as a state of war (8–11, 17–19). I am quite aware that these passages in chapters 2 and 3 are standardly interpreted as references to the right to punish Charles II in an armed revolt. Be this as it may, the very terms Locke uses to describe the offenders who may be 'destroyed' are the terms used to describe, and so dehumanize Amerindians in the books in Locke's library.[12] Offenders are characterized as 'wild Savage Beats'

---

[10] Bodleian, Locke MS. c. 6, fols 213, 216 and c. 30; *Records BPROSC, II.* 200, Cheves ed., *Shaftesbury papers,* 171–3, 193, 266–7, 311, 352, 381–2, 400, 432. The Agrarian law of June 21, 1672 is in William J. Rivers, *A sketch of the history of South Carolina to the close of the proprietary government by the revolution of 1719* (Charleston, 1856), 358. See Herbert R. Pascal, 'Proprietary North Carolina: a study in Colonial government' (Ph.D. dissertation, University of North Carolina, 1961).

[11] For the war of 1679 see M. Eugene Sirmans, *Colonial South Carolina* (Chapel Hill: University of North Carolina Press, 1966), 3–75. For the use of just war arguments, see Francis Jennings, *The invasion of America: Indians, colonialism and the cant of conquest* (New York: W. W. Norton, 1975) 105–28.

[12] For example, John Smith, *A description of New England* (London: 1616). See, in general, Robert F. Berkhofer, *The white man's Indian: images of the American Indian from Columbus to the present* (New York: Knopf, 1978).

who 'may be destroyed as a *Lyon or a Tyger*' (11, 16). In section 10 the natural right of the governments of England, France and Holland to punish or put to death 'an Indian' who violates natural law is put forward as the proof and illustration of this violent doctrine.

The second major conclusion Locke draws from the premise that America is a state of nature is that appropriation of land may take place without consent. Appropriation without consent is the main argument of chapter 5. The sections are carefully organized to prove and substantiate it. Nor is it surprising that Locke took such care in presenting his argument, for it is a departure from his earlier views, from the views of earlier natural law writers, and from the fundamental principle of western law: *Quod omnes tangit ab omnibus tractari et approbari debet* (what touches all must be approved by all).[13]

Appropriation without consent has given rise to more commentary than any other argument in Locke's political philosophy. The problem is to show how appropriation can take place given the background premise that everyone has a natural right to the means of preservation.[14] This is a problem generated in part and in theory by Filmer's criticism of the role of consent to property in Grotius' theory, but in some of the secondary literature the background premise is overlooked and it is then mistaken as solely a problem of justifying the division of English and European societies into propertied and propertyless classes.[15] The fact that the chapter is organized around a contrast between Europe, where appropriation without consent is not permitted because political societies exist, and America, where appropriation without consent is permitted because it is a state of nature, is rarely mentioned. That the argument justifies European settlement in America without the consent of the native people, one of

---

[13] For Locke's earlier view that property must be based on consent, see 'Morality', Bodleian, MS. Locke c. 28, fols 13–40. For his predecessors see James Tully, *A discourse on property: John Locke and his adversaries* (Cambridge: Cambridge University Press, 1980).

[14] For the background premise and the full theoretical framework of Locke's argument see Tully, *A discourse on property*, 53–95; Richard Ashcraft, *Locke's Two treatises of government* (London: Hyman, 1987), 81–150; Gopal Sreenivasan, *The limits of Lockean rights in property* (Cambridge: Cambridge University Press, forthcoming); Stephen Buckle, *The natural history of property* (Oxford: Oxford University Press, 1991).

[15] For typical misinterpretations along these lines see Jeremy Waldron, *The right of private property* (Oxford: Oxford University Press, 1989); G. A. Cohen, 'Marx and Locke on land and labour', *Proceedings of the British Academy*, 71 (1985) 357–89; Neal Wood, *John Locke and agrarian capitalism* (Berkeley: University of California Press, 1984). For refutation, see chapter 4 above, Ashcraft, *Locke's Two treatises*, and Sreenivasan, *The Lockean limits*, for a detailed refutation of Cohen and Waldron.

the most contentious and important events of the seventeenth century and one of the formative events of the modern world, is normally passed over in silence. On the other hand, among scholars who specialize in the European dispossession of Amerindians reference to Locke's argument is commonplace.[16]

In the first section of chapter 5 Locke introduces appropriation without consent as the problem he endeavours to solve in the chapter (25, lines 16–19), and he says he has solved it in the middle and final sections (39 and 51). The appropriation of common fruits and nuts, fish and game, and vacant land by means of individual labour is legitimate and creates a property right in the products as long as they do not spoil and there is enough and as good left in common for others. No other forms of exclusive property are recognized and all land that is not actively under cultivation is said to be vacant. Appropriation without consent continues until money is introduced, land becomes scarce, and there is no longer enough and as good for others. Until then, 'there could be no doubt of Right, no room for quarrel' (39), and 'no reason of quarrelling about Title, nor any doubt about the largeness of Possession it gave' (51). Illustrating his solution throughout with examples drawn from America, Locke confidently concludes that any person could appropriate in-land vacant land in America without consent (36):

let him plant in some in-land, vacant places of *America*, we shall find that the *Possessions* he could make himself upon the *measures* we have given, would not be very large, nor, even to this day, prejudice the rest of Mankind, or give them reason to complain, or think themselves injured by this Man's Incroachment.

The 'Controversie about . . . Title' and the 'Incroachment on the Right of Others' (51) by the 'Quarrelsom and Contentious', driven by 'Covetousness' (34), which Locke constantly refers to and claims to settle, raged across Europe and America from the early sixteenth century to well after 1690. These were controversies over title in the new world among competing European powers, jurisdictional disputes among the colonies, between colonists and their royal or proprietary governors, traders versus planters, and all of these against the aboriginal peoples who had been there for over 12,000 years.

---

[16] See William Cronon, *Changes in the land: Indians, colonists and the ecology of New England* (New York: Hill and Wang, 1983); and n. 7 above.

Much of Locke's work for the Boards of Trade and Carolina concerned these disputes.

By the early seventeenth century the accepted justification for the assertion of sovereignty in European international law was the discovery, occupation and defence of any part of America not already occupied by a Christian ruler, as long as the settlement was warranted by a charter or grant. Settlement and defence were said to constitute occupation and long usage, the oldest and most widely recognized principle of legal title in the world.[17] This served as a justification relative to other European nations, establishing the monopoly right of a particular European nation to treaty with the native nations within its sphere of influence to the exclusion of other European nations. It did not justify the assertion of sovereignty over the native nations or even the claim to establish co-sovereignty or trading arrangements with them. These relations with the ancient nations of America require a second step.[18] One answer to this further justificatory step was to ignore the Amerindians and to characterize America as *terra nullius*, a vacant land (a condition the principle of occupation and long usage requires). Another strategy was to downgrade the status of the aboriginal peoples to that of beasts or savages so no juridical recognition was required. Often a royal grant would simply grant explorers and invaders the right 'to subdue, occupy and possesse' the inhabitants, 'getting into us the rule, title, and jurisdiction', as Henry VII unsuccessfully commissioned John Cabot.[19]

The rationalizations in royal charters and inter-European agreements were out of touch with the real world of seventeenth-century America. The European newcomers were outnumbered by the natives and dependent upon them for food, trade, and survival. Under these conditions some form of recognition of and accommodation to aboriginal title was required. The natives understood themselves to be self-governing nations exercising sovereign authority over their people and territory, and with a far better claim to occupancy and long usage than any recent European settlement huddled on the coastline could muster. Accordingly, the indigenous nations signed numerous international peace and friendship treaties

[17] See references at n. 7 above.
[18] Slattery, *Ancestral lands*, 26; and Chief Justice John Marshall, part IV below.
[19] In Richard Hakylut, *Voyages touching the discovery of America* (London: Hakylut society, 1850), 21–2.

with European nations, in which they granted rights of trade and use over some of their territory and agreed to co-existing or parallel sovereignty in other areas, and asserted, time after time, their inalienable sovereignty. The classic presentation of this view is in many of the treaties between the Haudenosaunee (Iroquois) Confederacy and the Dutch, English and French nations. The First Nations represent it by a belt of two parallel rows of wampum:[20]

These two rows [of wampum] will symbolise two paths or vessels, travelling down the same river together. One, a birch bark canoe, will be for the Indian people, their laws, their customs and their ways. The other, a ship, will be for the white people and their laws, their customs, and their ways. We shall travel together, side by side, but in our own boat. Neither of us will try to steer the other's vessel.

This view is the basis of all treaties the First Nations made with European governments and their descendants.

A prevalent rival view was that sovereignty resides wholly in a European Crown to which Amerindians are subject. Amerindians have natural rights only to their goods and the small amounts of land they had under active cultivation at the time of contact, and these rights are subject to European law. As the English began to settle and plant, and not just trade, they began to argue that the Amerindians neither occupied and used in the appropriate manner the lands they claimed, nor did they live in political or civil societies. Hence, most of the land was vacant, no consent was required for its use, and the colonists claimed they signed formal treaties, not out of recognition of aboriginal rights, but only when necessity demanded it to mollify the wild and threatening natives.

The proponents of these rival views came into conflict in the 1630s. The first major quarrel began in 1633 as a jurisdictional dispute between Boston, led by John Winthrop, and Plymouth, led by Roger Williams. Williams argued that the royal patent did not convey title to Indian land and that the only legitimate means of possession was by treaty with Amerindian nations in order to acquire rights of usufruct on their property, as he did in Rhode Island and the Dutch

---

[20] Grand Chief Michael Mitchell of the Mohawk Council of Akwesasne, 'An unbroken assertion of sovereignty', in *Drumbeat: anger and renewal in Indian country*, ed. Bryce Richardson (Toronto: Assembly of First Nations, Summerhill Press, 1989), 105–37. For the treaties of the Haudenosaunee Confederacy and the recognition of native sovereignty see Francis Jennings, ed., *The history and culture of Iroquois diplomacy* (Syracuse: Syracuse University Press, 1985), xiv–xv. For Crown support of native sovereignty see part IV below.

in New York. Governor Winthrop replied that the Indians possessed only what they cultivated; the rest was open for appropriation without consent. The second major contention was the claim brought against the colony of Connecticut by the Mohegan Indians for sovereignty over their traditional lands. It began in the 1670s, appeals were made to the Privy Council in London, and litigation continued for 100 years. What was at stake in these celebrated cases was nothing less than the legitimacy of English settlement in America. They, in turn, were surrounded by innumerable other land disputes throughout the colonies between 1630 and 1690. In addition, two devastating wars against the Indians were connected to these disputes: against the Pequot, 1636–7, and against the Narragansett, 1674–5 (King Philip's War).[21]

In this contentious context appropriation by cultivation and without consent began to be employed to justify the dispossession of Amerindians of their traditional hunting and gathering territories. Some of the major authors are Samuel Purchas, the editor of Hakylut's *Travels* (1629), John White in Virginia (1630), Robert Cushman and Francis Higginson in New England, John Cotton, who replied point-by-point to Roger Williams, Governor Winthrop, and the lawyers for Connecticut in the Mohegan appeals to the Privy Council.[22] The arguments and the very terms used in the pamphlets are strikingly similar to chapter five of the *Two treatises*. No author puts forth an account that is as theoretically sophisticated as Locke's, but the basic terminology, premises, and conclusions for such a theory are present. Locke added his own knowledge of colonial affairs and of the sophisticated analyses of money, labour, and productivity by the

---

[21] For Roger Williams and John Winthrope see Moynihan, 'The patent and the Indians' (n. 7 above) and Jennings, *The invasion of America*, 128–46. For the Mohegan nation *v.* the Colony of Connecticut see J. H. Smith, *Appeals to the Privy Council from the American plantations* (New York: 1950), 417–42. For the wars against the Pequot and Narrangansett nations see Jennings, *The invasion of America*, 177–326.

[22] Samuel Purchas, *Hakluytus Posthumus or, Purchas his pilgrimes* (London: 1625), IV, bk 9, ch. 20; John White, *The planters plea* (London: 1630), Robert Cushman, 'Reasons and considerations touching the lawfulness of removing out of England into parts of America', 1621, in *Chronicles of the Pilgrim fathers of the colony of Plymouth*, ed. Alexander Young (Boston: Charles C. Little, 1844), 239–53; Francis Higginson, *New Englands plantation* (London: 1631), in *Massachusetts historical society proceedings* 62 (1929); John Cotton, 'John Cotton's answer to Roger Williams', *The complete writings of Roger Williams*, 7 vols. (New York: Russell and Russell, 1963), II; John Winthrop, 'Reasons to be considered, and objections with answers', *Winthrop papers*, 2 vols. (*The Massachusetts historical society* 1931) II, 138–45; *Winthrop's Journal*, ed. J. K. Hosmer (New York: 1908), 293–5.

mercantile writers of the Restoration to create the powerful theory in chapter 5.[23]

Let me now illustrate this with a number of quotations that are similar to the more familiar arguments of chapter 5. Replying directly to the argument that it is illegitimate to 'enter upon the land which hath beene soe longe possessed by others [Indians]', Winthrop writes, 'that which lies common, and that neuer been replenished or subdued is free to any that possesse and improue it'. This is a 'natural right' that holds 'when men held the earth in common [,] every man sowing and feeding where he pleased'. He illustrates this with the same biblical reference Locke uses (38). In contrast, a 'civil right' to jurisdiction over a whole territory only comes into existence after population increase and the enclosure of land make unused land scarce.[24]

Williams argued that hunting and land-clearing certainly consti- tute use and occupation and, therefore, Amerindians have title to their traditional lands: they 'hunted all the Countrey over', he wrote, 'and for the expedition of their hunting voyages, they burnt up all underwoods in the countrey, once or twice a yeare'.[25] To circumvent this defence, Williams' opponents deployed the argument that only sedentary agriculture and improvement constitute the kind of use that gives rise to property rights and, therefore, hunting and gathering lands may be looked on as vacant wasteland.

'We did not conceive that it is a just Title to so vast a continent, to make no other improvement of millions of acres in it, but onely to burne it up for a pastime', Cotton rejoined.[26] 'As for the Natiues in New England', Winthrop explained, 'they inclose noe Land, neither have any setled habytation, nor any tame cattle to improue the Land by, and soe have no other but a Naturall Right [i.e. in the products of their labour]'.[27] 'The Indians', Higginson concurs, have no right to their traditional lands because they 'are not able to make use of the one-fourth part of the Land, neither have they any settled places . . . nor any ground as they challenge for their owne possession, but change their habitation from place to place'. Since they possess very little land, America is *vacuum domicilium*, a 'vacant' or 'waste' land, and so *Vacuum Domicilium cedit occupanti*.[28] 'In a vacant soyle', Cotton

---

[23] As I have sought to show in other chapters of this volume Locke addressed other problems and contexts as well in chapter 5.   [24] Winthrop, *Winthrop papers*, 140–1.
[25] Cited by John Cotton in 'John Cotton's answer', 2: 46–7.   [26] Cotton, *ibid.*, 47.
[27] Winthrop, *Winthrop papers*, 141.   [28] Higginson, *New Englands plantations*, 316.

points out to Williams, 'he that taketh possession of it, and bestoweth culture and husbandry upon it, his right it is'.[29] Enunciating a principle similar to Locke's famous proviso in section 27, Winthrop concludes, 'soe . . . if we leave them [Amerindians] sufficient for their use, we may lawfully take the rest, there being more than enough for them and us'.[30]

It is clear, therefore, that two functions are served by situating America in a state of nature. First, Amerindian political organization is disregarded and replaced by a so-called natural system of individual self-government, thereby dispossessing Amerindian governments of their authority and nationhood and permitting Europeans to deal with them and punish them on an individual basis. Second, the Amerindian system of property over their traditional territory is denied and it is replaced by a so-called natural system of individual, labour-based property, thereby dispossessing Amerindians of their traditional lands and positing a vacancy which Europeans could and should use without the consent of the first nations. As we have seen, this 'agricultural' dispossession argument was usually advanced with the qualification that, from the colonists' perspective, at the time of first European appropriation there was enough and as good land left for the aboriginal peoples.

Locke was aware that the native peoples did not govern themselves in the wholly individual and independent manner laid out in his description of the state of nature, but were organized politically into nations. However, he describes their national forms of government in such a way that they are not full 'political societies' and thus native Americans can be dealt with as if they are in a late stage of the state of nature. In chapter 8 he asserts that, although Amerindians are called 'nations' (41) and are ruled by elected 'Kings' (108), they fail to meet the criteria of a distinct political society. The reason for this is that their kings 'are little more than *Generals of their Armies*', who, although 'they command absolutely in War', in peacetime and in internal affairs 'they exercise very little Dominion, and have but a very moderate Sovereignty, the Resolution of Peace and War, being ordinarily either in the People, or in a Council' (108, cf. 1.131). They lack the European institutions that, according to Locke, constitute the universal criteria of political society: an institutionalized legal

---

[29] Cotton, 'John Cotton's answer', 2: 47.   [30] Winthrop, *Winthrop papers*, 141.

system, institutionalized judiciary, legislature and executive (87), and the sovereign right to declare war and peace removed from popular control and lodged exclusively in the hands of the King or 'federative' authority (144–8).

The reason Amerindians do not have these institutions is that they have no need of them. They have 'few Trespasses, and few Offenders', 'few controversies' over property and therefore 'no need of many laws to decide them' (107). As a result, they settle the few disputes they have on an ad-hoc and individual basis, as in the state of nature (107). They have few disputes because they have limited and moderate amounts of property. In turn, the explanation for this, which explains their whole system, is that they have limited and fixed desires: 'confineing their desires within the narrow bounds of each mans smal propertie made few controversies' (107). Their desires are limited and they have 'no Temptation to enlarge their Possessions of Land, or contest for wider extent of Ground' because they lack money and large population which activate the desire to possess more than one needs (108). That is, they lack the acquisitive desire to enlarge their possessions that leads to disputes over property and thus to the need for a distinct political society with an established system of property law to settle them. Locke sums this up in *The third letter concerning toleration* (cited in the editor's note to the *Two treatises* 2.108):

Let me ask you, Whether it be not possible that men, to whom the rivers and woods afforded the spontaneous provisions of life, and so with no private possessions of land, had no inlarged desires after riches or power, should live in one society, make one people of one language under one Chieftain, who shall have no other power to command them in time of common war against their common enemies, without any municipal laws, judges, or any person with superiority established amongst them, but ended all their private differences, if any arose, by the extemporary determination of their neighbours, or of arbitrators chosen by the parties.

The typical form of Amerindian government encountered by Europeans was a confederation of nations presided over by an assembly of the national chiefs.[31] A nation was governed by a council or longhouse of chiefs (sachems) from the internal clans. Each nation had a clearly demarcated and defended territory, a decision-making

---

[31] This is a simplification of a complex range of political organizations. For an introduction, see Anthony F. Wallace, 'Political organisation and land tenure among Northeastern Indians 1600–1830', *Southwestern journal of anthropology* 13 (1957), 301–21.

body, a consensus-based decision-making procedure, and a system of customary laws and kinship relations. There were few religious sanctions (in marked contrast to New England), no standing army, bureaucracy, police force, or written laws. They lacked the state-centred European society, yet they performed the functions of government as many Europeans observed. '[T]he wildest Indians in America', Roger Williams noted, 'agree upon some forms of Government . . . [and] their civill and earthly governments be as lawfull and true as any Governments in the World'.[32]

Hence, like many European writers, Locke highlights three features of Amerindian political organization to the neglect of the customary system of government that underlies them. He interprets the war-chief from a European perspective as a kind of primitive and proto-European sovereign and he stipulates that native popular (non-delegated) government, over matters of war and peace, is by definition not a political society. But, the war-chief was, and still is, a temporary military commander with no political authority and who can be, and often is, talked down by a political authority, such as a clan mother. Of course, Europeans often took the war-chief as the sole leader in order to undermine the authority of the traditional councils (and perhaps because they were accustomed to the fusion of military and political rule in one person in the colonial lieutenant-governors and governors-general). Second, the chiefs and the council often appointed ad-hoc arbitrators of justice. The ad-hoc procedure may be a source of Locke's concept of individual self-government, but he overlooks the appointment procedure and the unwritten yet orally transmitted system of customary law and sanctions that govern it. Third, he emphasizes the lack of crime and litigation in Amerindian communities, and he explains this by reference to their limited material possessions and their limited desires, as did many observers. Yet, he disregards the national, clan, and family systems of community property and distribution that underpin these features.

With respect to property, the territory as a whole belongs to the nation and jurisdiction over it is held in trust by the chiefs.[33] It is inalienable and the identity of a nation as a distinct people is inseparable from their relation to and use of the land, animals, and

---

[32] Williams, 'The bloody tenant . . .', in *Complete works* 3: 250.
[33] See Wallace, 'Political organisation and land tenure'; Tim Ingold, D. Riches, and J. Woodburn, eds, *Hunters and gatherers: property, power and ideology*, 2 vols, ii (New York: St Martins Press, 1988); and part IV below.

entire ecosystem. Although the land belongs to them, it is more accurate to say, as the Inuit stress, that they belong to the land. Clans and families have a bundle of matrilineal rights and responsibilities of use and usufruct over land for various uses. That is, property rights and duties inhere in the clans and apply to activities and to the geographical location in which the activities take place, not, in the first instance, to the products of the activities. The activities include hunting, trapping, gathering berries, non-sedentary agriculture, clam bed cultivation, fishing, and so on. The distribution and trade of the products is governed by custom and kinship tradition. When the coastal Indians made property agreements with the settlers, as Williams explained to Winthrop, they were granting them rights of co-use of the land, not rights to the land itself (which was inalienable).[34] Finally, families and individual family members own their goods, yet there is a casual attitude towards possessions and an overriding custom of sharing and gift-giving. From the Amerindian point of view, therefore, appropriation without consent is expropriation without consent.

In his depiction of Amerindian property, Locke highlights one specific form of activity – industrious labour and the products of industrious labour – and does not recognize the native system of national territories, the bundle of property rights and responsibilities in activities and their locales, and the customs governing distribution. If he had recognized these forms of property, as Roger Williams and many others who signed treaties did, European settlement in America without consent would have been illegitimate by his own criteria of enough and as good. In addition, Locke has a further reason not to recognize the traditional property of the Amerindians. The argument for dispossession by agricultural improvement was often supplemented by the natural law argument for just conquest if the native people resisted.[35] But, in Locke's theory of conquest (written for another purpose) the conqueror has no title to the property of the vanquished (180, 184). The conqueror has no right 'to dispossess the Posterity of the Vanquished, and turn them out of their Inheritance, which ought to be the Possession of them and their Descendents to all Generations'. Therefore, if the Amerindians had property in their traditional land

---

[34] Cronon, *Changes in the land*, 61.
[35] The conquest justification of European sovereignty is spurious because the Amerindians did not surrender and the European–Indian wars do not meet the criteria of conquest in international law (Davis, 'Aspects of aboriginal rights in international law', 37–40).

conquest would not confer title over it. However, as Locke repeats twice in this section, in the case of conquest over a people in the state of nature, 'where there . . . [is] more *Land,* than the Inhabitants possess, and make use of', the conqueror, like 'any one[,] has liberty to make use of the waste' (184); thereby bringing his theories of conquest and appropriation into harmony.

In the second half of chapter 5 the concepts of property and political organization in the state of nature are shown to play a further and equally important role. Because the Amerindian political and property system is tied to a world of limited desires and possessions it is unsuited to the development of modern states and systems of property that Locke unfolds in the second half of the chapter. The dynamic development unleashed by the expansion of human desire for possessions after the introduction of money leads to interminable property disputes and so to the need to set up modern states to regulate and govern property relations. From this perspective, Amerindian societies are, as we have seen, defined by the specifically European institutions they lack and by superimposing on them the rudiments of individual, labour-based property, which plays such a prominent role in Locke's theory of historical development. To this we now turn.

WORLD REVERSAL: PROPERTY AND POLITICAL SOCIETY IN A CIVILIZATION OF COMMERCE AND IMPROVEMENT

Locke's theory of the historical development of politics and property comprises the following stages: different degrees of industry among individuals account for differences in possessions in the pre-monetary stage of nature. Money and trade are gradually introduced, spurring the growth of population and the applied arts. An elastic desire for more than one needs comes into being, uprooting forever the pre-monetary economy of limited desires and needs. People seek to enlarge their possessions, either by honest industry or by preying on the honest industry of others, in order to sell the surplus in the market for a profit. All available land becomes occupied and put to use. To solve the quarrels and insecurities that inevitably follow people set up political societies with institutionalized legal and political systems to regulate and protect property.

Each stage in the development of a modern system of what is now called surplus production and accumulation is defined by contrast to the Amerindian system of 'underproduction' and 'replacement consumption'.[36] First, the ethic of 'industriousness' that drives and legitimates the process is defined contrastively as superior to Amerindian land use. Although god gave the 'World to men in Common', he did not mean that they should leave it 'common and uncultivated', but rather that they should 'draw from it' the 'greatest conveniences of life'. Accordingly, he 'gave it to the Industrious and Rational, (and *Labour* was to be his *Title* to it;)' (34). Amerindians are then said to draw less than one one-hundredth the number of conveniences from the land that the English are able to produce (41). Second, Locke sets up cultivation as the standard of industrious and rational use, in contrast to the 'waste' and lack of cultivation in Amerindian hunting and gathering, thus eliminating any title they might claim (37, 41, 42, 43, 45, 48). The planning, coordination, skills, and activities involved in native hunting, gathering, trapping, fishing, and non-sedentary agriculture, which took thousands of years to develop and take a lifetime for each generation to acquire and pass on, are not counted as labour at all, except for the very last individual step (such as picking or killing), but are glossed as 'unassisted nature' and 'spontaneous provisions' when Locke makes his comparisons (37, 42, 108 note); whereas European activities, such as manufacturing bread, are described in depth (42, 43). Moreover, the 'industrious' use or labour that gives rise to property rights is equated with European agriculture, based on pasturage and tillage (42), thereby eliminating Amerindian non-sedentary agriculture as a type of use and subverting any title that might have been derived from it.

The coastal Indians lived in villages and engaged in non-sedentary agriculture. Several of the English settlers sought to expropriate the agricultural lands of the natives, for this eliminated the hard labour of clearing land themselves.[37] To justify expropriation, they argued that the Indians, who left their cornfields for the clam beds each year, neither tilled nor fenced, and who let the fields rot and compost every

---

[36] For these concepts see Marshall Sahlins, *Stone age economics* (Chicago: Aldine-Atherton, 1972).
[37] See Washburn, 'The moral and legal justifications for dispossessing', 23–5 (n. 7 above); Jennings, *The invasion of America*, 58–84; James P. Ronda, 'Red and white at the bench: Indians and the law in Plymouth Colony 1620–91', *Essex Institute historical collections* 110 (1974), 200–15; and Peter Thomas, 'Contrastive subsistence strategies and land use as factors for understanding Indian–white relations in New England', *Ethnohistory* 23 (1976), 1–18.

three years, for purposes of soil enrichment, did not cultivate the land in the proper fashion, and, therefore the land was open for use by others. 'They [the Indians] are not industrious', Robert Cushman explained, 'neither have they art, science, skill or faculty to use either the land or the commodities of it; but all spoils, rots, and is marred from want of manuring, gathering and ordering'.[38] Locke elevates this justification of expropriation to the status of a law of nature (38):

if either the Grass or his Inclosure rotted on the Ground, or the Fruit of his planting perished without gathering, and laying up, this part of the Earth, notwithstanding his Inclosure, was still to be looked on as Waste, and might be the Possession of any other.

The second contrast is between the limited desires of Amerindians and the unlimited desire of the English to accumulate possessions. When this is not mistaken for a contrast between bourgeois and proletarian motivation in the secondary literature it is often taken to be an astute observation on the difference in motivation of individuals in non-market and market societies; an anticipation of Adam Smith.[39] It is now possible to define Locke's contrast more specifically.

In section 37 the desire for more than one needs is said to follow from the introduction of money and population increase. This acquisitive motivation is contrasted with the pre-monetary motivation of Amerindians (cf. 108). As he famously writes in section 48, without money and a world trading system that develops with it, and so the hope of selling one's surplus on the market for money, no one would have the reason or motivation to enlarge their possessions (48):

Where there is not something both lasting and scarce, and so valuable to be hoarded up, there Men will not be apt to enlarge their *Possessions of Land*, were it never so rich, never so free for them to take. For I ask, What would a Man value Ten Thousand, or an Hundred Thousand Acres of excellent *Land*, ready cultivated, and well stocked too with Cattle, in the middle of in-land Parts of *America*, where he had no hopes of Commerce with other Parts of the World, to draw *Money* to him by the Sale of the Product? It would not be worth the inclosing.

---

[38] Cushman, 'Reasons and considerations touching the lawfulness of removing out of England', 243 (n. 22 above).

[39] For example in the fine article by John Dunn, 'Bright enough for all our purposes: John Locke's conception of a civilized society', *Notes and records of the Royal Society of London*, 43 (1989), 133–53.

On the other hand, once money and world commerce are introduced, the motivation of the same person will be transformed and they too will seek to enlarge their possessions: 'Find out something that hath the *Use and Value of Money* amongst his Neighbours, you shall see the same Man will begin presently to *enlarge* his *Possessions*' (49).

Locke's argument comprises three claims: Amerindians have limited desires and so no motivation to acquire more than they need; the introduction of a world commercial market ushers in the desire and reason to acquire more than one needs; and this new acquisitive rationality shows itself in the acquisition of land in order to sell the products for money. Leaving aside Amerindian pre-monetary motivation for the moment, the latter two claims need to be qualified. First, it is not true that the introduction of money and world commerce invariably leads to the desire for enlarged possessions of land. The Amerindians had been trading with Europeans for over 100 years when Locke wrote the *Two treatises*. Certainly this gave them the incentive to increase their fur-trapping and to kill animals beyond the limits their replacement needs had previously set. There is no evidence however that they desired to turn to private property in land and market-oriented agriculture. Quite the contrary. They were quite satisfied to trade with the Europeans and to preserve their traditional ways.[40] Furthermore, after 300 years of coercion, not only by market forces but also by missionaries and successive governments to destroy their traditional way of life and to assimilate them to a system of private property, market agriculture, and acquisition, they show few signs of motivational transformation.[41]

Second, it is not an accurate generalization even for all Europeans. The French *Canadiens* in New France traded with the Indians in a world market for at least as long as the English. Yet they did not develop a desire to enlarge their possessions of land and turn to agriculture. They preferred to engage in the fur-trade and adapt to native ways.

Nonetheless, from Locke's perspective that the Amerindians had no property in their traditional lands, Amerindian claims to land and

---

[40] See A. J. Ray, *Indians in the fur trade: their role as hunters, trappers and middlemen in the lands southwest of Hudson Bay 1660–1870* (Toronto: University of Toronto Press, 1974), 68–9; Cronon, *Changes in the land*, 97–9; Bruce Trigger, *Natives and newcomers: Canada's heroic age reconsidered* (Montreal: McGill–Queen's University Press, 1985), 164–225.

[41] J. R. Miller, *Skyscrapers hide the heavens: A history of Indian–white relations in Canada* (Toronto: University of Toronto Press, 1989).

their contention that colonists must purchase land from them would appear to be proof that they had acquired the desire to enlarge their possessions, not by honesty industry, but by illegitimate means. They would appear to be the 'Quarrelsom and Contentious', driven by 'covetousness' (34) to ingross more than they could use (31). Many of the colonists argued in exactly this way, claiming that the Indians had no desire for land until they learned they could make a profit by selling it to the newcomers. Then the Indians invented fictitious land deeds and sold them many times over to the unsuspecting settlers. Since the Indians had no records of fixed property in land, the conflicting claims were shrouded in mystery and this led to endless disputes over title. So, the colonists continued, even if they wished to recognize Amerindian title, it turned out to be impossible in practice. The colonists concluded that the only sure and indisputable title was thus occupation and cultivation.[42]

Locke's analysis of motivation should also be seen as an observation on the disputes which arose among the English settlers themselves over their insatiable desire to enlarge their possessions. There were two ways to act on the acquisitive desire to enlarge one's possessions of land in the colonies: by agricultural production for the market or by turning to trade with the Indians and to various 'deed-games' in order to avoid the work of agricultural production and the high rents the proprietors levied, and to reap the benefits of acquiring land which was valuable due to its growing scarcity. The latter type of land acquisition was a major cause of contention among the colonists, not only in New England but also Carolina and Virginia.[43] The colonists of Carolina were so outraged by the system of absentee landlords and high rents that Shaftesbury and Locke had established by the constitution of 1669 that they finally revolted and overthrew the constitution in 1719. When John Norris wrote a justification of this revolt against the constitution Locke had helped to design and establish he cleverly based his argument on the *Two treatises of government.*[44]

[42] This is the view presented by John Bulkley, *An inquiry into the right of the aboriginal natives to land in America*, 1725, xvi, xli, discussed below, part III. For a different view of the 'deed games' over Indian land see Jennings, *The invasion of America*, 128–46.

[43] See Bodleian, Locke MS. c. 6, fols 215–16; Cheves, ed., *Shaftesbury papers*, 13–32, 195, 248, 284, 466–8.

[44] John Norris, *The liberty and property of British subjects asserted in a letter from an assembly man in Carolina to his friend in London* (London: 1726). See Sirmans, *Colonial South Carolina*, 29–31. For the extent of Locke's authorship of *The constitution of Carolina*, see J. R. Milton, 'John Locke and the fundamental constitution of Carolina' (unpublished MS.).

The introduction of money and commerce leads to the situation where all available land is under cultivation (40). People are thus no longer free to hunt, gather, and cultivate as they please, but are compelled to live in the system of surplus production and accumulation (36). Locke presents two arguments to justify the extinguishment and replacement of the earlier system of limited production and replacement consumption. First, money is said to be introduced by 'mutual consent' into a system of pre-monetary trade of perishables for durables such as shells [i.e. wampum], pebbles, metal or diamonds (46–7). This hypothesis seems to be based on his knowledge of trade with Amerindians and it is fairly accurate. Amerindians adapted remarkably quickly to trade with the Europeans, often to their advantage, well into the nineteenth century in some cases.[45]

Locke sometimes presents the mutual consent to money as the sole justification required for the putting of all land under commercial cultivation and the extinguishment of the freedom people originally had to hunt, gather, and cultivate as they pleased, on the assumption that agreement to money entails agreement to the consequences (36, 50). However, his major justification is that the market system produces a greater quantity of conveniences (the standard laid out in 34). The presentation of this justification takes up the central sections of the chapter (37–44).

In his first comparison, enclosure and agriculture are said to require one-tenth the amount of land as hunting and gathering to produce the same quantity of conveniences (37). Locke then revises the ratio to one one-hundredth:

> For I aske whether in the wild woods and uncultivated wast of America left to Nature, without any improvement, tillage or husbandry, a thousand acres will yield the needy and wretched inhabitants as many conveniences of life as ten acres of equally fertile land doe in Devonshire where they are well cultivated?

It can be seen from the quotation that the comparison is made from the perspective of the system of commercial agriculture, not from an impartial standpoint. The quantity of conveniences each system produces is an irrelevant standard to measure the Amerindian system, since, as Locke knows, the system is designed to produce

[45] See James Axtell, *The invasion within: the contest of cultures in colonial North America* (Oxford: Oxford University Press, 1981) and references at notes 40–1.

limited (replacement) conveniences (36, 48). Also, Amerindian cultivation is overlooked. In addition, the inhabitants are said to be 'needy' and 'wretched' but this would only be the case if they had acquired a desire for more than they need. Finally, he claims that an English farmer in effect leaves 90 acres to mankind in common, relative to the hunter and gatherer who uses 100 acres, because he cultivates only 10 acres (37).[46] This is slightly disingenuous because he points out in section 49 that the same person will be motivated to enlarge his possessions. Hence, it appears that Locke is comparing the two systems either without regard to the standard of replacement, which he knows governs the Amerindian system (36, 48, 107–8), or on the assumption that the native peoples acquired the post-monetary desire for more than one needs.

The sustained argument for the superiority of commercial agriculture begins at section 40. 'Nor is it so strange', he opens, 'that the *Property of labour* should be able to over-ballance the Community of Land'. The reason is that '*Labour . . . puts the difference of values* on every thing'. He states that nine-tenths of the conveniences that are useful to 'the Life of Man', and therefore of value, are the effect of the improvement of labour whereas only one-tenth are due to unimproved nature. This ratio is then adjusted up to 99 parts out of 100 and illustrated with a questionable comparison of the American Indians who, 'for want of improving it [the soil] by labour, have not one hundredth part of the Conveniences we enjoy: And a King of a large and fruitful Territory there feeds, lodges, and is clad worse than a day labourer in *England*' (41). Again, the argument presupposes a universal desire to acquire conveniences since people would not value conveniences above all else, nor perhaps even possess this concept, and thus not use up all the land in labouring to produce them, unless they possessed an elastic desire for them.

The thesis that labour creates conveniences of value and benefit to mankind is illustrated in the next section with a contrast between the products of hunting, trapping, and gathering and the labour-intensive products of a commercial society (42). He then rounds his argument off with another comparison with American Indians. Here value and benefit are defined even more explicitly and narrowly as

---

[46] Cf. Winthrop, *Winthrop papers*, 139, for a similar comparison. Thomas, 'Contrastive subsistence strategies' (n. 37 above) figures that natives and newcomers used about the same amount of land.

how much a 'convenience' will fetch on the market as a commodity (43):

An Acre of Land that bears here Twenty Bushels of Wheat, and another in *America*, which, with the same Husbandry, would do the like, are, without doubt, of the same natural, intrinsick Value. But yet the Benefit Mankind receives from the one, in a Year, is worth 51 and from the other possibly not worth a Penny, if all the Profit an *Indian* received from it were to be valued, and sold here; at least, I may truly say, not 1/1000.

It seems clear, therefore, that the central sections on labour, value, and commodities are designed to legitimate and to celebrate the superiority of English colonial market agriculture over the Amerindian hunting, gathering, and replacement agriculture that it forcibly displaced. The destruction of centuries-old native American socio-economic organizations and the imperial imposition of commercial agriculture is made to appear as an inevitable and justifiable historical development. It is justified, according to Locke, because native Americans had no rights in the land, consented to the market system in agreeing to the use of money, and desired the change because the use of money changed their motivation. Furthermore, they are better off because the European market system produces 'more conveniences' – a manifestly partial standard that continues to be used down to this day to measure and legitimate the non-native socio-economic systems of North America.

The question-begging standard of 'more conveniences' is also common in the pamphlet literature of the early seventeenth century.[47] For all the confidence these writings convey, they were written against a backdrop of considerable doubt. Long before Marshall Sahlins pointed out the bias in the standard employed, some colonists were raising the same sort of doubts and objections.[48] In the *New English Canaan* (1632), Thomas Morton, like Locke, observed that Amerindians had a few needs and these they were able to satisfy with a minimum of work, leaving them with more leisure time than the colonists. When the colonists alleged that the Indians were therefore poorly clothed, needy, and lazy, Morton replied that perhaps they should be seen as rich and the colonists as poor: 'Now since it is but foode and rayment that we that live needeth . . . why should not the Natives of New England be said to live richly, having no want of

---

[47] See references at n. 22 above.   [48] Cronon, *Changes in the land*, 78–81.

either'.[49] Pierre Biard, a Jesuit of New France, compared the limited desires of Amerindians with the insatiable desires of settlers, as did Locke, and drew a similar conclusion:[50]

their [Amerindians'] days are all nothing but pastime. They are never in a hurry. Quite different from us, who can never do anything without hurry and worry; worry, I say, because our desire tyrannizes over us and banishes peace from our actions.

The normative difference that Locke draws between the two systems is defined further by his contrast between improvement and waste. 'Land that is left wholly to Nature, that hath no improvement of Pasturage, Tillage, or Planting, is called, as indeed it is, *wast*; and we shall find the benefit of it amount to little more than nothing' (42). Similar contrasts run throughout the colonial literature.[51] The juxtaposition gives the impression that land which is not put under labour intensive cultivation for the market is wasted or is not used beneficially. Those who fail to improve the land and take this attitude towards it are looked upon as neither rational nor industrious, and sinful in not heeding god's injunction to appropriate and improve (34, 35).[52]

The impression is false. Amerindians did not 'waste' the land; they used it in different and, in a number of respects, more ecologically benign ways.[53] According to their religious beliefs, all of nature is a world infused with spiritual power and humans are one family of spirits among many with no superior status. Consequently, they tend to seek adjustment to a natural world that is alive and of infinite value independent of human labour. The idea that nature is a wasteland of no value until it is 'improved' by commercial agriculture is sacrilegious for them. The New Englanders on the other hand, with their Christian voluntarism, saw themselves above the rest of nature and under an injuction to subdue and improve it for human purposes.[54] The ethic of improvement underwrites an exploitive stance towards

49 Thomas Morton, *New English Canaan*, 1632, in Charles F. Adams, ed., *Publications of the Prince Society*, 14 (Boston: 1883), 175–7. For reactions to Morton, see Richard Drinnon, *Facing west: the metaphysics of Indian hating and empire building* (Minneapolis: University of Minnesota Press, 1980).
50 Pierre Biard, S. J., 'Relation', in *The Jesuit relations and allied documents . . . 1610–1791*, 73 vols., ed. Reuben G. Thwaites (Cleveland: 1896–1901), III, 135.
51 See references at n. 22 above.
52 Roger Williams reversed this, arguing that the colonists were sinful in appropriating without consent (*Complete Works* 2: 40).   53 Cronon, *Changes in the land*.
54 Axtell, *The invasion within*, 15–19, 131–78.

nature in the name of 'greater conveniences for mankind' and stigmatizes any other stance as wasteful.[55]

The dynamic process that is set in motion by the introduction of money and world trade leads to the expansion of private property and surplus production until available land is under production. The disputes over property that follow cannot be solved by the ad-hoc and individual forms of adjudication available in the state of nature. At this historical juncture people agree to establish political societies in order to regulate and protect their property (123–6). Thus, by definition, a political society only comes into being on the basis of, and to govern, a regime of private property created by expanding needs and intensive agricultural production for the market (45):

(where the Increase of People and Stock, with the *Use of Money*) had made Land scarce, and so of some Value, the several *Communities* settled the Bounds of their distinct Territories, and by Laws within themselves, regulated the Properties of the private Men of their Society, and so, *by Compact*, and Agreement, *settled the property* which Labour and Industry began.

The formation of 'states and Kingdoms' is defined by a series of contrasts to Amerindian society (38, 45). Since American Indians lack the dynamic system of market-oriented property they have no need for the institutions of a political society to regulate it, and therefore they do not have governments; 'For in Governments the Laws regulate the right of property, and the possession of land is determined by positive constitutions' (50). In an even more ethnocentric conclusion, the system of modern states and commercial property is identified with civilization itself – 'those who are counted the Civiliz'd part of Mankind, who have made and multiplied positive Laws to determine Property' – in explicit contrast to American Indians (30).

In addition to conferring greater conveniences on the members of society, the system of political society and property is said to increase the power or hardness of that society *vis-à-vis* its neighbours. Locke introduces this mercantile theme at the end of his demonstration of the superiority of agriculture and industry over hunting, trapping, and gathering (42):

---

[55] See Carolyn Merchant, *Ecological revolutions: nature, gender and science in New England* (Chapel Hill: University of North Carolina Press, 1989) for a somewhat similar argument.

This shews, how much numbers of men are to be preferd to the largenesse of dominions, and that the increase of lands and the right imploying of them is the great art of government. And that Prince who shall be so wise and godlike as by established laws of liberty to secure protection and incourage-ment to the honest industry of Mankind against the oppression of power and narrownesse of Party will quickly be too hard for his neighbours.

If we read this brief and incomplete remark in the light of Locke's supervision of the old colonial system and his other writings on colonial policy and the art of government, I believe it is possible to locate chapter 5 in a larger context than I have done thus far. After 1674 England's chief rival was France. Shaftesbury and Locke turned their attention to how England and the Protestant states could contain and win out against this powerful competitor for hegemony over the resources of the non-European world. In 1689, with the English throne securely in the hands of a Protestant prince who shared this vision and led England into the Nine Years' War, Locke insisted that the contest with France must be the first concern of policy.[56] The centre of gravity of the struggle with France was America, where the English colonies were surrounded by the French fur-trading routes and military alliances with the Indian nations to the east and north.

There were two major differences between the French and the English in America. France had a small population spread over a large area whereas England had a larger population concentrated along the coast. Second, France established a non-agriculture, fur-trading empire in America and conformed, to a large extent, to Amerindian hunting, trapping, and gathering customs. The English in the colonies brought their agricultural system with them. I conjecture that Locke refers to these two differences in section 42: 'This shews, how much numbers of men are to be preferd to largenesse of dominions, and that the increase of lands [i.e. increase in the productivity of lands – JT] and the right of imploying of them is the great art of government'.

Therefore, I would like to suggest tentatively that in arguing for the superiority of commercial agriculture over Amerindian hunting, trapping, and gathering Locke may also be arguing for the superior-ity of English colonization over the French fur-trading empire. The

[56] James Farr, 'John Locke on the Glorious Revolution: a rediscovered document', *The Historical Journal* 28, 2 (1985), 385–98, 395–8.

recommendation of the chapter as a whole may be the following. Not only do the English colonists have every right to settle there, but also, if they settle down to agricultural surplus production, and if the king regulates, encourages, and employs them properly, imperial England 'will quickly be too hard' for the French empire, based as it is on what Locke has argued to be the comparatively inefficient, underproductive, wasteful, and out-moded fur-trapping system of the Amerindians. More research on the colonial documents is needed to test this hypothesis.

DISSEMINATION

We have seen how Locke's concepts of political society and property are, among other things, a sophisticated theoretical expression of the basic arguments of early colonial writers. Let us now ask if the colonists in turn employed Locke's arguments in their continuing struggle to justify English settlement in native America.

The litigation, mentioned above, between the colony of Connecticut and the Mohegan Indians continued into the eighteenth century and it was considered to be 'the greatest cause that ever was heard at the [Privy] Council Board'.[57] The Mohegans claimed to be a distinct political society with sovereignty over their traditional lands. Hence the Royal Charter could not confer sovereignty over their land to the colony of Connecticut. The only way the colony could gain legitimacy would be for the English nation to negotiate an international agreement with the Mohegan nation in accord with international law. The Privy Council ruled in favour of Mohegan sovereignty in 1705 and again in 1743.[58]

In 1725 the Reverend John Bulkley of Colchester, Connecticut published a book by Roger Wolcott, the late Governor of Connecticut, entitled *Poetical meditations*, and included an article he wrote, entitled 'An inquiry into the right of the aboriginal natives to the land in America'. It is a refutation of the Mohegans' claim to political society and property in their traditional lands based in its entirety on Locke's *Two treatises*. He brings out and presses into service exactly those contrasts I have sought to bring to light in this paper, illustrating each step in the argument with a quotation from Locke.[59]

---

[57] Smith, *Appeals to the Privy Council*, 418 (note 21 above).   [58] *Ibid.*, 434.

[59] John Bulkley, *An inquiry into the right of the aboriginal natives to the land in America*, in Roger Wolcott, *Poetical meditations* (New London: 1726), i–lvi. Bulkley's essay was published

Everyone agrees, Bulkley begins, that the natives have some property rights. The great question is how extensive are they. The defenders of the Mohegans claim that they have a right to all the land and that Europeans must acquire it by compact. But this is false (xvi). Either the Amerindians are in a state of nature or in political society. If they are in state of nature, then the only property they have is that acquired by labour, improvement, and rudimentary exchange. Labour starts and limits property (xxiv). Since the Amerindians had plenty and no motive to acquire more than they needed, they did not cultivate or till (xxviii). It is thus knavish and ignorant to assume they had large tracts of land. They had only a few spots of enclosed and cultivated land.

Furthermore, he continues, the Indians did not have civil societies: they lack laws, established judges, and a legislature (xxx). Their chiefs are simply generals of their armies. Nonetheless, he takes up the counterfactual hypothesis that the Indians did form political societies (xxxv). If they set up political societies by compact, then either they went on to settle property among themselves or they did not. Since they lacked commerce and money, they had no incentive to depart from their natural property of catching and gathering. What inducement or motive was there, he asks, to fix a property in land when they had such a 'rude, mean, inartful way of living' (xl)? Others argue on the contrary that they did have settled property. But this happened only after the English arrived when the Indians saw the advantages of claiming large tracts of land for the purpose of sale (xli). To settle these later claims we would need clear records of fixed property, but none exist. Native claims, such as the Mohegan claims, are shrouded in darkness and lead to disputations (xliii). On the other hand, he roundly concludes, the English had an 'undoubted right to enter upon and impropriate all such parts as lay waste or unimproved' (liii).

When the Mohegan dispute was heard again in 1743 commissioners Horsmanden and Morris restated the case for Mohegan sovereignty. In an acidic commentary William Samuel Johnson

separately later in the century. For Bulkley and the rivalry among colonists for Mohegan land, see Richard Bushman, *From Puritan to Yankee: character and social order in Connecticut 1690–1765* (Cambridge, Mass.: Harvard University Press, 1967). For the Mohegan's long struggle, which is in the courts again (1991), see John DeForest, *History of the Indians of Connecticut from the earliest known period to 1850* (Hartford: 1853). Since Bulkley's arguments follows the sections of the *Two treatises* discussed above I have given only a brief recapitulation of it below.

employed the Locke–Bulkley Eurocentric concept of political society to undermine their claim:[60]

When the English treated with them [Amerindians] it was not with Independent States (for they had no such thing as a Civil Polity, nor hardly any one circumstance essential to the existence of a state) but as with savages, whom they were to quiet and manage as well as they could, sometimes by flattery; but oftener by force. Who would not Treat if he saw himself surrounded by the Company of Lyons, Wolves or Beasts whom the Indians but too nearly resembled . . . but you would not immediately call them an independent State (though independent enough God knows) . . . This notion of their being free States is perfectly ridiculous and absurd. Without Polity, Laws, etc. there can be no such thing as a State. The Indians had neither in any proper sense of the words.

Fifteen years later in Europe the same kind of argument was written into the law of nations. In 1758 Emeric de Vattel (1714–67) stipulated that agricultural improvement and a political society with established laws are necessary conditions for the recognition of sovereignty and nationhood in international law. Accordingly, the Indians of North America not only lacked sovereignty but they also failed in their natural duty to cultivate the soil. Employing these familiar Lockean concepts he concluded that the establishment of 'various colonies upon the continent of North America' has been 'entirely lawful':[61]

The cultivation of the soil . . . is . . . an obligation imposed upon man by nature . . . Every Nation is therefore bound by the law of nature to cultivate the land which has fallen to its share. There are others who, in order to avoid labour, seek to live upon their flocks and the fruits of the chase . . . Now that the human race has multiplied so greatly, it could not subsist if every people wished to live after that fashion. Those who still pursue this idle mode of life occupy more land than they would have need of under a system of honest labour, and they may not complain if other more industrious nations, too confined at home, should come and occupy part of their lands . . . The peoples of those vast tracts of land roamed over them rather than inhabited them . . . [W]hen the Nations of Europe, which are too confined at home, come upon lands which the savages have no special need of and are making no present and continuous use of, they may lawfully take possession of them and establish colonies in them.

---

[60] Smith, *Appeals from the Privy Council*, 434–5, note 109 (note 21 above).
[61] Emeric de Vattel, *Le droit des gens, ou principes de la loi naturelle* (1758), *The law of nations or the principles of natural law*, tr. Charles G. Fenwick (Washington: Carnegie Institute, 1902), I. viii. 81, I. xviii. 207–10.

The 'agricultural' or 'improvement' justifications presented by Locke and Vattel were widely cited throughout the eighteenth and nineteenth centuries to legitimate settlement without consent, the removal of centuries-old aboriginal nations, and war if the native peoples defended their property. Vattel's *The law of nations* was selected as a classic of international law in 1902 and thereby became an authoritative source of international law for the modern world. The arguments that the aboriginal peoples are not self-governing nations and have property only in the products of their labour, and that the 'civilized part of mankind' have the right to appropriate and 'improve' their territories in the name of 'greater conveniences' continue to be used in the courts, legislatures, and public opinion.[62]

The agricultural argument was only one of many justifications for dispossession and English settlement in native America. When it was used it was often accompanied by an agreement or deed (registering the property under English law) and some kind of payment, whether this was only to mollify the Amerindians or to recognize that they possessed rights the agricultural argument denies.[63] More common was the practice of treaties and deeds of land transfer between non-natives and natives on the explicit assumption that the native peoples had rights of property over their traditional territories, and, therefore, could alienate property to the settlers by agreement. Treaties of this type were popular with the Dutch and English, and especially the land speculation companies that invaded the Ohio valley in the eighteenth century.[64] Also, as we have seen, the original agricultural arguments of the 1630s were deployed against the treaty-based property claims of Roger Williams and his followers.

   The classical presentation of this second type of justification is *Plain facts: being an examination into the rights of the Indian nations of America to their respective countries, and a vindication of the grant for the Six United Nations . . .*, 1781, by Samuel Wharton. As the subtitle reveals, Wharton sought to vindicate the land purchases he had negotiated

---

[62] See James Tully, 'Placing the *Two treatises*', in *Political discourse in early modern Britain: Essays in honour of John Pocock*, ed. Nicholas Philipson and Quentin Skinner (Cambridge: Cambridge University Press, 1992). For a recent example see Hamar Foster, 'The Saanichton Bay Marina Case: Imperial law, colonial history and competing theories of aboriginal title', *UBC Law Review* 23, 3 (1989), 629–50, 642–7.

[63] Jennings, *The invasion of America*, 128–35. For more detail on this and part IV see James Tully, 'Placing the *Two treatises*' (n. 62 above).

[64] Robert A. Williams, *The American Indian in western legal discourse*, 233–304 (n. 7 above).

with the Haudenosaunee (Iroquois) Confederacy against the counter, charter-based claim of the colony of Virginia. The important feature of this famous tract for our present purposes is that he cites Locke, among others, in defence of his conclusion that 'the aborigines of America have an absolute exclusive right to the countries they possess'. This (alienable) right is based on the natural law of preservation, where the right to their territories is then the necessary means to preservation, and on title from occupancy. Following Blackstone's interpretation of Locke, Wharton holds that Locke's labour criterion is met by occupation alone; an act of occupation being a degree of bodily labour.[65] The *Two treatises* is thus used to defend aboriginal property rights in order to validate English property in America based on consent by individual treaties with Indian sachems, in competition and contradiction with the use of the *Two treatises* by Bulkley and others to deny aboriginal property rights in order to validate English property in America based on settlement and cultivation without consent.

It appears to me, for reasons given above, that Wharton and Blackstone are incorrect to assume that occupation, or hunting and gathering, meets Locke's criterion of labour or 'due use'. Nonetheless, Wharton is correct in arguing that, on Locke's account, native Americans, like everyone, have the right to the means of preservation derived from the natural law of preservation (section 25). However, it does not follow that this right takes the form of a natural right to their hunting, gathering, and non-sedentary agricultural lands. This Locke expressly denies. These lands are vacant. Rather, in tacitly consenting to the use of money the aboriginal peoples consented to the system of commercial agriculture, and so their natural right to the means of preservation must be realized in this system: that is, by turning to commercial agriculture and trade themselves, by working for others or, if they are physically unable to labour, by local poor relief. If this is correct, then Locke's proposal to grant Indians individual tracts of land in Carolina is consistent with the *Two treatises*.

A third non-native title to land in America was a grant from a colonial assembly, on the assumption that jurisdiction was vested in the assembly (either without regard to the native nations or as a result

---

[65] Samuel Wharton, *Plain facts: being an examination into the rights of the Indian nations of America to their respective territories* (Philadelphia, 1781), 7, 15.

of treaties with them). Wharton's *Plain facts*, for example, is written against the claim advanced by Virginia, and supported by Thomas Jefferson, of jurisdiction over the same territory which Wharton claimed to have purchased from the six Nations (who, in turn, claimed it in virtue of their earlier conquest of the Delaware and Shawnee nations).[66] Like the other two titles, the independent right of a colonial assembly to grant property was also justified with reference to the *Two treatises*. John Otis, in the *Rights of the British colonies asserted and proved*, 1764, based his justification of colonial independence and jurisdiction on Locke's argument that people may leave their home country and set up independent political societies by consent.[67]

ABORIGINAL SOVEREIGNTY

Standing above and sovereign over these conflicting claims to land in native America stands the official title of the British Crown (and the French Crown). The doctrine of Crown title not only denies the legitimacy of the three titles mentioned above. It is also a complete repudiation of the concepts of Indian or 'non-state' property and political society of the *Two treatises*. The official Crown title, as we have seen in the Privy Council decision in the Mohegan nation case, is that the aboriginal peoples of North America are sovereign, self-governing nations with exclusive jurisdiction over and ownership of their territories.[68] Since they were never conquered, their juridical status as self-governing nations continues through the arrival of Europeans and co-exists with British and French sovereignty. Accordingly, the only legitimate non-native titles to land in America are those derived from nation-to-nation treaties of cession negotiated by the Crown and the sachems of the appropriate first nations (thereby recognizing their respective sovereignties), in a public ceremony and without duress. The Crown then grants the ceded land to colonists and, in exchange, agrees to protect the first nations on their Indian Lands from foreign invasion (by the French and Spanish) and from encroachment by settlers and land speculators,

---

[66] Williams, *The American Indian*, 259–71, 289–305.
[67] John Otis, *Rights of the British colonies asserted and proved* (Boston: 1764), 25–31.
[68] See Chief Justice John Marshall below; Russell Barsh and James Youngblood Henderson, *The road: Indian tribes and political liberty* (Berkeley: University of California Press, 1980); Bruce Clark, *Native liberty, Crown sovereignty: the existing aboriginal right of self-government in Canada* (Montréal: McGill–Queens University Press, 1990).

bearing the three invalid titles mentioned above, as long as the sun shines and the rivers flow.

The underlying premise that the native nations could come under the protection of another sovereign without forfeiting their own sovereignty, laws, and forms of government was based on the old 'continuity' principle of international law, which, ironically, was given one of its clearest formulations by Vattel in *The law of nations*.[69] Moreover, the continuity of a nation's legal and political institutions after the arrival of another sovereign, even in the counterfactual case of conquest, was an article of faith to every Briton, for the pre-Norman institutions of parliamentary government and Common law were understood to have continued unscathed through the Conquest by King William in 1066 and the imposition of Feudal law.[70]

This official doctrine obviously rests on the Crown's acknowledgement of the power of the first nations, especially the Haudenosaunee Confederacy, and of the dependency of the British in America on them for survival and military support against the French. It was proclaimed by the Crown throughout the seventeenth and eighteenth centuries and formally stated in the Royal Proclamation of 7 October 1763, as the Crown sought to consolidate its control and centralize colonial-Indian relations.[71] The Proclamation explains that 'great Frauds and Abuses have been committed in purchasing Lands of the Indians, to the great Prejudice of our Interest, and to the great Dissatisfaction of the said Indians', and states:

[I]t is just and reasonable and essential to our Interest, and the Security of our Colonies, that the several Nations or Tribes of Indians with whom We are connected, and who live under our Protection, should not be molested or disturbed in the Possession of such Parts of Our Dominions and Territories as, not having been ceded to or purchased by Us, are reserved to them, or any of them, as their Hunting grounds . . .

The Crown doctrine comes quite close to recognizing the aboriginal peoples as they recognize themselves: that is, as we have seen, as

[69] Vattel, *The law of nations*, I. v. (n. 61 above).
[70] See Tully, 'Placing the *Two treatises*' (note 62 above).
[71] For the Royal Proclamation and its context, see Jack Stagg, *Anglo-Indian relations in North America to 1763 and an analysis of the Royal Proclamation of 7 October 1763* (Ottawa: Department of Indian Affairs and Northern Development, 1980), Jack Sosin, *Whitehall and the Wilderness* (Lincoln: University of Nebraska Press, 1961).

independent, self-governing nations in a treaty relation of co-existence with the British and French nations in America. The native leaders reaffirmed their nationhood and independence in the hundreds of treaties with the British and French. As Minivavana, a Chippewa leader, typically informed Alexander Henry at Michilimackinac in 1761,[72]

> Englishman, although you have conquered the French, you have not yet conquered us. We are not your slaves. These lakes, these woods and mountains, were left to us by our ancestors. They are our inheritance, and we will part with them to no one.

The person in the best position to know the political status of the American Indians in the eighteenth century was Sir William Johnson, the Superintendent of Indian Affairs for the Northern half of British North America, who had negotiated the treaties of the mid-century. He informed London on numerous occasions as the Royal Proclamation was being prepared that,[73]

> The Indians of the Ottawa Confederacy . . . and also the Six Nations, however their sentiments may have been misrepresented, all along considered the Northern parts of North America, as their sole property from the beginning . . . I must beg leave to observe, that the Six Nations, Western Indians, etc., having never been conquered, either by the English or French, nor subject to the Laws, consider themselves as a free people.

The Crown title recognition of the aboriginal peoples as self-governing nations with exclusive jurisdiction over and ownership of their territories was entrenched in the Federal constitutional law of the United States by Chief Justice John Marshall in *Worcester v. the State of Georgia* in 1831. After rejecting an agricultural argument for dispossession based explicitly on the *Two treatises* in *Johnson and Graham's Lessee v. M'Intosh* in 1823, Marshall bases his recognition of native nationhood in *Worcester* on the explication of the Royal Proclamation of 1763, backed up by an extensive survey of treatises

---

[72] Cited in Alexander Henry, *Travels and adventures in Canada and the Indian territories between the years 1760 and 1776* (New York: I. Riley, 1809), 44. See Dorothy V. Jones, *License for empire: colonialism by treaty in early America* (Chicago: University of Chicago Press, 1982). For the continued assertion of native sovereignty see Richardson, ed., *Drumbeat: anger and renewal in Indian country* (note 20 above).

[73] Sir William Johnson to the Lords of Trade, Nov. 13, 1763 and n.d., in O'Callaghan, ed., *Documents relative to the colonial history of the state of New York* 7: 575, 665 (n. 20 above). See Francis Jennings et al., *The history and culture of Iroquois diplomacy: an interdisciplinary guide to the treaties of the Six Nations and their league* (Syracuse: Syracuse University Press, 1985).

between the Crown and the early United States and the Indian nations. He explains:[74]

America, separated from Europe by a wide ocean, was inhabited by a distinct people, divided into separate nations, independent of each other and the rest of the world, having institutions of their own, and governing themselves by their own laws.

He goes on to argue that their status as 'nations' and 'states' was never extinguished but in fact recognized and affirmed by the treaties. The 'several Indian nations' are 'distinct political communities, having territorial boundaries, within which their authority is exclusive', and their 'right to all the lands within those boundaries . . . is not only acknowledged, but guarantied [sic] by the United States'.[75] In addition, while coming under the protection of the United States necessarily restricted their right to trade with other nations, it also places an obligation on the United States to protect Indian sovereignty over their own territory and affairs:[76]

the settled doctrine of the law of nations is, that a weaker power does not surrender its independence, its right to self-government, by associating with a stronger, and taking its protection. A weak state, in order to provide for its safety, may place itself under the protection of one more powerful, without stripping itself of the right of self-government, and ceasing to be a state. Examples of this kind are not wanting in Europe. 'Tributary and feudatory states', says Vattel, 'do not thereby cease to be sovereign and independent states, so long as self-government and sovereign and independent authority are left in the administration of the state.'

The Royal Proclamation of 1763 remains part of Commonwealth constitutional law and it is entrenched in the Canadian constitution: in section 25 of *The Constitution Act, 1982*.[77] Also, Chief Justice Marshall has been cited many times in Canadian constitutional law as the authority on the Royal Proclamation. Notwithstanding, the constitutionally protected property and self-government of the first nations have been transgressed innumerable times by the United States and Canadian governments in a 'long train' of abuses and

[74] *Worcester v. the State of Georgia* (1832), 6 Peter 515 (U.S.S.C.) in John Marshall, *The writings of John Marshall upon the federal constitution* (Boston: James Monroe and Co., 1839), 419–48, 426. (6 Peter 542). [75] *Ibid.*, 442, 445. (6 Peter 557, 559). [76] *Ibid.*, 446 (6 Peter 560).
[77] *The Constitution Act, 1982* (Schedule B to Canada Act 1982 [U.K.]) section 25. 'The guarantee in this Charter of certain rights and freedoms shall not be construed so as to abrogate or derogate from (ne porte pas atteinte) any aboriginal treaties or other freedoms that pertain to the aboriginal peoples of Canada including (a) any rights or freedoms that have been recognised by the Royal Proclamation of October 7, 1763 . . .'

injustices. Indian lands have been taken without the form of consent required by the Royal Proclamation and international law, treaties have not been honoured, no treaties have been signed for over one-half of Canada (and thus this land remains under native sovereignty), and the native peoples have been involuntarily subjected to non-native government.[78]

If, therefore, Locke is wrong about the nature of property and government in non-state and specifically Amerindian societies, as I have argued; and if the aboriginal peoples, the British Crown, Chief Justice Marshall, International law,[79] and Canadian and United States constitutional law are right in claiming that Amerindians are self-governing nations with ownership of their territories; then it follows from the central theory of government of the *Two treatises* itself that they have the right to defend themselves and their property, with force if necessary, against these injustices, as the Haida, Gitksan and Wet'suwet'en, Lubicon Cree, Kanesatake, Mohawk, James Bay Cree, and Innu of Labrador, among others, are currently doing.[80] Further, if aboriginal property and self-government (sovereignty) are guaranteed in the constitution and constitutional law, as the evidence shows, and if these are denied and violated in practice; then, by the theory of limited constitutional government and rule of law of the *Two treatises*, and of liberal theories descended from it, every citizen has the right to support, with force if necessary, the first nations in their constitutional struggle to bring 'arbitrary' government to abide by the 'settled, standing laws' they have been 'delegated' to uphold.[81]

[78] There is no substitute for the legal–historical study of individual treaties and nations. For an introduction see Georges Erasmus, 'Introduction', in *Drumbeat: anger and renewal*, 1–43 (n. 20 above), and J. R. Miller, ed., *Sweet promises: a reader on Indian–White relations in Canada* (Toronto: University of Toronto Press, 1991).

[79] See John Howard Clinebell and Jim Thomson, 'Sovereignty and self-determination: the rights of native Americans under international law', *Buffalo Law Review*, 27 (1978) 669–712.

[80] See, respectively, Paul Tennant, *Aboriginal peoples and politics: the Indian land question in British Columbia 1849–1989* (Vancouver: University of British Columbia Press, 1990); Gisday Wa and Delgam Uukw, *The spirit in the land* (Gabriola, BC: Reflections, 1989); John Goddard, *The last stand of the Lubicon Cree* (Vancouver: Douglas & McIntyre, 1991); Geoffrey York and Loreen Pindera, *The People of the Pines: The warriors and the legacy of Oka* (Toronto: Little, Brown, 1991); Boyce Richardson, *Strangers devour the land*, 2nd edn. (Vancouver: Douglas and McIntrye, 1991); Marie Wadden, *Nitassinan: the Innu struggle to regain their homeland* (Vancouver: Douglas & McIntyre, 1991).

[81] For the theory see Locke, *Two treatises* 135, 137, 149, 168, 210, 240–3, and chapters 1 and 10 of this volume. For a statement of the constitutional struggle by the Chief of the Assembly of First Nations see Ovide Mercredi, 'Aboriginal peoples and the constitution', in *After Meech Lake: lessons for the future*, ed. David Smith, et al. (Sasktoon: Fifth house publishers, 1991), 219–23.

Consequently, as in many struggles for justice over the last three hundred years, Locke's enduring delegation theory of constitutional government, limited by the popular rights to dissent from and resist abuses of political power, is able once again to criticize and transcend the ideological constraints he placed upon it and serve to expose injustice and justify resistance to it. What could be a more fitting tribute at the tercentenary of the *Two treatises* than its self-critical use to expose and justify public action against a monumental injustice, at the base of two allegedly liberal societies, that the concepts of property and political society in the *Two treatises* have served to cover over and legitimate for far too long.

Governing subjects

CHAPTER 6

Governing conduct: Locke on the reform of thought and behaviour

INTRODUCTION

This is a working chapter.[1] The claims it embodies are provisional and tentative. The hypothesis laid out in the chapter is that a new practice of governing conduct was assembled in the period from the Reformation to the Enlightenment. My aim is to describe this ensemble of power, knowledge, and habitual behaviour at the point, 1660–1700, when its relatively enduring features consolidated, and from the perspective of one person who described, evaluated, and partly constructed it: John Locke. This mode of governance links together probabilistic and voluntaristic forms of knowledge with a range of techniques related to each other by a complex of references to juridical practices. Its aim is to reform conduct: to explain and then deconstruct settled ways of mental and physical behaviour, and to produce and then govern new forms of habitual conduct in belief and action. Finally, this way of subjection, of conducting the self and others, both posits and serves to bring about a very specific form of subjectivity: a subject who is calculating and calculable, from the perspective of the probabilistic knowledge and practices; and the sovereign bearer of rights and duties, subject to and of law from the voluntaristic perspective. The whole ensemble of knowledge, techniques, habitual activity, and subjection I will provisionally call the juridical government.

Aspects of this have been studied by Michael Foucault in *Surveiller et punir: naissance de la prison* (1975). He isolated and distinguished two complexes of power and knowledge, the juridical and the disciplinarian.[2] The former assembled around the spread of secular and Canon

---

[1] In memory of Michel Foucault.
[2] For comparisons and contrasts of these two forms of power and knowledge see Michel Foucault, *Discipline and punish*, tr. Alan Sheridan (New York: Vintage Books, 1979), pp. 177–183; and 'Two lectures', in Michel Foucault, *Power/knowledge*, ed. Colin Gordon (New York: Pantheon Books, 1980), 92–108.

Law from the twelfth century and the latter around the dispersion of techniques of discipline and normalizing from the early seventeenth century. There are important similarities, that would repay close study, between these two concepts and Gerhard Oestreich's distinction between constitutionalism and social discipline in *Neostoicism and the early modern state*, and this in turn is based on an older dichotomy used by Friedrich Meinecke and Otto Hintze.[3] Foucault's concern was to show how the disciplines, both as bodies of knowledge – the sciences of man – and as practices of fostering and administering individual and collective life, are, by the nineteenth century, heterogeneous with respect to juridical knowledge and practices. My concern is, rather, to show the tangled nest of relationships between these two before their separation. I want to suggest that the techniques, functions, and forms of knowledge, centred on the norm or statistical regularity, of the disciplines emerged out of the expanded demands placed on the older juridical complex in the mercantile age.

By placing the juridical features of early modern thought and action in the centre of my study I seek to revive and question the thesis advanced by Nietzsche in the second essay of *On the genealogy of morals*.[4] He argued that any genealogy of the modern subject, who is both calculable in his behaviour (and so the object of the explaining social sciences and their administrative practices) and sovereign, the bearer of rights and responsibility (and so the subject of the political, legal, and moral sciences and their legal and political practices), must predominantly refer to the secular and church penal practices of the early modern period. I want to explore some of the complexities of this thesis by focusing on the late seventeenth century; and, secondly, to question his conclusion that the product of this long process is the individual conscience. If my study is correct, just the opposite is true. The new practice of governing was an attack on the conscience, as both too radical and too submissive, and an effort to create habits that would replace the conscience and guide conduct.

This government by reform was put into practice in response to four problems of governability in the early modern period. The first

[3] Gerhard Oestreich, *Neostoicism and the early modern state* (Cambridge: Cambridge University Press, 1982).

[4] Friedrich Nietzsche, 'Second essay: guilt, bad conscience and the like', in *On the genealogy of morals*, tr. Walter Kaufmann and R. J. Halliday (New York: Vintage Books, 1969).

three problems were how to govern the labouring classes; what form of rule would end the civil and religious wars that swept Europe for 100 years and claimed 30 per cent of the population; and how to administer global relations of commercial exploitation, colonization, and military power. The fourth problem provided the means to organize the other three into an overall political strategy. In 1648 the consolidating early modern states faced each other as independent and sovereign powers in a situation of uncertainty and military–commercial competition. This predicament of balance of powers, as it was called, marks the threshold of modernity. The Anglo–Dutch war showed that war could now be global and that it would be primarily concerned with the commercial interests of states, not with religion. To compete it was necessary to construct a vast military–diplomatic ensemble capable of protecting and extending commercial relations. The key to this 'power' was, as everyone argued, the enhancement of the wealth and strength of the nation. This required a way of solving the first three problems: so to govern trade, manufacturing, labour, religion, and so on as to bring about riches and strength, which, in turn, would increase military power. The formation of the welfare–warfare state was thus a response to this strategic situation, as many contemporaries noted:[5]

> But some nations having departed from the ancient simplicity of living contented with productions of their own countries and having by navigation and trade, raised themselves to wealth, power and increase of inhabitants; it thereupon grew necessary for other nations to fall into like methods, lest otherwise they should have been a prey, as well as a derision to them whom trade hath rendered mighty and opulent.

Mercantilism is the name we give to government policies that sought to solve the problems in all four areas and to coordinate them by means of the law.[6] However, it involved more than an extension and intensification of the law: it marked, and sometimes masked, the transition to the new practice of governing. If the juridical apparatus is partly a response to these problems of governability it is also the way

[5] C. K., *Some seasonable and modest thoughts partly occasioned by, and partly concerning the East Indian Company* . . . (Edinburgh, 1696). Cited in Lawrence A. Harper, *The English navigation laws: a seventeenth century experiment in social engineering* (New York: Columbia University Press, 1939), 233.
[6] For a survey of mercantilism see Eli Heckscher, *Mercantilism*, tr. M. Shapiro, ed. E. F. Soderlund, 2nd edition (2 vols., London: Allen and Unwin, 1955 [1st edition, 1931]).

in which new types of knowledge were employed in dealing with these problems.

The religious wars that swept Europe were partly a response to and partly the carrier of the rule of faith controversy. This was the great struggle over the 'true' faith that rapidly deepened to an intellectual battle over the grounds for rational belief or assent in matters of faith. This was the most important question in a person's life not only because it involved eternal salvation or damnation, but also because the answer could bring persecution or the duty to take up arms in this world. This radical questioning of the foundations of belief spread throughout European knowledge, or linked up with independently provoked questioning in other areas of knowledge. The revival of scepticism aided these processes, which, by the end of the sixteenth century, had undermined the orthodox certainties and ushered in a general sceptical or legitimation crisis. In throwing into question the regimes of knowledge that had supported traditional ways of governing in politics, church, and university, the intellectual crisis delegitimated the ways of governing that were under siege on the battlefields as well.

Politically, the centre of this crisis was the presupposition that it was the role of government to bring about the good life; to propagate the true faith and inculcate virtue. Yet, as everyone from Montaigne onwards realized, this was the cause of religious and civil wars, for there were three conflicting views concerning the true faith. The seventeenth century provided a solution to this problem of what kind of government is possible if diversity in religious–moral belief is ineradicable. The answer, from Lipsius to Locke, was that the objective of government is preservation of life, not religion. Every school from natural law to scepticism could agree on this. Preservation was thus articulated in three ways as the objective of the early modern state: preservation of the population from internal and external attacks by war and war-preparation; preservation of the life, subsistence, discipline, and health of the population; and preservation of the rights and duties of subjects compatible with or derivable from the underlying objective of the preservation of life. Another way of putting this is to say that humanism, natural law, and republicanism came to terms with *raison d'état* practice in the seventeenth century, classically with Lipsius, Grotius, and Harrington. This modern political project, where life itself is wagered on our political technology, is the informing principle of mercantile practice.

The dissolution of the legitimation crises in other areas of knowledge coalesced around new criteria of rational belief that Richard Popkin has termed 'constructive scepticism'.[7] This comprises two distinctive types of knowledge: probabilistic and voluntaristic. These were employed in a multiplicity of ways in the policies of the early modern states, from Montchretien to Petty, and so came to be constitutive of the new practice of government. Indeed, one of the reasons why a consensus began to emerge around the new epistemological foundations, by the the time of Boyle, Locke, and Newton, was that these two types of knowledge gradually became invested in a host of practices of the consolidating state.

Locke is a good guide to the juridical way of governing because he was involved in the problems of governability, as a member of the Board of Trade, and of knowledge, as a philosopher.[8] This chapter is therefore centred on Locke's work, and is divided into four sections: governing belief, governing action, three practices of governing, and the penalized self.[9]

GOVERNING BELIEF

The first feature of the new way of governing is the rejection of any theory that assent or belief is governed by a natural disposition (or telic faculty) to the true or the good. This theory of a naturally dispositional conscience is replaced by an account of the conscience as a completely non-dispositional power of judgement, and of the mind as a blank tablet, indifferent to true and false, good and evil. Belief then ought to be governed by a new criterion, the weight of the evidence, but, as Locke argues, it is in fact governed by acquired dispositions.

The two questions concerning the grounds that ought to govern assent, and what in fact does govern it, dominate the 150-year

---

[7] Richard Popkin, *The history of scepticism from Erasmus to Spinoza*, revised editon (Berkeley: University of California Press, 1979), 129–50. Popkin does not take into account the role of voluntarism in the formation of constructive scepticism. For a consideration of constructive scepticism as a response to the broad crisis, see Theodore R. Rabb, *The struggle for stability in early modern Europe* (Oxford: Oxford University Press, 1973), and Marc Raeff, *The well-ordered police state: social and institutional change through law in the Germanies and Russia 1600–1800* (New Haven: Yale University Press, 1983).

[8] Locke served on the Board of Trade from October 1673 to December 1674 and from May 1696 to June 1700.

[9] My greatest debt in this chapter is to Ed Hundert and his classic article, 'The making of *homo faber*: John Locke between ideology and history', *Journal of the History of Ideas* (1972), 2–22.

intellectual struggle of the Reformation. As I have mentioned, it was not only the question of what one must believe in order to be saved. Because most sects believed theirs to be the true religion and that it was a primary Christian duty to take up arms to defend and extend their religion, there was also the political–military question of life and death. Several other factors contributed to this legitimation crisis: the effects of global conquest, the revolutionary changes in science, the developments in the mechanical arts, and so on. However, the religious wars and the multifaceted repercussions in the realm of knowledge seem to me to be the major provocation which rendered assent and its foundations problematic. The seventeenth-century quest for certainty and grounds for assent, from clear and distinct ideas to innateism, is a response to this problem in all areas of knowledge.[10]

Locke's *Essay concerning human understanding*, as well as the second draft (*Draft B*), is addressed explicitly to this issue:[11] 'to search out the Bounds between Opinion and Knowledge; and examine by what measures, in things, whereof we have no certain knowledge, we ought to regulate our Assent, and moderate our Persuasions'. Also, Locke's interest began with the specific religious and moral question of assent and gradually developed to comprise, and in a sense invent, a general epistemological context covering all areas of knowledge.[12] Further, the criteria of assent advanced in the *Essay* constitute the solution to the crisis.[13] The criteria, and the concept of assent itself, are foundational for the modern concept of rational belief. They now govern our mental conduct in science, law, history, and religion, to cite the conclusion of the most recent research.[14] This is partly

[10] For the concept of legitimation crisis that I use here see James Tully, 'The pen is a mighty sword', *British Journal of Political Science*, 13 (1983), 489–509.

[11] John Locke, *An essay concerning human understanding*, ed. Peter Nidditch (Oxford: Clarendon Press, 1975), 1.1.3. Compare John Locke, *Draft B of Locke's essay concerning human understanding*, ed. Peter Nidditch (Sheffield: University of Sheffield, 1982), 2, p. 37.

[12] The early drafts of the *Essay*, A and B, were written for a group of friends who met at Exeter House in 1670–1 to discuss problems of 'religion and morality', as James Tyrrell noted in the margin of his copy of the *Essay* next to Locke's reference to these meetings in the Epistle to the reader (*Essay*, 7). As Locke explains, the religious and moral questions could not be solved until the epistemological questions of assent were settled.

[13] This is the conclusion of the study by Henry G. van Leeuwen, *The problem of certainty in English thought 1630–1690* (The Hague: Martinus Nijhoff, 1963); and, earlier, Paul Hazard, *The European mind: 1680–1715*, tr. J. Lewis May (Harmondsworth, Middlesex: Penguin, 1973); and, of course, Voltaire, 'Treizième lettre', in *Lettres philosophiques*, ed. F. A. Taylor (Oxford: Basil Blackwell, 1976), 39–45.

[14] Barbara Shapiro, *Probability and certainty in 17th century England* (Princeton: Princeton University Press, 1983); Douglas Patey, *Probability and literary form: philosophic theory and literary practice in the Augustan age* (Cambridge: Cambridge University Press, 1984), 27–35.

because the *Essay* was so influential in the Enlightenment, but also because it is a survey of the way in which the reconceptualization of assent was taking place in these other fields. Most important of all, the new account of assent forms part of the juridical practice of governing, and it contains its own mechanism of dissemination, as I will presently show.

The theories under attack in the *Essay* are teleological, dispositional or participant accounts of assent. They hold that there are either innate ideas (knowledge) or innate dispositions that predispose us to assent to the true or the good and dissent from the false or evil; these are standardly in propositional form. These inclinations may require sensation or even ratiocination to activate them, but they are independent of and prior to either. Almost all the immediate critics of Locke's attack on the theory of innate ideas reassert it in one form or another, with John Norris, the Malebranchean occasionalist, excepted. Innumerable examples could be cited from religious and philosophical literature prior to the publication of the *Essay*, as John Yolton has shown.[15]

In many respects the best presentation of the dispositional theory is the *Treatise concerning eternal and immutable morality* by Ralph Cudworth, the leading Cambridge Platonist. It was written prior to the *Essay* and published posthumously in 1739. It is a refutation of a *tabula rasa* theory of the mind. Cudworth's target is of course the nondispositionalists prior to Locke: Thomas Hobbes, Walter Charleton, Nathaniel Culverwel, Samuel Parker, and, primarily, Pierre Gassendi, who had launched a famous assault on the dispositional theory of Lord Herbert of Cherbury.[16] However, let me cite Henry Lee, because his response to the *Essay*, *Anti-scepticism*, is one of the best guides to precisely what the blank tablet hypothesis displaced. Published in 1702, it is a detailed commentary on and refutation of the *Essay*. He writes:[17]

---

[15] John Yolton, *John Locke and the way of ideas* (Oxford: Oxford University Press, 1956). John Norris's book is *Cursory reflections upon a book call'd An essay concerning human understanding* (1690).

[16] Thomas Hobbes, *Leviathan* (1651), chs 1–6; Walter Charleton, *Physiologia Epicuro-Gassendo-Charletonia, or a fabrick of science natural, upon the hypothesis of atoms* (1654), bk 3, ch. 15; Nathaniel Culverwel, *Of the light of nature*, ed. John Brown (Edinburgh, 1857), ch. 11, 121–41; Samuel Parker, *A free and impartial censure of the Platonick philosophy* (1666); Pierre Gassendi, *Syntagma philosophicum*, in *Opera Omnia* (1658), I, 90–3; Edward Lord Herbert of Cherbury, *De Veritate*, tr. M. H. Carre (Bristol, 1937). For the English non-dispositionalists, see Yolton, *John Locke and the way of ideas*, 30–48. For Gassendi's response to Lord Herbert see Popkin, *The history of scepticism*, 151–9. [17] Henry Lee, *Anti-scepticism* (1702), 5.

the *Soul* of man is so framed by the Author of Nature, as not to be equally
disposed to all sorts of perceptions, to embrace all propositions with an
indifferency, to judge them true or false; but *antecedently* to all the Effects of
Custom, Experience, Education or any other *Contingent* Causes, it is *limited* to
perceive by certain external Motions or Impressions, is necessarily *inclined* to
believe some Propositions *true*, others *false*; some actions *good*, others *evil*: and
so is not altogether like a *rasa tabula*, on which you may set any impression
indifferently . . . Because it's presupposed with such inclinations and
dispositions . . .

The innate knowledge or disposition provides the foundation for
knowledge and especially for moral knowledge. A person assents to a
proposition *because* he or she is naturally inclined towards truth and
goodness, just as a stone naturally tends to its natural home, the earth.
As in all forms of teleological explanations, the action, assent, is
explained by its natural tendency to a certain result or end, true
belief. Leibniz' commentary provides good examples of teleological
explanations.[18]

There were two general types of teleological theories of assent. The
individualist and politically subversive one was put forward by
Puritans and radicals, especially during the English Civil War period.
Here, the natural conscience is a dispositional faculty with which one
judges the moral goodness or evil of one's actions. Yet conflicting
moral and religious beliefs are conscientiously held. Therefore, how
does one distinguish an erring conscience from a true one? The radical
Puritan's answer is that those with a regenerate conscience do not err
because the grace or spirit of god moves their assent from within; and
secondly, they know that they are regenerate or elect by virtue of an
inner assurance or grace. The conscience is thus sovereign and cannot
be subordinated to any authority or authoritative external criteria.
As Catholic opponents would say, these radical Protestants had set up
their conscience as a new pope. This radical puritanism is similar in
kind to the equally subversive animistic, hermetic, and pantheistic
political and scientific movements that justified belief by reference to
an inner force, and rejected accepted criteria. These movements were
all called 'enthusiastic' because they appealed in different ways to a
god within. They were subversive because they undermined appeals

[18] G. W. Leibniz, *New essays on human understanding*, tr. Peter Remnant and Jonathan Bennett
(Cambridge: Cambridge University Press, 1981), 79, 80, 84, 86.

to accepted authority, advanced a radical kind of subjectivity, and legitimated the right of the people to speak and act for themselves.[19]

'Enthusiasm' was used in a pejorative sense, and a massive intellectual assault was waged on all its forms, especially after 1660. Locke attacked this radical theory as early as 1660, and he added a chapter on enthusiasm to the fourth edition of the *Essay*. It is based on arguments he had worked on over a twenty-five-year period. The motivation for publication may have been the revival of pantheistic radicalism around John Toland and Locke's desire to disassociate his philosophy from it.[20] As he describes it, 'Firmness of persuasion is made the cause of believing, and confidence of being in the right, is made an argument for truth.'[21] He argues that it is a purely subjective and so non-verifiable ground of assent. As always, Locke's concern is that enthusiasm could be used to justify persecution of religious dissent.[22] This separates Locke from the mainstream Anglican and latitudinarian refutations of enthusiasm, which were used to justify

[19] The classic treatment of these radicals is Christopher Hill, *The world turned upside down* (Harmondsworth, Middlesex: Penguin, 1972). For the animistic scientific movement, see M. C. and J. R. Jacob, 'The Anglican origins of modern science: the metaphysical foundations of the whig constitution', *Isis*, 71 (1980), 251–67; David Kubrin, 'Newton's inside out: magic, class struggle and the rise of mechanism in the west', in Harry Woolf, ed., *The Analytic spirit* (Cornell: Cornell University Press, 1981), 96–122; and Carolyn Merchant, *The death of nature: women, ecology and the scientific revolution* (San Francisco: Harper and Row, 1981). For the establishment attack on the radical dispositionalists as 'enthusiastic', see Morris Berman, *The reenchantment of the world* (New York: Bantam, 1981), ch. 1–2; M. Heyd, 'The reaction to enthusiasm in the seventeenth century', *Journal of Modern History*, 53 (1981), 258–80; Michael Spiller, 'Concerning natural and experimental philosophie', in *Meric Casaubon and the Royal Society* (The Hague: Martinus Nijhoff, 1980); Frederic Burnham, 'The More–Vaughan controversy: the revolt against philosophical enthusiasm', *Journal of the History of Ideas*, 35 (1974), 33–49; and Brian Easlea, *Witch-hunting, magic and the new philosophy 1450–1750* (New Jersey: Humanities Press, 1980), 89–154. For the radical puritan doctrine of the conscience, see William Perkins, *A discourse of conscience*, in *William Perkins: 1558–1602, English puritanist*, ed. T. F. Merrill (1966), 31–2, 61; William Ames, *Conscience with the power and case thereof* (London, 1639), bk 11, 10.
[20] For Locke and Toland, see below, part III.
[21] *Essays*, 4.19.12. For Locke's early work on enthusiasm see 'On enthusiasme' (1682), Bodleian, MS. Locke f. 6, fo. 205, in R. I. Aaron and J. Gibb, *An early draft of Locke's Essay* (Oxford: Clarendon Press, 1936), 119–21. Locke's earliest political writings, the two Latin and English manuscripts in support of monarchical absolutism (1660–1), are in response to a radical dispositional defence of toleration on the basis of the sovereignty of natural conscience by Edward Bagshawe in *An essay in defence of the Good Old Cause* (1660). See John Locke, *Two tracts on government*, ed. Philip Abrams (Cambridge: Cambridge University Press, 1968). I have discussed this in my introduction to John Locke, *A letter concerning toleration* (Indianapolis: Hackett Publishing Company, 1983). See also John Colman, *John Locke's moral philosophy* (Edinburgh: Edinburgh University Press, 1983), 9–29; and Edmund Leites, 'Conscience, casuistry and moral decision: some historical perspectives', *Journal of Chinese philosophy*, 2 (1974), 41–58.   [22] *Essay* 4.19.12.

persecution of the enthusiasts (nonconformists).[23] This campaign was so successful that the charge of enthusiasm could be used to discredit any appeal to a 'subjective' criterion of assent. Even Descartes' 'clear and distinct ideas' and Leibniz' teleology were branded as enthusiastic.[24]

If this type of theory, that god or immanent gods govern assent directly, was too subversive, the second type of theory was too submissive. In this traditional or 'Aristotelian' view, the conflicting yet firmly held beliefs that lunged Europe into war were caused by bad customs and education.[25] Although assent naturally tends to true beliefs, this tendency can be deflected and overridden by bad mental habits acquired by custom or education. Therefore, an authority is required to guide the pupils to the truth and to educate them so their innate dispositions develop into good operative mental habits.[26]

The innate and dispositional theories underpinning established religion and morality are the sole target in the early *Draft B* of the *Essay*. By the time of the *Essay* the same strategy is used to refute any form of innateism, including the Aristotelian–scholastic sciences of the universities.[27] The two standard arguments of universal assent and ready assent are shown to be false – and, even if they are true, they do not prove innateness.[28] Locke's main argument, however, is

---

[23] I therefore demur at the tendency to assimilate Locke's political and religious thought and action to that of the latitudinarians. See Neil Wood, *The politics of Locke's philosophy* (Berkeley: University of California Press, 1983). Locke and Shaftesbury were revolutionary defenders of toleration of nonconformity, not latitudinarians. See my introduction to *A letter concerning toleration* and the literature referred to there.

[24] See Steven Shapin, 'Of gods and kings: natural philosophy and politics in the Leibniz–Clark disputes', *Isis*, 72 (1981), 187–215; Easlea, *Witchunting*, 158–64.

[25] Cf. John Locke, *Two tracts*, 160.

[26] This is reasserted by Locke's major critics: Henry Lee, *Anti-scepticism*, 4–12; Edward Stillingfleet, *Discourse in Vindication of the Doctrine of the Trinity . . .* (1696, 1697 [2nd edition]), ch. 10; William Sherlock, 'A digression concerning connate ideas or inbred knowledge', in *A discourse concerning the happiness of the good man and the punishment of the wicked in the next world* (1704), 124–65; Thomas Burnet, *Remarks upon an essay Concerning human understanding* (1697). (Two further sets of *Remarks* followed in 1697 and 1699).

[27] *Essay* 1.2, 4.7.

[28] *Essay* 1.2. I demur at Yolton's suggestion that Locke does not attack innate dispositions but only innate ideas (*John Locke*, 53). It is clear from *Essay* 1.2.5–10, 22 that Locke explicitly attacks the dispositional view as well. Yolton seems to rely on Locke's comment on Thomas Burnet's *Third remarks upon an Essay concerning human understanding* (1699): 'I think noe body but this Author who ever read my book could doubt that I spoke only of innate ideas for my subject was the understanding and not of innate power . . .' (Noah Porter, 'Marginalia Locke-a-na', *New England and Yale Review* 7 (1887), 33–49, 45. It is clear from the context (pp. 38, 44) that this 'faculty' or 'power' is just the non-dispositional power of judgment Locke uses throughout the *Essay* and his other writings. Compare Colman, *John Locke's moral philosophy*, 51.

that the appeal to custom and education to explain why some fail to assent to propositions others take to be innate puts the authority in the dispositional theory in the same position as the individual in the enthusiast theory. That is, the proponent of a certain set of first principles will have no criteria to appeal to except their innateness, yet this is what is in question.[29]

Locke's strategy for undermining this 'established opinion' and so 'pulling up the old foundations of knowledge and certainty' is the following.[30] He denies that there is a distinction between assent based on innate principles and dispositions and assent based on custom and education. Principles or ideas and dispositions that are said to be innate are, in fact, the *product* of custom and education. By being called 'innate' or 'divine' and 'first principles' they are insulated from examination and taken on 'trust' or on 'authority'.[31] This concept of 'trust' is of course the central target of the *Essay*.[32] Children are taught them 'as soon as they have any apprehension', and their teachers 'never suffer those propositions to be otherwise mentioned, but as the Basis and Foundation, on which they build their Religion or Manners'. In this way they come to be taken for granted and to 'have the reputation of unquestionable, self-evident and innate Truth'.[33] They become riveted in the understanding.[34] Not only principles and dispositions to believe become entrenched in this way, but also a whole 'hypothesis' such as the Aristotelian–scholastic one.[35] The innateist or dispositional hypothesis itself became established by custom and education, and was then used to justify taking certain principles on trust, according to Locke.[36]

Therefore, custom, education, and fashion in fact govern assent. This is just the surface of Locke's analysis of governing assent. The actual techniques of education and custom will be discussed below since they are employed in the new practice of governing. The investigation of the factors that do govern assent, as opposed to those

---

[29] *Essay* 1.3.20. *Draft B*, 7, pp. 57–8. Compare Locke's identification of dispositionalism with enthusiasm in his marginal comments on Burnet's *Third remarks* (Porter, 38). See also Colman, *John Locke's moral philosophy*, 57; and R. S. Woolhouse, *Locke* (Minneapolis: University of Minnesota Press, 1983), 16–26.   [30] *Essay* 1.2.1, 1.4.23.

[31] *Draft B*, 8–10, pp. 58–65; *Essay* 1.3.20–7, 4.7.11, 4.20.18.

[32] *Essay*, Epistle, p. 7, 1.3.24, 27, 1.4.23, 4.20.17.   [33] *Essay* 1.3.22.

[34] John Locke, *Draft A of Locke's Essay concerning human understanding*, ed. Peter Nidditch (Sheffield: University of Sheffield, 1980), 42, pp. 148–9, *Essay* 4.20.9.

[35] *Draft A*, 42, pp. 150–1, *Essay* 4.20.11.

[36] *Draft B*, 10, pp. 61–5, *Essay* 1.3.26, 1.4.24, 1.2.1, 4.7.11.

that ought to, was carried out by Locke throughout his lifetime. This was part of a widespread analysis of *de facto* grounds of assent that accompanied the legitimation crisis in Europe.

Thus, the dispositional 'hypothesis' is an established form of knowledge and it, in turn, supports authorities or elites in religion, science, and politics. This political perspective is, as Leibniz comments, the major argument against dispositionalism and it is a constant theme in Locke's writings.[37] The classical summary is at 1.4.24:[38]

And it was of no small advantage to those who affected to be Masters and Teachers, to make this the Principle of *Principles*, That Principles must not be questioned: For having once established this Tenet, That there are innate Principles, it put their Followers upon a necessity of receiving some Doctrines as such; which was to take them off from the use of their own Reason and Judgement, and put them upon believing and taking them upon Trust, without further examination: in which posture of blind Credulity, they might be more easily governed by, and made useful to some sort of men, who had the skill and office to principle and guide them. Nor is it a small power it gives one man over another, to have the Authority to be the Dictator of Principles, and Teacher of unquestionable Truths; and to make a Man swallow that for an innate Principle, which may serve to his purpose, who teacheth them.

Both the 'natural conscience' and the innate dispositions are hence exposed as dispositions acquired by education and the workings of custom.

As early as 1660 Locke began to analyse how religious elites, especially Anglicans and Catholics, used the innateist approach to gain power, dominate the laity, and justify the suppression of dissent by persecution.[39] The 100 years of war were caused by religious and political elites using allegedly dispositional knowledge to justify the inculcation of conflicting principles in their followers, including the duty to take up arms to defend and spread the true faith.[40] As Locke summarizes:[41]

And he that shall deny this to be the method, wherein most men proceed to the assurance they have, of the truth and evidence of their principles, will, perhaps, find it a hard matter any other way to account for the contrary

---

[37] Leibniz, *New essays*, 74, 107.   [38] Compare *Draft B*, 13, pp. 72–3.
[39] *Two tracts*, 118–19, 158–61, 210; and Tully's introduction, *A letter concerning toleration*, 1–16.
[40] *Two tracts*, 158–61; *A letter concerning toleration*, 42–3.
[41] *Essay* 1.3.27, *Draft B*, 10, p. 64.

tenets, which are firmly believed, confidently asserted, and which great numbers are ready at any time to seal with their blood.

The genealogy of belief formation, summarized at 1.3.22–6, therefore begins to explain the central problem of the Reformation period: the situation of contradictory beliefs held with confidence and a readiness to go to war to defend them. Developing such a comprehensive explanation is one of the major aims Locke set himself in the *Essay*.[42]

The intellectual weapon Locke advances to destroy these established bodies of knowledge and power in religion, politics, and science is 'suspension and examination'; that is, to suspend the judgement and examine the grounds for and against any proposition before assenting to it. This is what the dispositional theory blocks, and so it serves as a 'false foundation' to legitimate unquestioning acceptance of authority.[43] 'Suspension and examination' *versus* 'trust and authority' is the intellectual demand of the Reformation, cutting across religious lines.[44] The *Essay* opens with this formula, but it receives its most famous statement in what is one of the most reworked sections of book 1: 'The great difference that is to be found in the Notions of Mankind is from the different use they put their faculties to, whilst some (and those the most) taking things upon trust, misemploy their power of assent, by lazily enslaving their minds, to the Dictates and Dominion of others, in Doctrines, which it is their duty carefully to examine; and not blindly, with an implicit faith, to swallow.'[45]

The early critics of the *Essay* charged that it undermined religion and morality. These critics were Anglicans, and what they meant was that it undermined established religion.[46] As we have seen, this is true,

---

[42] *Essay* 1.1.2, *Draft B*, 2, p. 38. A similar genealogy is developed in *Draft A* in the discussion of assent (42, pp. 148–57), as I noted above. This forms the basis of *Essay* 4.20.7–18 (see below). It is not reproduced in *Draft B*, but it is reworked in 'Study', Bodleian, MS. Locke f. 2, fos 87–90, 91–3, 95–6, 97–100, 100–1, 114–17, 118–22, 124–40 (beginning on 26 March 1677). Reprinted in Peter King, *The life and letters of John Locke* (2 vols., London: H. Colburn and R. Bentley, 1830), vol. I, 171–203, 188–92. For a similar analysis of Locke's radical attack on innate ideas see John Biddle, 'Locke's critique of innate principles and Toland's deism', *Journal of the History of Ideas* 37, 3 (July–September 1976), 411–22.

[43] *Essay*, Epistle, 10.

[44] For a recent and perceptive discussion of this constitutive intellectual contest of the Reformation see Walter Rex, *Essays on Pierre Bayle and religious controversy* (The Hague: Martinus Nijhoff, 1965), especially 9–42.

[45] *Essay* 1.4.22. For Locke's drafts of this famous sentence, see R. I. Aaron, *John Locke* (Oxford: Clarendon Press, 1972 [1937]), 59.

[46] For the response to the *Essay*, see H. O. Christophersen, *A bibliographical introduction to the study of John Locke* (Oslo, 1930) and Kenneth MacLean, *John Locke and the literature of the eighteenth century* (New York: Russell and Russell, 1962); and Yolton, *John Locke*.

and it was in fact Locke's intention. Defenders of the *Essay* were often dissenters or tolerant Anglicans like Samuel Bold.[47] However, the critics based their charge on a much more fundamental claim. In sweeping aside the old foundations, Locke had swept aside all foundations. If the mind were not disposed in some way to the truth or the good, then it must be indifferent, and so all our knowledge is the product of custom and education. This argument of *indifferency*, and hence of relativism, is advanced by almost all of Locke's critics. As Henry Lee states it:[48] 'The true state of the question seems to me this, whether the minds of men are so framed, as to be just like white paper, equally capable of any letters or characters, indifferently disposed to believe any proposition true or false, any actions good or bad?' Locke is our best guide to the transition to new foundations of knowledge in the seventeenth century because he accepts this radical indifferency, 'for white paper receives any character', and attempts to construct a new way to govern assent rationally.[49]

Having swept away the epistemological foundations of the *ancien régime*, in both its radical and conservative variants, Locke reconstructs belief on the blank and indifferent *tabula rasa* that remains. He considers two solutions. The first is advanced by the latitudinarians and the experimental scientists, and is accepted in a broad range of disciplines by the late seventeenth century, as Henry van Leeuwen and Barbara Shapiro have shown. Locke ultimately rejects it and, as we shall see, develops a different explanation of how assent is governed.

The first solution is that if belief is not governed by innate tendencies, because there are no such occult forms *in re*, then assent is, or at least ought to be, governed by and proportional to the grounds that can be adduced in its support after a thorough examination. The 'force of the better argument' and 'the weight of the evidence' are the external criteria, accessible in theory to all, on which rational belief is

---

[47] Samuel Bold, *Some considerations on the principle objections and arguments which have been published against Mr Locke's Essay* (1699).

[48] Henry Lee, *Anti-scepticism*, 12. Compare William Sherlock, *A discourse*, 161–2, where he accuses Locke of promoting atheism: 'for if all the knowledge we have of God, and of Good and Evil, be made by ourselves, atheists will easily conclude that is only the effect of education and superstitious fears; and satisfy themselves that they can make other notions, more for the ease and security of life'. James Lowde, *A discourse concerning the nature of man* (1694), 54–5. Most of the criticisms brought against Locke had already been made by Cudworth, and the non-dispositional theory placed in the context of the revival of Greek atomism (*A treatise*, bk 4, 127–35, 214–22, 286–7).   [49] *Essay* 1.3.22.

grounded and by which it is governed. As Locke summarizes this 'mechanical' concept of rationality:[50]

the mind if it will proceed rationally, ought to examine all the grounds of probability, and see how they make more or less, for or against any probable proposition, before it assents to or dissents from it, and upon due balancing the whole, reject, or receive it, with a more or less firm assent, proportionably to the preponderancy of the greater grounds of probability on one side or the other.

Two changes have taken place here relative to the dispositional view. First, the faculty of judgement, which makes the probability calculations, has been cleansed of any telic properties. It is a purely non-dispositional power of judging that is indifferent to the object of judgement; void of intrinsic causal efficacy.[51] It is, as Leibniz notes, the revival of the nominalist concept of a faculty: a power which could not in itself have a necessary causal tendency, as the Aristotelian–scholastic had posited, because this would bind god's omnipotence.[52] Locke's whole attack on 'faculties' is a rejection of the Aristotelian–scholastic concept of a teleological faculty and the reworking of a nominalist concept of faculty as an indifferent capacity.

The second change is that almost all our beliefs are viewed as probable as opposed to certain.[53] A few propositions remain that are certain, and here a person gives full and ready assent. However, the 'ready assent', and so the certainty, is based on either the comparison of the subject and predicate of a proposition, as in *A* is *A* (intuition), or in the comparison of one proposition with another, as in strict entailment (demonstration). This small class of propositions comprises knowledge in the proper sense of the word. Once the component ideas are understood and the comparison is made, assent is ready, certain, and involuntary.[54] However, the vast majority of reasoning is concerned not with certain knowledge but with 'belief' or

---

[50] *Essay* 4.16.5.

[51] Locke possessed this concept of judgment as early as 1660, when he described the conscience as nothing but the power to judge the good or evil of one's actions. See *Two tracts*, 138, *Essay* 1.3.8, 4.14.4; Porter, 'Marginalia Locke-a-na', 35, 38. Compare Colman, *John Locke's moral philosophy*, 12–26; and Lee, *Anti-scepticism*, 5.

[52] Leibniz, *New essays*, 174 (comment on 2.21.6).

[53] Compare Margaret Osler, 'John Locke and the changing ideal of scientific knowledge', *Journal of the History of Ideas* 31 (1970), 1–16.

[54] *Essay* 1.2.18, 4.2.1–9, 4.7.2, 4.7.10. Note that certainty depends on comparison, not on 'self-evidence' or 'clear and distinct' ideas; Locke thus tries to avoid a subjective, Cartesian criterion.

'opinion'; that is, 'knowledge' (as I will continue to use the term in this wider sense) that is only probable.[55] Here, assent cannot be based on a comparison of the ideas themselves, but rather 'something extraneous to the thing I believe', and the grounds cannot induce certainty, but only degrees of assurance.[56]

The criteria of probable belief, or 'grounds of probability', are two fold. The first is conformity with what we already know, in Locke's strong sense, have observed, or have experienced. The second is reliable on the 'testimony of others, vouching their observation and experience'. The criteria in accordance with which their testimony is to be judged are the following:[57]

---

[55] *Essay* 1.1.5, 4.14–15.

[56] *Essay* 4.15.4. This and the following sections of book 4 of the *Essay* that I refer to here follow fairly faithfully *Draft A*, 32–42. The main sources of Locke's ideas of probable assent are almost certainly Robert Boyle and Pierre Gassendi. Locke's account of probability in *Draft A* is similar to Gassendi's account of criteria of assent in part 1 of *Syntagma philosophicum* (1658). Locke apparently did not own *Syntagma*, but he quoted from it, and he did own Thomas Stanley, *The history of philosophy* (4 vols., 1655–62), vol. III of which contains *Syntagma*. (See Richard Kroll, 'The question of Locke's relation to Gassendi', *Journal of the History of Ideas* 45, 3 (July–September 1984), 339–61. It is also possible and indeed highly probable that Locke was familiar with the work on probable assent in England when he wrote *Draft A* (1670): William Chillingworth, *The religion of protestants* (1633); John Tillotson, *Rule of faith* (1666); Joseph Glanvill, *The vanity of dogmatizing* (1661), and *Scepsis scientifica* (London, 1665).

John Wilkins, *Of the principles and duties of natural religion* (1675) is too late for *Draft A* yet very similar on assent. Richard Burthogge, *Organnum vetus & novum or a discourse of reason and truth* (1678), is probably the closest to Locke. He went on to defend Locke in *An essay upon reason and the nature of spirit* (1694). Boyle's main works on probable assent were published after 1670: *Some considerations about the reconcileableness of reason and religion* (1675); *A discourse of things above reason* (1677). However, as early as 1667 Locke noted Boyle's praise of Gassendi (Bodleian, MS. Locke f. 14) (see E. A. Driscoll, 'The influence of Gassendi on Locke's hedonism', *International philosophical quarterly* 12 (1972), 87–110, 87–9). These authors are discussed by van Leeuwen, *The problem of certainty*, and Shapiro, *Probability and certainty*, supra n. 13, 14. Richard Tuck also discusses a group of writers who introduced probability into political writing in England in the 1640s (*Natural rights theories* [Cambridge: Cambridge University Press, 1979], 101–18). Both Leibniz and Lee suggest that Locke's views on assent and other issues were influenced by Gassendi. See further below, and Margaret Osler, 'Providence and divine will in Gassendi's views on scientific knowledge', *Journal of the history of ideas* 44, 4 (October–December 1983), 549–60, 560; Gabriel Bonno, 'Les Relations intellectuelles de Locke avec la France', *University of California publications in modern philosophy* 38 (1955), 37–264, 237–42.

Other possible sources of Locke's concept of probability are: Cicero, *Academica* II. 20–48 (Cicero's defence of Carneades' constructive scepticism); Sextus Empiricus, *Outlines of Pyrrhonism*, first published in early modern Europe in 1562 and available to Locke in Stanley, *History of philosophy*; and [Pierre Nicole and Antoine Arnault,] *La Logique ou l'art de Penser* (Paris, 1662), bk 4, chs. 13–16. For the early modern influence of *Academica*, see Charles Schmitt, *Cicero scepticus* (The Hague: Martinus Nijhoff, 1972); for Empiricus, see Popkin, *The History of scepticism*.   [57] *Essay* 4.15.4.

1. The number. 2. The Integrity. 3. The Skill of the Witnesses. 4. The Design of the author, where it is a Testimony out of a Book cited. 5. The consistency of the parts, and the circumstances of the relation. 6. Contrary testimony.

A proposition is judged relative to these criteria and the proportional degree of assent given to it, 'from full assurance and confidence, quite down to conjecture, doubt and distrust'.[58]

The concept of probability that is introduced here dominates the *Essay*. The *Essay* in fact is a celebration that this form of knowledge 'is sufficient to govern all our concernments'.[59] The type of probability is epistemological: judging reasonable degrees of belief relative to the evidence or grounds. It is not aleatory probability concerned with statistical regularities of natural or human phenomena. The epistemological concept was used in the early modern period from the thirteenth century onwards in an increasing number of disciplines. The use of both types of probability increased in the first part of the seventeenth century and, in addition, Blaise Pascal formulated a theory of probability.[60] From a dispersion of early modern sources probabilistic reasoning came to predominate in a wide range of disciplines by the late seventeenth century, gradually changing them into their modern forms. However, one context that must be considered central is the rule of faith controversy. In the thousands of pamphlets and books that constitute this debate, these criteria are partly formed and employed to justify rational religious belief. Specifically, a consensus gradually developed in England around the assumption that faith is belief, not knowledge, and that these criteria make it reasonable to believe that Revelation is the word of god, based on the testimony of witnesses and the evidence of miracles.[61]

Secondly, these criteria undercut any appeal to authority in the old sense of the word, as Locke immediately points out.[62] In Anglican and

---

[58] *Essay* 4.15.2.

[59] *Essay* 1.1.5, not in *Draft B*. This signals that a demonstrable ethic is not a necessary part of his moral theory.

[60] Ian Hacking, *The emergence of probability* (Cambridge: Cambridge University Press, 1984 [1975]). For a corrective to Hacking's hypothesis that the emergence of the *concept* of probability marked an abrupt discontinuity see below, concerning the role of voluntarism in widening the scope of probability, and Patey, *Probability and literary form*, 266–73.

[61] *Essay* 4.18–19 summarizes the consensus. Compare 'Faith and Reason', Bodleian, MS. Locke f. 1, fos 412–32, in W. von Leyden, ed. *John Locke: essays on the laws of nature* (Oxford: Clarendon Press, 1954), pp. 274–81. The important studies by Popkin, van Leeuwen, and Shapiro have barely scratched the surface of this controversy (*supra* n. 7, 13, 14).

[62] *Essay* 4.15.6.

Catholic casuistry, a belief is probable because it is not demonstrable, and so religious authorities advance different and sometimes contradictory opinions about it. A contemporary authority then weighs the various authoritative opinions and applies them to particular cases (as in, for example, the Jesuit doctrine of probabilism).[63] But this whole schema came under severe strain with the sceptical crisis, as can be seen in the remarkably sceptical and unsure *Ductor Dubitantium or the rule of conscience* by Jeremy Taylor.[64] The new criteria mitigated the threat of extreme scepticism, as Popkin has argued. It also forced the enthusiast to regulate his assent by these criteria and so relinquish his certainty and admit 'reasonable doubt'. But the price for this was that any putative claim to authority could itself be examined and scrutinized by these criteria. The leading latitudinarians were willing to pay this price, however, because it toppled the basis of certainty in religious belief that had led to confrontation and placed all the different sects in the realm of opinion and 'latitude'. They assumed that it would thus be unreasonable not to conform to a simplified and more liberal Anglicanism.[65] Locke, although he accepted and refined these criteria from the predominantly latitudinarian context, as van Leeuwen has shown, drew exactly the opposite conclusion. Precisely because certainty in religious belief is not possible on these criteria, it would be unreasonable to force dissenters to conform.[66]

The rule of faith controversy is not, however, foundational for the development of this kind of reasoning. The controversy is carried on in terms drawn from legal reasoning and practices of early modern Europe. The conscience is conceptualized as an 'inner tribunal', a 'court of appeal', and so on, and the criteria are drawn from juridical discourses and practices. In addition, when the experimental scientists of the Royal Society employ these criteria, reference is often made to trial and judicial reasoning. The central concepts of this probable form of reasoning – 'evidence', 'proof', 'probability', and

---

[63] See Patey, *Probability and literary form*, 58–61; and C. W. Slights, *The casuistical tradition* (Princeton: Princeton University Press, 1981); Hacking, *The emergence of probability*, 18–30.

[64] Jeremy Taylor, *Ductor dubitantium or The rule of conscience*, in *The whole works of Jeremy Taylor* (10 vols., London, 1751 [1970 reprint]), ix–x. For the importance of Taylor see H. Baker, *The wars of truth: studies in the decay of Christian humanism* (1952); Robert Hoopes, 'Voluntarism in Jeremy Taylor and the Platonic tradition', *The Huntington Library Quarterly*, 13 (1950) 341–54; Leites, 'Conscience, casuistry and moral decision', *supra* n. 21.

[65] For a similar argument see Heyd, 'The reaction to enthusiasm', *supra* n. 19.

[66] *Essay* 4.16.4. This sceptical justification of toleration is the main theme of *The third letter concerning toleration*, thus separating Locke decisively from the latitudinarians.

'testimony' – were gradually constructed in the context of the spread of the inquisitorial methods of justice throughout Europe from the condemnation of the trial by battle of 1215 to the great codification in the French ordinance of 1670.[67] In England, where the accusatory system lived on after 1215 in the jury trial, concepts of evidence, testimony, and probability developed in the non-jury, inquisitorial institutions of the law. In the 1670s there was an important and unsuccessful attempt to impose these criteria on the jury in the Bushel case.[68] This perhaps marks the transition of the old idea of the jury as partial witnesses, drawn from the neighbourhood of the crime, to the modern, quasi-inquisitorial view of the jury as impartial judges of the evidence. The most systematic treatment of these criteria prior to Locke's *Essay* in England is the work of Sir Matthew Hale, the leading legal theorist of the Restoration. The first modern theory of evidence is written by a lawyer, Baron Geoffrey Gilbert (1674–1726), and is based on the criteria laid out in the *Essay*.[69] Therefore, although this form of reasoning begins to be applied in all fields of knowledge, and is universalized by Locke in England and Bayle on the continent, its concepts are drawn from the reasoning and practices of the inquisitorial institutions of early modern Europe.[70] It is not surprising that Richard Burthogge calls Locke's probable reasoning 'judicial assent' and Locke refers to it as *Argumentum ad judicium*.[71]

Locke's first analysis of probable reasoning is that assent is necessarily governed by the grounds of probability that are available and in accordance with which judgement is made. This made belief

---

[67] A. Esmein, *A history of continental criminal procedure with special reference to France* (Boston: Little, Brown, 1913), 183–288. For one aspect of the development of probability in a juridical context see John H. Langbein, *Torture and the law of proof* (Chicago: University of Chicago Press, 1977).

[68] This trial could hardly have been of more importance to Locke since the jury, against the entreaty of the judge, acquitted William Penn and William Mead of the charge of unlawful assembly under the anti-dissent Conventicle Act. The jury were imprisoned and fined but then acquitted by Chief Justice Vaughan. For the importance of this case, see J. B. Thayer, *A preliminary treatise on evidence at the common law* (Boston: Harvard University Press, 1898), 166–70.

[69] Geoffrey Gilbert, *The law of evidence* (1756). For Gilbert's importance and his relation to Locke, see Theodore Waldman, 'Origins of the legal doctrine of reasonable doubt', *Journal of the History of Ideas* 20, 3 (June–September 1959), 289–316.

[70] For Pierre Bayle in this context see Ed James, 'Pierre Bayle on belief and evidence', *French studies* 27 (1973), 395–404. In 1699 John Craig attempted to quantify Locke's criteria of probable assent: 'A calculation of the credibility of human testimony', *Philosophical transactions of the Royal Society* 21 (1699), 359–65.

[71] Burthogge *Organnum vetus*, 44; *Essay* 4.17.22.

involuntary, like knowledge and perception, and Locke used it in this way to justify toleration.[72] However, as he corrected himself in *Draft A*, belief must be in some sense voluntary, or ignorance and error would not be faults, and infidelity would not be a sin.[73] It is at this point that he introduced the power to suspend one's assent and examine the grounds for it. The concept, perhaps adapted by Locke from Gassendi, is the foundation of intellectual liberty or freedom of thought.[74] Once the examination is carried through, assent still necessarily closes with, and in proportion to, the available grounds of probability. It is, as he says, 'the nature of the understanding constantly to close with the more probable side': 'a man, who has weighed them, can scarce refuse his assent to the side on which the greater probability appears'.[75] This is so not because the judgement is partial or internally related to the truth. The judgement is impartial and external to it. Rather, it is the new mechanical properties, the 'weight' of the evidence, and the 'force' of the argument that cause assent. The manifest probabilities govern assent by acting as 'inducements' and 'motives'.[76]

There is an important Enlightenment ideal here: once our beliefs are carefully examined in the light of rational criteria we will come to agree. The old superstitions and authorities will give way to an age of reason. However, as a result of his analysis, Locke is forced to reject this hypothesis on four grounds. First, the great majority, because of their conditions of work, cannot examine the proofs of their beliefs. Secondly, often those who have the ability are not able to exercise it owing to political repression, as with the Hugenots. Thirdly, people may have the opportunity yet lack the will, usually out of laziness.[77]

The fourth and most important reason for wrong assent is that even when the probabilities 'are plainly laid before them', some people give their assent 'to the less probable opinion'.[78] This happens because they have the 'wrong measures of probability'. These are of four types: the first is taking an opinion as a first principle, as knowledge, and thus as a certain criterion for judging other beliefs. This is, of course, our old friend the innate principle, riveted in the understanding, and Locke repeats how custom and education

---

[71] John Locke, *An essay concerning toleration* (1667), Bodleian, MS. Locke c. 28, fos 21–32, fos 21–2.   [73] *Draft A*, 42, p. 156; *Essay* 4.20.16.
[74] See Kroll 'The question of Locke's relation', and Bonno, 'Les relations intellectuelles', p. 241–2, *supra* n. 56.   [75] *Essay* 4.20.15.   [76] *Essay* 4.15.4, 4.20.1.
[77] *Essay* 4.20.1–6.   [78] *Essay* 4.20.7.

establish it there.[79] The second wrong measure is a whole 'wrong hypothesis', again fixed in the understanding in the same way. Here Locke's target is the Aristotelian–scholastic professors, whose conceptual framework will allow a different role for grounds of probabilities.[80] The third wrong measure of probability is a 'prevailing passion'. For example, 'Let never so much Probability hang on one side of a covetous man's reasoning; and money on the other; and it is easie to foresee which will out-weigh.'[81] The fourth and most insidious wrong measure of probability is, not surprisingly, authority. By 'authority' Locke means the general phenomenon of the Reformation of yielding one's assent to the beliefs of one's political or religious group:[82] 'I mean, giving up our assent to the common received opinions either of our Friends, or Party; Neighbourhood or country. How many men have no other ground for their tenets than the supposed honesty, or learning, or number of those of the same profession.'

Locke realizes in the course of this analysis, which takes place over twenty-five years, that these arguments refute his initial claim that assent is mechanically governed by the external proofs. As John Passmore has argued, from his examples Locke is forced to realize that these four non-rational factors can govern assent even in the face of the manifest right measures of probability.[83] This is true in all four cases, although the prevailing passion case is the most obvious: 'Tell a man passionately in Love that he is jilted; bring a score of witnesses of the falsehood of his mistress, 'tis ten to one but three kind Words of hers, shall invalidate all their testimonies.'[84]

Therefore, the modern rationalist's belief that the weight of the evidence and the force of the better argument will govern our belief once we have critically examined is false. These are just what they appear to be: mechanical metaphors with no causal efficacy. Assent is governed by non-rational factors; by passion, custom, and education. Locke tries to save the rationalist assumption in this old part of the *Essay* from which I have been quoting by saying that people who give in to these wrong measures have not really examined their beliefs.[85]

---

[79] *Essay* 4.20.8–10.   [80] *Essay* 4.20.11.   [81] *Essay* 4.20.12.

[82] *Essay* 4.20.17. This is again identified as the cause of the division of the world into warring religious factions (4.15.6).

[83] John Passmore, 'Locke and the ethics of beliefs', Dawes Hicks Lecture, British Academy, 1978. I am indebted to this fine piece of analysis even though I disagree with parts of it.

[84] *Essay* 4.20.12.   [85] *Essay* 4.20.18.

But this is contradicted by his own examples. Richard Burthogge attempted to save the theory by arguing that the mind has a natural disposition not to assent to incongruous propositions in virtue of 'a certain sensible reluctance' or 'pain' annexed to it.[86]

Some time between 1671 and 1677 Locke abandoned the idea that assent would be automatically governed by the probabilities that we have seen him struggling with in the oldest part of the *Essay*. In a manuscript in 1677 he constructed his alternative: for the mind to be governed by the right measures of probabilities, it is necessary to develop an artificial inclination or passion to suspend, examine, and assent in accordance with the correct grounds. Men must be educated to 'covet truth', to develop a 'love' or passion for it.[87] This is then added to the fourth edition of the *Essay* in book 4, chapter 19, 'Of enthusiasm', contradicting the claims of the old chapter 20, which repeats the early *Draft A*. Assent is governed by passions, and thus he 'that would seriously set upon the search of Truth, ought in the first place to prepare his mind with a love of it'. The one mark of having acquired this passion for truth is 'not entertaining any proposition with greater assurance than the Proofs it is built upon will warrant'. Now, there is no mention that to do otherwise after examination might be 'impossible', as before. Rather, all the 'surplusage of assurance' beyond what the proofs warrant 'is owing to some other affection, and not to the love of truth'.[88]

Locke's project from this point on was to develop an educational practice that would form mental 'inclinations' or 'relish' to examine and assent in accordance with the probable proofs, i.e. with the new form of reasoning. This is laid out in the *Conduct of the understanding*, intended as a chapter of the *Essay* but published posthumously, and *Some thoughts concerning education*. This 'passion' or 'love' is in fact a kind

---

[86] Burthogge, *Organnum vetus*, 39–40.

[87] 'Study', March 1677, *supra* n. 42. Locke was in France from 1675 to 1679 hiding from arrest for his anonymous call for revolution, *A letter from a person of quality to his friend in the country* (1675). In this French period Locke changed his views on a number of central issues, including the determinants of assent, and then incorporated these into the second to fifth editions of the *Essay*. There is a second Gassendi connection here as a result of Locke meeting François Bernier, Gassendi's able disciple. See F. Bernier, *Abrégé de la philosophie de Gassendi* (1678). For this Relationship see Driscoll, 'The influence of Gassendi', and Bonno, 'Les relations intellectuelles', *supra* n. 56. In addition, Locke began to assimilate the ideas of Pierre Nicole and Pascal during this period (see below). Locke's pre-1675 analysis of the role of custom and education remains with the latitudinarian and Baconian context studied by van Leeuwen, *The problem of certainty*, and Wood, *The politics of Locke's philosophy*, *supra* n. 13, 23.   [88] *Essay* 4.19.1.

of mental habit, acquired by education and capable of withstanding and eroding the habits formed by the old education, which were falsely claimed to be innate.

GOVERNING ACTION

The attack on the old way of governing physical behaviour and the construction of a new governor are analogous to the treatment of mental behaviour. The dispositionists held not only that men are disposed to assent to the good and to dissent from the evil, but also that they are disposed to act towards good and away from evil. This behavioural disposition, as with its mental counterpart, could be deformed by bad customs and education, giving rise to vicious habits, and thus the same justification for practical guidance by teaching, penance, and discipline followed. Practical principles were thus distinguished from speculative principles by the fact that once they were assented to they tended to influence one's conduct. As Henry Lee stated it:[89]

> The true question is whether human nature be not so constituted by the provident author of it, as to be more inclined to the observance of some rules of action, for the promoting of their own and the happiness of all mankind, than to the breach of them. Or, in other words, whether all men or any one man is free from all sense of duty, and indifferent to all sorts of action.

Locke, like the anti-dispositionalists before him, argues that there are no innate practical principles and no innate dispositions to act in accordance with them; or, as he argues against Thomas Burnet, there is no disposition to assent to and tend towards good acts directly.[90] Again, this was taken to undermine religion and morality, and to encourage atheism.[91] The account of conduct put forward by Locke is a synthesis of two powerful traditions in the seventeenth century: voluntarism and hedonism. I call this synthesis penalism for reasons that will become obvious. Ralph Cudworth argued that these two traditions provided the intellectual framework for the revolution in thought and action he observed occurring around him.[92] Locke's role

---

[89] Lee, *Anti-scepticism*, 12. Compare: Leibniz, *New essays*, 90; Lowde, *A discourse concerning the nature of man*, preface; John Sergeant, *Solid philosophy asserted against the fancies of the ideists* (London, 1697), 224; Burnet, *Third remarks*, 4, 7–8.

[90] *Draft B*, 4–8; *Essay* 1.3; *Essays on laws of nature*, 137–45.

[91] Lee, *Anti-scepticism*, 17; Burnet, *Third remarks*, 4. Compare Yolton, *John Locke and the way of ideas*, 29, 39, 68.   [92] Cudworth, *A treatise*, bks 1–2, 1–75.

was to build on earlier syntheses, especially by Pierre Gassendi, Samuel Pufendorf, and Robert Boyle, to construct both an explanation of conduct and a theory for governing conduct.[93]

Voluntarism, or Ockhamism, and Intellectualism, or Thomism, are the two major theological traditions of the early modern period.[94] Intellectualism is a synthesis of Aristotelian and Christian thought. Its classic presentation is the *Summa theologiae* of Saint Thomas Aquinas. Aquinas emphasized god's reason and intellect over his will and omnipotence. God created the universe in accordance with reason and thus it is a rational and purposive order governed by the law of reason or eternal law. In addition, god created Aristotelian essences, causes, or forms which incline things towards their ends; that is, acting in harmony with eternal law. It is possible by reason to know the nature or essence of things and from these definitions to demonstrate the necessary relations among things, and so to understand the relational and purposive order of nature.

In 1277 a number of propositions drawn from Aristotle and positing necessary relations in nature were condemned in Paris and Oxford. A similar anti-Aristotelian move had been made a century earlier in Islamic theology. This condemnation can be taken as a rough starting-point for early modern voluntarism. It was formed initially in opposition to Intellectualism in the generation after Aquinas, by Duns Scotus and William of Ockham. The central tenet of voluntarism is that Revelation clearly states that the Christian god created the world out of nothing; it is a creation, not a product made in accordance with a plan. The emphasis is on god's omnipotence and his free will, not his reason. Therefore, to say that god created the

[93] For Gassendi's voluntarism, see Osler, 'Providence and divine will', *supra* n. 56, and for his hedonism L. T. Sarasohn, 'The ethical and political philosophy of Pierre Gassendi', *Journal of the History of Philosophy* 20, 3 (July 1982), 239–61. For Pufendorf's voluntarism see *The law of nature and nations* (1672), ed. J. Barbeyrac, tr. B. Kennett (London, 1729), 2.3.20, and Leibniz's response, in 'Opinion on the principles of Pufendorf' (1706), in *The political writings of Leibniz*, tr. Patrick Riley (Cambridge: Cambridge University Press, 1972), 64–77. For Boyle's voluntarism, see *A free inquiry into the vulgarly received notion of nature*, in Robert Boyle, *The works*, ed. T. Birch, intr. D. McKie (6 vols, Hildesheim, Georg Olms, Verlagsbuchhandlung, 1965), v, 158–255. See J. E. McGuire, 'Boyle's conception of nature', *Journal of the History of Ideas*, 33 (1972), 523–42; and Eugene M. Klaaren, *Religious origins of modern science* (Grand Rapids, Michigan, Eerdmans, 1977).

[94] For these two traditions see Francis Oakley, 'Medieval theories of natural law: William of Ockham and the voluntarist tradition', *Natural law forum*, 6 (1961), 65–84, and *The political thought of Pierre D'Ailly: the voluntarist tradition* (New Haven: Yale University Press, 1964); Steven Ozment, *The age of reform 1250–1550* (New Haven: Yale University Press, 1980), 22–73.

world in accordance with reason, either in the Platonic sense of an independently existing order, or in Aquinas' sense of god creating a rational order which then embodies necessity, is to limit god's omnipotence. The universe is a contingent creation of god's will. Any necessary laws or natures would equally limit god's omnipotence and free will. Thus, god acts directly on nature, which is made up solely of his creatures and the order he wills on them.

It follows that 'nature' is simply contingently related particulars and the 'laws of nature' are observed regularities which god could change any time. There can be no *a priori* knowledge of the necessary and immanent relations in nature, because these do not exist. Knowledge of 'nature' must be *a posteriori* observation of individuals and generalizations. These generalizations will be 'hypotheses' that describe the regularities and, because the relations among things are contingent, they will be probable, not certain. Thus, the voluntarist tends to be nominalist and empiricist. Knowledge of kinds will be of what Locke calls their 'nominal essences'; of observed correlations of properties.

A number of remarkable studies in the post-war period have shown that the revival of voluntarism during the Reformation provided the intellectual foundations for the development of modern science in the seventeenth century.[95] At the centre of this movement are Pierre Gassendi and Robert Boyle, two influences on Locke. In addition, the features of voluntarism that I have listed run through the writings of the members of the Royal Society, especially John Wilkins and Joseph Glanvill.[96] The Leibniz–Clarke correspondence is a classic confrontation between an intellectualist and Clarke's defence of Newton's voluntarism.[97] The practical consequence of the displacement of intellectualism by voluntarism is the elevation of use, as opposed to understanding, as the goal of science. 'Understanding' is

---

[95] Michael Foster, 'The Christian doctrine of creation and the rise of modern natural science', *Mind*, 43 (1934), 446–68 and 'Christian theology and modern science of nature II', *Mind*, 45 (1936), 1–28 are the original articles. Francis Oakley, 'Christian theology and the Newtonian science: the rise of the concept of the laws of nature', *Church History* 30, 4 (December 1961), 433–57; McGuire 'Boyle's conception of nature'; Osler, 'Providence and divine will', and 'Descartes and Charleton on nature and God', *Journal of the History of Ideas* (September 1979), 445–56; Klaaren *Religious origins*. The best full-length study is R. Hooykaas, *Religion and the rise of modern science* (Edinburgh: Scottish Academic Press, 1984 [1972]).

[96] Glanvill, *Scepsis scientifica*, 211–12; John Wilkins, *Of the principles and duties*, ch. 11.

[97] See McGuire, Boyle's conception of nature', and Shapin, 'Of gods and kings'.

no longer possible because there is no rational, *a priori* order to understand. Secondly, certain knowledge is beyond our reach because there are no necessary relations that our knowledge identifies. It follows that our knowledge is predominantly probable, in the two senses of *likely to occur*, as in natural regularities, and *likely to be true*, as in epistemic probability. Thus the spread of voluntarism is an important factor in the development of probability. Coupled with the seventeenth-century sense of mediocrity, due to loss of understanding and certainty, is an equally strong countervailing feeling of being able to use and control nature.[98] Although this is usually identified with Bacon, it should, I believe, be placed in this broader context. The sense of god's omnipotence and man's mediocrity can be seen clearly in the analysis of 'hypothesis' in the writings of Joseph Glanvill and Robert Boyle.[99] These writings also stress the goal of use and control, and Boyle's manuscript on hypothesis articulates the modern identification of explanation and prediction. Moreover, the theme of use *versus* understanding is addressed by Locke in a 1677 manuscript and then woven into the fabric of the *Essay*.[100]

The intellectualist tradition also provides the basis for the view that man has an innate disposition to assent and act in accordance with reason; that is, with natural law. Men have, as Aquinas classically stated it, 'a certain share in the divine reason itself from which they derive a natural inclination to such actions and ends as are fitting'.[101] It is this kind of theory that we have seen Locke's critics put forward. Some actions are intrinsically good or evil and man is naturally inclined towards the former and away from the latter. For the voluntarist, on the other hand, good and evil cannot be necessary

[98] See, especially, Merchant, *The death of nature*, 164–236, and Hooykaas, *Religion and the rise*, 67–75.

[99] Glanvill *Scepsis scientifica*, 211–12; Robert Boyle, in Richard Westfall, 'Some unpublished Boyle papers relating to scientific method', *Annals of Science*, 12 (1956), 63–73, 107–17. For the voluntarist conception of hypothesis see Robert Kargon, *Atomism in England from Hariot to Newton* (Oxford: Clarendon Press, 1966), 106–18. For Locke on hypothesis, see *Essay* 4.12.9–15; L. Laudan, 'The nature and sources of Locke's views on hypothesis', in *Locke on the human understanding*, ed. I. C. Tipton (Oxford: Oxford University Press, 1977), 149–62.

[100] 'How far and by what means the will works upon the understanding and assent', Bodleian, MS. Locke f. 2, fos 42–55, in R. I. Aaron and Gibb, *An early draft of Locke's Essay* (Oxford: Clarendon Press, 1936), 84–90. The justification for studying the understanding with which the *Essay* opens is that the understanding gives man 'Advantage and Dominion' over nature (1.1.1). He then moves on to attack the possibility of understanding and to advance use (1.1.5–6). Compare 4.12, 4.14.2 and Wood, *The politics of Locke's philosophy*, 94–121.

[101] Aquinas, *Summa theologiae*, 1a qu. 93, art. 1, *resp.*

properties of actions because this would limit god's freedom. Good and evil are rather external evaluations of actions relative to a law or standard. 'Evil is', as Ockham classically stated, 'nothing other than doing something opposite to that which one is obliged to do.'[102] What one is obliged to do is obey the will of god expressed in divine law. Obligation to divine law is based on its being god's will, not on its being rational, as with Aquinas. Secondly, because there is no necessary and rational moral order in which we participate by virtue of our reason, the way to know divine law is through Revelation, where god has revealed his will. God could even change the definition of good and evil if he willed. However, this would be an expression of his absolute power (*potentia absoluta*), like miracles. Customarily, he governs by his ordinary power (*potentia ordinata*), and this is the reason for the regularity in our moral and natural universe. He has even created us in such a way that our powers of probable reasoning can play some role in discovering divine law. But this is a different concept of reason from that of the Thomists, and it is a contingent and not necessary feature of the universe.

This ethical voluntarism complemented the spread of epistemic and ontological voluntarism in both Protestant and Catholic theology during the Reformation. It is articulated by the young Grotius, Samuel Pufendorf (who is attacked by Leibniz), Jeremy Taylor, Robert Sanderson, Walter Charleton, Pierre Gassendi, Robert Boyle, Richard Cumberland, Thomas Hobbes, and Nathaniel Culverwel, among others.[103] The religious motivation here is particularly clear in a work such as Nathaniel Culverwel's *Of the light of nature* (1657). He attacks the whole intellectualist tradition as embodying the sin of pride. God has imprinted no innate ideas or dispositions in man, nor does man share in any way, especially through his reason, in god's divine reason. The mind is a 'blank sheet' and all our knowledge is based on simple observation. Man does not participate in god's essence, which is unknown and omnipotent. Man is as the vessel to the potter: all of mankind could be annihilated without touching god's

---

[102] William of Ockham, *Super quatuor libros sententiarum* II, qu. 5 H.
[103] Hugo Grotius, *De jure praedae* (1868 [1604]), ch. 2; Jeremy Taylor, *Ductor dubitantium*, in *Works*, IX, 333–40; Robert Sanderson, *De Obligatione conscientae* (1660), 4th lecture, pp. 5–6; Walter Charleton, *The darkness of atheism dispelled by the light of nature* (1652), ch. 10, 1; Robert Boyle, *Some considerations about the reconcileableness of reason and religion*, in *Works*, IV, 151–91, 162; Thomas Hobbes, *Leviathan* (1651), bk II, chs 30–1; Richard Cumberland, *A treatise on the law of nature*, tr. J. Maxwell (London, 1672), 320. For a fuller account see n. 94, 95.

essence. Man, and even the soul, is 'infinitely distant from him'.[104] Similar voluntaristic themes are present in Boyle's writings. Cudworth summarized the voluntarists in this way:[105]

divers Modern Theologers do not only seriously, but zealously contend . . . *That there is nothing Absolutely, intrinsecally, and Naturally Good and Evil, Just and Unjust, antecedently to any positive Command or Prohibition of God; but that the Arbitrary will and Pleasure of God,* (that is, an Omnipotent Being devoid of all Essential and Natural Justice) *by its Command and Prohibitions, is the first and only Rule and measure thereof.* Whence it follows . . . that whatsoever God can be supposed to do or will will be *for that reason* Good or just, because he wills it.

Locke grew up in this Calvinist and voluntaristic milieu, and his early writings are dominated by the double theme that both the obligation and content of natural law are derived from god's will. The morality of things is not an intrinsic property, but their conformity or disconformity to a law that makes known the law-maker's will.[106] In the latter half of the 1670s, while in France, Locke began to integrate his natural law voluntarism with the revival of Greek hedonism.

Hedonic moral philosophy was introduced into the seventeenth century along with the revival of the Greek atomism of Epicurus, Democritus, and Lucretius. Atomism served as a useful hypothesis for the experimental sciences, but it threatened to lead to atheism. Hobbes, for example, argued that once god had created the universe of matter in motion he had left it alone to run by its own efficient causes. Gassendi, Charleton, Glanvill, and Boyle all argued that god was not only necessary to set matter in motion but also, because there were no causes in nature, to keep it in motion. Thus, voluntarism could absorb the atomistic hypothesis and retain god's providence. A parallel synthesis of Epicurus' hedonic moral philosophy was achieved by Gassendi and Charleton. Accepting the notion of pleasures and pains as the springs of human action, they added three Christian elements to Epicurus' theory: a providential god, the immortality of the soul, and heaven and hell as the reward and

---

[104] Culverwel, *On the light of nature*, 125–40, *supra* n. 16.   [105] Cudworth, *A treatise*, 9–11.
[106] This interpretation has been put past doubt by Francis Oakley and Elliot W. Urdang, 'Locke, natural law and God', *Natural Law Forum*, 11 (1966), 92–109. I disagree with some details but not with their overall argument. My major difference is that Oakley and Urdang do not treat the syncretism of natural law with the revived hedonism that is at the heart of Locke's ethical theory after 1676. See also von Leyden, *Essays on the law of nature*, 43; and Philip Abrams, introduction, *John Locke, Two tracts on government* (Cambridge: Cambridge University Press, 1967), 69–74.

punishment for good and evil behaviour. 'Thus he [Locke]', Baker writes, 'not only crowns the anti-authoritarian protest with which Bacon had opened the century, but also brings to a full cadence that incisive attack with which William of Ockham had initiated the revolt against scholasticism.'[107]

Locke, building on Gassendi, brings these two traditions together in the following way.[108] First, from hedonism, he defines natural 'good and evil' as 'nothing but Pleasure or Pain, or that which procures pleasure or pain to use'.[109] Secondly, although man has no innate disposition to moral conduct, he does have empirically verifiable motives – 'attractions' and 'repulsions' – to pleasures and from pains. This is then linked to voluntarism by a new concept: *moral good and evil.*[110]

Morally Good and Evil then, is only the Conformity or Disagreement of our voluntary Actions to some Law, whereby Good or Evil is drawn on us, from the Will and Power of the Law-maker; which Good and Evil, Pleasure or Pain, attending our observance, or breach of the law, by the Decree of the Law-maker, is that we call *Reward* and *Punishment.*

[107] Baker, *The wars of truth*, 186. The great texts of the synthesis of voluntarism and epicurean hedonism are Pierre Gassendi, *De vita et moribus Epicuri* (1647), *Philosophiae Epicuri Syntagma*, 1649; F. Bernier, *Abrégé* (1978) and *The Discourses of happiness, virtue, and liberty collected from the learned Gassendi* (1699); Thomas Hobbes, *Leviathan* (1651); Walter Charleton, 'Apology', *Epicurus's morals* (1656), and *The darkness of atheism dispelled by the light of nature* (1652). See Charles T. Harrison, 'The ancient atomists and the English literature of the 17th century', *Harvard studies in classical philology* 45 (1934), 1–74; Thomas Mayo, *Epicurus in England* (Dallas, 1934); Kargon, *Atomism in England*, 63–93 (*supra* n. 99); Frederick Vaughan, *The tradition of political hedonism from Hobbes to J. S. Mill* (New York: Fordham University Press, 1982).

[108] I am greatly indebted to Driscoll's study of the influence of Gassendi on Locke's hedonism (*supra* n. 56).

[109] *Essay* 2.20.5. Compare 2.20.2, 2.21.42. Pleasure and pain are first discussed in this way in July 1676: 'Pleasure and pain', Bodleian, MS. Locke f. 1, fos 325–47, in von Leyden, *Essays on the law of nature*, 263–72. Compare *Essay* 2.7, 2.8.13, 4.3.6. Note that pleasures and pains are mental states for Locke. Compare letter to Molyneux, *Correspondence*, IV (1655).

[110] *Essay* 2.28.5. This synthesis is first introduced in a manuscript, of 1687, that was intended as chapter 21 of the first edition of the *Essay*: 'Of ethick in general', Bodleian, MS. Locke c. 28, fos. 146r–152r. It is printed in King, *Life of Locke*, II, 122–33. However, an important section is omitted, which is reprinted in von Leyden, *Essays on the law of nature*, 72. Earlier attempts to combine voluntarism with hedonism are made in the hedonic manuscripts of the late 1670s to early 1690s: 'Pleasure and pain' (1676); 'Happynesse' (September 1676), Bodleian, MS. Locke f. 1, fos. 445–7, in Driscoll, 'The influence of Gassendi", 101–2 (*supra* n. 56); 'Happynesse' (October 1678), Bodleian, MS. Locke f. 3, fos 304–5, in King, *Life of Locke*, I, 216; 'Thus I think' (1685–9?), Bodleian, MS. Locke c. 28, fos 143–5, in King, II, 120–2; 'Ethica' (1692), Bodleian, MS. Locke c. 42, fo. 224 and 'Morality', Bodleian, MS. Locke c. 28, fos 139–40, both in T. Sargentich, 'Locke and ethical theory', *Locke Newsletter*, 5 (1974), 24–31.

A voluntary act is *moral* relative to a law that is the will of the law-maker, as in voluntarism. It is good or evil because obeying or disobeying the law brings on reward or punishment; that is, pleasure or pain, and, by definition, good or evil. The moral goodness of a voluntary action is its 'rectitude' and moral evil its 'pravity' or 'obliquity'.[111] Moral good and evil are like natural good and evil in virtue of their relation to pleasure and pain. They are unlike them, or a special case, in virtue of referring only to voluntary acts and pleasure and pain in the form of rewards and punishments attached to a law.

Let me call such an ensemble of law-maker, laws, punishments, and rewards and the schedule of morally good and evil acts a juridical apparatus.[112] There are three types of this apparatus. The first comprises god, divine or natural law, the reward of heaven and the punishment of hell, and the schedule of sins and duties. Conscience, or judgement, compares an action to divine law to determine if it is a sin or duty.[113] This providential apparatus is one of the great governing mechanisms of the early modern European church and state. The practice associated with it is attrition: the fear of divine punishment (hell) and the hope of divine reward (heaven) are necessary to motivate people to act in accordance with the moral and legal systems. Every theorist, with the important exceptions of Richard Overton and Pierre Bayle, held that belief in providentialism must underline any stable social order.[114] It was, of course, deeply entwined in a multiplicity of practices in early modern Europe and partially enforced in this world by the penitential and disciplinary

---

[111] *Essay* 2.28.6, 15–16; 1.3.8. This distinction between right – the relation of an action to a law – and good – the relation of an action to pleasure and pain – is brought out clearly in 'Voluntas' (1693), Bodleian MS. Locke c. 28, fo. 114, in von Leyden, *Essays on the law of nature*, 72–3 and Colman, *John Locke's moral philosophy* (Edinburgh, 1983), 48–9. I am indebted to the fine work of von Leyden and Colman even though my interpretation differs in some respects. Von Leyden argues that Locke fails to reconcile hedonism and voluntarism, and Colman argues that Locke is not a voluntarist with respect to the content of natural law.

[112] I include within the term 'apparatus' discursive and non-discursive (techniques, institutions, etc.) elements.   [113] *Essay* 2.28.7–8.

[114] Richard Overton, *Mans mortallitie* (Amsterdam, 1643). Pierre Bayle argued against Antoine Arnauld's providential argument that fear of divine punishment is a necessary condition of social order and began to explore the radical possibility of a society of atheists, thus contesting the whole providential apparatus of Christianity. Pierre Bayle, *Pensées diverses sur la comete* (1682). See Rex, *Essays on Pierre Bayle*, 52–67; and for providentialism see D. P. Walker, *The decline of hell* (London: Routledge and Kegan Paul, 1964). I am indebted here to many discussions with David Wootton.

powers of the churches. This is why, according to Locke, atheists cannot be tolerated. They have no motive to obey the law or keep their promises if they calculate that they can avoid secular punishment; only fear of an omniscent, punishing god will govern their conduct in these circumstances.[115] Conversely, and this is Locke's toleration, belief in *any* providential god will do (hence the scandal associated with the publication of the first *Letter concerning toleration.*[116])

Although Locke always held that providentialism was a necessary condition of social order, he also realized that it was the major cause of social disorder.[117] Two false beliefs had been introduced into Christianity by the various priests; that there is only one right way to worship god, and that it is a Christian duty to take up arms to protect and spread the true faith. Since this duty was enforced by teaching the providential threat of eternal damnation for non-compliance, the pastorate of each faith were powerfully motivated to take up arms. The priests inculcated these beliefs to gain power, and the overall consequence had been 100 years of European wars. This is a fairly common analysis of the age of religious wars. Locke's solution in the *Letter concerning toleration* is to correct the two 'false' beliefs: god tolerates many ways of worship, and faith is to be spread by persuasion, not arms. Now, one faces divine punishment for using coercion in matters of faith. This would have removed the cause of religious war and legalized dissent while preserving providentialism as an instrument of social control. However, it would also have disestablished the Anglican Church and delegitimated the penal practices of all churches, and so it was decisively rejected.[118]

The second juridical apparatus involves the state: the sovereign or law-maker, the laws, the rewards and punishments of the penal system, and the codes of legal and illegal acts.[119] This is the foundation of political theory and practice in the early modern period. The gradual juridicalization of society against feudal and city particularism and trial by battle includes the military and penal institutions that developed around this apparatus, and the great legal schools of

---

[115] *A letter concerning toleration*, 47, 51. See Tully, introduction, *A letter concerning toleration*, 8.
[116] See the establishment attack on the *Letter* by Thomas Long, *The letter for toleration decipher'd and the absurdity of an absolute toleration demonstrated* (1689).
[117] John Locke, *Two tracts*, 158–61.
[118] See Jonas Proast, *The argument of The letter concerning toleration briefly considered and answered* (London: 1690). See the tell-tale argument in Joseph Glanvill, *The zealous and impartial protestant*, 3.   [119] *Essay* 2.28.7, 9.

Thomism, voluntarism, and humanism that constructed juridical
discourses to administer and justify it, as well as to legitimate
resistance to its absolutist variant. By the mid-seventeenth century
the hegemonic sovereign of this apparatus was no longer the feudal
lord, the Empire, free city, estate, or Catholic Church, but the
consolidating state.[120] Every political writer from the University of
Bologna in the twelfth century to Locke, and even to Hegel, held,
correctly, that this apparatus of legal relations *constituted* political
society; that it was the 'constitution' of political society. (We still call
our fundamental laws our 'constitution', even though other relations
are more fundamental now, and our moral and political theories are
still trapped in these juridical discourses.) The state juridical
apparatus is the model for this concept of governance: power is
exercised by a sovereign body through the law and by means of
punishments and rewards in order to bring about a certain kind of
conduct.[121]

   The third, and for Locke the most effective governor, is what I will
call the 'humanist' juridical apparatus. Every society, culture, group,
or party has its intersubjective opinions about appropriate and
inappropriate belief and action. These are promulgated by the
community through what he calls the laws of 'reputation', 'fashion',
or 'opinion'. Judged by their conformity to or disagreement with the
laws of reputation, actions are called virtues or vices. The rewards
and punishments attached to these laws and enforced by the
community are praise and blame, acclaim and opprobrium, honour
and dishonour, and so on.[122]

Thus the measure of what is everywhere called and esteemed *Vertue* and *Vice*
is this approbation or dislike, praise or blame, which by a secret and tacit
consent establishes itself in the several Societies, Tribes and Clubs of men in
the world; whereby several actions come to find Credit or Disgrace among
them, according to the Judgment, Maxims or Fashions of that place.

I call this juridical apparatus 'humanist' because what Locke has
done here is to translate humanism, its virtues and vices and motives
of honour, praise, glory, and reputation, into his juridical framework.
Humanism is not – as many argued then and still do now – an

[120] J. H. Shennan, *The origins of the modern European state: 1450–1725* (London: Hutchinson,
      1974).
[121] See, Tully, 'The pen', 498–502, and introduction to *A letter concerning toleration*, 11–16.
[122] *Essay* 2.28.7, 10–13.

alternative form of political theory and practice.[123] It is one type of juridical governance. As he states in his correspondence, and as we see below, all politico-ethical regimes fall within these three great ensembles of knowledge and techniques.[124]

The humanist juridical apparatus is the most effective *de facto* governor of belief and action. People do not seriously reflect on god's punishment and, if they do, they dream of making reconciliations concerning present sins. With respect to the law of the Commonwealth 'they frequently flatter themselves with the hopes of Impunity'. But no one can escape the punishment of the censure and dislike of the company he or she keeps. Nor is there one person in 10,000 strong enough to bear up under the constant ill opinion of their friends. 'This is a burthen too heavy for human sufferance: And he must be made up of irreconciliable Contradictions who can take pleasure in company, and yet be insensible of Contempt and Disgrace from his Companions.'[125]

Locke first mentions these three laws in a manuscript written in 1678.[126] It is clear by the context that he is beginning to draw into his juridical framework the powerful analysis of belief and behaviour in the terms of interests and reputation carried out in France, especially the analysis by Pierre Nicole.[127] From as early as his famous 'Diana' letter of 1659 Locke was deeply involved in the rich English analysis of the determinants of belief and action.[128] This tradition, which as Neil Wood has shown, is Baconian in inspiration, took interest, party,

---

[123] A contemporary statement of the view that civic humanism or classical republicanism is different in kind from juridical government is presented by John Pocock, 'Virtues, rights, and manners: a model for historians of political thought', in J. G. A. Pocock, *Virtue, commerce, and history* (Cambridge: Cambridge University Press, 1985), 37–50. This difference is based primarily on distinctive features of the *languages* of republican and juridical political thought: of virtues and vices and of rights and obligations respectively. As important as this difference unquestionably is, however, in *practice*, and even in some features of its language, early modern republicanism is a strategy of juridical governance of conduct, not an alternative to it, as Vico stresses in his *New science* (1725). See Jeffrey Barnouw, 'The critique of classical republicanism and the understanding of modern forms of polity in Vico's *New science*', *Clio* 9, 3 (1980).
[124] *Correspondence*, Letter of James Tyrrell, IV, letter 1309, 110–13.   [125] *Essay* 2.28.12.
[126] 'Adversaria', Bodleian, MS. Locke f. 247–8, in Aaron and Gibb, *An early draft*, 93. 'Law' (1678), Bodleian, MS. Locke, f. 3, fos, 111–12. See also *Draft A*, 25 and *Draft B*, 158. The tripartite classification is crystal clear in 'Of ethick in general' (1687), *supra* n. 110. Compare von Leyden, *Essays on the law of nature*, 67–8.
[127] For the French analysis of interests and reputation see Nannerl Keohane, *Philosophy and the state in France* (Princeton: Princeton University Press, 1980), 262–317.
[128] *Correspondence*, I, letter to Tom (1659), 81. Compare *Draft A*, 24–6; *Draft B*, 157–62; 'Of study', in King, II, 188.

custom and education as the determinants of conduct, as we have seen.[129] In his first period of political exile, 1675–9, Locke began the process of standing back from these two modes of analysis and working them into his deeper tripartite juridical apparatus. Here is a classic statement on reputation from this period:[130]

The principal spring from which the actions of men take their rise, the rule they conduct them by, and the end to which they direct them, seems to be credit and reputation, and that which at any rate they avoid, is in the greatest part shame and disgrace . . . this puts men upon school divinity in one country and physics and mathematics in another; this makes merchants in one country and soldiers in another . . . Religions are upheld by this and factions maintain, and the shame of being disesteemed by those with whom one hath lived, and to whom one would recommend oneself, is the great source and director of most of the actions of men . . . He therefore that would govern the world well, had need consider rather what fashions he makes, than what laws; and to bring any thing into use he need only give it reputation.

This explanation of virtue and vice was immediately attacked by James Lowde, and later by the third Earl of Shaftesbury and many others, as moral relativism.[131] This, however, was Locke's point. The humanist juridical apparatus provided an explanation of the cultural diversity of moral practices which Europe's global expansion had uncovered, refuting the old consensus justification of natural law.[132] Secondly, it explained, along with providentialism, the division of Europe into warring factions, and so the sceptical crisis. The only moral principle that is in fact culturally invariant is preservation of the community, and this is all that is required as an empirical foundation for the new natural law theory centred on preservation.[133]

---

[129] Wood, *The politics of Locke's philosophy*, 94–107.

[130] 'Credit, disgrace', Bodleian, MS. Locke f. 3, fos 381–2, December 1678, in King, *Life of Locke*, I, 203. The passage is a paraphrase of Pascal, *Pensées* (1670), 821 (Lafuma numbers).

[131] James Lowde, *A discourse concerning the nature of man* (1694). In the preface Lowde attacked *Essay* 2.28.11. Locke replied in the 2nd edition, 2.28.11 note. Shaftesbury linked Locke's voluntarism and his relativism: 'Thus virtue, according to Mr Locke, has no other measure, law, or rule, than fashion and custom; morality, justice, equity, depend only on law and will, and God indeed is a perfectly free agent in this sense; that, free to will anything, that is however ill: for if He wills it, it will be made good; virtue may be vice, and vice virtue in its turn, if he pleases. And thus neither right nor wrong, virtue nor vice, are anything in themselves; nor is there any trace or idea naturally imprinted on human minds. Experience and our catechism teach us all!' Third Earl of Shaftesbury, *The life: unpublished letters and regimen of A. A. Cooper . . .*, ed. B. Rand (New York: Macmillan, 1900), 403–4.

[132] *Essay* 1.3.10. Locke abandoned universal consent as the basis of morality as early as the *Essays on the law of nature*.

Thirdly, it provided a means of relativizing both humanist and Aristotelian ethics.[134] I have been unable to find a parallel to this remarkable conceptual innovation in the seventeenth century. Although this strategy explains and accepts culturally relative moralities, it does not lead to a complete moral relativism. Divine law remains as the true standard of morality, as Locke emphasized in the second edition of the *Essay* in response to Lowde.

The problem of how one comes to know divine law by the use of reason still remains, as Locke's critics point out. I want to mention one solution that Locke rejects, in order to explicate one further feature of the providential apparatus. To bring natural law philosophy in line with the new voluntaristic concept of reason and the experimental sciences, Cumberland argued that god had attached to natural law natural punishments and rewards in this world. The hangover that follows from overdrinking, for example, is a punishment god annexed to overdrinking because it is a sin. It follows that one can work back from empirical observations of the pleasures and pains that result from human actions to hypotheses of what natural laws must be. Hobbes had moved in this direction, as had Samuel Parker and Joseph Glanvill.[135] Henry Lee puts this theory forward in a self-revelatory way, citing Cumberland's proof that there are 'natural advantages' annexed to morally good acts: 'health, strength, beauty, long-life, wisdom, memory, honour, riches, power, ease of mind and inward pleasure'.[136]

James Tyrrell attempted to draw Locke into this (latitudinarian) movement, but he rejected it for two reasons.[137] First, it assimilated a moral law to a descriptive law of natural phenomena and thus to what is not, properly speaking, a law but merely a regularity.[138] Here Locke is following Boyle's *A free inquiry into the vulgarly received notion of nature*.[139] Such an assimilation leads, as Locke was well aware, to a kind of deistic necessitarianism, and elides the necessary features of a law: that it applies to voluntary actions and is enforced by the free will

---

[133] See n. 209 and accompanying text below.

[134] 'Of Ethick in General', 124–6, *supra* n. 110.

[135] Samuel Parker, *A demonstration of the divine authority of the law of nature and of the Christian religion* (1681); Hobbes, *Leviathan*, 2.31, 406–7.

[136] Lee, *Anti-scepticism*, 12. Of course, to disagree with Hobbes, these are not the only rewards.

[137] James Tyrrell, *A brief disquisition of the law of nature, according to . . . Dr Cumberland's . . . Latin treatise* (1692). In the preface, Tyrrell attempts to align Cumberland and Locke.

[138] *Essay*, 2.28.6.

[139] Boyle, *Works*, IV, 367. Compare *Christian virtuoso* 5, 46.

of the law-maker. Without this, there is no substantive distinction between natural and moral good, as Locke stresses in 'Of ethick in general'. The second reason for rejecting it is that it could be and was used by the latitudinarians to justify the use of coercion against dissenters.[140]

With these three apparatus (Christian or providential, sovereign, and humanist) in hand, we can turn to the explanation of conduct. Locke argues that the fact of both global and historical moral relativity refutes the theory that there are either innate practical principles or innate dispositions to them. The defining feature of a practical as opposed to a speculative principle is that it affects our activity. This is not because we are disposed to act in accordance with it or because we incline towards good and away from evil action. Rather, what guides action is our basic motivation set: 'a desire of Happiness, and an aversion to misery . . . do constantly . . . operate and influence all our actions, without ceasing'. These are 'the constant Spring and motives of all our Actions', but they are 'inclinations of the appetite to good, not impressions of truth on the understanding'.[141] Therefore, for a practical principle to influence action it must be related to man's empirically verifiable motivations. This is done by making a practical principle a law within one of the three juridical apparatus. This is what Locke means when he says that every practical principle requires a reason which justifies it.[142] This justification appeals to a reason or ground from which the practical principle can be deduced and which is its foundation. Thus, there are three foundations of, for example, the principle that men should keep their compacts, corresponding to the three juridical apparatus. Locke's statement is thus worth quoting in full because it brings voluntarism, hedonism, and the three ethnical systems together into a comprehensive penalism:[143]

That Men should keep their Compacts, is certainly a great and undeniable Rule in Morality. But yet, if a Christian, who has the view of Happiness and Misery in another Life, be asked why a Man must keep his Word, he will *give* this as a *Reason*: Because God who has the Power of eternal Life and Death, requires it of us. But if an *Hobbist* be asked why; he will answer: Because the Publick requires it, and the *Leviathan* will punish you, if you do not. And if

---

[140] This is brought out most infamously in Samuel Parker, *A discourse of ecclesiastical politie* (1670). See Locke's Letter to Tyrrell, *Correspondence*, IV, letter 1309, 110–13.
[141] *Essay* 1.3.3.   [142] *Essay* 1.3.4.   [143] *Essay* 1.3.5.

one of the old *Heathen* Philosophers had been asked, he would have answer'd: Because it was dishonest, below the Dignity of a Man, and opposite to Vertue, the highest Perfection of human Nature, to do otherwise.

Of course the Christian apparatus is the 'true ground of morality' because the Law-maker is god, the author of truth, and the rewards and punishments, heaven and hell, are the greatest pleasures and pains.[144]

Given this, what governs human action? As in the case of assent, Locke's first answer is a deterministic one. An individual's judgement of the greater good in view determines the will. This appears in the first edition of the *Essay* and in a number of the manuscripts.[145] It is conformable with his penalism but, like the first account of probabilities determining assent, conduct is necessarily governed by whatever greater good is ready to hand. Locke asked William Molyneux to solicit comments on the first edition and William King replied, pointing out the determinism of this argument.[146] Locke then reworked the argument, in continual correspondence with Molyneux, and published a new and definitive account in the second edition. The materials for the new account were already available in manuscripts of the 1670s, so he probably published the first chapter 21 without much thought and from an old manuscript. The new account, like the account of assent, appears to be indebted to Gassendi, just as the first is, it seems, to Hobbes.[147]

Locke argues that his first view cannot be true, because if it were everyone who has considered Christianity would be an unfailing Christian in practice. This is so since they would be aware that heaven

[144] *Essay* 1.3.6 (lines 11–12 added in edition in response to Lowde's charge of relativism). Burnet doubts the efficacy of the juridical apparatus: 'Do we not see men every day, in spite of laws external or internal, divine or human, pursue their lusts, passions and vicious inclinations? Though they have not only the terrors of another life to keep them in awe and order, but see before their eyes God's gibbets, whips, racks and torturing engines'. Locke replies: 'What! Whilst they have the terrors of those things as unavoidable for that action before their eyes.' Porter, 'Marginalia Locke-a-na', 43.

[145] *Essay* 2.21.29, 1st edition. The sections of the 1st edition of 2.21 that were omitted by Locke in the later editions are reprinted by Nidditch in the *Essay*, 248–73.

[146] Locke to Molyneux, 20 September 1692, *Correspondence*, IV, letter 1538; Molyneux to Locke, 15 October 1692, IV, letter 1544 (contains King's comments); Locke to Molyneux, 15 July 1693, IV, letter 1643 (contains new chapter outlines for 2nd edition of 2.21). See Molyneux's own criticisms, letter 1579.

[147] For Locke's apparent debt to Hobbes in his first account see S. Lamprecht, *The moral and political philosophy of John Locke* (New York: Columbia University Press, 1918), 89, 98. For his debt to Gassendi in the second account see Bonno, 'Les relations intellectuelles', 241–2; and Driscoll, 'The influence of Gassendi', 108, *supra* n. 56.

and hell outweigh all other good and evil, and so they would be motivated to live a Christian life to gain infinite pleasure and avoid infinite pain. Yet it obviously is true that everyone who has considered Christianity is not a practising Christian, therefore the greater good in view does not determine the will.[148]

In this self-criticism, precipitated by William King, Locke argues that the criticism holds even if heaven, hell, and the immortality of the soul are only probable, not certain. All voluntarists hold this view, because heaven and hell are contingent features of the universe. Locke opens the *Essay* by equating faith with opinion, not knowledge, and re-emphasizes this in the response to Stillingfleet's intellectualist assault on the *Essay*.[149] Here he employs a variant of Pascal's wager, a decision–theoretic form of probable reasoning that had actually developed in England prior to the *Pensées*.[150] Locke's source however seems to be the *Pensées*.[151] This argument contains two types of probable reasoning: (1) assessing the grounds of probability for the belief that Revelation is the word of god and, therefore, that heaven and hell exist and the soul is immortal (the kind of reasoning we have seen in the section on assent), and (2) calculating the relative weights of goods: that is, a probability calculus of pleasures and pains (the form of probable reasoning most closely connected to the juridical apparatus since it is a matter of weighing the relative pleasures and pains of the three systems of punishments and rewards). Once Locke had mastered the concept of probability in 1676, he realized that a demonstrable ethics was no longer necessary: probability and opinion are sufficient for all our concernments.[152]

How is it, then, that people can have the greater good in view yet

---

[148] *Essay* 2.21.31, 38.
[149] *Essay* 1.1.3. Compare 4.18; 'Faith and reason', August–September 1676, Bodleian, Ms. Locke f. 1, fos. 412–32, in von Leyden, *Essays on the law of nature*, 272–81; and Biddle, 'Locke's critique of innate principles', 421–2, *supra* n. 42.
[150] For example, in Chillingworth, *The religion of Protestants* (1633), in *Works* (1844), 203–4. See van Leeuwen, *The problem of certainty*, 30.
[151] The first appearance of the wager is in his journal, 29 July 1676 (reprinted in Aaron and Gibb, *An early draft*, 81–2). Locke then used it in several places in the *Essay*. For Locke's relation to Pascal see John Barker, *Strange contrarieties: Pascal in England during the age of reason* (Montreal: McGill–Queen's University Press, 1975), 36–7, 48–9, 50–6.
[152] The point of Locke's journal entry on the wager is that a demonstrable ethics is unnecessary to morality. Compare 'Faith and reason' (1676), *supra* n. 61; Locke's reply to Tyrrell's request for a demonstrable ethic, *Correspondence*, IV, letter 1309; and *Essay* 1.1.5, 2.21.70 (part 1, n. 60). Pascal's wager is at *Pensées* 418 (Lafuma numbers). For a modern reconstruction see Hacking, *The emergence of probability* , 63–72.

not be moved by it, if pleasure and pain, happiness and misery, are the constant springs of human action? The answer is that the greater good is absent and ''tis against the nature of things, that what is absent should operate, where it is not'.[153] A residual disposition or occult force acting at a distance was lurking in the first theory and is now removed in the second edition. What determines the will, therefore, must be something present, and this is *uneasiness*. This now becomes the immediate determinant that always governs behaviour. It is first introduced in 2.20.6 of the second edition, contradicting the old view three passages earlier. Locke had immense difficulty defining the concept of uneasiness and continued to refine it throughout his manuscripts and correspondence. Pierre Coste, who translated the *Essay* into French, warned the reader that there were no French equivalents and used 'inquietude'. Again, there is an earlier manuscript on uneasiness and, secondly, the possibility of a connection with Gassendi.[154]

Uneasiness is any present mental or physical *pain* to which is always joined a desire equal to the pain.[155] Since desire is always uneasiness for some absent good, in reference to any pain felt, the absent good is the ease of pain. This simple mechanism can explain the attraction of an absent positive good as well, without invoking any occult forces. An absent positive good (heaven, honour, etc.) does not in itself cause desire equal to its greatness of pleasure because it cannot, in itself and at a distance, cause 'pain for it'. A present pain, and so an uneasiness, must be 'raised' for an absent positive good before a person can be moved towards it. 'And therefore', Locke concludes, 'absent good may be looked on and considered without desire' unless and until an uneasiness has been raised for it.[156] 'I am forced to conclude, that *good*, the greater good, though apprehended and acknowledged to be so, does not determine the will, until our desire, raised proportionably to it, makes us uneasy in the want of it.'

Since it is this micro-mechanism of pain that determines the will, it is wrong to call Locke a voluntaristic hedonist, or to suggest that he makes pleasure the motive force of action. The term 'penalism'

---

[153] *Essay* 2.21.37.

[154] For 'uneasiness', see 'Will, pleasure, pain' (July 1676), Bodleian, MS. Locke f. 1, fos 317–19, in Aaron and Gibb, *An early draft*, 80; 'Pleasure and pain' (August 1676), in von Leyden, *Essays on the law of nature*, 263–72, 269–70; *Correspondence*, v (1798) (a clarification intended for the 4th edition).

[155] *Essay* 2.21.31.   [156] *Essay* 2.21.35.

captures both the penal features of the theory and the centrality of 'ease of pain' as the basic human drive. Even the infinite pleasures and pain of heaven and hell can be contemplated without desire or aversion until a person has cultivated an uneasiness for heaven and made it part of his or her happiness.[157] Then, a person will be moved not directly by pleasure but by a present pain or uneasiness he or she has acquired for it. This is because all present pain makes a necessary part of our misery whereas absent good does not make a necessary part of our present happiness.[158] 'Though, as to pain, that they are always concerned for; they can feel no *uneasiness* without being moved. And therefore being *uneasie* in the want to whatever is judged necessary to their Happiness, as soon as any good appears to mark a part of their portion of happiness, they begin to desire it.'

This little penal mechanism is partly implanted in the mind by god. The pain and uneasiness annexed to hunger is set in place by god to motivate humans to seek preservation. The pain of sexual lust is implanted by god to drive men to marriage and reproduction:[159] '*it is better to marry than to burn*, says St *Paul*; where we may see, what it is that chiefly drives men into the enjoyments of a conjugal life. A little burning felt pushes us more powerfully, than greater pleasures in prospect draw or allure.' However, the vast majority of our uneasinesses are acquired, such as the uneasiness for 'Honour, power or Riches', and produced by custom and education.[160] The concept of uneasiness now becomes the instrument to link the will to the juridical apparatus and so to explain and reform conduct.

Before Locke turns to this he adds one final feature. Uneasiness solves the problem of the absent good but not the problem of determinism, for now it determines the will. Locke thus introduces a power of the will to suspend the solicitations of present unease and to examine which course of action will lead to the greatest pleasure. The power is the freedom of the will and the foundation of liberty.[161] 'For during this suspension of any desire, before the will be determined to action, and the action (which follows that determination) done, we have the opportunity to examine, view and judge, of the good or evil of what we are going to do.' Once the judgement is made, and an uneasiness aligned with its object, the will is determined.

There is a direct parallel with this account of behaviour and the

---

[157] *Essay* 2.21.36–8.   [158] *Essay* 2.21.43.   [159] *Essay* 2.21.34.   [160] *Essay* 2.21.45.
[161] *Essay* 2.21.47.

earlier account of belief. With respect to assent we have the power to suspend our acquired and customary determinants of judgement and to examine the grounds of probability. Here, we have the power to suspend our acquired and customary determinants of the will and to judge our course of action in accordance with grounds or measures of pleasure and pain, good or evil. Then, behaviour follows. As Locke states, god himself is determined by what is best, and it is therefore no abridgement of our freedom to say that we are determined by what we judge to be the best. Freedom consists in suspension and examination.[162]

This new account provoked a response by Locke's close friend the Dutch Arminian, Phillip van Limborch. The correspondence that followed is the clearest expression of two views of intellectual liberty in the late seventeenth century.[163] Limborch argued that after a practical judgement is made the will remains 'indifferent'; free to act or not to act in accordance with it. This autonomy of the will, which follows Descartes, is more voluntaristic than in Locke.[164] Locke had held this view in 1660 when he justified imposition of religious uniformity in England. If practical judgement, and hence conscience, is separate from the will, then dissenters can be forced to conform to religious practice without compromising their religious beliefs, since conformity requires only an act of the will. They can be said to enjoy freedom of conscience or 'inner' belief. What the dissenters wanted was freedom of religious practice, not just inner faith, and they broke with the long-standing Protestant separation of judgement and will. They argued that practical judgement is non-contingently linked to and determines the will, so that freedom of conscience entails freedom of practice. To impose uniformity on dissenters is to force them to compromise their beliefs and so to commit the sin of hypocrisy.

---

[162] *Essay* 2.21.48–52. For the parallel between suspending assent and the will compare part I above and Passmore, *The ethics of belief*. For the similarity with Gassendi see Bonno, 'Les relations intellectuelles', 241–2, and Driscoll, 'The influence of Gassendi', 108–9, *supra* n. 56. For the introduction of suspension and examination with respect to the will, see Locke, 'Will, pleasure, pain' (1676), *supra* n. 154.

[163] *Correspondence*, VII, 268–70, De Beer introduces the Limborch–Locke controversy, which runs from 2881 to 3200. For a summary of the debate over the indifferency of the will from Descartes to Anthony Collins, see A. O. O'Higgins, introduction, *Determination and freewill* (The Hague: Martinus Nijhoff, 1977).

[164] This is the sixth difficulty in the sixth set of objections urged against Descartes' *Meditations on first philosophy*. Note how Norris, *Cursory reflections*, *supra* n. 15, following Malebranche, takes the indifferency line against Locke: pp. 16–17. For attacks on Descartes' voluntarism, see Cudworth, *A treatise*, 27–9 and Lowde, *A discourse*, 59–68, *supra* n. 48.

Therefore, they have a right and a motive to resist imposition. When Locke moved to the defence of dissent in 1667 he put forward this view to justify toleration, as did John Owen, the Master of Christ Church and indefatigable defender of dissent. Therefore, in England the theory that the judgement determines the will was associated with the revolutionary struggle for toleration, and the indifferency theory with latitude and uniformity.[165] What Limborch, and presumably Descartes, wanted was the opposite: a theory that would justify intellectual freedom for minorities without entailing any disorderly consequences in the realm of practice. This kind of objection had been advanced earlier by King and Molyneux. Locke added yet another section to chapter 21 in the fifth edition in which he explicitly rejected the indifferency theory of the will.[166]

The moral judgement involved in examination is an exercise in probable reasoning; of weighing the relative pleasures and pains of possible actions: 'Judging is, as it were, balancing an account, and determining on which side the odds lies [sic].'[167] The judgement of *present* pleasures and pains cannot be mistaken: 'Things in their present enjoyment are what they seem; the apparent and real good are, in this case, always the same.' If the pains of honest industry and of starving with hunger and cold are set before us, 'no body would be in doubt which to chuse'.[168] Misjudgement arises because things are called good or bad in a double sense: with respect to the pleasure or pain of the action, and with respect to the pleasure or pain *consequent* to the action. We cannot help but be concerned with and desirous of these future pleasures and pains, and so they make part of our happiness.[169] However, we misjudge the weight of future or consequential pleasures and pains relative to the present ones. Future goods are at a disadvantage, and so their relative pleasure misjudged, because they are absent or unfamiliar. Hence, even when one suspends present uneasiness, the closer and more familiar causes us to misjudge; to employ wrong measures of good and evil, analogous to wrong measures of probability:[170]

because the abstinence from a present pleasure, that offers itself, is a Pain, nay, oftentimes a very great one, the desire being inflamed by a near and tempting object; 'tis no wonder that that operates after the same manner

---

[165] See Tully, introduction to *A letter concerning toleration*, 5–7.
[166] *Essay* 2.21.71, 283.16–284.21.   [167] *Essay* 2.21.67. Compare 2.21.47, 52, 53.
[168] *Essay* 2.21.58.   [169] *Essay* 2.21.61.   [170] *Essay* 2.21.64.

Pain does, and lessens in our Thoughts, what is Future; and forces us, as it were, blindfold into its embraces.

It is not only that people misjudge absent good but, more important-ly, that they make their judgements relative to a subjective and inconstant standard. Their moral standard is their background, acquired uneasiness for some things and against others which Locke calls mental 'relish'.[171] This is another concept that dates from 1678. It denotes those acquired uneasinesses that are fairly stable or habitual, as opposed to violent or contingent uneasinesses.[172] Because these are subjective and various, people pursue different life plans and place happiness in different things. Therefore, moral judgement is subjective and relative: 'The mind has a different relish, as well as the Palate; and you will as fruitlessly endeavour to delight all men with Riches and Glory, (which yet some men place their Happiness in), as you would to satisfy all men's hunger with cheese and lobster'. To different men, happiness and misery, good and evil, are found in different pursuits as a result of their different mental relish or taste.[173]

People choose correctly here because we all seek happiness and what counts as pleasure is relative to our background relish. What saves Locke from relativism is the nature of heaven and hell. These pleasures and pains infinitely outweigh all others, and this for every palate:[174] '[Heaven] being intended for a state of Happiness, it must certainly be agreeable to every one's wish and desire: Could we suppose their relishes as different there as they are here, yet the Manna in Heaven will suit every one's Palate'. Locke offers two proofs of this; one from Revelation, which appears to be a paraphrase of Gassendi, and the second is an empirical argument from the fact that we are never satisfied with earthly pleasures to the possibility of some future happiness that satisfies all desire.[175]

Relish is the acquired mental habit in virtue of which specific ways of thinking and acting are pleasant to the agent. There is, in turn, a fairly settled range of uneasiness for these ways of thinking and acting. Relish is the mechanism that brings absent goods within one's view of

---

[171] *Essay* 2.21.57.   [172] 'Happynesse' (1678), in King, *Life of Locke*, I, 216.
[173] *Essay* 2.21.55.   [174] *Essay* 2.21.65.
[175] 'Happynesse', in King, *Life of Locke*, I, 216 (*Psalms* 16: 11). This appears in 2.121.29 of the 1st edition and 2.21.41 of the 2nd. For the parallel with Gassendi, see Driscoll, 1972, 100. See 'Pleasure and Pain', in von Leyden, *Essays on the law of nature*, 269, and 'Happynesse' (26 September 1676), Bodleian, MS. Locke f. 1, fos 445–7, in Driscoll, 'The influence of Gassendi', pp. 101–2 for unease of earthly happiness.

happiness, renders them desirable, and thus disposes the agent to them.[176] When people are governed by this standard in thought and action, they are acting in accordance with their overall desire for happiness. This utilitarian and hedonic search for happiness is how they ought to act; 'the inclination, and tendency of their nature to happiness is an obligation, and motive to them'.[177] Moral error is not so much misjudging relative to one's habitual relish but acquiring a relish that does not lead to the greatest or true happiness. Since the relish is acquired, it is malleable and so capable of reform. Relish is in fact the disposition to judge and act in specific ways, acquired by custom and education and exposed in Locke's attack on the various dispositional theories.[178] 'Fashion and common Opinion having settled wrong Notions, and education and custom ill Habits, the just values of things are misplaced, and the palates of men corrupted'. It is possible to reform corrupt palates and implant new habits to govern conduct. 'Pains should be taken to rectify these [habits]; and contrary habits change our pleasures, and give a relish to that, which is necessary, or conducive to our Happiness'.

Locke now lays out his reform project. Man has the power to change the pleasantness or unpleasantness that accompanies physical and mental action. The relish of the mind is malleable like that of the body.[179] Actions are pleasing or displeasing with respect to the performance of them and with respect to the rewards and punishments annexed to them. The first step is to suspend *de facto* desires and to examine the consequences of actions using the probabilistic reasoning of weighing future pleasures and pains. This kind of probabilistic reasoning is best exemplified in Pascal's wager, and Locke now introduces it in his most polished presentation. He concludes:[180]

The Rewards and Punishments of another life, which the Almighty has established, as the enforcements of his Law, are of weight enough to determine the Choice, against whatever Pleasure or Pain this life can shew, when the Eternal state is considered but in its bare possibility.

Heaven and hell are thus the 'true foundations' of morality because they outweigh all other pleasures and pains.

The second step in an examination is 'due consideration' of the pleasures and pains reason has discovered.[181] By this, Locke means

---

[176] *Essay* 2.21.55, 57.   [177] *Essay* 2.21.52.   [178] *Essay* 2.21.69.   [179] *Essay* 2.21.69.
[180] *Essay* 2.21.70. Compare 1.3.13, 2.2160.   [181] *Essay* 2.21.45, 69.

that the person should reflect repeatedly and silently on the end until it has become fixed in his mind. In *Some thoughts concerning education*, which is the application of this theory to the education of gentlemen, he explains this step in the formation of a young pupil. To imprint on the mind a true notion of god and instill love and reverence, it is necessary to tell the pupil that god hears, sees, and governs all and rewards those who obey. No questions are permitted, and the pupil is to consider this in silent and simple prayer morning, noon, and night.[182]

These two steps are insufficient in themselves to break an old relish or to create a new one for the virtues that have heavenly rewards. If they were sufficient his original theory would have been true. Reason 'recommends' and consideration gives a certain pleasant colour to the action. This is true for Pascal as well and they both introduce into their theories at this point the modified Aristotelian step that one becomes virtuous and finds pleasure in doing virtuous acts by practising the virtues. For Locke, as for Pascal, this process is analyzed mechanistically, not teleologically, as with Aristotle. The third step, what Pascal calls *la machine*, is called by Locke 'use and practice'.[183]

By the continual repetition of an activity it gradually becomes both habitual and pleasurable. As with 'Bread and Tobacco' so with 'vertue too'. Summing up, Locke writes: 'reason and consideration at first recommends, and begins their trial, and use finds, or custom makes them pleasant'. Therefore, it is continual repetition that makes activities pleasant. 'But the pleasure of the action itself is best acquired, or increased, by use and practice'. 'Repetition', as he explains, 'wears us into a liking, of what possibly, in the first essay, displeased us'. The key, then, to governing conduct is the formation of mental and physical habits, the acquisition of which will, in turn, recommend things to us that reason is impotent to do. 'Habits have powerful charms, and put so strong attractions of easiness and pleasure into what we accustom our selves to, that we cannot forebear

---

[182] *The educational writings of John Locke*, ed. James Axtell (Cambridge: Cambridge University Press, 1968), 136, pp. 241–2. The force of constantly repeating ideas until they are imprinted on the mind is explored in the *Essay* (2.10.6).

[183] *Essay* 2.21.69. Compare the final section of 'Happynesse' (1678), on acquiring virtue by 'use and practice' in King, I, 220. In Locke, use and practice immediately precede the wager argument (2.21.69–70), whereas in Pascal they follow it (419, compare 125, 126).

to do, or at least be easy in the omission of actions, which habitual practice has suited, and thereby recommends to us.'

To summarize, the problems of war, ungovernability, and the legitimation crisis gave rise to the question of what factors govern thought and action. One powerful answer was 'interest'; a concept that took on its modern form in this period, especially in France. Locke rejected this because what a person takes to be his or her interest is constituted by a more fundamental factor: custom and education. This is the Baconian answer. Locke took this two steps further. First, custom and education do not govern conduct, but rather the habits formed by them. Habit is understood not as it had been previously, against a background of teleological nature and human nature, but against the view of man as a malleable blank tablet, indifferent to manipulation. Reason and interest are not as powerful as mental and physical habits.[184] Locke's life-long analyses are brought together in this final form for the first time in chapter 33 of book 2, added to the fourth edition of the *Essay*. He opens by rejecting the argument that 'self-love' or interest explains belief and action (probably thinking of Pierre Nicole).[185] Secondly, he says that 'education' and 'custom', and to some extent 'interest', describe a process but do not explain it. The correct answer is that custom, in the sense of repetition, establishes habits of thinking (assent), of willing, and of bodily movement that govern conduct.[186]

Custom settles habits of thinking in the understanding, as well as determining in the will, and of motions in the Body; all of which seems to be but trains of motion in the animal spirits, which once set a going continue on in the same steps they have been used to, which by often treading are worn into a smooth path, and the motion in it becomes easy and as it were Natural.

Once these habits are formed, reason is powerless.[187] The only way to break them is, as we have seen, to set up counter-practices that make probabilistic reasoning and virtuous action habitual.

Locke then analysed the processes of custom and education into the practice of training by continuous repetition and due consideration. This is how principles and dispositions that are said to be innate come to be implanted habits. His deepest insight, however, was his

---

[184] *Education*, 110, 215.

[185] *Essay* 2.33.2. In 1677 Locke had translated three essays by Pierre Nicole: *On the existence of a God, On the weakness of man, On the way of preserving peace.* See John Locke, *Discourse translated from Nicole's Essays* (1828). The second of these articles is one of many examples of analysis in the terms of self-interest or *amour-propre*.   [186] *Essay* 2.33.6.   [187] *Essay* 2.33.13.

discovery that this process of habit formation is governed by the three juridical apparatus, especially the humanist one. As we have seen, a human being, in virtue of his or her sociability, takes pleasure in company and in the approval of peers. The means to this pleasure, and to avoid the pain of disrepute, is to think and act in ways that are taken to be virtuous and praiseworthy by one's peers. Habits are gradually formed and so the customs of various societies reproduced. Thus, the humanist juridical apparatus is, by 'tacit consent', invested in and constitutive of our most basic social practices. The appeal to praise and blame, good- and ill-repute, is used explicitly to govern in the educational systems. The appeal to love of reputation is the means of drawing the student into ways of thinking and acting that gradually become habitual. Once these habits are settled we cannot bear the reproach with which we are punished for unconventional opinions. By this means, authorities secure their domination, pass off their legitimating beliefs as sacred and innate, and so precipitate a century of wars.[188] The most absurd beliefs and practices can become the object of reverence in this way, says Locke, coming close to Nietzsche:[189] 'In history he shall see the rise of opinions, and find from what slight, and sometimes shameful occasions, some of them have taken their rise, which yet afterwards have had great authority, and passed almost for sacred in the world, and borne down all before them'.

THREE PRACTICES OF GOVERNING

I want to turn now to Locke's account of how these three apparatus had been used to govern conduct; and, secondly, how they could be used to govern the reform of conduct and to establish a new mode of domination and subjection.

The operation of the providential apparatus, the first practice of governing, is explained in the *Reasonableness of Christianity* (1695). It builds upon two early manuscripts: 'Of ethick in general' (1687), intended as a chapter of the *Essay*, and the earlier 'Faith and reason' (1676). Locke published the *Reasonableness* in response to *Christianity not mysterious* by the radical deist John Toland.[190] Toland argued that

---

[188] *Essay* 1.3.22–7.   [189] 'Of Study', in King, *Life of Locke*, I, 202–3.
[190] For Toland and Locke, see Biddle, 'Locke's critique of innate principles', 417–22, *supra* n. 42; M. Jacob, *The Newtonians*, 201–51, and *The radical enlightenment* (London: George Allen and Unwin, 1981).

Scripture, not popes, councils, or tradition, must be the guide in ethics. Given this, there are two positions, the first being that reason is 'the instrument, but not the rule of our belief'. On this view, which he rejected, the mysteries of the Gospel are taken to be either contrary to reason or above reason, yet are nonetheless accepted on faith. In both of these cases, 'the several doctrines of the new Testament belong no further to the enquiries of reason than to prove 'em divinely reveal'd, and they are properly mysteries still'. He rejected this view. Reason must be the *rule* and not merely the *instrument* of belief; or, as he put it, 'reason is the only foundation of all certitude'.[191]

The instrumental view Toland rejects here is Locke's view in chapter 18 of book 4 of the *Essay*, worked out in 1676 and similar to Boyle's argument. Faith is opinion or 'belief', not knowledge, yet it has the highest degree of assurance.[192] Nothing in faith can contradict intuitive or demonstrably certain knowledge, but the number of these truths is very slight in any case. If faith appears to contradict belief, on the other hand, then we must accept faith.[193] The reason for this is that faith has a higher degree of assurance, because 'whatever GOD hath revealed, is certainly true; no doubt can be made of it'. Therefore, 'an evident *Revelation* ought to determine our assent even against Probability' because Revelation is 'another principle of Truth, and Ground of assent'. The role of reason in ethics is instrumental: to judge in accordance with the grounds of probability (witnesses, miracles, etc.) if Scripture is divine Revelation or not (and to interpret): 'it still belongs to *Reason*, to judge of the Truth of its being a Revelation, and of the significance of the words, wherein it is delivered.'[194] This classic voluntarist account of reason in ethics undercuts the old authorities and enthuasiasm. It also undercuts the use of reason to judge the content of Scripture, in opposition to Toland and the radical deists.

Toland's work was taken to be an extension of Locke's work by Bishop Stillingfleet.[195] Locke wrote the *Reasonableness* to distance himself from Toland and, in the final triumph of his voluntarism, to show that reason, in the sense of demonstration, could not provide an independent foundation for morality. He argued that the rationalists

[191] John Toland, *Christianity not mysterious* (1696), 5–6.
[192] 'Faith and Reason' (1676), in von Leyden, *Essays*, 272–84. Robert Boyle, *A discourse of things above reason*, in *The works of Sir Robert Boyle*, ed. T. Birch (1772), D. McKie, 6 vols. (Hildesheim, Olms, 1965–6), IV.   [193] *Essay* 4.18.5, 9, 11.   [194] *Essay* 4.18.10, 9, 8.
[195] Edward Stillingfleet, *A discourse in the vindication of the doctrine of the trinity* (1697), 273.

have the argument upside down: reason cannot be an independent rule for judging Christian ethics because Scripture is the foundation of our moral reasoning, and this because Scripture has spread and become habitual for thought and action by the historical operation of the providential juridical apparatus.

The use of reason prior to Christianity failed to produce an ethical system. All the pagan philosophers could do was teach how to use their moral vocabularies, virtues, and vices, and to back this up with praise and blame. The diversity of moral codes shows that there has been no rational consensus except on the rule of preservation. These rational systems are useless because they are too complex for the majority to understand. The pagan philosophers only discovered those moral principles that coincide with conveniency. Even if they had discovered all the moral principles, these would not constitute a morality because they lack the 'force of law', 'obligation', and sufficient motivation. They would be obeyed only when it was convenient; when praise and blame and one's relish were in conformity with them. For these to be a 'true' morality, the laws must be made for all of us, not by us, by a law-maker who has 'punishing power'.[196]

Therefore, revelation is a necessary condition of morality. Christianity as revealed by Jesus is the true morality. First, it revealed a law-maker, his laws and duties, and his punishments and rewards applicable to and understandable by all. This is 'the true ground of morality'.[197] Clearly, it provides the strong motivation that the pagans with their rewards of praise for virtue could not. With Christ's revelation of heaven and hell 'interest is come about to her [virtue] and virtue is visibly the most enticing purchase and by much the best bargain'.[198] The obligation that only the providential apparatus can provide seems to point in two directions. Sometimes Locke says we have an obligation to obey god because his rewards and punishments bring true happiness and misery. At other times, the obligation is founded on the law being the will of the omnipotent creator.[199] However, when Locke argues in this latter way, he standardly adds, as a traditional voluntarist would not, reference to god's rewards and

---

[196] *Reasonableness of Christianity*, in *The works of John Locke* (Germany: Scientia Verlag Aalen, 1963 [1823]), VII, 88–90, 93; 'Of ethick in general', in King, *Life of Locke*, II, 124–5, 130–1.
[197] *Reasonableness*, 87, 90, 92.   [198] *Reasonableness*, 94.
[199] *Essay* 1.3.5–6; 'Voluntas', 1693, in von Leyden, *Essays on the law of nature*, 72; 'Of ethick in general', 130; *Reasonableness*, 89–90.

punishments. Thus, the theory of obligation as well is neither pure voluntarism nor pure hedonism but what I have called penalism.

Locke now turns from the pagan philosophers to the rationalist tradition in Christendom. Christian philosophers have come closer to demonstrating ethics than the pre-Christians, but this is not because, as they assume, they have an independent rule of reason to test moral principles. It is rather because their first principles are derived from revelation. We grow up with the Gospel from the cradle. It seems 'natural' to us and we take it for 'unquestionable truths'. Rationalists think they have discovered the foundations of morality, but they only 'confirm' revelation. We would be lost without it. Revelation is the foundation of reason, of what we take to be 'self-evident':[200]

A great many things which we have been bred up in the belief of, from our cradles, (and are notions grown familiar, and, as it were, natural to us, under the Gospel) we take for unquestionable obvious truths and easily demonstrable; without considering how long we might have been in doubt or ignorance of them, had Revelation been silent. And many are beholden to Revelation, who do not acknowledge it. It is no diminishing to Revelation, that reason gives its suffrage too to the truths Revelation has discovered. But it is our mistake to think that because reason confirms them to us, we had the first certain knowledge of them from thence; and in that clear evidence we now possess them. The contrary is manifest . . .

Thus, god spreads Christianity by the same mode of governance as other opinions are spread. Jesus revealed the providential apparatus, and it slowly spread and sank in as people considered its force.[201] Even Islam is an offshoot of this historical process.[202] It became part of European education, thus enforcing it with the humanist apparatus, and so gradually thinking and acting in accordance with the Gospel has become 'second nature', the foundation of our rationality.[203] What the Enlightenment, prefigured in Toland, called reasonable is just acquired dispositions to think and act in accordance with Scripture. Hence the title: the *Reasonableness of Christianity*. The rationalist, whether the Thomist-scholastic or the new deist, is inside the language-game: he or she takes for granted the principles and ways of acting that the voluntarist explains as having been laid down by the normal operation of the juridical apparatus. For Locke, then,

---

[200] *Reasonableness*, 88, 90–1. Compare 'Faith and reason', in von Leyden, *Essays*, 275–80.
[201] *Reasonableness*, 93–4, 92, 86.   [202] *Reasonableness*, 86.
[203] Compare *Essay* 1.3.22, 1.4.9: 'if the Fear of absolute and irresistible Power set it [the idea of God] on upon the Mind, the *Idea* is likely to sink the deeper, and spread the farther'.

the providential juridical apparatus governs conduct, laying down its own causal and rational grounds of obedience as it proceeds.[204]

When Locke writes in the *Reasonableness* that the self-evident principles on which Christian philosophers base their demonstrations come from Scripture, he is thinking, I believe, of the non-trivial, demonstrable principles advanced in the *Essay*. The sample of demonstrably certain, non-analytic knowledge he presents is precisely the providential apparatus:[205] 'He also that hath the idea of an intelligent, but frail and weak Being, made by and depending on another, who is eternal, omnipotent, perfectly wise and good, will as certainly know that man is to honour, fear and obey God, as that the Sun shines when he sees it'. This is repeated to illustrate his non-syllogistic form of demonstration and then it is put forward as the foundation of demonstrable ethics.[206] Although the existence of an omnipotent, creating god can be demonstrated by reason, experience, and reflection alone, his providence and laws cannot, according to Locke and voluntarists generally.[207] Nor can Christian ethics be deduced from scholastic maxims: "'Tis from Revelation we have received it [Christianity], and without Revelation these *Maxims* had never been able to help us to it.'[208]

Once we see that the Christian rationalist is starting from revealed providentialism, it is possible to draw some conclusions about natural law. Specifically, it is possible to deduce the principle that mankind ought to be preserved from the providential premises; this can be confirmed by revelation and by observation of early culture. A basic set of rights and obligations can then be derived from this one law within its juridical framework, as Locke shows in the *Two treatises of government* and as I have argued elsewhere, thus justifying and giving a normative structure to the seventeenth-century politics of preservation.[209]

Nietzsche is thought to be the first to suggest that some of the processes of rationalization in thought and action that we call

---

[204] *Reasonableness*, 87–92. [205] *Essay*, 4.13.3. [206] *Essay* 4.17.4, 4.3.18.
[207] *Essay* 4.10. [208] *Essay* 4.7.2.
[209] The basic premise that mankind ought to be preserved is deduced from the providential apparatus by Locke first in 1681, 'Preservation' (August 1681), Bodleian, MS. Locke f. 5, fos 88–91, in King, *Life of Locke*, I, 228–30. This is worked out in the *Two treatises of government*, book 2, section 6. See James Tully, *A discourse on property* (Cambridge: Cambridge University Press, 1980). Preservation is said to enjoy universal consent in 'Of ethick in general' in King, *Life of Locke*, II (125), and to be the fundamental moral principle in *Education* (116) and the *Two Treatises* (2.135).

modernity, which are now habitual, are the continuation of Christianity by other means.[210] This hypothesis has been supported by the work of Michael Foster, Francis Oakley, Robert Hooykaas, and a new generation of historians of science and politics.[211] They specify, however, that it is a particular type of Christianity which lies at the seventeenth-century foundations of modern science and politics – voluntarism, and that voluntarism is the theological expression of the creative god of Revelation. What this study seems to suggest is that Locke and some of his contemporaries were thinking along similar lines.

Once the foundational nature of Scripture is understood, it is unnecessary and irrelevant to demonstrate ethics, because the Gospel provides a 'perfect body of ethics': 'reason may be excused from that enquiry, since she may find man's duty clearer and easier in Revelation than in herself'.[212] How do we know Scripture is true? As we have seen, the assessment of the evidence for Scripture being a divine revelation in accordance with the new grounds of probability shows that it is probably a divine revelation, and thus rational to believe. This probability is in turn sufficient, given the overwhelming pleasures and pains of heaven and hell, to provide reason and motivation to become Christians. But, first, how does one know that what god says is true, since we have no independent criterion? Locke says we know solely in virtue of its being the word of god.[213] When Thomas Burnet responded to the *Essay* by claiming Locke was a voluntarist, as the third Earl of Shaftesbury was to do more famously, and challenging Locke to make it explicit, he put this question of truth to him.[214] Locke replied in a brief appendix to his first response to Bishop Stillingfleet. This response is standardly taken to be a case of Locke dodging the question.[215] But he clearly answers the question and, in so doing, admits his voluntarism. He says that god does not lie, because lying is a weakness. Thus, truth follows from omnipotence. Any law of the almighty is for that very reason true.[216]

---

[210] F. Nietzsche, 'What is the meaning of ascetic ideals?', in *On the genealogy of morals*, section 27, 160.   [211] See above, nn. 93, 95 and Merchant, *The death of nature*, 192–235.

[212] Locke to Molyneux, 5 April 1696, *Correspondence*, v, 2059. Compare letter to Tyrrell, IV, 1309.   [213] *Reasonableness*, 92, *Essay* 4.18.10.

[214] Thomas Burnet, *Remarks upon an essay concerning humane understanding* (1697). For the third Earl of Shaftesbury see n. 131 above.

[215] See Oakley and Urdang 'Locke, natural law', 106, *supra* n. 106.

[216] Locke, *An answer to remarks upon an essay concerning human understanding*, in *Works*, IV, 186–9: 'Whether an infinitely powerful and wise Being be veracious or no; unless falsehood be in such reputation . . . that . . . lying [is] to be no mark of weakness and folly' (187); 'Whoever sincerely acknowledges any law to be the law of God, cannot fail to acknowledge also, that it hath all the reason and ground that a just and wise law can or ought to have' (p. 188).

This voluntarist thesis that truth *is* the word of the most powerful is driven home in the late work *A discourse of miracles* (1702). The problem here is how to know that the miracles, which are evidence for the belief that Scripture is the word of god, are god's work. The criterion for an extraordinary event being a miracle from god is 'the carrying with [an extraordinary event] the marks of a greater power than appears in opposition to it'.[217] Therefore, god's omnipotence is the ultimate ground of both the truth of and assent to Christianity:[218]

His power being known to have no equal, always will, and always may be, safely depended on, to show its superiority in indicating his authority, and maintaining every truth that he hath revealed. So that the marks of a superior power accompanying it, always have, and always will be, visible and sure guide to divine Revelation; by which men may conduct themselves in their examining of revealed religions, and be satisfied which they ought to receive as coming from God.

This voluntarism runs through the other two juridical apparatus: the sovereign civil power decrees and enforces what is and is not a crime; the community wills and enforces virtue and vice.[219]

The second practice of governing is the use of the humanist apparatus in the education of elites. This is laid out in *Some thoughts concerning education* and *On the conduct of the understanding*. The aim is to inculcate habits of probabilistic reasoning and virtuous behaviour, habits that will replace 'old custom'. The programme is based on the new view of human nature: the gentleman's son is considered 'only as white paper, or wax, to be moulded and fashioned as one pleases'.[220] The governor's objective is 'to fashion the carriage, and form the mind; [to] settle in his pupil good habits, and the principles of virtue and wisdom'.[221] The key to good habits is not the memorization of rules, as it had been, but practice, because, 'As in the body, so in the mind; practice makes it what it is', and 'most even of those excellencies, which are looked on as natural endowments, will be found, when examined into more narrowly, to be the product of exercise, and to be raised to that pitch only by repeated actions'.[222] By 'practice' he

---

[217] *A discourse of miracles*, in *Works*, IX, 256–65, 259.

[218] *A discourse of miracles*, in *Works*, IX, 263; *cf: Essay* 4.19.15, 4.16.13; *Reasonableness*, in *Works*, VII, 86–7.

[219] 'Of ethic in general', in King, *Life of Locke*, II, 130–2. This is one of the major themes of the *Essay*: 2.28.14, 2.32.11, 17, 3.5, 3.9.8–11, 3.10, 3.11.25. The doctrine is summarized at 4.4.10. See Tully, *Discourse*, 8–27.

[220] *Education*, ed. James Axtell (supra, n. 182), 216, p. 325.   [221] *Education*, 94, p. 198.

[222] John Locke, *Of the conduct of the understanding*, in *Works*, III, 4, p. 214. Locke wrote this as an addition to the fourth edition of the *Essay*, but it was not published until 1706. For the role of practice forming mental and physical habits, compare 28, pp. 255–7, and *Education*, dedication, 2, 10, 17, 32, 41, 42, 64, 66, 70, 94, 105, 185.

means the continual repetition of mental and physical behaviour until it becomes habitual and pleasurable.

This assault on the Renaissance techniques of memorizing rules, and its replacement with education as habit formation by repetition and drill, by 'exercises', is part of a much broader dispersion of techniques of discipline by drill throughout Europe from roughly the time of the revolutionary reform of training in the Dutch army in the 1590s.[223] The second transformation marked by Locke's practice theory of education is the replacement of corporal punishments by praise and blame as the major techniques of habit formation and reformation.[224] Of course, he still advocates the use of the whip, but not as often as earlier theorists. The main rewards and punishments are esteem and disgrace. Once love of credit and apprehension of disgrace are instilled, these can be manipulated to train the child.[225] The very first step is thus to cultivate a love of reputation in the pupil; this provides the basis for subtle, detailed, and closely supervised governing of drill and repetition.[226]

As we have seen, the first idea to be imprinted on the mind is the providential apparatus, the foundation of virtue.[227] Then, Christian virtues, with a strong stress on the mercantile and neo-stoic virtues of discipline and industry, are impressed by constant repetition and praise and blame.[228] Mental habits are formed in the same manner. Just as in the training of animals, the mind can be made 'obedient to discipline' and 'pliant to reason' and so 'habits woven into the very principles of his nature'.[229] Natural philosophy is taught by studying the various 'hypotheses', which are probable, not certain. Since the sciences only treat of body, the other half of nature, spirit, should be taught by inculcating the Bible, preferably in the form of an epitome. This should precede and provide the foundation for natural philos-

---

[223] In addition to Foucault, *Discipline and punish*, 135–95, see the important article and review of the literature on this issue from Weber onwards by Murray Field, *The structure of violence* (Beverly Hills: Sage Publications, 1977), 169–204.

[224] See Margaret J. M. Ezell, 'John Locke's images of childhood: early eighteenth century response to *Some thoughts concerning education*', *Eighteenth Century Studies* 17, 2 (Winter 1983–4), 139–56, 152–3.

[225] *Education*, 56, pp. 52–3: '*Esteem* and *Disgrace* are, of all others, the most powerful Incentives to the Mind, when once it is brought to relish them. If you can once get into Children a Love of Credit, and an Apprehension of Shame and Disgrace, you have put into them the true Principle, which will constantly work, and incline them to the right.' Compare 57, p. 153.   [226] *Education*, 61, pp. 155–6.

[227] *Education*, 136, pp. 241–2. Compare 61, p. 156.

[228] *Education*, 33, 38, 42, 64, 70, 103–5, 110, 185.   [229] *Education*, 34, p. 138; 42, p. 146.

ophy.[230] Theology in the juridical sense is the basis for all other areas of knowledge as well.[231] The fundamental principle of politics and morality is the preservation of mankind. The best training for applying this principle in politics is the practice of caring for animals.[232]

In the *Conduct* Locke lays out the central mental habits. He says that a person's ability to reason varies in accordance with his occupational practices, with, of course, the labourer on the bottom and the person with this new education on top.[233] The habit of reasoning with probabilities is to be learned early by use and exercise in mathematics and bookkeeping and by studying Chillingworth's sermons.[234] The two primary habits of suspension and examination are taught in order to break old prejudices. Locke suggests developing an 'indifferency' to assent, like the sceptic, then a passion to close with the truth after examination. Since 'tyranny' of passion is the greatest problem, only counter-passions, formed by detailed training, can guard against or cure it.[235]

Although not everyone has the time and leisure for this, everyone can learn their calling and the rudiments of the after-life by exercises on Sunday. The basics of theology – god, duty and the possibility of a future life – can be absorbed by everyone. As Locke stresses in the *Reasonableness*, Christianity is a simple ethic for the poor who labour; an ethic of discipline, industry, honesty, and sobriety. All that is required is the Gospels, training on Sundays, and practice, as the Huguenot peasants have proven in adverse conditions in France.[236] The simplified and austere neo-stoical Christianity renders casuistical authorities unnecessary. The final step in this direction, which played such an enormous role in the eighteenth century, is the argument that there is not one right answer in any moral situation, and that therefore god rewards effort and sincerity, not sophistication.[237]

---

[230] *Education*, 190–4.   [231] *Conduct*, 4, p. 214.   [232] *Education*, 116, pp. 225–7.

[233] *Conduct*, 3, pp. 208–13.

[234] *Conduct*, 6–7, pp. 222–5; *Education*, 188, 210–11, pp. 296, 319–21.

[235] *Conduct*, 11–12, pp. 230–3; 45, pp. 284–8.

[236] *Conduct*, 9, pp. 225–7; *Reasonableness*, p. 98.

[237] See Letters to Denis Grenville, *Correspondence*, I, 328, 374, 426; *Essay* 2.21.47, 3.10.12. The argument that sincerity, not true knowledge, is the key Christian virtue is one of the main arguments of *A letter concerning toleration*. It is first introduced by Locke to justify toleration in *An essay concerning toleration* (1667). It leads to Bayle's famous paradox in the *Pensées diverses*. For the role of sincerity in the eighteenth century, see Leon Guilhamet, *The sincere ideal* (Montreal: McGill–Queen's University Press, 1974).

The humanist technique is thus used to educate by habituation and to implant the providential apparatus. To borrow a phrase from Thomas Kuhn, it is a 'disciplinary matrix' which, through love of reputation, reproduces itself, governing even the new elites it trains and legitimates. In the eighteenth century this practice of education, premised on the pupil as malleable raw material, gradually became more popular than either the Augustinian model of the pupil as fallen or the model of the pupil as innately good.[238] In addition to the schools and dissenting academics, it was carried forward in the crazy-quilt of practices set up in the late seventeenth century to moralize and discipline all segments of the population, not only the gentry, by organizations such as the Society for the Promotion of Christian Knowledge.[239]

The third practice of governing is the legal apparatus of the early modern state. I want to look at this in the case of Locke's report to the Board of Trade in 1697 on reform of the poor law system. The problem the Board faced was 'the multiplying of the poor' and, consequently, 'the increase of the tax for their maintenance'.[240] Gregory King had just submitted his famous report showing that the majority of the population was dependent to some extent on parish poor relief. In addition, others published calculations of the increase in poor rates since 1660. Since the Restoration over seventy proposals had been put forward to correct the system of houses of correction and work. This system had been used since the 1550s not only, as earlier, to support the surplus population but to 'correct' and 'reform' the poor in 'virtue' and 'industry'. Indeed, many of the early houses of correction and work were disbanded monasteries in which monastic discipline continued. The system fell into disrepair during the Civil War and early Restoration. By the time Locke wrote there were roughly 200 workhouses spread throughout the country.[241] Here is his solution.

[241] For a survey of the major proposals, see F. M. Eden, *The state of the poor* (3 vols., London, 1797). Also, Dorothy Marshall, *The English poor in the eighteenth century* (London: Routledge & Kegan Paul, 1926); E. M. Leonard, *The early history of English poor relief* (Cambridge: Cambridge University Press, 1900).

[238] Ezell, 'John Locke's images of childhood', 140–2.

[239] See Hundert, 'The making of homo faber', *supra* n. 9; Dudley Bahlman, *The moral revolution of 1688* (New Haven: Yale University Press, 1957); Leo Radzinowicz, *A history of English criminal law and its administration from 1750* (2 vols., New York: Macmillan, 1956), II, 1–29; M. G. Jones, *The Charity School Movements* (London: Archon, 1964 [1938]).

[240] John Locke, *A report of the Board of Trade to the Lords Justices respecting the relief and employment of the poor* (1697), in H. R. Fox Bourne, *The life of John Locke* (2 vols, London, 1876), II, 377–91, 377–8.

The cause of the problem is not 'scarcity of provisions nor want of employment' but rather 'nothing else but the relaxation of discipline and the corruption of manners'. This is so because virtue is always joined to industry and vice to idleness. He then lays out a vast scheme to use the disciplining practices of the law, the Royal navy, the houses of correction and work, the compulsory apprenticeship system, deportation, and control of travel by passes and badges to make the poor docile with respect to the law and useful in employment.

There are three classes of people on relief: those who can do nothing towards their own support; those who can do something but not all; and those who could be self-maintaining yet have either large families or claim they cannot find work and engage in begging. The first remedy for the last sort of 'begging drones' who live upon others' labour is the strict enforcement of the Elizabethan poor laws. These provide for parish houses of correction, punishment of vagabonds, compulsion of the able-bodied to work, apprenticeship for children, support for impotent paupers, and the enforcement of poor rates by parish overseers, guardians, and justices of the peace. In addition, a new law is required. All able-bodied men over fourteen and under fifty caught begging outside their parish in the maritime counties without passes are to be seized and taken to the nearest seaport. They are to be kept at 'hard labour' until one of his majesty's ships arrives and then placed in three years' service 'under strict discipline', at soldier's pay (minus subsistence cost) and punished with death for desertion. If the beggar is maimed or over fifty, he is to be sent to the closest house of correction for three years of hard labour.[242]

To upgrade the houses of correction the master should receive his pay from what the 'inmates' produce. The local justice of the peace is to inspect them and if any are 'not at all mended by the discipline of the place', he is to order longer and more severe discipline. Nobody is to be dismissed without 'manifest proof of amendment, the end for which he was sent'. If a beggar has a forged travel pass, he shall lose his ear the first time and 'be transported to the plantations, as in the case of felony' for a second offence. This means in effect, as Locke points out in the *Two treatises*, that he has the status of a slave.[243]

If a female over fourteen is found begging outside her parish, she is to be returned and the person who reports her is to be rewarded out of

---

[242] *Report*, 378. All following quotations from the *Report* unless otherwise noted.
[243] *Two treatises*, 2.23.

her poor relief. If she is caught a second time, or is more than five miles from her parish the first time, she is to be taken to the closest house of correction for three months' hard work and 'due correction'. Boys and girls under fourteen caught begging out of their parish are to be sent to the workhouse, 'soundly whipped', and worked until evening. A second offence, or being more than five miles out of their parish, is to be met with six weeks of hard labour in the workhouse.

The local parishioners are compelled to employ those who claim they cannot find work and to give them a small wage. If these men refuse to work, they are to be placed aboard one of his majesty's ships for three years, their wages going to the parish. For women with children and the elderly, 'being decayed from their full strength', part-time work is to be organized in woollen and other manufacturing. This 'shows us what is the true and proper relief of the poor'. It consists in 'finding work for them and taking care they do not live like drones upon the labour of others'.

The main targets of this proposal are the children of the labouring poor, who are a 'burden to the parish' and are 'maintained in idleness'. Children of three to fourteen are to be sent to working schools in each parish, thus freeing the mother for labour. The children will be better provided for than at home, 'and from infancy be inured to work, which is no small consequence to the making of them sober and industrious all their lives after'. Diet will consist in a 'belly full of bread daily' and, 'if it be thought needful, a little warm water-gruel in winter'. These schools will thus reduce the parish-relief and, with proper management, aim for maintaining themselves out of the products of child labour. Locke's friend Thomas Firmin was experimenting with making his workhouses profitable throughout this period. Children will come to work because, echoing the *Essay*, the alternative is starvation.[244] Various kinds of manufacturing appropriate to local needs are to be instituted. Another advantage is that the children 'may be obliged to come constantly to church every Sunday . . . whereby they may be brought to some sense of religion'. At the age of fourteen, the disciplined and industrious young men and women are to be placed in compulsory apprenticeship with local manufacturers and landlords until the age of twenty-three. Locke then outlines an elaborate system of managers, guardians, overseers,

[244] *Essay* 2.21.58.

beadles, and justices of the peace which, by a series of interlocking monetary and legal rewards and punishments, makes it in the interest of each to enforce the whole process of reform and habituation.

Locke's proposal is similar to about one hundred others written between 1660 and 1760. In addition, Locke wrote notes on a system of work, relief, and correction for colonial settlement.[245] His reform proposal was not instituted nationally, but it was applied almost immediately in Bristol and it continued to influence projects to reform the poor throughout the eighteenth century. Indeed, it continued to be praised until the time of the Webbs. The importance of the document is that it displays the objectives of the new mode of governing: to deconstruct old customary ways of life and to produce new ones. The aim is to use the law, the navy, corporal punishment, the threats of divine punishment, economic incentives, and the activity of repetitious labour, from age three onwards, to fabricate an individual who is habituated to obedience and useful labour. It should not be forgotten that the overseers and guardians were drawn into this system as well. Further, the governing of each individual is integrated into the collective welfare–warfare policy of increasing the strength of the mercantile state by means of passes, badges, apprenticeship, the use of the navy, and the type of work done in each workhouse. It is out of these houses and their experimentation in moulding human behaviour that many of the early factories, reformatories, and public schools developed.[246]

Locke's proposal was republished in 1790 with a preface that captures the spirit of this juridical practice of governance:[247]

the object of republishing [Locke's report] is to explain, and, if possible, procure strength and permanency for a system of parochial economy, congenial to the sentiments of Mr Locke, who appears from the whole tenor of his reasoning in that memorial, to be convinced that rewards and

---

[245] See Ernesto De Marchi, 'Locke's *Atlantis*', *Political Studies* 3, 2 (June 1955), 164–5. Part of the journal entries is reprinted in Charles Bastide, *John Locke, ses théories politiques et leur influence en Angleterre* (Geneva, 1970 [1906]), Appendice 1, 'Les projets de réforme sociale de Locke', 377–9.

[246] Austin van der Slice, 'Elizabethan houses of correction', *Journal of the American institute of criminal law and criminology* 27 (May–June 1936 – March–April 1937), 45–67; E. Furniss, *The position of the labourer in a system of nationalism* (New York: A. M. Kelley, 1965 [1920]); Rusche and Kirchheimer, 24–52; Sidney Pollard, *The genesis of scientific management* (Cambridge, Mass.: Harvard University Press, 1965), 163–97; Sidney and Beatrice Webb, *English local government: English poor law history*, pt 1, *The old poor law* (London: Longmans, Green & Co., 1927), 102–20.   [247] John Locke, *Report* (London, 1790), preface, viii.

punishments, and the mixing habits of industry with principles of religious duties, were the best and surest means of effecting that reformation in the manners of the people, which in those days was judged essential to the strength and safety of the nation; and which in our time, from the great increase of profligacy and dissoluteness of the lower order of people, is become a more pressing object of national concern.

The work of Michael Ignatieff and Michel Foucault has thrown light on the dispersion of these techniques of governing in eighteenth-century England and France.[248] Foucault argued that the social science disciplines that explain and are employed to administer and reform the behaviour of individuals and of populations of modern states have their roots in the diverse reform projects of the early modern period. He distinguished this disciplinarian power and knowledge from juridical power and knowledge because the former refers behaviour to a norm or statistical regularity, and adjusts it relative to criteria of normality and abnormality. In contrast, the juridical refers to the law and criteria of legality and illegality and is primarily repressive. However, it should by now be clear that the techniques of reform and behavioural fashioning of the disciplines developed partly out of a long tradition of using the law to reform, and not simply to repress. Secondly, if we ask in what conceptual framework the concept of a law of human behaviour as a statistical regularity emerged, the answer is the juridical combination of a voluntaristic theory of observed regularities in nature and the probability theory that we see with Boyle and Pascal. And we should not be surprised to see systematic attempts to explain, predict, and administer people in accordance with these two forms of knowledge, and with the techniques of the juridical apparatus, by political economists such as John Graunt, William Petyt, Charles Davenant, John Cary, and Pieter de la Court.[249]

'True politics', Locke states, summarizing the juridical mode of

---

[248] M. Ignatieff, *A just measure of pain: the penitentiary in the industrial revolution 1750–1850* (New York: Pantheon, 1978). For the use of Locke's providential and humanist governors in eighteenth-century education see Jones, *The charity school*, especially 5.

[249] John Graunt, *Natural and political observations . . . made upon the bills of morality* (1662); William Petyt, *Political arithmetick, or a discourse concerning the extent and value of land, peoples, buildings . . .* (1690), Charles Davenant, *An essay on the probable methods of making a people gainers in the balance of trade* (1699); John Cary, *An essay towards regulating the trade and employing the poor of this kingdom* (1717); Pieter de la Court, *Considérations sur L'État, ou la balance politique* (1662). See Michael Hunter, *Science and society in Restoration England* (Cambridge: Cambridge University Press, 1981), 118–34.

domination, 'I look on as a part of moral philosophy, which is nothing but the art of conducting men right in society and supporting a community amongst its neighbours.'[250] Section 116 of *Education* illustrates one further aspect of this new politics of reform. As we have seen, the practice of toleration was intended, *inter alia*, to undercut the religious motive for warfare. In section 116 Locke moves against the second great early modern war motive – the Renaissance humanists' glorification of warfare and the identification of military achievements with heroic virtue. This motivation is the product of two habit-forming practices: teaching children to delight in inflicting pain and, secondly, the central position of the history of battles and martial virtue in the humanists' curriculum. 'By these steps unnatural cruelty is planted in us.' These are to be replaced by practices that instill habits of care and compassion and an overall concern with preservation. In section 71 he stresses that the population must still be trained to fight wars, but now in a more disciplined, controlled manner – where war is a rational instrument of the policy of preserving the state in a condition of international rivalry, not an arena where virtuous acts are performed and glory achieved. Thus, the new model of governance involves, and is perhaps best exemplified in, the incremental bureaucratization of violence in this period and the integration of warfare into the rationalizing state.[251]

THE PENALIZED SELF

I want to ask, finally, what kind of self is produced by subjection to a way of governing action that aims at forming habitual mental and physical conduct. The answer is provided by Locke himself, who added an important chapter on personal identity to the second edition of the *Essay*.

Locke located the identity of the person or self solely in consciousness, and not in substance, thus making his most radical departure from his predecessors. The self or person is constituted by consciousness alone, and this is consciousness of sensations and perceptions. The '*Self*', he writes, 'is that conscious thinking thing . . . which is sensible, or conscious of Pleasure and Pain, capable of Happiness or

---

[250] Draft letter to the Countess of Peterborough (1697), Bodleian, MS. Locke c. 24, fos 196–7, in *Education*, 395–6.
[251] See William H. McNeill, *The pursuit of power* (Chicago: University of Chicago Press, 1981), 117–85.

misery, and so is concern'd for its *self*, as far as the consciousness extends.'[252] Although the 'person' or self is conscious of all sensations of pleasure and pain, it is constituted by consciousness of voluntary actions; that is, those actions the self is conscious of having performed. Secondly, the concern for self that is part of consciousness is primarily concern for rewards and punishments, pleasures and pains, attached to voluntary actions. Therefore, he concludes, 'self' only belongs to voluntary agents capable of a law: it 'is a Forensick Term appropriating Actions and their Merit; and so belongs only to intelligent agents capable of a Law, and Happiness and Misery'. This subjectivity is founded in the constitutive 'concern' or uneasiness of self for happiness.[253] 'All which is founded in a concern for Happiness, the unavoidable concomitant of consciousness, that which is conscious of Pleasure and Pain, desiring that that Self, that is conscious, should be happy'.

Thus, the penalized self is for Locke the ontological self. As he says, 'In this *Personal Identity* is founded all the Right and Justice of Reward and Punishment; Happiness and Misery, being that, for which every one is concerned for *himself*'. On judgement day everyone 'shall receive his doom', on the basis of this self that is the consciousness of having performed voluntary actions for which he can be held accountable.[254] Therefore, the self which is concerned about, and thinks and acts with continual reference to the juridical apparatus, is the ontological self: 'And to receive Pleasure or Pain, i.e. Reward or Punishment, on account of any such Action, is all one, as to be made happy or miserable in its first being'.[255] The self whose thought and action is always guided by a concern to be rewarded by the juridical apparatus and to avoid its punishment is the kind of self god created.

Locke could assume that this penalized self was constituted prior to the juridical apparatus that governs and subjects it. We should ask, rather, if this self, so familiar to us in its relative regularity and law-abidingness, is not a product of centuries of subjection to juridical governance. Is it not a form of subjectivity that continues to be imposed on us in virtue of the juridical mode of governance being invested in our social practices? This is a regime that not only subjects us in our everyday practices but also governs even modern states, as

---

[252] *Essay* 2.27.17.   [253] *Essay* 2.27.26. Compare 2.27.9, 14, 25.   [254] *Essay* 2.27.18.
[255] *Essay* 2.27.26.

Hobbes dreamed, like a 'mortal God'. For what is said to be the fundamental governor of the conduct of the modern world but the apparatus of deterrence, with its threat of nuclear annihilation for misconduct?[256]

[256] I would like to thank John Dunn, Guy Laforest, Edmund Leites, David Norton, Quentin Skinner, and Charles Taylor for their helpful comments, and Vivian Pelkonen and Adam Jones for typing several drafts. I am pleased to acknowledge the assistance of the Social Sciences Research Subcommittee of McGill University.

CHAPTER 7

Rights in abilities[1]

In contemporary political philosophy the question of property or rights in one's abilities is posed within a broader problematic of property or rights over things. This problematic comprises three main concepts: (1) the self or subject and its capacities, abilities, powers, or talents; (2) the products of the exercise of abilities on nature; and (3) nature or natural resources on which abilities are exercised. Since the publication of John Rawls' *A theory of justice* eighteen years ago, philosophers have advanced three solutions to this set of problems; that is, three ways of relating selves and abilities, their products, and natural resources.

The first solution, self-ownership, is that abilities are necessarily or constitutively related to the self and, in virtue of this necessary relation, the self can be said to be in a juridical relation of ownership to its abilities. This in turn is said to ground the values of autonomy, individual liberty, and inviolability of the person. From these premisses two opposed conclusions have been drawn. One is that inequalities of private property in products and natural resources follow from self-ownership.[2] The other is that liberal socialists should accept these premisses of self-ownership, and so the values of autonomy and individual liberty, but go on to show that 'partial egalitarianism' in products and natural resources is derivable from them.[3]

The second solution, the disengaged self, is that abilities are only contingently related to the self and, in virtue of this contingent

---

[1] A paper delivered at the conference on *Liberalism and the moral life*, conference for the study of political and social thought, City University of New York, 8–10 April 1988.
[2] Robert Nozick, *Anarchy, state, and utopia* (New York: Basic Books, 1974).
[3] G. A. Cohen, 'Socialist equality and capitalist freedom', in Jon Elster and K. Moene, eds, *Work, markets, and social justice* (Oxford: Oxford University Press, 1987); James Grunebaum, *Private ownership* (London: Routledge and Kegan Paul, 1987).

relation, abilities can be said to be in a juridical relation of being 'common assets' of the community. On this disengaged conception of identity, for the community to exercise some sort of rights over the abilities of members is not in any way to violate the autonomy of persons, or to treat them as means, as the self-ownership school claims, precisely because the abilities are not constitutive of persons. From these premises of common assets it is possible to justify a more egalitarian distribution of products and natural resources, thus grounding the values of welfare and equality.[4]

In the third or communitarian solution, the self and its abilities are necessarily related, as in the self-ownership solution. However, the 'self' is not the individual exerciser of abilities, but the community in which the abilities are developed, nurtured, and exercised. Further, to provide a space for liberal concerns of individual liberty, communitarians argue that the juridical relation between individual exerciser and her abilities is one of being the 'guardian' of her abilities, but not the 'owner', as in the self-ownership solution, nor the mere 'repository', as in the disengaged solution. In this way, the individual guards her abilities in the sense of having a say over the uses of these abilities in the dialogue of the community in which individual goods and the common good come to be articulated, adjudicated, and sustained.[5]

Summarizing, therefore, the manner in which the question of rights in abilities is posed and answered within these three solutions, there are three constitutive concepts – self, abilities, and community – and two types of relation among them: (1) relations of identity between self and abilities, which as we have seen, are either necessary or contingent; and, as a consequence, (2) relations of property or rights in abilities, which are of ownership, repository, or guardianship.

My aim in this chapter is not to provide another solution within this problematic but to enable us to stand back and thus to free us slightly from this recent yet now customary way of thinking about property *via à vis* self, abilities, and communities. I do this by means of a survey of five ways that selves, abilities, and communities can be

---

[4] John Rawls, *A theory of justice* (Oxford: Oxford University Press, 1971); and Ronald Dworkin, 'Equality of resources', *Philosophy and public affairs* 10 (1981), 283–345.

[5] Michael Sandel, *Liberalism and the limits of justice* (Cambridge: Cambridge University Press, 1982), 79, 97; I am also indebted to discussions with Charles Taylor for my understanding of this position.

conceptualized and related. These five games or practical systems of constituting and relating selves, abilities, and communities can then be used as objects of comparison to throw light on, and to loosen the hold of the conventional way of thinking about rights in abilities in contemporary political philosophy as outlined above.

Three exercises in the freedom of critical thought with respect to our current way of thinking are involved in the following survey. First, it shows the multiplicity of ways in which self, abilities, and community can be both construed and related. This enables us to see clearly the limitations of the three contemporary solutions: where they are appropriate and where their shared language conceals the diversity of ways of organizing selves, abilities, and communities, and, in so doing, constrains our political imagination. Second, the five practical systems are arranged historically to highlight the singularity and historical contingency of the current concept of a right in abilities, thus making it less obvious, less to be taken for granted, and so itself more open to question. Third, once the features of the current concept are clarified it is possible to bring to light a basic problem with the concept of a right in *productive* abilities. Some of the forms of organization of selves, productive abilities, and communities in the workplace are incompatible with the kind of arrangement of selves, abilities, and communities necessary for agents to exercise the rights which they are said to have in their productive abilities. Therefore, it is not surprising that many of the great struggles during the last two hundred years over the organization of work have been attempts to overcome this incompatibility; to establish practices of rights in the workplace.

Before proceeding to the survey, it is necessary to outline the features of abilities which make up a practical system. Abilities presuppose capacities that they realize or set in motion. To have acquired an ability is to be able to engage in a range of thought and action, to participate in a practice with others. The acquisition and exercise of abilities, therefore, involves the training and education of mental and physical capacities over time in rule-governed activities until the exercise of abilities becomes more or less customary. Moreover, in virtue of having and exercising an ability, of being a practitioner in a practice, one acquires an identity, a self, or a form of subjectivity. For example, to have keypunching, mill-working, or teaching abilities is just to be a keypuncher, mill-worker, or teacher. (Of course, it does not *necessarily* follow from abilities being necessarily related to forms of subjectivity or selfhood that these forms of subjectivity constitute the complete or even predominant identity of a person, since it is possible, for example, to be a teacher without this exhausting one's identity.)

Finally, all five examples concentrate on one class of capacities or abilities: abilities exercised in work or productive abilities. These abilities have been at the centre of struggles waged in the language of rights since at least the seventeenth century. However, it is only since the early nineteenth century that they have been thought of as 'labour-power': that is, as capacities or abilities which, along with their corresponding forms of subjectivity, are separable from the persons who bear them and from the communities in which they are exercised to such an extent that the relations among self, abilities, and community have become problematic. To see the singularity of construing abilities in this disengaged way, let us contrast it with the first practical system, that of handicraft.

HANDICRAFT

In a craft system workers are not separated from their instruments of production. 'On the whole', Marx remarks, 'the worker and his means of production remained closely united, like the snail with its shell'.[6] In addition, the concept of an ability separable from its agent, exercise, and practice is inapplicable. The 'abilities' in virtue of which one is a craftsperson are the craft as a whole, consisting of many skills inseparable from their appropriate tools. The craft community, like any practical system of work, comprises the following types of relation: (1) relations of training and exercising productive capacities, which in this case constitute the apprenticeship system with its technical knowledge and techniques of working embodied in practice; (2) relations of governance among workers which, in the craft system, tend to be the same as the hierarchical relations of producing (the master both governs apprentices and directs them in their work); and (3) relations of communication among members. Since each member acquires and exercises the skills of the trade or craft as a whole, there are no separate, specialized abilities and, consequently, no division of labour within a trade: 'the entire exclusion', writes

---

[6] Karl Marx, *Capital*, vol. 1, trans. Ben Fowkes, intro. Ernest Mandel (New York: Vintage, 1977), 480; all citations from Marx will use the page numbers of this edition.

Marx, 'of division of labour in the workshop' (477).[7] Thus, in this system there is no labour-power as a commodity. What the merchant buys is a product or complete service from a trade or guild; 'he could not buy labour as a commodity' (479).

The differences are obvious between those concepts of self, abilities, and community, and of the relations among them appropriate to the craft system, and those conventionally used in our current debate. Indeed, the craft system could not be translated into the terms of our debate without doing violence to this craft form of productive life. Thus, it can be used to loosen the grip of contemporary conventions of thought. In addition, it should not be seen as simply a dissimilar historical curiosity. Several features of some contemporary forms of social organizations can be illuminated by using the language of crafts to disclose similarities, as, for example, Thomas Kuhn and Michael Polanyi have shown with respect to modern scientific communities, and ecologists with respect to ourselves as inhabitants of our ecological habitats.

The transition to the second example can now be made by employing the craft game as an object of contrast to throw light on the concept of labour-power, which is absent in the craft way of producing but constitutive of contemporary ways of construing the producing subject. Along with his contemporaries, Marx introduced the terms 'labour-power' (*Arbeitskraft*) and 'capacity for labour' (*Arbeitsvermägen*) and defined them as 'the aggregate of those mental and physical capabilities existing in the physical form, the living personality, of a human being, capabilities which he sets in motion whenever he produces a use-value of any kind' (270). Not only are abilities abstracted from practice in this remarkably abstract defini-tion, but, one step back from that, the capacities that exist in potential in the person and are set in motion in the exercise of abilities. Further, the labourer self-consciously stands in a juridical relation to her labour-power of owner to commodity. This reflexive form of juridical self-identity is, as Marx points out, a peculiarly möbius-like, contorted mode of disengaged subjectivity. The labourer has the right to alienate her labour-power like any other commodity but, on the other hand, she cannot sell it completely for indefinite time, unlike other commodities, since this would transform her identity from a free subject to a slave. Hence, the labourer 'manages both to alienate his

---

[7] In contrast, there is a division of *trades* within society; see Marx's 'general rule', 477, n. 36.

labour-power and to avoid renouncing his rights of ownership over it' (271).

The familiar historical conditions necessary for this game of rights and labour-power to take place are the separation of the labourer from the means of production and the existence of relations of commodity exchange between the labourer and the owner of the means of production. However, it is clear from a contrast with the craft example that another, less studied condition is the reflexive disengagement of the self from craft, abilities, and capacities, and the complementary self-understanding of the relation between self and capacities as a peculiar type of property, yet not full property. How did this transformation from craftsperson to labourer take place?

In the craft system the rights and (mostly) duties of property do not penetrate the craft community but attach to the guild as a juridical unit. The guilds and trades are self-governing, and the regime of law regulates the network of guilds, services, trades, and crafts for the sake of the public good – the wealth and power of the early modern state. This mercantile political community is the second practical system.

THE MERCANTILE SYSTEM

Labour in the mercantile system is understood as a resource that can be utilized to strengthen the state by contributing to its wealth and power. As John Bellers wrote in 1699, 'regularly labouring people are the kingdom's greatest treasure and strength'.[8] The state in turn is understood as a power locked in a zero-sum, balance-of-powers game of military and commercial rivalry with other European states over the conquest, colonization, and exploitation of the non-European world. This way of thinking about politics developed during the period of European state-building in the seventeenth and eighteenth centuries. In order to strengthen and improve the state it is necessary to promote, regulate, and coordinate the productive activities of the population, by means of law. This 'improvement' of the productivity of labour requires not only legal and administrative regulation, but also the development of knowledge of the history of trades, of demography, of the conditions of work, and thus the beginnings of political economy, statistics, international relations, and demo-

---

[8] John Bellers, *An essay toward the improvement of physick . . . with a proposal for employing the poor in a college of industry* [1699] (London, 1714), 124.

graphics. The labouring selves in this game, if they are to be fit members of the political community, able to labour or to fight, have to be cared for, in the terms of their health, manners, and education, and directed to productive labour which, in turn, is integrated into the mercantile strategies of a 'welfare–warfare' state (to use Lawrence Stone's apt phrase).

The use of the word 'labour' in the documents of this system in its first century show that it means neither abilities nor capacities but a whole producing activity organized into trades and crafts. Subjects are thought of as members of trades with the right and duty to work, not as labourers with rights in abilities. The community in this practical system, therefore, is a political society governed by legal relations specifying duties and rights. Members are political subjects, subject to the law in virtue of their identity as a member of a trade (hence the crazy-quilt of legislation to bind subjects to apprenticeship regimes). The various trades or producing activities of members are common assets of the political society, to be used for the 'improvement' of the society as a whole.

The policies of improvement have now become the self-sustaining and destructive processes of modernization and some of the mercantile legislation that set them in motion has been dismantled.[9] However, it would be a mistake to see all aspects of this political organization of selves, labour, and community as things of the past. This practical system forged political relations between development of productive abilities and the interests of states that remain constitutive features of all modern states, even though productive abilities are now construed differently. Consequently, the analysis of rights in abilities should be broadened to include consideration of relations of political power that partly structure the system of rights in abilities in order to constitute a political community in which subjects are induced to acquire certain productive abilities, through the educational system, and to exercise them in specified ways, by means of neomercantilist strategies designed to coordinate scientific and industrial activity with the interests of the state. This kind of analysis would provide the context for an important question which is difficult if not impossible to pose within the conventions of the current discussion of rights in abilities; namely, 'How can the growth of

---

[9] Marx Raeff, *The well-ordered police state* (New Haven: Yale University Press, 1983), 11–43, 251–7.

capabilities be disconnected from the intensification of power relations?'[10]

THE JURIDICAL POLITY

The third example is a form of organization characteristic of the transitional period between the distintegration of the handicraft system and the appearance of a system of manufacturing based on a division of labour in which abilities abstracted from practise are present and rights of ownership are attached to them. Several important changes occurred in the later mercantile age that provided the foundations for specialized systems of manufacturing. First, Europeans learned two lessons from the Dutch army reforms of the 1590s. The complex tasks of soldiering can be broken down into a succession of minute and detailed behavioural movements and a 'raw recruit' can be trained and eventually habituated into becoming a soldier by endless repetition of these movements in drills and exercises. The other lesson is that soldiers, when they are organized into a disciplined unit, constitute a power or force different from and greater than the sum of its parts.[11] The second change was the experimentation in decomposing simple tasks into discrete, repetitive steps and applying these techniques to children, from the ages of three to fourteen, in the workhouses and poorhouses of early modern Europe. The reformers discovered the extreme malleability of children; how, by repetition and discipline, they can be 'inured to labour', which, John Locke writes, 'is of no small consequence to the making of them sober and industrious all their lives'.[12] Locke's contemporary, Bellers, argues that, 'children are more like clay out of the pit, and easy to take any form they are put into'.[13] The workhouses were prototypes for the division of labour in factories and for the scientific management of the workers.[14]

---

[10] Michel Foucault, 'What is Enlightenment?' in *The Foucault reader*, ed. Paul Rabinow (New York: Pantheon, 1984), 48. For the historical formation of the global complex of mercantilist states, see Paul Kennedy, *The rise and fall of the great powers* (London: Unwin Hyman, 1988).

[11] Murray Feld, 'Middle class society and the rise of military professionalism: the Dutch army, 1589–1609', *Armed forces and society* 1 (1975), 419–42; William H. McNeill, *The pursuit of power* (Chicago: University of Chicago Press, 1982), 117–43.

[12] John Locke, *A report of the Board of Trade to the Lords Justices respecting the relief and employment of the poor* [1697] (London, 1793), 10–11.

[13] John Bellers, *A proposal for raising a college of industry* (London, 1696), 40.

[14] Sidney Pollard, *The genesis of scientific management* (Cambridge, MA: Harvard University Press, 1965).

Moreover, the representation of the body and eventually the mind as machines helped to articulate this mechanization of human behaviour and thinking. Political economists began to write about the political community, not in the terms of families, estates, and trades, but in the terms of populations, with their statistical laws of birth, marriage, productivity, and death; and of political economy as an applied science that could guide political intervention in this realm. Finally, the closed practices of trades were opened up by the well-known Baconian movement to compile histories of trades. The aim was to appropriate the technical knowledge embodied in the practice of each mechanical art, to write it down in books, and to teach it to technicians and scientists independent of and in abstraction from the actual activity of the trade, thus providing conditions for the modern division of the workforce into engineers, managers, and labourers.[15]

These changes are given expression in sections of Locke's educational writings and his *Report to the Board of Trade*. At the centre of his analysis is the premise that an individual is 'only as white paper or wax to be moulded and fashioned as one pleases'.[16] Since each individual desires to avoid pain or punishment and to seek reward or pleasure, one can be led to engage in mental or physical behaviour by the application of punishments and rewards. As a result of the continual repetition and practice of any complex behaviour, suitably broken down into operational parts, the individual becomes accustomed and habituated to it, eventually finding pleasure in it.[17] One system of rewards and punishments that Locke lays out to apply in order to reform the 'relaxation of discipline and the corruption of manners', to uproot the vice of idleness, and to implant the virtue of industry is the use of bodily rewards and punishments in the workhouse system. His proposal for reform of the national system of workhouses was praised as a model for reforming and habituating children and adults to labour right up to the Webbs. As his 1793 editors remarked,

Mr Locke appears to be convinced that rewards and punishments, and the mixing of habits of industry with principles of religious duties, were the surest

[15] Carolyn Merchant, *The death of nature* (San Francisco: Harper and Row, 1980), 164–253.
[16] John Locke, *The educational writings*, ed. James Axtell (Cambridge: Cambridge University Press, 1968), 325.
[17] John Locke, *An essay concerning human understanding*, ed. Peter Nidditch (Oxford: Oxford University Press, 1975), 2.21.69–70: 280–2.

means of effecting that reformation of the manners of the people, which, in those days, was judged essential to the strength and safety of the nation.[18]

Once the labouring subject was conceptualized as a repository of productive capacities that could be trained into mechanical abilities by the repetition of simple operations, some mercantilists went on to argue that it is the role of government to apply these techniques in production. 'Labour', William Petyt recommends, 'is capital material, raw and undigested, to be committed into the hands of the supreme [political] authority, in whose prudence and disposition it is to improve, manage, and fashion it to more or less advantage'.[19] However, this view is fairly uncommon. The form of political subjectivity appropriate to being governed by law in the political community remained, and remains, different in kind from the form of subjectivity in the workplace. The political subject is not considered as a patient, a passive resource open to manipulation and utilization. She is conceptualized as a free agent, an active, self-governing subject, possessing the abilities appropriate to the exercise of rights and duties. A political subject is one who is capable of consenting to and dissenting from, and even of rebelling against, the rule of law on the basis of judgement.

This distinctive language-game of the self-governing subject, which is common to both civic humanist and juridical, nonabsolutist political texts of the period, is particularly noticeable in the place where one would expect it to disappear: that is, in the legal relation between government and the labouring subject. Here, as we all know, the labouring subject stands to the law not as a resource to techniques of exploitation, but as self-governing agent with rights over one's labouring activity to a law that regulates the activity as a whole. Locke writes, 'The *Labour* of his Body, and the *Work* of his Hands, we may say, are properly his . . . the unquestionable Property of the Labourer. . . . Man . . . being Master of himself, and *Proprietor of his own Person*, and the Actions or *Labour* of it . . .'[20]

This refusal to treat *political* subjects, even in their labouring activities, as passive and malleable repositories of capacities, as the

---

[18] John Locke, *A report*, preface. For more thorough investigations of the material referred to in sections 2 and 3 of this paper, see Michel Foucault, *Discipline and punish*, trans. Alan Sheridan (New York: Pantheon, 1977), and chapter 8 above.

[19] William Petyt, *Britannia lanquans* (London, 1680), 238.

[20] John Locke, *Two treatises of government*, ed. Peter Laslett (Cambridge: Cambridge University Press, 1967), sections 27, 44: 305–6, 316.

labouring self is in the emerging political economy literature, appears also in the picture which Locke presents of the way a ruler governs labouring activity in society as a whole. The ruler confronts and seeks to coordinate from the outside a complex collection of craftspeople already organized by trade.[21]

The self and abilities to which juridical relations of rights and duties apply, and the way that they apply (mediated by the free play of consent and dissent), thus are different from the self and abilities to which relations of production begin to apply in the workhouse and in the science of political economy. Although, that is, something like the conception of labour-power is present in the malleable conception of the producing self, it is not connected in any way to the language of rights, with its distinctive conception of human agency. In fact, they are incompatible. The juridical subject who has the abilities to exercise rights and duties *is* able to govern herself and master her labouring activities in relations with others. As long as this self-governing conception of human agency is constitutive of the language of rights it is impossible to predicate rights of ownership directly to labour-power, since the malleable human agent, or rather patient, in whom alienable labour-power is conceived to inhere lacks the agency and hegemony over her abilities that the exercise of rights presupposes.

To overcome this incompatibility, and so link rights to labour-power, as we do in the modern world, recourse is needed to a game of rights in which, when agents alienate a right, they also alienate, so to speak, the right to the working conditions necessary to acquire and exercise the abilities involved in the practice of rights. They abjure their self-governing form of subjectivity. The paradigm of this way of thinking about rights is of course the early modern right to consent unconditionally to absolute monarchy or to sell oneself voluntarily into slavery. The person who becomes a slave in this way ceases to be sovereign over herself in the same manner as a person who sells her labour-power ceases to be sovereign over her abilities. This non-Lockean way of thinking about rights was readily available to early modern Europeans since it was widely used in the explanation and justification of both the slave trade and of obedience to the absolutist state.[22]

---

[21] John Locke, *Two treatises*, section 43: 316. See James Tully, *A discourse on property: John Locke and his adversaries*, 104–31, 135–45.

[22] For the absolutist tradition of rights see Richard Tuck, *Natural rights theories* (Cambridge: Cambridge University Press, 1980), esp. 52–4, 101–42. I am indebted to Richard Tuck for making this point in a discussion of the argument.

With the separation of the worker from the means of production, the owner of the means of production, the capitalist, came to control the production process. It is within this new organization of selves, productive abilities, and community that the techniques and conceptions of a tractable and utilizable labouring self came to be applied. This system of manufacture incorporating a division of labour provided the conditions for the application of rights to labour-power.

THE DESPOTIC DIVISION OF LABOUR

A large number of people are assembled together under the command of a capitalist to produce a commodity in the manufacturing system. They make up, Marx writes, 'a productive mechanism whose organs are human beings' (457). Co-operation, in contrast to the craft system, is based on a division of labour: 'Not only is the specialized work distributed among the different individuals, but the individual himself is divided up and transformed into the automatic motor of a detail operation' (481). The specialized labourers are appendages of the workshop, 'living automatons', according to Dugald Stewart, 'employed in the details of the work'.[23]

The result of this form of co-operation is twofold (just as in the Dutch army reform): an increase in individual productive power and the creation of a new productive power that is the property of the collectivity. Marx writes: '[a] new power arises from the fusion of many forces into a single force, [and] social contact begets in most industries a rivalry and a stimulation of the animal spirits, which heightens the efficiency of each individual worker' (443). This shows, Marx continues, 'that man, if not as Aristotle thought, a political animal, is at all events a social animal' (444). The collective productive power is not only greater than the sum of the individual labour-powers; it is based on capabilities that are brought into being and compelled into operation in virtue of being a part of the co-operative mechanism: 'the worker strips off the fetters of his individuality, and develops the capabilities of his species' (447). The new powers the labourer develops are appropriate only to his specific function and make sense only in light of the whole: 'The one-sidedness and even the deficiencies of the specialized individual worker become *perfections* when he is part of the collective worker' (469).

Here the worker is treated as the repository of labour-power as pure

---

[23] Dugald Stewart, *Lectures on political economy* [1800], in *The collected works*, ed. Sir William Hamilton (Edinburgh, 1855), 8: 318, cited in Marx, 418, n. 40.

capacities. She is not the owner of abilities or skills since these only come into being after she has become a part of the co-operative process. Henri Storch notes in 1815:

The worker who is the master of a whole craft can work and find means of subsistence anywhere; the other (the manufacturing worker) is only an appendage who, when he is separated from his fellows, possesses neither capabilities nor independence, and finds himself forced to accept any law it is thought fit to impose.[24]

Further, the technical and managerial knowledge, will, and judgement once embodied in the worker's craft are here separated from the specialized worker and embodied in the work system as a whole. The deskilled labourer 'is brought face-to-face with the intellectual potentialities of the material process of production as the property of another and as a power which rules over him' (482n). In 1824, anticipating Harry Braverman, William Thompson observes:

The man of knowledge and the productive labourer come to be widely divided from each other, and knowledge, instead of remaining the handmaid of labour in the hand of the labourer to increase his productive powers . . . has almost everywhere arrayed itself against labour. Knowledge becomes an instrument capable of being detached from labour and opposed to it.[25]

A right of ownership was attached to one's labour-power in the course of the late eighteenth and early nineteenth centuries as this specializ-ed division of labour became common. However, the rights transac-tion between labourers and capitalists, which, as Marx points out, appears as a legitimate market exchange (280), conceals the additional abnegation of the labourers' abilities to govern their own activities. Their rights-exercising abilities are replaced by the government of the productive system and their capacities become open for use and consumption. This deconstruction and fragmenta-tion of the self was criticized by many observers. Adam Smith puts it this way:

the understandings of the greater part of men . . . are necessarily formed by their ordinary employments. The man whose life is spent in performing a few simple operations . . . has no occasion to exert his understanding. He generally becomes as stupid and ignorant as it is possible for a human

[24] Henri Storch, *Cours d'économie politique* (Paris, 1823), 1: 204, cited in Marx, 482.
[25] William Thompson, *An inquiry into the principles of the distribution of wealth* (London, 1824), 274, cited in Marx, 482, n. 44; compare Harry Braverman, *Labor and monopoly capital* (New York: Monthly review, 1974).

creature to become. His dexterity at his own particular trade seems . . . to be acquired at the expense of his intellectual, social and martial virtues.[26]

Yet, Smith continues, this stupid and ignorant form of subjectivity, constituted by the division of labour system, must be accepted, and so justified, for the sake of improvement. 'But in every improved and civilized society, this is the state into which the . . . great body of the people, must necessarily fall, unless government takes some pains to prevent it.'

It may be that there is no formal contradiction in alienating the form of subjectivity required to exercise a right in the act of alienating a right in an ability (labour-power), as the absolutist tradition has always argued. But even here Rousseau opens the *Contrat social* with argument that it involves a contradiction (as the contorted nature of the right itself suggests).[27] Even so, Smith points to what might be called a pragmatic incompatibility. The labourers who spend most of their lives in this type of practical system tend to develop a form of selfhood which renders them less able to acquire the capabilities necessary to exercise the rights on which the legitimacy of the system rests. The sociological conditions of work undermine the legitimacy of the organization of work by blocking the presupposed character formation.

Smith's criticism of the division of labour is, as John Pocock has rightly emphasized, expressed in terms of its destruction of the civic humanist concept of human agency; of developing the abilities necessary to exercise the civic virtues.[28] This shows that there are two distinct yet complementary criticisms – juridical and civic humanist – of the specialized division of labour available to us; at least to those of us who do not share the view of Smith and his followers that civic virtues and human rights can be suppressed or curtailed in the name of improvement or modernization. The great struggles of resistance

---

[26] Adam Smith, *An inquiry into the nature and causes of the wealth of nations*, 2 vols, ed. R. H. Campbell, A. S. Skinner, and W. B. Todd (Oxford: Clarendon Press, 1976), II, V.i.f.50: 781–2, cited in Marx, 483. Smith recommends that government mitigate, and even prevent, the debilitating effects of the division of labour by means of an appropriate system of public education (v.i.f.53–7: 784–6, discussed by Marx, 484–5).

[27] Jean-Jacques Rousseau, *Du contrat social*, ed. Ronald Grimsley (Oxford: Oxford University Press, 1972), Livre I, ch. 4, 108–13.

[28] J. G. A. Pocock, 'The mobility of property and the rise of eighteenth-century sociology', and 'Virtues, rights, and manners', in his *Virtue, commerce, and history* (Cambridge: Cambridge University Press, 1985), 37–51, 103–25; I am indebted to John Pocock for his comment on this section of an earlier draft of this article and to the work of Istvan Hont and Michael Ignatieff for my understanding of Adam Smith.

against this system of work standardly take the form of claims of workers to exercise rights in the relations of governance within the workplace. The rights to limit the working day, to unions, to health, safety, and environmental committees, to daycare facilities, and to self-management all involve the establishment in the workplace of practices in which workers can develop and foster the abilities of self-governing agency that they have always in fact refused to abjure.[29] The current discussion of agency, summarized at the beginning of this essay, tends to be carried out in abstraction from the specific communities in which rights are actually exercised and alienated, and so fails to investigate the incompatibility of rights-agency and this widespread system of self, productive abilities, and community.

A second feature of the system of division of labour that is not questioned in the contemporary problematic, as a consequence of its individualist premises, is the collective power or ability that is brought into being through co-operation. Although this ability inheres in the co-operative whole, it is said to belong to the capitalist. The reason why it cannot be attributed to the workers as a corporate subject is that their community identity is constituted by, and so the object of, the co-operative process rather than being the constitutor, and so the subject of the co-operative process. This inversion of corporate popular sovereignty comes out clearly in the way that Marx criticizes the system in the traditional juridical language of political agency.

The system, he says, is 'despotic' (i.e. absolutist), organized along the lines of a modern army (450). The workers do not object to co-operation itself, but rather to the imposition of it on them by another. The 'interconnection between their various labours confronts them' as the 'will of being (the capitalist) outside them, who

---

[29] For struggles against and criticisms of 'despotic' forms of the division of labour in the nineteenth century see Christopher Lash, 'The sociology of liberty in recent historical writing', working paper for the seminar on republicanism, University of Rochester, 1988 (unpublished; I am much indebted to this fine analysis), and Richard Ashcraft, 'A Victorian working class view of liberalism and the moral life', the conference on *Liberalism and the moral life*, City University of New York, 8–10 April 1988 (unpublished). Note also that Marx describes the struggle to regulate the length of the working day as the victory of legal relations over the power of productive relations to determine relations of governance in the workplace (415–16). (Marx's analysis in this chapter [10] calls into question the validity of the criticism that he fails to distinguish between instrumental relations of producing and social relations among workers.)

subjects their activity to his purpose'. The unification and the relations between individual functions, he writes, 'are not their own act' (449–50). Marx's criticism of the co-operative structure is thus the familiar Rousseauian demand that the constitution of the roles and relations of a co-operative community should be the act of the constituents themselves. The corporate body should constitute and govern the relations that regulate the members in their work, not vice versa. Yet this presupposes the practices necessary to foster and sustain a corporate political community of workers that the operation of the productive process tends to undermine, just as in the case of individual agency. Hence, this organization of work is also incompatible with community self-government, and, in capitalist and socialist countries, its atomizing effects have been met by struggles for community control.[30]

Many criticisms of modernity as fragmented and one-dimensional have been based on this specialized system as a paradigm of modern organizations. Recently, Marxists have even suggested that the celebration of fragmentation and deconstruction in postmodern thought and action is itself a form of subjectivity constituted by the development of capitalism along these lines.[31] Be this as it may, for Marx, as for Charles Babbage, this organization of work was superseded in the second half of the nineteenth century by a new way of organizing self, abilities, and community.

THE AUTOCRATIC REGIME OF AUTOMATION

In the final example, machines replace the worker, thus forming the basis of the co-operative structure: 'a collective working machine' (502). Once human skills had been broken down into mechanical, mental, and physical operations in the division of labour system, these operations were gradually taken over and performed by industrial machines and computers. Here the worker confronts a self-contained or 'objective' productive process constituting a 'vast automaton, composed of various mechanical and intellectual organs, acting in uninterrupted concert . . . [and] all of them being subordinated to a

---

[30] For recent work on community self-government, see Joshua Cohen and Joel Rogers, *Democracy* (Middlesex: Penguin, 1986); I am indebted to Joshua Cohen's helpful criticism of this aspect of a rough draft of the article.

[31] For an interesting discussion of this phenomenon, see Peter Dews, *Logics of disintegration* (London: Verso, 1987).

self-regulated moving force' (544). A system of applied scientific research and development, rationalized along the same mechanical principles, reflexively monitors the working and improvement of the production process. Rationalized procedures of management and investment perform the functions of capital.

What constitution of abilities and subjectivity does this practice involve? Since specializations are performed by machines, there is no division of labour based on productive skills. The labourer's role is to attend, to mind, to watch, and to 'monitor', as Marx puts it. This is, he writes, 'undemanding' work, which requires little or no apprenticeship or muscle power, so it tends to 'level' and 'equalize' the workforce, thus drawing in women and children. Divisions are based on gender and age (517–20).

Marx claims that 'the automaton itself is the *subject*, and the workers are merely conscious organs, coordinated with the unconscious organs of the automaton, and together with the latter, subordinated to the central moving force' (544–5). In particular, the intensity and duration of work are constituted by the system, limited only by 'the resistance offered by man, that obstinate yet elastic natural barrier' (527). Consequently, the worker contributes neither labour-power nor skill but, rather, her time; and the struggle is over its intensity and duration. Of course, abilities are required to tend and feed the automaton, such as information-processing and the like. However, according to Marx, to concentrate on abilities, as in the other producing games, and in our current debates, is to miss the constitutive features of this system: that it uses and exploits human time (526–43). And that is to say that the rights workers have in this way of life are rights of ownership in time.

The form of subjectivity or identity one has in virtue of participation in this practice has two obvious aspects. The first is what might be called a 'time-consciousness'. This is a heightened and reflexive self-awareness of one's life and activity as essentially time, construed as a process which can be programmed and managed in various ways to maximize its intensity (in the aestheticization of everyday life) or its duration (in our endless practices of prolonging life). The dominant measure of freedom is the use of 'free time'.

The second feature of this form of subjectivity is a unique type of disengaged consciousness, of watching, attending, or 'monitoring'. Perhaps an exemplary picture of this today is the worker watching her screen at a work station in an office, at home, in a missile silo, or at a nuclear power plant. The worker is isolated from and lacks solidarity with other workers. If the workers have a sense of community, it is not inherent in the production process but is supplied, as we know, by other poles of identity: ethnicity, language, politics, sports, and so on. Further, the worker in her work is constituted as a being standing in the world as watcher to thing watched. The thing watched is an automatic or cybernetic system independent not only of the worker's will and knowledge but also, unlike the detail worker, independent of the worker's labour-power. She is a watcher and relayer of information. The peculiar type of spectatorial disengagement creates a self-understanding of powerlessness, since none of the worker's powers seems to play a role in the autonomous productive process. Nor is there a sense that any individual or class is sovereign over the system – quite the opposite.

The understanding of politics as anonymous and self-regulating systems and of citizens as powerless to engage in these political processes are well known manifestations of the effects of this beyond the workplace. (So too is the opposite, Faustian sense that the world is itself a process to be endlessly programmed by man.) Finally, the identity of the 'minimal' or standing-back self, disengaged and apart from politics, and relating to it (as to other areas of one's own life) as spectator and monitor, unable to commit, can be partly explained as effects of this organization of work.[32]

Marx argues that this 'autocratic' regime of automation, as he calls it, could be overthrown. The associated workers could be the 'dominant subject', rather than the object, thus realizing Aristotle's dream, in which,

if every tool, when summoned, or even by intelligent anticipation, could do the work that befits it, just as the creations of Daedalus moved of themselves, or if the weavers' shuttles were to weave of themselves, then there would be no need either of apprentices for the mastercraftsmen, or of slaves for the lords.[33]

The associated workers could easily work in different yet simple jobs in the system, thus abolishing the one-sidedness caused by specialization. They could also shorten the working day and control its intensity, thereby increasing their free time, the new measure of

[32] See Christopher Lasch, *The minimal self: psychic survival in troubled times* (New York: Norton, 1984), and Shoshana Zuboff, *In the age of the smart machine: the future of work and power* (New York: Basic Books, 1988). [33] Aristotle, *Politics* 1253b32–40, cited in Marx, 532.

freedom. Free time could then be used for education in how to organize the relations of governance and production appropriate to automation (617–19).

Here is yet another way of thinking about types of subjectivity, abilities (to use time), and community, best understood and assessed in the light of the autocratic regime of work it is written to challenge. Like the other examples, this one can be used to draw attention to the sheer multiplicity of communities in which we as moderns are subjects, as Smith phrases it, in our 'ordinary employments'. Further, these samples also can be used as objects of comparison to show where our present, conventional concepts fail to describe clearly both the specific forms of domination and subjection of different practical systems and the specific games of contestation and freedom open to us to modify them.[34]

CONCLUSION

In liberalism, we speak of rights, liberty, and community. We also discuss the self-governing forms of subjectivity or agency, and the range of abilities of deliberation, judgement, discussion, and action required in the exercise of rights, liberty and community in practice. Yet, when we examine our producing practices we see that the way they are organized, and so the forms of subjectivity and the types of abilities they foster, undermine the development of agency and abilities necessary to engage in liberal practices of rights, liberty, and community.

This would not matter to liberals if politics and labour were two separate realms. But they are not. For, as we have seen in the Introduction, it is taken for granted in liberal theory that rights attach to productive powers, thus linking the two realms, and liberal theories of the moral life of autonomy and community are founded on different interpretations of this right over productive abilities. As a consequence, the labouring agent with rights over abilities is discussed in the terms of agency of the language of rights, liberty, and community. As we have seen in our five samples, this conceals the reality that the producing agent and her ability are not as the liberal language game presupposes. Rather, she possesses, in virtue of being

---

[34] I would like to thank Hudson Meadwell and the scholars acknowledged *en passant* in previous footnotes for their comments on successive versions of this article.

engaged in the productive practice, a different form of subjectivity and range of abilities which, in turn, disable her from developing the identity and abilities necessary for the full exercise of rights, liberty, and community.

Once we see how the use of the liberal language of rights, liberty, and community hides and thereby legitimates the productive systems of modernity which undermine the social conditions necessary for engaging in the practices of rights, liberty, and community, there are two possible courses of action. One could concede that a right over labour-power does not bestow on its holder the full range of self-governing agency that rights standardly presuppose. Or, one could investigate the ways in which we could transform the relations of governance in our diverse producing practices into relations of governance appropriate to agents exercising rights and liberty in community.

CHAPTER 8

Progress and scepticism

Many of the great thinkers of the European Enlightenment advanced two closely related beliefs. The first was that the societies in which they lived possessed or were about to possess properties that made them different from all other societies in history and thus distinctively 'modern'. The second was that these modern features gave rise in turn to a second equally distinctive aspect of their societies: their 'progressive' nature. Two hundred years later we continue to believe that we live in societies that are 'modern' in roughly the sense given to this word during the Enlightenment. However, we tend to doubt and in fact to be highly sceptical of the belief that modern societies are progressive.

Four deeply troubling characteristics of our century are standardly said to have provided good reason for the rise of scepticism and disillusionment with respect to progress. The horrors of two world wars shattered the belief advanced by Adam Smith (1723–90), Immanuel Kant (1724–1804), Marie-Jean Condorcet (1743–94), and Jeremy Bentham (1748–1832) that modern societies tend to peace. Our experience with war and militarism since 1945 has, if anything, increased scepticism. Over 30 million have died in the hundreds of wars since 1945; enough nuclear, biological, chemical, and conventional weapons have been built and deployed to exterminate most forms of life on the planet many times over; and our militarized international relations sustain an ever-increasing arms trade. The resulting global military–scientific–industrial complex is deeply embedded in the fabric of every modern society and, as Charles-Louis de Secondat Montesquieu (1689–1755) forewarned, it seems to be self-sustaining. Further, this complex is not some pre-modern atavism, but a structure which involves our most advanced and modern natural, social, and military sciences.

The second set of problems that has engendered robust scepticism about progress is the wide range of ecological damage, pollution, and destruction caused by the very features of modern societies that were claimed to support the progressive control of nature. In recent years it has been scientists working in the ecological sciences who have done the most to draw attention to the way modern societies squander resources and destroy rather than control nature. Third, in the so-called third world, high levels of famine, starvation, and hunger, coupled with the most brazen forms of oppression and exploitation, fly in the face of the predictions of Smith and Kant that the spread of modern markets and European imperialism would lead to 'improvement' for non-Europeans. This feature alone has caused much of the world's population to see the belief in progress as an ideology which has served to legitimate the continued exploitation of the third world by the first. The fourth characteristic is the failure of modern capitalist and socialist societies to cope with the domestic problems that the Enlightenment claimed they were uniquely suited to solve: unemployment and poverty, debt, corruption in politics, lack of political participation, human rights abuses, violence and crime, illiteracy, and the spread of 'modern' diseases such as cancer, heart disease, toxic poisoning, stress, and so on.

As Lewis Mumford concluded in his review of Charles Beard's *A century of progress* (1932), 'progress is the deadest of dead ideas . . . thoroughly blasted by the facts of twentieth-century experience'. Christopher Lasch pointed out in his recent lectures on progress that writers who still profess allegiance to progress do so as a matter of faith rather than belief, and out of fear of the consequences of giving it up rather than consideration of the evidence.[1]

These four sets of problems, therefore, have given rise to a sceptical attitude to the belief in progress which has legitimated and secured allegiance to modern civilization for almost two hundred years. This predicament often leads, as we know, to the degenerative extremes of either a cynical attitude toward the modern societies in which one must live and work but which one no longer respects or admires, or to a blind and dogmatic adherence to progress in the face of our problems. Fortunately, however, it also has ushered in a healthy resistance to and examination of the concept of progress in all areas of modern society. The aim of this examination has been to clarify how

[1] Christopher Lasch, 'The idea of progress in our time', McGill University, November 1987. The quotation from Lewis Mumford was cited in this fine public lecture.

our belief in progress has led us to overlook, and so fail to question, those forms of modern thought and action which sustain and reproduce the four sets of problems we need to address.

There is scarcely a university discipline that has not been touched by the sceptical examination of the ways in which its procedures may rest on the uncritical acceptance of progressive assumptions inherited from the Enlightenment. This questioning has been most intense in the social sciences, for many of them were constituted during the Enlightenment and thus the sceptical attack seems to question their basic status as sciences. We have also seen the growth of the philosophy of science and social science as a separate discipline in which these debates are carried on. Further, scepticism itself, as an independent epistemology and moral and political philosophy, has become one of the fastest growing areas of contemporary philosophy. Finally, the broad cultural movement of postmodernism is probably best seen as an attempt to construct an ethos based on permanent scepticism that would replace the modern ethos of progress. Indeed, postmodern writers argue that in their scepticism towards the present they are more faithful to the spirit of the Enlightenment than the defenders of progress.

The current reflection on progress is not a continuation of the long-standing debate over whether or not modern societies are progressive. This debate is a constitutive feature of modernity, from the debate over the ancients and moderns during the early years of the Royal Society through the Enlightenment to the views of Thomas Henry Huxley (1825–95) and Oswald Spengler (1880–1936), and on to Robert Nisbet, *History of the ideas of progress* (1980). Since the writers in this debate use the procedures of critical reflection that are defining features of modern thought they do not provide an independent means of questioning these procedures. Within this debate the question marks are not placed far enough down. Therefore, the current discussion of progress seeks to go one step further: to bring to light and call into question the language and forms of thought that both defenders and critics of progress share. These conventions, taken for granted in the course of the debates, are basic constituents of modern thought.

In the following two sections, accordingly, I will survey some of the major conventions of the language of progress which we have inherited from the Enlightenment. Of the many uses of the word 'progress' the one which has become most common is closely related to 'construction' and its cognates. Progress as construction consists in two parts: types of 'development' inherent in modern societies and forms of thinking and knowing in the natural and human sciences that are said to be characteristically modern. Modern forms of thought in the sciences are related to development in society by the application of the human sciences to administer and govern modern societies and by research, development, and application in the natural sciences. These features make up a picture of progress as the increasingly successful co-ordination of modern forms of thought and the rational control of natural and social processes.

This is not a comprehensive definition of progress, but, rather, one picture of progress that has tended to captivate us and to elbow aside other ways of thinking about progress over the last 200 years. It captivates us because it informs what we might call the language of progress: that is, the broad range of vocabulary and conventional linguistic usages that we, as children of the Enlightenment, continue to employ in our thinking and acting even when we attempt to take a critical stance to progress. As Ludwig Wittgenstein commented in 1930, 'Our civilization is characterized by the word "progress". Progress is its form rather than making progress being one of its features. Typically it constructs.'[2]

To clarify this picture of progress, and thereby enable us to free ourselves from its hold, I will present synoptic historical sketches of the two sets of conventions the language of progress comprises. The first set of conventions represent progress as reform and gradual improvement. This view of progress was established in the early Enlightenment, from the mid-seventeenth century to the French Revolution. The second, progress as unintended and dialectical, was developed in reaction to the first, from the late-eighteenth century to the present. Our current language of progress and the picture of progress sustained by our continued use of this language are an amalgam of these two. As we will see, even the most sceptical critics of progress tend uncritically to employ some of these conventions in their criticisms and so become entangled in the very language of progress they seek to clarify.

---

[2] Ludwig Wittgenstein, *Culture and value*, ed. G. H. von Wright, tr. Peter Winch (Oxford: Basil Blackwell, 1980), 7.

PROGRESS AS REFORM AND GRADUAL IMPROVEMENT

A *picture* held us captive. And we could not get outside it for it lay in our language and language seemed to repeat it to us inexorably.[3]

The early Enlightenment view of progress as reform and gradual improvement was developed in response to the crisis caused by the wars of religion which engulfed Europe from the 1560s to 1648. At the centre of the project of reform and reconstruction was the systematic use of techniques of sceptical doubting (inherited from the ancient sceptics and introduced into European thought by Michel de Montaigne [1533–92]) to disengage from blind assent to custom, opinion, and the dogma of religious and scholastic authorities. Adherence to these authorities was said to be a major cause of the religious wars and of the blindness to advances being made in the mechanical arts and the new, non-Aristotelian science associated with Galileo Galilei (1564–1642). Once people had suspended their assent to traditional and authoritative beliefs, they would examine them in accordance with criteria of rational assent until they reached ideas that were indubitable. These ideas would provide the foundations of knowledge on which the new natural and moral sciences would be constructed, each step being systematically examined in accordance with the criteria of rational assent. Further, the 'ideas' that were assembled in this way were understood to 'stand for' or to 'represent' their objects. The new way of thinking, accordingly, consisted of three parts: 1. systematic and shared procedures for doubt and examination, 2. the view of rational thought as cumulative construction on foundations that had passed the test of rigorous doubt, and 3. knowledge (or ideas) as representing its object domain. All disagreements of Thomas Hobbes (1588–1679), Pierre Gassendi (1592–1655), René Descartes (1596–1650), John Locke (1632–1704), and Isaac Newton (1642–1727) rest on agreement in these three assumptions.

This tripartite picture was related to the following concept of rational control. Accurate theoretical representations – of the workings of nature, of the human body and its motivational mechanisms, of human interaction, of the circulation of money and the balance of power, and so on – were to be constructed step by step

---

[3] Ludwig Wittgenstein, *Philosophical investigations*, tr. G. E. M. Anscombe (Oxford: Basil Blackwell, 1988), no. 115.

and applied to reform and to improve the 'human condition', systematically monitoring the effects of each reform to correct the original projection and to guide the next reform in a cumulative manner. The modern applied sciences and the human sciences of political economy, statistics, demography, education, medicine, ballistics, and psychology emerged within this general framework in the seventeenth and early-eighteenth centuries, from Antoine de Montchrétien (1575–1621) and William Petty (1623–87) to René Louis d'Argenson (1694–1757) and Claude-Adrien Helvetius (1715–71). These applied sciences are related in turn to the efforts of early modern states to increase their populations and improve their health, and to organize and increase their production and trade. The aim of this new comprehensive government of the basic productive and biological processes of the population was to 'strengthen' the state and increase its wealth so it could hold out in the commercial and military rivalry among European states. These states in turn were locked in a balance of power system and in competition for control over the resources and labour of the non-European world. The new comparative political economy, from the comparative analysis of European states by Samuel Pufendorf (1632–94) to the great *Encyclopédie* edited by Denis Diderot (1713–84) and Jean d'Alembert (1717–83), provided ever more accurate and utile knowledge of the global possessions of the European colonial systems.

The last but not least convention of this picture of progress was the understanding of the person as a malleable *tabula rasa* or blank tablet, without any innate ideas or natural dispositions. The individual was said to acquire dispositions to think and act in habitual ways by a process of continual repetition of the activity itself. The only constant and reliable dispositions humans possess was said to be a causal inclination or motive to be concerned for one's self; that is, to seek pleasure and avoid pain. This provided a powerful explanation of human behaviour and a model for reform. Accordingly, by the judicious application of various types of pleasures and pains, or rewards and punishment, an individual could be induced to engage in repetitive exercises of modern forms of thinking and behaving until these movements became habitual, and eventually pleasurable in themselves. Educational and legal reform consisted in applying these techniques to break down traditional ways of thought and action, to inculcate the new tripartite way of critical thought and to apply it in different activities. Also included was the systematic reform of work habits in the poorhouses of early modern Europe, so the poor would grow up with settled habits of industriousness and inured to labour. The moral and political sciences were reconstructed around the individual calculating the pleasures and pains associated with the courses of action open to her or him.

Although these conventional assumptions continue to be deeply lodged in modern thought and action, willy-nilly, they have been shown to be dubious by many of the major philosophers of the twentieth century, including Maurice Merleau-Ponty, Ludwig Wittgenstein, Thomas Kuhn, and Charles Taylor.[4] The three-part account of knowledge rests on a straightforward misunderstanding. Our most critically reflective activity of doubting any proposition rests on the non-reflective uses of innumerable other words which are not doubted in the course of subjecting the proposition in question to doubt. Thus, our knowledge does not rest on foundations which have themselves been grounded by some doubting procedures. Rather, our doubting procedures themselves rest in a nest of judgements that are not doubted at all in the course of our enquiries. As Wittgenstein sums up this point: 'All testing, all confirmation and disconfirmation of a hypothesis takes place already within a system. And this system is not a more or less arbitrary and doubtful point of departure for all our arguments: no, it belongs to the essence of what we call an argument. The system is not so much the point of departure, as the element in which arguments have their life.'[5] Further, the assumption that language is a representational medium and that knowledge consists in clear and distinct representations of what it represents has been shown to be an overly simplified account of language and knowledge. 'Representing' is one thing we do with language, but there are innumerable other things we do with language, even when we are engaged in the specialized and reflective activity of representing.

These criticisms from various quarters help us to see the captivating image of the knowing subject that the three assumptions held in place. It is a subject disengaged from customary and traditional beliefs, from language itself, and standing apart from the world as representer to object represented. The ascetic attraction of this god-like image of disengagement and radical autonomy has been explained in many

[4] See Charles Taylor, 'Overcoming epistemology', in *After philosophy: end or transformation?*, ed. Kenneth Baynes (Cambridge, Mass.: MIT Press, 1987), 464–88.
[5] Ludwig Wittgenstein, *On certainty*, tr. Denis Paul and G. E. M. Anscombe (Oxford: Basil Blackwell, 1974), no. 105.

ways. In addition, the picture of reform and improvement has been shown to contain the same view of the acting subject, disengaged from the world and standing in an instrumental relation to it as controller to thing controlled. This too has been shown to be overly simplified and untenable. Even our specialized activities in which we do exercise control always rest in and presuppose a horizon of natural relations which we do not control and on which we depend.

Accordingly, critics have gone on to draw attention to the limits of human knowledge and control, to stress the extent to which we are, in knowing and acting, engaged in and dependent upon language and the world. They have also turned this argument around and shown that many of our problems in theory and practice in the twentieth century derive from continuing to think and act as if we could gain this kind of disengaged knowledge and control.[6]

As important as these criticisms are, they tend to overlook one striking feature of European intellectual history. Almost all the criticisms our contemporaries have advanced were made by the major thinkers of the late-eighteenth and nineteenth centuries. However, these thinkers used the very limitations of human knowledge and control they discovered as a basis on which to construct an even more Faustian concept of progress. Many of our contemporary critics, far from criticizing this new, dialectical concept of progress, continue to work within and sustain its conventions.

PROGRESS AS UNINTENDED AND DIALECTICAL

The concepts of knowledge and rational control of the early Enlightenment were criticized in the period from roughly 1780 to 1850. The concept of rational control as comprehensive reform and improvement was associated with enlightened absolutism in France from Cardinal duc de Richelieu (1585–1642) and Jean-Baptiste Colbert (1619–83) to Simon Linguet (1736–94) and Louis XVI and with the mercantile system in England. Adam Smith, Condorcet, Bentham, and Emmanuel Joseph Sieyès (1748–1836) all argued that modern commercial societies with representative political institutions and the division of labour were far too complex to know or to control

---

[6] Fritjof Capra, *The turning point* (New York: Bantam Books, 1983), Carolyn Merchant, *The death of nature: Women, ecology, and the scientific revolution* (San Francisco: Harper and Row, 1980).

in this way. Indeed, they argued that the attempt to exercise this type of control failed and stifled improvement. Progress could be achieved precisely by not attempting to bring it about as a project. Rather, progress and the wealth of nations are the unintended and unplanned consequences of leaving individuals more or less alone to pursue their enlightened self-interest in the constraints of the division of labour in civil society and representative government. On this view, progress occurs behind the backs of the agents involved, by means of a hidden hand or, as G. W. F. Hegel (1770–1831) phrased it, the cunning of reason. Thus, the three features that most of the earlier thinkers considered essential – comprehensive knowledge, control, and habituating each member of society to work for the common good – were said to be unobtainable, unnecessary, and inimical to progress. The philosophers of the late Enlightenment and of the age of Reaction disagreed over how much co-ordination and invigilation was required *of* the autonomous processes in which mankind found itself constrained to live and work, but all agreed these were the natural limits on planning and control.

As we can see with hindsight, these later thinkers simply took for granted the organized forms of thought (the scientific disciplines) and the political, economic, and technical institutions that the earlier reformers had constructed. These appeared to be quasi-autonomous processes that were tending in a progressive direction without an overall director. The political act which symbolized this transition from modern to contemporary thought was the execution of Louis XVI. The absolute monarch, who stood above the law, was replaced by the republic, in which every one was equally subject to the laws of politics, economics, science, and the division of labour, and moved in a progressive direction by this very subjection.

The theorists went on to show how the conditions over which humans had no control were moving them, in spite of themselves, in a progressive direction. Individuals caught up in the dependency relations of the market – which automatically rewarded economically rational behaviour and punished irrational behaviour – would gradually become disciplined, polished, and enlightened, without the need for moral education. Their selfish pursuit of unlimited wants would bring about the greatest good of the greatest number. As markets spread around the globe governments would become economically interdependent and war would no longer be in their self-interest. Even wars would lead unintentionally to peace. Citizens, experiencing the cost and destructiveness of war, and thinking only of their self-interest,would curb military spending and adventurism through a free press and representative government. Thus, as Kant was able to sum up this whole line of thought in *Perpetual peace* (1795), supposing humans to be devils, the unintended consequences of their dialectical unsocial sociability were leading them to scientific and material progress and to perpetual peace.

These progressive thinkers did not stop at grounding the mechanisms of progress in the institutional structures of modern societies. Charles Darwin (1809–82) claimed to find such a mechanism in the natural world. Further, all of human history was understood as an unplanned progressive development passing through four stages. Since no other society in recorded history has ever understood itself in the terms of progress, but, rather, usually in the natural cycles of growth and decay, historical progress was said to occur behind the backs of the people involved. This entrenchment of progress in a fundamental historical process proved attractive to the generation of philosophers who grew up in the age of Reaction after the French Revolution. The failure of the Revolution and the Terror were seen to be the result of sweeping away the traditional structures of French society and the imposition of abstract reform. This enabled critics as diverse as Edmund Burke (1729–87), Joseph de Maistre (1753–1821), Hegel, Claude-Henri Saint-Simon (1760–1825), Isidore Auguste Comte (1798–1857) and Karl Marx (1818–83) to interpret the Terror as the consequence of the earlier movement of progress, and to criticize it for its lack of historical and sociological understanding. Moreover, with their new historical and dialectical language of progress, this was an exercise in replacing one concept of progress with another. They could thus criticize the excesses of the Revolution, and indeed the whole 'slaughter-bench' of history, yet situate it as a necessary step in the progressive development of humanity.

This form of argument was shared by conservative and radical alike. Marx, for example, argued that the immediate unintended consequences of capitalism were regressive rather than progressive but that the consequence of these consequences was the unplanned development of the conditions for the overthrow of capitalism and progression to socialism. In this 'master–slave' dialectic, the unintended consequences of human action create and sustain the social and historical conditions that enslave mankind, but the overall tendency of this self-imposed 'subjection' is the progressive development of the human species in spite of itself. At its most optimistic, the mechanisms of progress will gradually produce a human animal capable of knowing these mechanisms and bringing them under a new and comprehensive form of rational control. From Condorcet's *Esquisse d'un tableau historique des progrès de l'esprit humain* (1795) to the latest cybernetic model of humans' place in society and nature, this utopian rationalization of present ills in the terms of their alleged future, progressive benefits knows no bounds.

The form of thinking characteristic of this dialectical concept of progress contains, in addition, two features not present in the earlier, tripartite conception. The first or 'critical' feature is to ask of any claim to know or to doubt, what are the 'conditions of possibility' for making such a claim or exercising such a doubt. This reflective step was employed to criticize the earlier view of knowledge by showing that there are background conditions for our reflexive activities of doubting and representing. The step, however, generates a paradox for two reasons: we are both the knower and the known, the subject and object of knowledge, and we claim both that our knowledge is limited and that we can know these limits. The paradox, or 'dialectical of finitude', as it is often called, appears in the sciences that were developed in the nineteenth-century on this form of thought: the attempt in the empirical sciences to account empirically for the transcendental conditions of possibility of the empirical field; in hermeneutics to make explicit the implicit horizons of explicit knowledge; and in phenomenology, to grasp conceptually the conditions of embodied or pre-conceptual knowledge.[7]

The second feature is the attempt to find some way to overcome the paradox. As we have seen in the new social theories, the sociological and historical conditions of possibility of human action were said to have a progressive bent. In an analogous manner, the solution was to claim that the epistemic conditions of knowing contained a dialectically progressive tendency. From Kant and Hegel through Friedrich Nietzsche (1844–1900) to Jürgen Habermas this feature has taken a variety of forms. It standardly involves the claim that, due to historical development, the present generation can see more clearly into the underlying conditions of human knowledge. For Habermas,

---

[7] Michel Foucault, *Les mots et les choses* (Paris: Éditions Gallimard, 1966), tr., *The order of things: an archaeology of the human sciences* (translator not named) (London: Tavistock Publications, 1970), 312–35.

tendencies to truth, rightness, and sincerity are built into the use of language and these are uniquely transparent to moderns. In the hermeneutical or interpretative sciences we are told that the condition of possibility of interpretation is an underlying inclination to clarity and truth. Even the sceptical Nietzsche posited, as the ground of his hermeneutics of suspicion, a natural drive of self-overcoming (*selbstaufhebung*). Thus, the first step is used to expose and criticize the unclarity, error, immorality, and insincerity of the age, whereas the second step claims to discover an underlying tendency to progress, as one stage or paradigm is typically said to correct and supersede in a more comprehensive form an earlier one.[8]

This language of progress as unintended and dialectical is deeply woven into contemporary ways of thought and action. Rather than replacing or superseding, it has become grafted on to the earlier language of progress as reform and gradual improvement. Thus, positivists and dialecticians, from the Vienna Circle and the Frankfurt School, tend to play the conventions of one language of progress against the other in an interminable twentieth-century debate on progress.

Over the last twenty years postmodern critics have subjected dialectical progress to extensive investigation and refutation. The most influential postmodern scholar has been Jacques Derrida, who initially applied his 'deconstructive' criticism to the work of one of the most important philosophers of science in the twentieth century, Edmund Husserl (1859–1938). The broad generalizations about the progressive tendencies of the unintended consequences of our scientific, industrial, military, and political institutions have been refuted by the four sets of problems I mentioned in the Introduction. The prevailing belief that knowledge develops in the natural and social sciences by one theory or paradigm superseding and comprehending its predecessor has been shown to be question-begging and inconclusive. Postmodern critics have exposed this dialectic of progress in all areas of our thinking, from the way we conceptualize scientific research and development and the way we organize the world into developed and developing nations to learning theory and the way we think about history. They have gone on to 'deconstruct' this last 'metanarrative' of the Enlightenment. The cumulative effect

---

[8] For a recent example of these two features, see Alasdair MacIntyre, *Whose justice? Which rationality?* (Notre Dame, Indiana: University of Notre Dame Press, 1988), 349–69.

of these criticisms has been to suggest that the progress the dialecticians claim to discover is rather a feature of the language they use.

CONCLUSION

The new postmodern sceptics have shown how we have become entangled in and bewitched by these two language games of progress over the last two hundred years. However, their way of thinking continues the most destructive features of both conceptions of progress. In criticizing the limits imposed on our thinking by progressive assumptions they assume that the only rational response to any limit or convention is to deconstruct and to overcome it. Thus, they see themselves as engaged in the endless task of 'overcoming' or 'overthrowing' self-imposed limits. Thus, any use of the word 'natural', 'limit', or 'foundation' needs to be exposed as something imposed by us and constraining us in what is essentially a wholly contingent universe, self, and society, open to infinite interpretation and manipulation.[9] They thus combine the radical contingency of the first view of progress with the ethics of overcoming of the second (without its progressive faith).

I scarcely need to say that this postmodern way of thought and action is not what we require today. Its activity of deconstruction is simply the reversal of the prevailing picture of progress as construction. We need a way of thinking which continues the best traditions of critical thought, not only from the Enlightenment but also from a much more cosmopolitan range of sources in order to continue this careful task of self-criticism of our reigning forms of critical thought. Moreover, as ecological and feminist scholars have stressed, we require a way of thinking that is able to recognize and to affirm the limits of our knowledge and action and the extent of our dependency on the natural world. Rather than a mistaken picture of our control *over*, we surely need to recover a sense of our appropriate place *in* the universe, which the Enlightenment swept away as a pre-modern superstition. As an increasing number of people have sought to remind us, we are one species among millions on an interdependent and fragile planet. And we are in a universe that was not made for us and which will long outlast our inevitable passing.

[9] A good example of this line of thought is provided by Richard Rorty, *Contingency, irony, and solidarity* (Cambridge: Cambridge University Press, 1989), part 1.

A line of argument which might lead in this direction is the current questioning of two further conventions of both conceptions and progress. These conventions, perhaps more than any others, cause us to overlook the complexity of what we are trying to understand and to assume a disengaged and transcendent viewpoint. The first is the widely held assumption that understanding consists in having a comprehensive theory which sets forth the essential features of the phenomenon in question. In the *Philosophical investigations* Ludwig Wittgenstein showed that this is a mistaken conception of understanding.[10] Any phenomenon we seek to understand is too complex to be grasped in a general schema which purports to lay out its essential features. The reason for this is that instances of a general phenomenon do not have the common and essential features this view presupposes. Rather, to put it negatively, they have complicated and overlapping similarities and relationships. If this is true, understanding cannot consist in possessing a general theory. It involves, rather, surveying and paying careful attention to the examples, and thus gradually acquiring a familiarity with them and their complex relations with one and another.

Let us take progress as an example. I have presented a brief survey of two examples of progress and drawn your attention to their similarities and dissimilarities. There are numerous other examples of progress and no one could claim to know what progress is until they had become familiar with additional samples. Moreover, a general theory of progress would necessarily overlook the complexity of my two examples, and *a fortiori*, the complexity of other examples, by treating a small number of features as if they were essential to and definitive of every instance of progress. A theory, by representing progress in this way, would thus cause us to overlook and therefore misunderstand the very phenomenon we seek to understand.

We can see that many of the sweeping generalizations that the great progressive thinkers put forward about the essential nature of knowledge, reason, science, society, history, and, of course, progress itself were based on this mistaken view. Unfortunately, many of the critics who have picked out errors in the earlier theories continue to construct even more abstract and misleading theories. Recently, for example, philosophers of science have put forward one theory after

---

[10] Wittgenstein, *Philosophical investigations*, nos 65–97. See James Tully, 'Wittgenstein and political philosophy', *Political theory* 17, 2 (May 1989), 172–204.

another of the essential nature of science. Critics such as Paul Feyerabend have demonstrated that for each theory of the essential rules of any science there is always a decisive counter-example. However, sharing the same assumption as their opponents, some critics (but not Feyerabend) have gone on to conclude that since science does not conform to any of the sets of rules or schemata advanced by the philosophers then it is not a rule-governed activity at all: anything goes. If they would abandon their common misconception, as Wittgenstein and Thomas Kuhn recommend, they could go on to survey the numerous examples of science available to them, to become familiar with the various and irreducible ways in which science is a rule-governed and non-anarchic activity, and thereby come to understand what science is.

Of course, we can always construct a theory or a generalization if we wish as long as we remember that it serves the limited and heuristic purpose of throwing light on a small number of features of the phenomenon at the expense of obscuring all others. Therefore, whereas the misidentification of understanding with theory directs us away from the multiplicity of the world and towards abstract and procrustean representations of it, Wittgenstein's argument directs us toward attention to and wonder at its irreducible diversity and our relations to it.

Wittgenstein complemented this with a second line of argument which I have used in my analysis of the two concepts of progress. All our enquiries, no matter how reflective and critical, always take place within some ways of thinking and acting that are taken for granted and not questioned. Being engaged in these 'language games' or 'forms of life', as he called them, is not some limit that needs to be deconstructed and overcome, nor does it render our knowledge defective in any way. The correct attitude, accordingly, to this prosaic and natural feature of the way we are in the world is acceptance: 'what has to be accepted, the given, is – so one could say – *forms of life*.'[11] (He does not mean that we must accept any given form of life, but questioning a given form of life involves the acceptance of others and not a transcendental standpoint.) As we have seen, the Cartesian activity of radical doubt – of the earlier conception of progress – overlooked the non-reflective and unquestioned forms of thinking and acting with words in which it was indeed grounded.

---

[11] Wittgenstein, *Philosophical investigations*, 226 and no. 23.

Although the post-Kantian thinkers were able to see this error in their predecessors, they mistakenly claimed that their own reflective activity of making explicit the unquestioned conditions of any claim to know was itself free of such conditions. Yet, their forms of reflection rested on and took for granted a whole range of conventions of the progressive form of life in which they thought and acted. Wittgenstein argued that the progressive forms of expression we have surveyed in this paper caused these great thinkers, and continue to cause us, to overlook and misunderstand the forms of life in which we are naturally engaged in all our reflective activities and thus to struggle against the natural way we are placed in the world as if it were some limit to be overcome.[12]

We are just beginning to appreciate the full significance of these two lines of argument. However, if we are to have a future in which we are able to address the four sets of problems that confront us, we will need to clarify and to set aside the conventions of the old language of progress which cause us to overlook and to perpetuate the activities which give rise to these problems. Hence, it seems that these two arguments will be as central to such a future as the arguments of Descartes and Kant were to the old age of progress. And, if we are fortunate enough to modify our destructive forms of life in time, there will be a different sense in which it will be right to call this future an age of progress.[13]

---

[12] Stephen Hilmy, *The later Wittgenstein* (Oxford: Basil Blackwell, 1987), 190–227.

[13] This paper is dedicated to Professor Charles Taylor, F.R.S.C., McGill University, who was unable to attend the Symposium.

Freedom and revolution

CHAPTER 9

Liberty and natural law

Part one is an analysis of Locke's concept of natural and civil liberty in the *Two treatises*. His account of liberty in the *Essay* is interpreted within the framework laid down in the *Two treatises*. I continue to believe that this early interpretation of natural and civil liberty is substantially correct and crucially important for understanding the formation of the concept of civil society or 'public sphere' in which citizens actively judge the policies of government in light of the public good. Whereas Hobbes and the absolutists argue that citizens alienate their independent political judgement as a condition of subjection, civic humanists uphold independent political judgement but tend to restrict its exercise to those directly engaged in government. Locke, in contrast to both, grants to citizens not in government the right to discuss and judge their governors in public, to dissent, and, if necessary, resist, when they transgress the public good.

However, as I worked on chapter 6 I came to see that the interpretation of Locke's natural law as 'rationalist' rather than 'voluntarist' was mistaken. I took Hobbes' extreme form of moral and legal voluntarism as a benchmark and assumed that any theory short of that was rationalist. But it became clear that Locke developed his theory of natural law within an intellectual context set by Pufendorf of 'mitigated' voluntarism in which the creation of the world is purely contingent, as in all forms of voluntarism, yet once it is created certain unalterable and rational rules of human conduct follow that god ordinarily binds himself to obey, as in rationalism. (Thus a rationalist like Grotius and a mitigated voluntarist like Pufendorf could reach similar conclusions from different premises.) In part 2, accordingly, I set aside the *Two treatises* and trace the development of Locke's thoughts on natural law and moral liberty in his other writings. He did not work out a coherent theory and, towards the end, despaired at reconciling god's omnipotence and human freedom. His thoughts remain complex, incomplete and inconsistent. The complexity of his work is intensified by his attempt to combine mitigated voluntarism with a hedonistic psychology and a probabilistic epistemology in a way which genuinely answers the threat of moral relativism laid out in book one of the *Essay*.

Moreover, turning back now to the *Two treatises*, in order to ground his philosophy of limited government Locke attempted to place more limitations on the divine and human will than voluntaristic absolutists such as Pufendorf needed to do, yet without recourse to the discredited teleological assumptions underlying rationalism. While hedonistic motivation and sanctions play central roles, the content of natural law is not derived from god's will but from the relation of God as maker to humans as his workmanship. Although god is free to destroy his creation if he wills, he nonetheless made humans for certain purposes which can be discovered by rational reflection on his workmanship, and natural duties and rights can be derived from them. These limit both individual human will and the will of the lawmaker (or government). Government is further limited by Locke's argument that absolute or arbitrary rule is not a legitimate form of government, and that consent and the rule of law are necessary conditions of legitimacy. Thus natural and human law in the *Two treatises* are inconsistent with his voluntaristic statements elsewhere that the will of the lawmaker backed up by sanctions *is* the law (see chapter 6). The way to clarify these complexities further is not to try to force the texts into the fixed categories of voluntarism and rationalism but to kick away the categories once they have served their purpose.

This chapter shows that the concept of a tradition, such as voluntarism or rationalism, should be used only heuristically to provide an initial representation of a text and a benchmark against which the text's originality can be measured. Unless an author is simply reproducing a tradition of working entirely within it, the unreflexive interpretation of a text solely in the terms of a tradition obscures what is most original and distinctive. This is especially true for an author such as Locke who is working with and within a number of traditions and combining elements from each in transformative ways. The understanding of a text that is gradually achieved by interpreting it in the light of various traditions eventually enables a person to turn around and see that the continued use of a tradition as an interpretive grid is an obstacle to further understanding.

LIBERTY FROM THE PERSPECTIVE OF THE TWO TREATISES

In section 18 of the *Philosophical investigations* Wittgenstein writes,

Our language can be seen as an ancient city: a maze of little streets and squares, of old and new houses, and of houses with additions from various periods; and this surrounded by a multitude of new boroughs with straight regular streets and uniform houses.

Our language of liberty can be seen this way too: the many ways we have to describe, explain, evaluate, question, and characterize liberty are the present interrelated descendents of styles or boroughs 'from various periods', some of which bear the stamp of Locke's contribution.

An account of liberty is a set of terms and a range of distinctions that are the expression of certain purposes, concerns or interests, of an author, group, class, people or so on. The terms and distinctions are partially *adopted* from the languages or traditions of political expression available to the author, the neighbourhoods of the city with which he or she is familiar (the achievement of intellectual community); and partially *adapted* by the author to articulate his or her concerns, thus making his or her distinctive contribution to the city (the achievement of intellectual freedom). By making the point or purpose of a depiction of liberty a necessary element I mean to bring into prominence the 'practical' nature of this kind of knowledge: its aim is not speculation nor understanding alone, but a certain kind of life or conduct. That is, the language the author employs is interwoven in human action, in the practice of liberty, and the way he or she adapts it is meant to alter that practice, by being accepted by the audience. This point has been made by Aristotle and Wittgenstein, and put beyond doubt by Taylor.[1]

To understand Locke's rendition of liberty, then, we will have to become familiar with the ways the terms and distinctions he employs are used by him and by other authors whose writings comprise the available languages of political expression. Describing similarities and dissimilarities will throw into relief what is conventional and what is original in Locke's account. Surveying this in the light of the practical context, the objects of concern to which Locke's argument is a response, will enable us to understand the purposes and concerns

---

[1] Aristotle, *Nicomachean ethics*, 1095a4–6, 1103b25–8, 1179a35–b2; Wittgenstein, *Philosophical investigations*, 23, 570; Charles Taylor, 'Neutrality in political science', in *Philosophy, politics and society*, 3rd series, ed. Laslett and Runciman (Oxford: Blackwell, 1967), 25–57.

that find expression in, and give significance to the terms and distinctions he uses. Finally, comparisons and contrasts with the ways we standardly talk and write about liberty today will help us to see where our thought runs parallel to Locke's, where his 'style' has left its mark on whole areas of our city, and where our thought diverges. There are continuities because we are citizens of the same city as Locke and discontinuities because there have been both conceptual additions and evacuations since Locke and new objects of concern (Locke was not concerned with totalitarian movements, for example, as was Berlin,[2] but with, *inter alia*, absolutism). My aim in approaching Locke in this manner is not only to understand but also to break up our sense of the ordinary with respect to liberty, to paraphrase Cavell; to broaden our horizons when thinking about liberty and thus to provide, to employ a term given a new lease on life by Rorty, edification.[3]

i

Of the three summaries or explanations of liberty that Locke provides in the *Two treatises* the most extensive is given at section 22 (spelling modernized; cf: 4, 57):[4]

The natural liberty of man is to be free from any superior power on earth, and not to be under the will or legislative authority of man, but to have only the law of nature for his rule. The liberty of man, in society, is to be under no other legislative power, but that established by consent, in the commonwealth, nor under the dominion of any will, or restraint of any law, but what the legislative shall enact, according to the trust put in it.

The major distinction is between natural liberty and liberty in society, or, as I shall call it, civil liberty. (When I wish to refer to both I shall use the term 'liberty'.) After each of the three explanations Locke concludes that liberty is not what Sir Robert Filmer, his great absolutist adversary, claims it is, namely, 'a liberty for every one to do what he lists, to live as he pleases, and not to be tyed by any laws' (22).

---

[2] Sir Isaiah Berlin, 'Two concepts of liberty', in *Four essays on liberty* (Oxford: Oxford University Press, 1979), 118–72.

[3] Stanley Cavell, *The claim of reason* (Oxford: Oxford University Press, 1979), 22; Richard Rorty, *Philosophy and the mirror of nature* (Princeton: Princeton University Press, 1979), 357–72.

[4] The numbers in brackets refer to section numbers of the *Second treatise*, and to the *First treatise* when preceded by a 1.

This shows, as Laslett and Dunn have always stressed,[5] that Locke wrote on liberty in response to Filmer's change that liberty is indistinguishable from licence. Thus, I want to examine Filmer's attack on natural liberty in order to provide the appropriate stage setting or, to keep with our original metaphor, urban topography for understanding Locke's response.

Filmer's writings are the most radical attack in the seventeenth century on the political premise that men are naturally free or have natural liberty. In the opening of *Patriarcha*, subtitled 'A defence of the natural power of kings against the unnatural liberty of the people', he singles out as his target the whole western political tradition that is based on man's natural liberty (53):[6]

Since the time school divinity began to flourish many of the Schoolmen and other Divines have published the opinion that: 'Mankind is naturally endowed and born with freedom from all subjection, and at liberty to choose what form of government it please, and that the power which any one hath over others was at the first by human right bestowed according to the discretion of the multitude.'

Filmer quite rightly associates natural liberty with the theory of popular sovereignty, that political power resides naturally in the people and only conventionally, by consent, in the government. He says the theory was first advanced by 'the subtle Schoolmen, who to be sure to thrust down the King below the Pope, thought it the safest course to advance the people above the King; that so the papal power may be more easily take place of the regal' (55). During the Reformation, 'upon the grounds of this doctrine, both Jesuits and some zealous favourers of the Geneva discipline [Calvinism] have built a perilous conclusion, which is, "that the people or multitude have power to punish or deprive the Prince if he transgress the laws of the kingdom"' (53). That is, natural liberty is secondly associated with early modern theories of revolution (see chapter 1 above). In the seventeenth century, Filmer continues, the 'Divines of the Reformed Churches have entertained it, and the common people everywhere tenderly embrace it' (53). He then goes on to criticize and to refute a number of the leading sixteenth and seventeenth century theories of natural liberty.

[5] Peter Laslett, ed. *Two treatises*, 25–67; John Dunn, *The political thought of John Locke* (Cambridge: Cambridge University Press, 1969), 43–77.
[6] The numbers in brackets refer to page numbers in *Patriarcha and other political works of Sir Robert Filmer*, ed. Peter Laslett (Oxford: Blackwell, 1949).

Thus, when Filmer set out to undermine the doctrine of natural liberty he attacked a four-hundred-year-old tradition that 'hath of late obtained a great reputation' (55) and which had been embraced by every major European movement including humanism. When Locke reasserted natural liberty, popular sovereignty, and the right of revolution against Filmer, he was able to draw on this rich and variegated mainstream tradition. From a contemporary viewpoint, Filmer was, as Locke characterizes him, 'a reformer of politicks' (1.106); Locke an advocate of 'the old way' (1.6).[7]

Filmer's assault on natural liberty consists in two parts. The first is the defence of absolutism; his Adamite theory of natural subjection. Christianity, prior to its perversion by thirteenth century Scholastics and their heirs, and prior to its contamination with pagan ideas of liberty, knew of only one example of natural liberty, and this the tragic liberty of Adam that led to the Fall and original sin. From that moment politics emerged in its unalterable form. God granted Adam absolute and unlimited domain over his family, including his wife, children, servants and slaves, and all land and animals in the world. This fatherly or patriarchal dominion was transmitted through eldest sons to every present monarch over every family in his kingdom and, in a collateral and subordinate manner, to every present father over his family (63). Because every father is under the absolute and arbitrary will of the monarch, there is no natural liberty (229).[8] However, as Locke points out, monarchs and fathers have absolute and unlimited liberty over their respective families (1.9). In the *First treatise*, Locke, like his friend Tyrrell in *Patriarcha non monarcha* (1681), advances a counter-interpretation of scripture that denies Adam's absolute dominion and reaffirms man's natural liberty.

The second arm of Filmer's attack consists in a series of brilliant criticisms of the doctrine of natural liberty. He marshals them in a singularly devastating form in his refutation of the most influential natural liberty theory of the seventeenth century, *The laws of war and peace* (1625) by Hugo Grotius. First, if men are naturally free, then they must have come together at specific times in history and unanimously consented to establish governments, but Grotius pro-

---

[7] This contemporary viewpoint is confirmed by James Daly, *Sir Robert Filmer and English political thought* (Toronto: University of Toronto Press, 1979), 163.

[8] 'Arbitrary' means that the exercise of the will need not be constrained by moral reasons; that action is justified by one's inherited authority, not by demonstrating that it is conformable to rational moral principles.

vides no evidence that this did or even could happen (273, 286–7). Locke attempts to meet this charge with a much more sophisticated historical and logical account in chapters 5 and 8 of the *Second treatise* and it need not concern us further here. Filmer's second point is that if each man is naturally free 'to live as he pleases', then we need to know the reason why he would consent to give up his freedom for the restraint and subordination of civil society; yet no reason is proffered (273–4). This problem of political obligation, which liberalism is still unable to answer, is stated by Filmer in a way similar to Wolff's criticism of all subsequent theories of natural liberty and consent in *In defense of anarchism*[9]: a man would be 'a madman, that being by nature free, would choose any man but himself to be his own governor' (286). Third, there is no reason for any man not to withdraw his consent when he thinks fit, and so 'it will be lawful for every man, when he please, to dissolve all government, and destroy all property' (274). Given the logical incoherence and anarchic consequences, Filmer thus rejects the premise of natural liberty and argues for natural subjection.

Locke's task in the *Second treatise* is to adapt the theory of natural liberty so it is invulnerable to Filmer's incisive and devastating arguments. We now want to know what sort of defences are available for adaptation from within the natural liberty tradition, so we can determine Locke's originality, and why he should be concerned to meet Filmer's criticism, so we can understand the practical point his adaptions or innovations serve. The magisterial surveys of the natural liberty tradition by Skinner and Tuck[10] show that Filmer, in his brief history, conflates two different schools.

The voluntarist school, stemming from William of Ockham, holds the belief that man has natural liberty and that liberty is the ability or power to do any possible thing one wills. From this premise that political power or sovereignty resides naturally in the people as part of their natural liberty, voluntarism developed into three subschools: conciliarism, radical individualism and absolutism. The conciliarists

---

[9] Robert Paul Wolff, *In defense of anarchism* (New York: Harper and Row, 1970).

[10] Quentin Skinner, *The foundations of modern political thought*, 2 vols. (Cambridge: Cambridge University Press, 1978); Richard Tuck, *Natural rights theories, their origin and development* (Cambridge: Cambridge University Press, 1979). For the authors mentioned below see Skinner I: 49–69, II: 113–78, 302–49; Tuck 17–31, 54–82, 143–74; Francis Oakley, *The political thought of Pierre D'Ailly* (New Haven: Yale University Press, 1964); and James Tully, *A discourse on property: John Locke and his adversaries* (Cambridge: Cambridge University Press, 1980).

argue that the natural power of preservation of the community as a whole is *delegated* by consent to form a mixed government that exercises this power in accordance with the will of the community, the common good. If the ruler pursues his own interest rather than the common good, he ceases to be the community's delegate and it has the right, through its representatives, to depose him and re-elect a new ruler. Although I am glossing Pierre D'Ailly's theory here, it is common to William of Ockham, Jean Gerson, Jacques Almain, and John Mair. The radical individualist argues that each individual delegates his power of preservation to form government and so may revolt and depose a ruler who fails to rule in accordance with the common good. Here I am thinking of the Christian humanism and voluntarism of George Buchanan and of Juan de Mariana. The absolutist voluntarist argues that since individuals have absolute liberty, they must be free to totally and irrevocably *alienate*, and not merely delegate, sovereignty by consent to form an absolute monarch (unlimited by any law). They claim that this is what rational men would do to avoid the anarchy of absolute liberty, and so men in society are understood to have done so. Civil liberty then consists in the ability to do as one pleases where the law permits. This justification of voluntary slavery and absolutism was popular in the late sixteenth century, in the slave trading absolutist regimes in Portugal and the Spanish Netherlands, and amongst absolutists during the English Revolution, classically with John Selden. Hobbes' theory of limited natural freedom, where man is not free to take his life and thus not free to alienate it to the sovereign, is a timid version of this theory. Since Filmer's absolute monarch, and fathers within the family, has absolute liberty, we might characterize his absolutism as natural subjection voluntarism.

The second or 'rationalist' natural law school of natural liberty, stemming from Aquinas, holds the belief that man has natural liberty but liberty is not defined as the ability to do as one pleases. Natural liberty is the ability to act in a way conformable to the law of nature: a set of objective and morally obligatory moral principles discoverable by and justifiable in the terms of reason that guide man to his natural end. The aim of the natural law school was to put moral and political philosophy on an objective foundation: natural law proscribes certain subjective practices (such as voluntary slavery) and enjoins others that voluntarism simply permits. The natural law school too is divided into delegation and alienation, collective and individual subschools. The first, Aquinas and Francisco Suarez, argues that the community as a whole alienates its natural law liberty to the sovereign, thus justifying limited absolutism: the sovereign is above civil law but under a moral obligation to enact laws conformable to natural law. Hugo Grotius, Samuel Pufendorf, and Richard Cumberland advance the individualist theory that individuals alienate their natural law liberty to execute the law of nature to preserve themselves to form an absolute sovereign limited by natural law. However, Grotius construed natural liberty as a set of exclusive individual rights of self-preservation and reduced natural law to the negative duty to respect the individual rights of others, thus reducing the sovereign's duty to the protection of exclusive rights, expletive justice, and emptying natural law of its role as a rule of distributive justice. The way was therefore open for the radical Levellers during the English Revolution to argue that these natural rights are inalienable and men only delegate by consent their natural power of protecting their rights to form a government. Revolution by individuals is thus justifiable when government transgresses individual natural rights.

I will make a number of finer distinctions below, but this is sufficient for the purpose at hand. Clearly, Filmer assimilates all these theories to the 'voluntarist' or absolute liberty school, denying the autonomy of the 'rationalist' natural law school and equating natural liberty with licence. He justifies this move by pointing out the inconsistencies in natural law as presented by Grotius (261–6). Locke's first task, then, is to reassert a consistent natural law theory of natural liberty and this he claims to have done in my initial quotation. Secondly, Filmer characterizes all these theories as revolutionary when, in fact, only the delegation theories are intentionally revolutionary (some alienation theories of natural law permit revolution *in extremis*). His justification of this move, which he makes astutely against both Hobbes and Grotius, is that the element of consent common to all these theories is inherently unstable and cannot but lead to revolution (246–7, 272–4). Although he agrees with Hobbes' absolutist conclusion, his point is that *no* theory of natural liberty and consent can support a stable regime; only natural subjection can guarantee order. Filmer is thus the forerunner of modern conservative critics of popular sovereignty, such as Hegel and other opponents of participation, who argue that it leads to the Terror, to unfreedom. Locke's second task is to show that the role of consent in his account of natural liberty is not only to protect liberty but also to provide the cement, and not the solvent, of a free political community: that is, to refute Filmer's criticisms of consent mentioned above.

Why, finally, was Locke concerned to advance a theory invulnerable to Filmer's assault? Filmer's works, written to justify absolute monarchy during the English Revolution, were published in 1679–80 during the Exclusion Crisis, the revolutionary situation that came to a head over Charles II's ultimately successful attempt to secure the ascension to the throne of his Catholic brother, James, Duke of York, later James II. Pressed into service to redescribe and evaluate these political events, Filmer's arguments justified James' ascension even though this entailed a Catholic monarch and the consolidation of the draft towards absolutism.[11] The Whigs, led by Shaftesbury, wished to exclude James and to place the Duke of Monmouth on the throne in order to defeat absolutism and a Catholic monarchy – the 'French disease' (Locke's code name for the *Two treatises* is *De morbo gallico*). Their aim was to introduce religious toleration for the Dissenters and to restore the co-ordinate sovereignty of king-in-parliament by revolution if necessary.[12] When parliamentary means failed the moderate Whigs 'trimmed' and the radical Whigs turned unsuccessfully to revolution. An aborted popular uprising in 1681–2 was followed by an unsuccessful plot to kidnap the king, a massive repression of the Whigs and their supporters by the Court, the flight of the revolutionaries, including Locke, to the Netherlands and the brutally quashed Monmouth rebellion in 1685.[13] Locke wrote the *Two treatises* to delegitimate James' ascension by undermining its Filmerian justification, to justify the Whigs' political aims by advancing his theory of liberty and popular sovereignty, and to justify the Whigs' political activity by writing his theory of revolution.[14] Even if Filmer's defence of absolute monarchy seemed extreme and untoward to contemporaries, it must have seemed the only alterna-

---

[11] J. P. Kenyon, *Revolution principles: the politics of party 1689–1720* (Cambridge: Cambridge University Press, 1977); J. R. Western, *Monarchy and revolution* (London: Blandford, 1972).

[12] See Mark Goldie, 'The roots of true Whiggism 1688–94', *History of political thought* 1, 2 (1980); J. R. Jones, *The first Whigs: the politics of the exclusion crisis, 1678–83* (Oxford: Oxford University Press, 1961).

[13] Peter Earle, *Monmouth's rebels: the road to Sedgemoor 1685* (New York: St. Martin's Press, 1977); Jones, *First Whigs*.

[14] Richard Ashcraft, 'Revolutionary politics and Locke's *Two treatises of government*', *Political theory* 8, 4 (1980), 429–87.

tive to many because his exposure of the anarchic implications of popular sovereignty appeared to be borne out by the Whigs' activity. Shaftesbury and his non-Conformist allies were constantly accused of fomenting rebellion and threatening a second English Revolution. That the acceptance of Locke's theory of liberty was crucially dependent upon his demonstration that it would not entail anarchy, as Filmer and the events of 1679–85 suggested, can be seen by the fact that Locke presents his set of arguments for the stability of a political community founded on liberty and consent *twice* in the *Two treatises* (203–10, 223–30).

With this survey of Locke's practical concerns, the theoretical problems confronting him, and the normative political vocabularies available to him, we are now in a position to understand the meaning and significance of the terms and range of distinctions that comprise his account of liberty.

ii

Locke uses the terms 'freedom' and 'liberty' in two senses: as a 'state' or condition of freedom and as an 'ability' or 'power' the exercise of which is the purpose or point of that condition or state (4, 59). In section 22, quoted above, he says natural liberty obtains when man is not under another's will and has natural law as his rule. Both the voluntarist and the natural lawyer agree that being under the will of another man is not the condition of freedom and that freedom is defined in opposition to this condition. But, Locke must show, against Filmer and voluntarists generally, that natural freedom is not therefore the state of being under one's own *unrestrained* or 'arbitrary' will but under one's own will and natural law. Like all natural lawyers, Locke does this by employing the two premisses concerning man's nature, one Aristotelian and the other Christian, that Aquinas developed: 'the proper function of man is acting in accordance with reason',[15] and 'men . . . [are] all the workmanship of one omnipotent and infinitely wise maker' (6). By 'reason' he means both man's faculty of reason and the rational moral principles discoverable by reason (natural law), and so he calls natural law 'the law of reason' (57) or simply 'reason' (6). Thus, the 'freedom then of man and

---

[15] John Locke, *Essays on the law of nature*, ed. W. von Leyden (Oxford: Clarendon Press, 1970), 113; *cf: Two Treatises*, 2.63.

liberty of acting according to his own will, is grounded on his having reason, which is able to instruct him in that law he is to govern himself by' (63). By the second premise, man, in acting in accordance with reason, is discharging his moral obligation to god, the author of man and the laws of reason (1.86, 6), and so participating in the divinely ordered, purposive universe.

Natural law is a set of objective moral principles that express what man ought to do and forebear, cross-culturally and trans-historically valid, independent of man's subjective will and discoverable by reason. Locke reasserted this venerable tradition in 1660 and defended it throughout his life. A brief survey of his defences will bring the major features of natural law into sharper relief. Against those such as Lord Herbert who believe that moral truths are innate, like the 'self-evident' doctrine of the American Constitution and twentieth-century intuitionism, Locke argues that this leaves morality without a rational foundation. To say that natural law is discoverable by reason, on the other hand, is to say that each moral principle can be given reasons that justify it; that natural laws are norms, not imperatives. He also takes issue with the sceptic, the obverse of the innatist, who, like Berlin and the pluralists today, believes that moral principles must be rationally justifiable but denies that this is possible. He is no less concerned to guard natural law against its greatest adversary, humanism: the view that moral principles are not objective in the natural law sense but, rather, grounded in intersubjective customs, mores, and practices, and so culturally and historically relative. This Renaissance tradition gained a strong foothold in seventeenth century English political thought, paradigmatically in James Harrington's *Oceana*, and it was used to characterize the Whigs' aspirations by Locke's ill-fated fellow conspirator, Sydney, in his *Discourses concerning government*.[16] In addition to the atheistic and hubristic tendency of the theory in implying that man, not god, is the author of values, Locke objects to its inherently conservative bent. It is difficult to see how a society's cultural practices and form of government could be rationally criticized; especially, as Locke stresses, in a country like Restoration England with its practice of religious uniformity and persecution of non-Conformity and no countervailing tradition of religious toleration to which one could

[16] For English humanism see J. G. A. Pocock, *The Machiavellian moment* (Princeton: Princeton University Press, 1975), 333–506.

appeal. (This is of course a problem that haunts contemporary 'practice' theories of society, law, morality, and reason.) Finally, the doctrine that morality has only a subjective foundation, and this in self-interest, utility, or self-preservation, enunciated by Hobbes and ultimately triumphant with the entrenchment of capitalism in the nineteenth century, is subjected to a scathing rout by Locke.[17] This should be enough to show that Locke's attachment to natural law is not instrumental but rationally grounded conviction, and, *en passant*, that a theory of liberty has its home within a skein of beliefs about human nature, law, reason, and so on.

The two Thomistic premises of the natural law tradition that man is naturally rational and created by god seem to entail an unacceptable conclusion. By the first premise, 'there cannot any one moral rule be proposed, whereof a man may not justly demand a reason' (*Essay* 1.3.4) and, by the second premise, man is morally obligated to obey the fundamental moral rules, because they are willed by his maker, god.[18] This is consistent only if god wills what we rationally discover to be morally good for man and this entails that god is not free to will for man what we would count as non-rational; 'that God himself cannot choose what is not good' (*Essay* 2.21.49). At first blush, this seems to limit god's freedom and so contradict our idea of god. The voluntarist school resolves this problem in a radical way that has left its indelible mark on our language of freedom. To save god's freedom they deny the premise that a necessary condition of a natural law, and so any law, is that it can be shown to be good for man. A law is a law if it is enacted by an authoritative lawgiver and promulgated. Thus, god's will is good, and just, *because* he wills it, and not because it is conformable to independent criteria of 'good' or 'just' that are rationally apprehendable by man. God is therefore free in the radical sense of making laws that determine right and wrong, good and evil, for man as he pleases. His justice is inscrutable and so accepted on faith, not reason. Natural law is a set of facts about human beings and scripture a set of ultimately arbitrary fiats. Civil law, in turn, is a law, and so just and good, *because* it is the will of the authoritative lawgiver,

---

[17] For these arguments see *Essays on the laws of nature*, 205–15; *An essay concerning human understanding* 1.3, 1.4; 2.28.10–12; 4.15.6; 4.16.4.

[18] *Essay* 1.3.4. For god's will, see 2.28.8, 4.3.18 and *Two treatises* 1.51–3, 2.6. All quotations from the *Essay* are from John Locke, *An essay concerning human understanding*, ed. Peter Nidditch (Oxford: Clarendon Press, 1975). The numbers in brackets refer to the book, chapter and section numbers of the *Essay*.

the absolute and hence 'arbitrary' monarch; just as the word of the father *is* the law of the household. This command or imperative theory of law is found today in secular form in majority will democracy and in legal positivism. (This explains as well why the voluntarist school were led to logical nominalism: the essence of a thing, or kind of thing, is what we name it to be.) Thus, their indifference theory of freedom of god and man to do as one lists is inseparable from their will theory of law and their project of making reason and faith or morals incommensurable.

Natural lawyers object to the way god's intellect (reason) is assimilated to his will in the voluntarist tradition. With their optimism concerning man's ability to come to rational agreement on the good life for man, they hold fast to the promise that there are rational criteria of the good for man that natural law, and so any law, must meet to be a law (in addition to it being promulgated by an authoritative lawgiver). God wills natural law *because* it is good for man; it is not good solely because god wills it. This is necessary if we are to be able to judge the goodness or justice, and so the validity, of civil law and thereby limit the sovereign. (This explains why this school were led to logical realism: the essence of a thing or kind of thing is 'what it is to be' (*Essay* 3.3.15).) Laws then are not imperatives but normative or 'ought' propositions for which reasons can be given. Divine law comprises natural law, promulgated by reason, and revelation which 'complements' but does not contradict reason. For the natural lawyer, god's laws are obligatory, but not just or good, because they are willed by god, thus saving god's essential role in morality (2.28.12). However, to save their optimistic view of man's moral reason, and thus justify limited government, they require a concept of freedom that is consistent with willing the good so god's and man's freedom is not compromised in acting in accordance with reason.

iii

The account of law and liberty in the *Two treatises* (57–63) is the employment of a much more detailed analysis presented in book 2, chapter 21 of the *Essay concerning human understanding*. Locke defines the will as a power or ability 'to order the consideration of any idea, or the forebearing to consider it; or to prefer the motion of any part of the body to its rest, and *vice versa* in any particular instance' (2.21.15).

The exercise of this ability or power in directing any action or its forebearance is 'that which we call volition or willing'. An action that follows from such a direction, where the agent has the power not to will that action, is voluntary; one that does not is involuntary. Liberty, like the will, is a power or ability, but 'a power in any agent to do or forebear any particular action, according to the determination or thought of the mind, whereby either of them is preferred to the other' (8). When the agent is not free not to do the action he wills then the action is 'necessary'. Thus the distinction between two powers, will and liberty (16), enables Locke to distinguish between voluntary and involuntary action, and free and necessary action respectively. If a man prefers to stay in a locked room, for example, his staying is voluntary but not free because necessary. Liberty comprises the will plus the power to do and not to do the action willed: freedom of choice and action (15).

So far Locke has presented a natural, in the sense of non-moral, account of liberty. He now constructs a moral concept of liberty on this base. He asks, if the will is the power of the mind 'to direct the operative faculties of a man to motion or rest', then 'what determines the will?' (29). He answers that the mind or intellect determines the will but the intellect in turn is determined by a 'motive', called 'uneasiness' or 'desire'. The distinction between two acts, willing and desiring, is initially introduced to make sense of the common problem of willing one thing and desiring another. Locke employs it to win a middle position between two extreme views. The voluntarist is free in so far as his will is unrestrained by reason or law. The extreme subjectivist version of this that Locke attacks (30), represented by Hobbes and Filmer,[19] is that the will is identical to desire, and an object of desire, and so of will, is good *because* it is desired or willed, as we have seen. Desire, not reason, determines what is good for man. Reason is simply an instrument for calculating the best means to satisfy one's *de facto* desires, freedom the doing what one desires, and the good life the satisfaction of desires.[20] This is the view that triumphed, *mutatis mutandis*, in classical utilitarianism and in the various theories of emotivism, non-cognitivism and value pluralism today. The opposite or objectivist view is that the will is determined not by desire but by what is objectively good, the 'greater good' (35).

[19] For Filmer see *Two treatises* 1.9; Thomas Hobbes, *Leviathan*, ed. C. B. Macpherson (Middlesex: Penguin, 1968) 1.6 (120, 128).
[20] Hobbes, *Leviathan*, 1.5 (115), 1.6 (129-30), 1.8 (139).

The will is identified with the intellect, as with Spinoza and Leibniz,[21] the intellect or reason discovers the good and this is contingently related to *de facto* desires. The idea of the good is causally efficacious in the sense of creating the requisite motivation. Freedom is following one's rational and autonomous will as we see for example in Kant.

Locke, like Aristotle, agrees with the subjectivist that desire accompanies willing (this is why they are confounded [9]), that one's *de facto* desires standardly determine the will and that we call their objects good (37). But he also agrees with the objectivist that there is a greater good discoverable by reason. However, the greater good does not *determine* the will or everyone exposed to the teaching of Christ would act like Christians (38). The 'present good', the satisfaction of an immediate uneasiness, standardly determines the will (40). What he denies to the subjectivist is that desires are beyond revision or rational evaluation. The desires men seek to satisfy are those which fit into his background conception of happiness: 'Happiness, under this view, everyone constantly pursues, and desires what makes any part of it: other things, acknowledged to be good, he can look upon without desire; pass by and be content without' (43). With our reason we can apprehend the 'greater good' and make it our conception of happiness so 'our desire, raised proportionally to it, makes us uneasy in the want of it' (35). Sheer force of rational will cannot do this; man requires the motivational inducement of the reward of heaven and punishment of hell to raise his desires so he finds happiness in doing the greater good (44, 60). Reason discovers what man ought to do and the picture of infinite happiness for the immortal soul, along with practice, provides the necessary fortitude for doing it and laying aside desires that lead to sin (46).

The 'source of all liberty' thus consists in this (47):

For during this suspension of any desire, before the will be determined to action, and the action (which follows that determination) done, we have opportunity to examine, view, and judge, of the good or evil of what we are going to do; and when, upon due examination, we have done our duty, all that we can, or ought to do, in pursuit of our happiness; and 'tis not a fault, but a perfection of our nature to desire, will, and according to the last result of a fair examination.

[21] See Leroy Loemker, *Struggle for synthesis: The seventeenth century background of Leibniz's synthesis of order and freedom* (Cambridge, MA: Harvard University Press, 1972), 130.

To be determined to the good by choice and judgement is not 'a restraint or diminution of freedom'; it is 'the end and use of our liberty' (48). To be determined by *de facto* desire is 'misery and slavery'. Locke does not say that acting in accordance with reason *is* freedom but, rather, that it is the purpose, 'perfection' or 'end' of freedom. The failure to do so is a failure to *use* liberty for the sake of which god gave it to man; for 'infinite perfection and happiness' (49). Therefore, like man's freedom, 'the freedom of the Almighty hinders not his being determined by what is best' (48). The 'hinge on which turns the liberty of intellectual beings' (52) is examination, 'consulting a guide' and 'following the direction of that guide' (50).

To consult a guide, to judge the good or evil of proposed courses of action, is to compare these actions to Divine law, either natural or revealed; 'the true touchstone or moral rectitude', of 'moral good or evil' (2.28.8). Given the variability and contingency of human affairs, there is not one right judgement of how to apply natural law to a given situation: a moral pluralism of means but not of ends.[22] The *moral* use of liberty involves 'obligation', to god to follow natural law or reason, and a 'motive', to gain eternal happiness (52). Locke has shown here what the voluntarist denies; that freedom and law or obligation are consistent. Hobbes, like all voluntarists, writes:[23]

RIGHT consisteth in liberty to do or forbeare; whereas LAW, determinith, and bindeth to one of them: so that law, and Right, differ as much, as Obligation, and Liberty; which in one and the same matter are inconsistent.

For the voluntarist, law is *regulative* of an antecedently defined freedom, restraining and opposing it. For Locke, as he puts it in the *Two treatises*, 'where there is no law there is no freedom' (57). Law is *constitutive* of freedom, perfecting or completing it as its final cause. Law is not the conventional means to control man's natural desire to do as he pleases; it is the natural guide to lead man to the fulfillment of his rational inclination to do the good. It follows that the role of civil law will not be to restrain naturally egoistic desires but to promote man's natural ratiocinative desire for the good life. What he says in the *Two treatises* is: 'Law, in its true notion, is not so much the limitation as the direction of a free and intelligent agent to his proper

---

[22] *Essay* 4.14, 4.16; *The correspondence of John Locke*, ed. E. S. DeBeer (Oxford: Clarendon Press, 1976), I, letters 328, 374, 426. [23] Hobbes, *Leviathan*, 1.14 (189).

interests, and prescribes no farther than is for the general good of those under that law' (57). Thus, following civil law in a rationally ordered polity is not the diminution of liberty but the realization of civil liberty: 'the end of law is not to abolish or restrain, but to preserve and enlarge freedom'.

The voluntarist notion of freedom runs parallel to Berlin's concept of 'negative' freedom, 'freedom from', and there is no question that, through Hobbes, the voluntarist view has deeply influenced our secular language games of pluralist and utilitarian freedom. Locke's natural law freedom to perfect our nature in performing our rational duties to god runs parallel to Berlin's concept of 'positive' freedom, 'freedom to'. Berlin wants to say that the philosophical foundation of the 'liberal' freedoms we enjoy today is the theory of negative freedom, and positive freedom historically the foundation of totalitarianism and arbitrary rule. However, if Locke is one of the theorists of liberalism, then Berlin has this part of our intellectual and practical political history the wrong way round. This can be seen not only in the difficulty he has in classifying Locke (124, 126, 147), but also in the important concession he makes in a footnote: 'belief in the absolute authority of divine or natural laws, or in the equality of all men in the sight of God, is very different from belief in freedom to live as one prefers' (129). For Locke, nothing is more important than 'positive' freedom because it is the means to salvation (60). The depth of Locke's analysis partly consists in his remarkable presentiment of the unrestrained individualism entailed by abandoning natural law liberty and embracing secular voluntarism:[24]

A dependent intelligent being is under the power and direction and dominion of him on whom he depends and must be fore the ends appointed him by that superior being. If man were independent he would have no law but his own will, no end but himself. He would be a god to himself and the satisfaction of his own will the sole measure and end of all his actions.

iv

Locke defused Filmer's first criticism of natural liberty 'for every one to do what he lists' by showing that there is a way of thinking about liberty which involves acting in accordance with one's will and 'within the bounds of the law of nature' (4). Now we want to know

[24] Ethica, Bodleian, MS. Locke c. 28, fo. 141.

how Locke answers Filmer's second criticism: why anyone would consent to abjure his natural liberty for the confines of civil liberty. To understand this we must start with his account of man in a pre-political condition, the state of nature.

The state of nature is a moral community constituted by natural law (128) and man is free in exercising his liberty or natural power in accordance with natural law and with rational choice where natural law is silent (4.59). Although there are three basic natural laws the one that does the majority of the work in Locke's political theory is 'mankind ought to be preserved' (135). This is divided into the negative service duty not 'to harm another in his life, health, liberty, or possessions', and the positive service duty to 'preserve himself' and 'when his own preservation comes not in competition . . . to preserve the rest of mankind' (2.6). Man's natural rights to things necessary for preservation follow from these natural duties with the consequence that rights of 'private' property are limited by the claims of others to preservation, 'the support and comfort of their being' (26). (The balancing of man's duty to preserve himself with the duty to ensure the preservation of others is worked out in chapter 5 of the *Second treatise*.) Part of the exercise of the liberty or power to preserve oneself and others is the duty, and so the right, to punish those who transgress natural law, by violence, theft (8) or by accumulating more than their share of the common (37). The 'execution of the law of nature is in that state, put into every man's hands' (7). Thus man has two natural powers or liberties the exercise of which is morally obligatory: to preserve himself and others and to punish violations of natural law (128). When men enter political society they give the *exercise* of their power of punishment and the *regulation* of their power of self- and mankind-preservation to the political society (129). These exercising and regulating powers are then 'entrusted' to the constitution of government they choose (131) and thus, by definition, political power is bounded by the end, preservation, for the sake of which men possessed it in the state of nature (171). Government is thereby under natural law in the same way man is in the state of nature (135).

This is an individualist theory of popular sovereignty. Political power or the state is simply the power that individual members entrust to their government; it is not something different in kind from man's natural power, as it is in the neo-Thomist and Calvinist traditions, or in Filmer's theory. It is an individualist adaptation of the natural law delegation tradition. Marx deploys a similar theory of popular sovereignty to undermine Hegel's mystification of the state in his *Critique of Hegel's philosophy of right*.[25] Locke's theory of popular sovereignty contains an important feature which can be illuminated by a contrast with Grotius and the natural rights theorists of the English Revolution who followed him. Grotius' state of nature is governed by natural law but the only natural law is the negative service duty to abstain from that which belongs to another.[26] The role of the state is therefore the negative one of expletive justice, the protection of contracts and private property and the punishment of crimes against persons. A negative theory of natural law thus yields the minimum or 'nightwatchman' state that protects individual rights, the forerunner of the version of liberalism represented today by Nozick's *Anarchy, state and utopia*.[27] For Locke, natural law also enjoins the preservation of others, and so government is entrusted with the positive duty of regulating the means of preservation, property relations (50, 120, 138). Distributive justice is thus a role of government and so, in this sense, Locke is a follower of Aquinas and Suarez and precursor of the version of liberalism represented today by John Rawls' *A theory of justice* and of democratic socialism.[28]

If we turn back to Locke's definition of civil liberty we see that we have covered one half of his account. Men possess civil liberty if their government enacts legislation 'according to the trust put in it' (22). The trust is that their political power will be employed in a way conformable to its original purpose, to natural law (12). The second condition is that political power is established by 'consent' (22). This means that each and every member of a political community must explicitly consent to join that society for him to become a member and for it to become a 'community' (96, 122). In consenting the member agrees to be bound by the majority, or by the majority of representatives if it is not a direct democracy, in framing a constitution and all further legislation (96). The citizens are not bound to the government but to 'the will of the society, declared in its laws', the 'publick will of the society' (151). The government can break its trust and so destroy civil liberty by legislative or executive action contrary to natural and established law, beyond their trust, or without the consent of the

[25] Karl Marx, *Critique of Hegel's philosophy of right*, ed. J. O'Malley (Cambridge: Cambridge University Press, 1970), 19–38, esp. 30.   [26] H. Grotius, *De Iure ac Pacis*, prol. 8.
[27] Robert Nozick, *Anarchy, state and utopia* (Oxford: Blackwell, 1974).
[28] John Rawls, *A theory of justice* (Oxford: Oxford University Press, 1972). For the Lockean socialists see Max Beer, *The history of British socialism* (London: 1921).

majority.[29] In either case civil liberty dissolves, the exercise of political power is 'arbitrary', power devolves back to the people and they regain their natural liberty and duty to punish the government for violating natural law through a revolution and to establish a new government (149, 222).

Locke's account of civil liberty is similar to republican or civic humanist theories in which political liberty consists of participation in a self-governing commonwealth. It contrasts with the theories of Hobbes and some modern rights theorists who define liberty in terms of the absence of law. Although Locke mentions the point that part of civil liberty comprises 'a liberty to follow my own Will in all things, where the Rule prescribes not', this is introduced primarily to distinguish civil liberty from being subject to the 'arbitrary Will' of a despot (22). It is not introduced, as in Hobbes, as the definition of liberty. In section 122 he lays it down that a person who simply obeys the law and does not positively engage in and consent to their political community is not a member of that society. The primary meaning he attaches to civil liberty is the condition of living under the rule of law established by the consent of the governed and limited by their trust (22). Living and acting in such a free commonwealth – whether one is acting in accordance with the law, and so performing one's duties to the public good, or acting where the law does not prescribe – is said to be the '*Liberty of Man, in society*' (22). Thus, with Locke, as with Milton, republican and contraction conceptions of political freedom join hands in common opposition to the disengaged and passive subjection offered by absolutists such as Hobbes and Filmer[30].

The strength of Filmer's criticism resides in his sharp contrast between the unrestrained natural liberty and communism of the state of nature and the confining conventional obligations one is subjected to in a political community. Confronted with these alternatives, the rational grounds of consent appear ephemeral indeed. Only an excessively bleak picture of how men would behave in such a natural condition, coupled with a countervailing picture of the security of

---

[29] *Two treatises*, 2.135, 1402, 153–6, 214–19, 222.

[30] For republican liberty see Quentin Skinner, 'The paradoxes of political liberty', in M. McMurrin, ed., *The Tanner Lectures on human values*, VII (Cambridge: Cambridge University Press, 1986), 225–50. This feature of Locke's account of civil liberty has been noted by Richard Ashcraft, *Locke's Two treatises of government* (London: Hyman and Unwin, 1987) 97–123, and Ruth Grant, *John Locke's liberalism* (Chicago: University of Chicago Press, 1987), 192–205.

302 FREEDOM AND REVOLUTION

political society could, as Hobbes saw, underpin a rationally grounded consent. But once we accept Locke's premise of natural liberty under natural law, Filmer's contrast loses its application and political society appears as a civilized development out of the state of nature, rather than a sharp break with it. Locke presents three reasons for consenting to join political society. First, since men tend to be partial to themselves and their friends in their judgements, the *ad hoc* administration of justice in the state of nature would be biased, thus tending to insecurity, fear, danger, and inconvenience (13, 123–6). Political society partly solves this by establishing a known and standing judge; the legislature, law, and judiciary (87–9). Second, following Grotius, men have a natural inclination for political community, not simply as a means to preservation but to enjoy it for its own sake (77). Men 'enjoy many conveniences, from the labour, assistance and society of others in the same community' (130) and find 'political happiness' (107). All man loses is his 'economic' liberty (contrary to many laissez-faire misinterpretations of Locke): 'he is to part also with as much of his natural liberty in providing for himself as the good, prosperity, and safety of the society shall require' (130, cf: 120). The third and decisive reason is that civil laws are just and an expression of the public will only if they are conformable to natural law (12). Their end is the 'public good' (3); the application of natural law to human societies grown complex by population increase, the rise of agriculture, trade, and manufacture and the introduction of money (38, 45, 116). Just as he perfects his liberty in choosing to be guided by natural law, so man preserves and enlarges freedom in consenting to be directed by civil laws 'to his proper interest' and 'general good' (57). The laws are the expression of a citizen's rational judgement, 'indeed are his own judgements, they being made by himself, or his representative' (88).

We can summarize these three reasons in the following way: political society is (1) good in the instrumental sense of being the best means to the end of security, (2) good for its own sake or intrinsically good in being a richer and more flourishing form of life, and (3) naturally good in the sense of being partly constitutive of the purpose for the sake of which man has liberty and reason. The argument turns, it seems to me, on consent being the exercise of one's natural liberty for the sake of the 'greater good', civil liberty, not, as with the voluntarist and Filmer, on it being the alienation of one's unlimited natural liberty for the sake of conventional security and absolutism.

The argument as a whole has two dimensions: life in political society is natural against the voluntarist belief that it is conventional and contrary to man's natural, unlimited liberty; and life in political society is free against Filmer's belief that it is servitude (2). Notwithstanding many dissimilarities, in this respect it is similar to Aristotle's argument in book 1 of the *Politics* against the sophists and Plato.

Locke's final task is to refute Filmer's charge that in a regime of civil or popular liberty the members would withdraw their consent, would dissent and revolt whenever the public good conflicted with their private interest. The reason for this is that a member's consent is based on his individual judgement that the government is governing in accordance with its trust, the public good, but, Filmer writes citing Aristotle, 'the multitude are ill judges in their own case' (94). Thus the partiality of individual judgement that provides a reason for entering a commonwealth would also justify frequent and biased dissent and rebellion. Filmer's comment on Hunton's theory of popular sovereignty in *A treatise on monarchy* (1643) is apposite: 'every man is brought, by this doctrine of our author, to be his own judge. And I also appeal to the consciences of all mankind, whether the end of this be not utter confusion and anarchy' (297). Locke cannot finesse this criticism because he accepts that men are partial in their judgements and uses it to partly explain why men enter political society and why they adopt the majority principle (98). Also, his account of civil liberty rests on the premise that continuing consent is based on individual judgement of government performance. He asks, 'who shall judge whether the prince [executive] or legislative act contrary to their trust?' and he answers, 'the people shall judge', 'every man is judge for himself' (240–1).[31] Filmer, like the revisionist critics of popular democracy today, seems to have caught Locke in an insoluble dilemma.

Many commentators have thought that Locke's response is that man's consent to join a political society puts him under a standing obligation to obey the law. What he says is that 'express' consent makes man a member and 'obliged to be and remain unalterably a

---

[31] It is important to see that the people are sovereign in the sense that they judge the legislature and the executive (151). The legislature does not judge the executive as in parliamentary or legislative sovereignty, nor does the judiciary judge, as in constitutional sovereignty. See Julian Franklin, *John Locke and the theory of sovereignty* (Cambridge: Cambridge University Press, 1978).

subject' until it 'comes to be dissolved' (121–2). All this does is distinguish between 'members', who expressly consent, and those resident aliens over whom the government has jurisdiction. This is no answer at all to Filmer's dilemma because the ground for the conviction that a government is 'dissolved' is the individual's judgement that the trust has been breached. The member is obligated in virtue of his consent only to what he consents to – government in accordance with the trust – and that it is such a government is a matter of judgement. Political obligation is thus based on the individual judgement that the government is worthy of one's consent and must be if civil liberty is to remain intact.

What Locke does is advance and defend criteria for judging that the trust is broken and government dissolved (121–22). The criteria are tailored fairly closely to English government and are designed to show that the executive, Charles II, has dissolved government and thus revolution is justified here and now (210, 222). His aim is of course to legitimate Whig revolution and reconstitution of a civil liberty commonwealth in 1681–2 *and* to demonstrate that this does not lay 'a ferment for frequent rebellion' (224). However, as Locke is well aware, establishing criteria for judgement does not answer Filmer's criticism because people may employ the criteria in a partial manner to justify revolt 'whenever they take offence' (223). Locke gives two reasons why he doubts Filmer's conclusion. First, if the people are 'ill-treated', they 'will be ready on any occasion to ease themselves of a burden that sits heavy upon them' in any form of government, including Filmerian absolutism (224). Because a popular legislature is responsive and open to judgements of the citizenry, *is* the articulation of their will (151), it is less likely to oppress and more open to claims of oppression than absolutism (107). Since the absolute ruler himself must be partial as well as irresponsible, absolutism foments revolt (90–4). People in popular governments will be partial, but, Locke believes like Aristotle, Machiavelli, and Marx, partial to liberty. 'Whatsoever cannot but be acknowledged to be of advantage to the society, and people in general, upon just and lasting measures, will always, when done, justifie itself' (158). Therefore, turning the tables on Filmer, the best guarantee of a stable polity is civil liberty (226).

Second, Locke again turns the conservative trump card of partiality against Filmer. People are generally partial to the *status quo*, will not rebel 'upon every mismanagement of publick affairs' (225), but will revolt only once 'the mischief grows general' (230) and 'the precedent and consequences seem to threaten all' (209). In these passages Locke is not denying the individual *right* to revolt, he is making a sociological observation about the conservative nature of revolutionary *motivation* (208). Although these reasons surely meet Filmer on his own turf, Locke is nonetheless concerned that the quest for order remain subordinate to the aspiration for liberty. He writes that the Filmerians say 'this doctrine is not to be allowed, being so destructive to the peace of this world' and responds: 'they may as well say upon the same ground, that honest man may not oppose robbers or pirates, because this may occasion disorder or bloodshed' (228).

v

I would like to make three concluding remarks. First, Locke's government has no authority to enforce a particular religion. Since men entrust only their powers of preservation, the attempt to impose religious conformity, or a particular moral vision of the good life, would constitute a breach of trust and, as he argues in *A letter concerning toleration*, justify revolution. The theory is thus a defence of religious liberty, a paramount concern of Locke's from 1668 onwards and a major aim of Shaftesbury's movement. Locke is liberal in the sense that religion, or morals, and politics are separate and the role of government is to ensure material well-being and individual civil and religious liberty. However, he is not a secular theorist but, rather, a theistic theorist.[32] The obligation to natural law is an obligation to god and the motivation is dependent upon belief in the immortality of the soul. Also, natural law and its derivative natural rights are derived from the relationship between man and god as his maker. Thus, if this theistic framework were removed liberty would become 'living as one pleases' and government a kind of voluntarist majoritarian absolutism. A secular rationalist version of Lockean liberty would require an 'ends' theory of rationality capable of deriving a rational law of preservation and natural rights from the human condition, and theories of moral and political obligation and motivation. As Locke foresaw, nothing remotely resembling this has

[32] For the emergence of secular political thought, see David Wootton, *Sarpi, atheism, and the social order* (Cambridge: Cambridge University Press, 1985).

been produced.[33] This is why Locke says in *A letter concerning toleration* that atheists cannot be members of political society.

Even though Locke's theory has had an immense and somewhat paradoxical influence on our western way of life, the only faithful attitude we can take to the original contribution as a whole is one of nostalgia. However, we can study it to understand how much of the fragmented ruins of liberty we cling to in desperation today once held together as a coherent and limited structure.

My second point is that Locke's account of liberty presupposes active, rational, and politically informed citizens willing to critically assess their government's performance and a responsive government. During the Exclusion Crisis such a citizenry existed to an extent perhaps unrivalled in English history. The aspiration articulated by Locke to base religion and politics on individual judgement – to have religious and political liberty – was put forward by men who had experienced it in the English Revolution, the Commonwealth and religious congregations.[34] Ever since Schumpeter's *Capitalism, socialism and democracy* (1942) social scientists have concluded that such a citizen is a myth (presumably exempting themselves).[35] It is of course a commonplace that present 'liberal' states have defaulted on this early promise of a 'public sphere' in which citizens bring claims and controversies forward, discuss and give expression to the public will.[36] As a result, they are more absolutist than Filmer could have imagined. Those who seek ammunition to confront these technocratic absolutisms, who are not satisfied with the liberty to do as one lists where the supervisory state chooses to leave them alone, would do well to re-search Locke's borough of our city of liberty.

Without the theological foundations, Lockean liberty still provides a theory of popular sovereignty and civil liberty as the exercise of critical political judgement about the public good. Foundations for this could be provided by a union with natural law's great rival, civic humanism, and this for two reasons. Civic humanists have always kept alive the argument that political judgement is developed

---

[33] John Dunn, *Political obligation in its historical context* (Cambridge: Cambridge University Press, 1980), 243–301.

[34] Jones, *First Whigs*, Ashcraft, '*Revolutionary politics*'; Iris Morley, *A thousand lives: an account of the English revolutionary movement 1660–85* (London: Andrew Deutsch, 1954).

[35] Joseph Schumpeter, *Capitalism, socialism and democracy* (New York: Harper and Row, 1950 [1942]), 250–84.

[36] Jürgens Habermas, 'The public sphere', *New German Critique*, 3 (1974), 49–55.

through the exercise of civil liberty. Secondly, Locke stigmatized humanism as conservative because the criteria for judgement are the intersubjective norms and customs of a society; what counts as a rational political argument is what can be justified in the terms of our established justificatory practices. What Locke is saying is that these practices themselves can be criticized, and this in the terms of an objective law of reason. Just because the theological framework for a substantive law of reason has ceased to be intersubjective for us does not mean that the heritage of critical reason now is simply saying what I please (as modern voluntarists tell us). Part of the crazyquilt of language-games, if not of institutions, that comprise our city is just the natural law tradition of popular sovereignty and liberty. Although now part of the suburbs, it could still provide the ground for justifying claims to liberty against the more established and dominant, but less liberal, practices of our political life.

Third, women were excluded from all these traditions of liberty. If we wish to continue to use these traditions the following critical steps need to be undertaken. The traditions of women writing on liberty need to be recovered and used to expose the male bias of mainstream conceptions of liberty, and to present women's ways of conceptualizing freedom. In addition, the histories of women's struggles for liberty need to be studied in order to become familiar with alternative practices of liberty, and to see how voluntarists, natural law, and humanist conceptions of liberty have been used in practice, and continue to be used, to silence and exclude women from the exercise of political and civil liberty. Finally, the distinctive ways in which contemporary women writers conceptualize liberty, agency, and rationality need to be recognized and affirmed, and not simply treated as 'supplements' to, or absorbed within, the conceptual framework of male traditions of liberty.[37]

LIBERTY FROM THE PERSPECTIVE OF THE ESSAY

John Locke lived in the century in which the modern natural and human sciences, which still form the horizons of much of our thought, were initially constructed. His *Two treatises of government* (1690) and *A letter concerning toleration* (1690) are major constituents of modern

---

[37] I would like to acknowledge my debt to the late G. A. Paul and to thank Herbert Hart for making Paul's excellent lecture notes on Locke available to me.

political thought, and *An essay concerning human understanding* (1690) is a landmark in the formation of modern philosophy, especially epistemology and psychology. In the course of writing these texts Locke also worked out his equally significant moral philosophy. He sought to advance an account of morality conformable to his epistemology and psychology and complementary to his analysis of the conditions of freedom and oppression in religion and politics.

Locke worked on his moral philosophy from the *Essays on the law of nature* (1662) to the *Paraphrases of the Epistles of St Paul*, written in the last years of his life. The various changes in his moral thinking are recorded in his published works, in the successive drafts of the *Essays*, written over eighteen years, in the changes he made to the five editions of the *Essay* published during his lifetime, in his Journal notes, and in his eight volumes of *Correspondence*. Since these are all now available to us, we are in a position to survey the development and final arrangement of his thoughts on morality.

One way to gain an initial picture of this large body of writing is to view it as an attempt to combine three modern movements in seventeenth-century philosophy. The first is called the school of 'natural jurisprudence' or 'juristic' morality because its members treated morality as a legal system: that is, a demonstrable body of universal laws promulgated by a lawmaker (god), backed up by rewards and punishments, grounded in each individual's concern for self-preservation, and free from any particular religion, thereby providing a minimal moral foundation on which Europeans of different religious persuasions could agree after 100 years of religious wars. Hugo Grotius, Thomas Hobbes, Baruch Spinoza, Samuel Pufendorf, and Gottfried Leibniz all worked on this great project. The second movement is the revival of Greek hedonism: the attempt to replace the scholastic psychology of innate dispositions and telic faculties with a mechanical model of human behaviour based on the causal motives of pleasure-seeking and pain-avoidance. This is associated with Pierre Gassendi, Walter Charleton, and Robert Boyle. The invention and elaboration of theories of probability in philosophy, law, history, statistics, and religion, associated with Joseph Glanvill, Blaise Pascal, and Antoine Arnauld, is the third school of thought.

Locke began to analyse morality in the terms of natural jurisprudence, hedonic psychology, and epistemic probability in the 1670s and published his first theory in the *Essay* in 1690. It was immediately seen as the most challenging and audacious moral philosophy in Europe and it continued to set the terms of debate for over a century. Readers were scandalized by the moral relativism his views seemed to entail. This charge is based in part on a misunderstanding of Locke's intentions, as he pointed out to James Tyrrell (*Correspondence* 4: 1309). The account of morality in the *Essay* is first and foremost a critical analysis and explanation of the development, functioning, and use, by moral elites, of different moralities. There is less emphasis on justifying one specific morality, yet this is the question his readers asked of the text. Locke wished to lay bare the workings of diverse moral systems, both within a confessionally divided and warring Europe, and throughout the world that Europeans had recently invaded and now sought to understand and control. Thus, let us survey his critical analysis before taking up the question of justification.

Locke's analysis of moral systems integrates his hedonism and his juristic model of morality. After defining 'natural' good and evil as nothing but pleasure and pain or the means of them, he went on to define 'morally good and evil' as (*Essay* 2.28.5):

only the conformity or disagreement of our voluntary actions to some law, whereby good or evil is drawn on us, from the will and power of the lawmaker; which good and evil, pleasure or pain, attending our observance, or breach of the law, by the decree of the lawmaker, is that we call reward and punishment.

This encapsulates the main features of his moral philosophy. The primary subject of morality is voluntary human action. No voluntary action is intrinsically moral or immoral, but only with reference to a law. A moral law is defined voluntaristically as the will of a lawmaker and enforced with rewards and punishments. The rewards and punishments administered for obedience and disobedience are the types of pleasures and pains, goods and evils, that any moral agent is concerned with in her/his voluntary action.

All systems of morality conform to this juristic-hedonic scheme. There are three types (*Essays* 1.3.5, 2.28). Morality and legality are identical in the first or 'Hobbist' system: the will of a political sovereign defines good and evil actions by means of law and enforces them by the rewards and punishments of the penal system. The second comprises all the reputation-based ethical systems – such as those of the Greek and Romans – in which the will of a moral community or group is tacitly expressed through the laws of public opinion, in the form of the conventional virtues and vices of the group, and these are sanctioned by the rewards of public honour, esteem or praise and the punishments of public dishonour, shame or blame. Locke conjectured that this is historically the most common and effective type of morality because not one in ten thousand can bear the pain of ill-repute or resist the pleasure of a good reputation among companions. The third type, of which Christianity is the exemplar, includes religious systems in which a god makes divine laws and backs these up with the reward of eternal life (heaven) and the punishment of damnation or annihilation (hell).

How does the moral agent engage in these systems? In Book one of the *Essay* Locke rejected the scholastic and humanist view that humans have an innate moral disposition to assent to and act towards some natural good and argued that the mind is like a blank tablet, morally indifferent and capable of receiving any imprint. Rather, humans have empirically verifiable motives to seek pleasure or happiness and to avoid pain or misery. In all moral action, these take the form of a basic 'concern' to find out and to obey the laws that will bring rewards and thereby avoid punishment; and this concern is both the motivation and obligation of moral agency (*Essay* 2.27.26, 2.21.52).

In the first edition of the *Essay* Locke wrote that a moral agent would always act for the greater good in view. His critics responded that this is empirically false: nothing is more common than the choice of a lesser yet closer good in full knowledge of a greater yet absent good. The will, he replied in the second edition, is not determined by the greater good in view but, rather, by present 'uneasiness': a desire to ease a present pain which always accompanies any present pain (*Essay* 2.21.31). This psychological mechanism also explains how people can be moved to pursue an absent or long-term good. By developing an uneasiness for it an agent is moved to pursue it in order to ease the present pain. Further, most of the types of uneasiness that govern our conduct, such as for honour, power, riches, or virtue, are acquired by what Locke calls 'use and practice' or custom. That is, by the repetition of ways of thinking and acting we come to acquire a habitual uneasiness for and, accordingly, a pleasure in them (*Essay* 2.21.69).

The reason why people find their happiness in diverse ways of life, such as riches or glory, is that they become accustomed, through repetition, to the constituent activities and thereby acquire a habitual uneasiness or mental 'relish' for them. This relish then serves as the ground on which they think and act morally. The use of the word 'relish' is meant to highlight the fact that moral judgements are as relative as judgements of taste in food (*Essay* 2.21.55). Once custom and repetition settle habits of thinking, willing, and bodily movement, these become 'easy and as it were natural', overpowering and shaping reason and interest (*Essay* 2.33, added to the fourth edition). Locke's practice theory of moral conduct is part of a tradition of reflection on the role of custom from Michel de Montaigne to Pascal.

It is now easy to see how this theory dovetails with his three systems of morality. From childhood onward novitiates are induced into moralities by means of a combination of praise and blame, bodily punishments and rewards, and threats of heaven and hell administered by authorities. Through drill and exercise the pupil becomes accustomed to canonical ways of thinking and behaving, eventually finding them pleasant (virtue becomes its own reward) and natural. As he puts it in *Some thoughts concerning education* (1693), the pupil is 'only as white paper, or wax, to be molded and fashioned as one pleases' (216).

Locke's analysis explains why Europeans believe that their acquired dispositions and conflicting moral beliefs are innate and natural, as their moral authorities conveniently teach them in order to get what they want: power and dominion. In addition, it explains the rise of political, moral, religious, and educational elites, the hold they have over their followers, and how they are able to mobilize millions of nominal Christians to take up arms to defend their conflicting 'true' moralities in the wars of religion. Consequently, one of the major aims of Locke's moral philosophy has been completed: a comprehensive account of how moral systems form moral subjects with the motivation and obligation to die in the defence and propagation of their morality for the sake of glory and heavenly reward (*Essay* 1.1.2, 1.3.22–7, 1.4.24).

The justification of moral reform is the second major aspect of Locke's moral philosophy. In response to the charge that his analysis of morality is deterministic, Locke replied, in the second edition of the *Essay* (2.21), that persons have the power to suspend their habitual ways of thought and action and to examine the pleasures and pains of proposed courses of action. The power to suspend and examine not only within the background relish of one's moral system but also, more reflectively, to suspend and examine one's moral system itself is the foundation of moral freedom. When acquired uneasiness to assent and act is suspended, examination involves the application of Locke's two types of probabilistic reasoning. Before outlining these, it is necessary to contrast them with the alternative form of moral reasoning in the seventeenth century in order to appreciate the importance of Locke's turn to probability.

The great project of the juristic school was to demonstrate a certain moral code from a few, unquestionable premises about god, concern for preservation, and the necessity of sociality. The natural laws and rights would be simple and universal enough to unite a religiously pluralistic Europe and so end the wars of religion. Locke agreed that the existence of a god could be demonstrated with certainty. Further, from the demonstrable premise of a god who made humans and of humans as god's workmanship, he claimed that it is possible to derive a few, certain universal duties and rights of preservation (*Essay* 4.3.18). The reason Locke and his contemporaries believed that morality could be demonstrable is their belief that moral concepts ('mixed modes' and 'relations'), like mathematical concepts, are conventional or made by the mind (3.11.16). The *Two treatises of government* is, *inter alia*, his anonymous attempt at such a demonstration.

However, Locke became sceptical of the demonstrability of the immortality of the soul and the existence of heaven and hell. Hence, even if such a code could be demonstrated, it could not provide moral motivation or obligation because we could not be certain that the rewards of heaven and the punishments of hell were attached to it. So, rather than continuing this project he turned to a different way of thinking about the rational foundation of morality, in which probability replaces demonstration.

His first step is to argue that most morality lies in the epistemic category of 'opinion', not 'knowledge', and thus is only 'probable', not demonstrably 'certain'. As a result, moral propositions are known not by the logic of demonstration but by weighing their degree of probability in accordance with the weight of the evidence, testimonies and arguments for them; and by carefully apportioning our degree of assent accordingly, from full assurance down to conjecture, guess, doubt, and distrust (*Essay* 4.15.2–4). The *Essay* is a synthesis of seventeenth-century work on this type of probability and a celebration of its usefulness in all areas of knowledge. His criteria of probability were widely adopted throughout the human and natural sciences.

If these criteria are applied to the testimony of witnesses and the evidence of miracles for the *Bible*, Locke explains in the *Essay* and *The reasonableness of Christianity*, then it is rational to believe with full assurance that the *Scripture* is a divine revelation. Moreover, to distinguish his view from the deism of John Toland, he claimed in the *Essay* 4.19 (added to the fourth edition) that it would be irrational to go on to apply the criteria of probability to the content of the *Bible*. Being a revelation, it is a separate and higher ground of assent.

Next, how do we know that Christian revelation is true? In his *Discourse of miracles* (1702) and reply to Thomas Burnet, Locke asserted, as Descartes had done earlier, it is evident from the miracles that the Christian god is the most powerful, and, therefore, because lying is a weakness, any word of the Christian god is *ipso facto* true. It follows that a demonstrable ethics is unnecessary: the Gospel provides a 'perfect body of ethics' and 'reason may be excused from that enquiry [demonstration], since she may find man's duty clearer and easier in Revelation than in herself' (*Correspondence* 5: 2059).

Once examination has shown that Christian revelation warrants the highest degree of assent, Locke's second step is to introduce his other type of probability calculation. Here, the moral agent weighs the pleasures and pains associated with each morality. The Bible states that the pleasures of heaven and the torments of hell of the all powerful Christian god far outweigh any other moral reward or punishment and that heavenly pleasures suit everyone's palate. To clinch the calculation Locke employs a version of Pascal's wager. Even if the existence of an afterlife is a 'bare possibility' it is hedonically rational to become a Christian: 'The rewards and punishments of another life, which the Almighty has established . . . are of weight enough to determine the choice, against whatever pleasure or pain this life can shew' (*Essay* 2.21.70). As he puts it in *The reasonableness*, with Christ's revelation of heaven and hell, 'interest has come about to her [virtue], and virtue is visibly the most enticing purchase and by much the best bargain' (*Works* 7: 94).

Although the *Bible* provides 'a perfect body of ethics', it is still necessary to use reason to clarify and interpret it. Thus, much of Locke's latest moral writing is concerned with developing and applying biblical hermeneutics (see *Paraphrases*). His interpretation is that Christian ethics are simple and so available to and applicable by any day labourer, without the need for religious casuists and moral philosophers. The central virtues are religious worship as one sees fit, sincerity, toleration, respect for rights, discipline, industriousness, and an overarching duty to preserve oneself and others (in opposition to the honour ethic and its glorification of war). This can be seen as a contribution to the moral affirmation of everyday life that swept across Europe in the early modern period.

The moral reform Locke advocated was to root out the scholastic and intolerant religious systems and to introduce his two types of moral reasoning and his simplified version of Christian ethics. In his educational writings he outlined a system that would weave these three into the very fabric of a student's nature by means of repetition and practice, and with the judicious application of praise and blame. In 1697 he presented a proposal to the Board of Trade for the reform of the manners of children and adults on poor relief. By forcing them into the local workhouses and subjecting them to a regime of simple, repetitive tasks of labour and the rudiments of Christian duties, backed up by gradations of physical punishments and rewards, the habits of virtue, sobriety, discipline, and industriousness could be instilled and their preservation assured.

Both aspects of Locke's moral philosophy were widely adopted in the eighteenth century. The irony is that the very forms of moral reasoning he recommended were used to expunge the soul and its final resting place which, for Locke, gave the whole enterprise its moral value.

CHAPTER 10

Political freedom

Three hundred years after the publication of the *Two treatises of government* and *A letter concerning toleration*, one aspect of Locke's thought continues to stand out in sharp contrast to the prevailing conventions of both seventeenth- and twentieth-century political theory. This is his hypothesis that institutionalized forms of government are derived from and perpetually rest upon the prior freedom of the people to exercise political power themselves (summarized at 2.171).[1] Locke had no doubt that it would 'seem a very strange Doctrine to some' in his own time (2.9). It is no less unconventional today. In the current debate between liberals and civic humanists, for example, the leading participants share the assumption that political freedom is derived from and rests upon basic institutions and traditions.[2] The aim of this paper is to enable readers to understand Locke's strange doctrine by drawing attention to its distinctive features, first by means of a synopsis and then by a series of contrasts with more conventional views.

I

Prior to the establishment of institutionalized forms of government, people are capable of exercising political power themselves in an ad-hoc manner: 'the *Execution* of the Law of Nature is in that State, put into every Man's hands' (2.7). The exercise of political power

---

[1] The numbers in brackets refer to treatises and section numbers of John Locke, *Two treatises of government*, ed. Peter Laslett (Cambridge: Cambridge University Press, 1970).

[2] John Rawls, 'Justice as fairness: political not metaphysical', *Philosophy and public affairs*, 14 (1985), 223–52; Richard Rorty, 'The priority of democracy to philosophy', M. Peterson and R. Vaughan, eds, *The Virginia statute of religious freedom* (Cambridge: Cambridge University Press, 1987); Michael Sandel, *Liberalism and the limits of justice* (Cambridge: Cambridge University Press, 1982); Charles Taylor, *Philosophical papers*, II (Cambridge: Cambridge University Press, 1985), 185–339.

comprises the abilities to know and to interpret standards of right (natural laws), to judge controversies concerning oneself and others in accordance with these laws, and to execute such judgements by punishments proportionate to the transgression and appropriate for purposes of restraint and reparation (2.7–12). Individuals are free to order their actions within the bounds of natural laws and are equal in the 'Power and Jurisdiction' to govern the actions of those who transgress these bounds (2.4, 2.6).

Since 'every one is Judge, Interpreter, and Executioner', this ad-hoc form of self-government, or individual popular sovereignty, does not run smoothly in practice (2.136). People disagree on a 'common measure to decide all Controversies between them' and they are reluctant to concede that a law is binding in their own case (2.124). They lack the motivation to participate in the ad-hoc adjudication and prosecution of disputes when the case does not concern them, and they tend to participate with passion and revenge when it does (2.125). Another reason people do not perform these duties of self-government is the danger involved in executing them against lawbreakers who forcefully resist the local arbitration proceedings (2.126; cf. 2.13, 2.136).

To overcome these difficulties people set up institutionalized forms of government. They place political power 'into the hands of the Community in all cases', and 'the Community comes to be Umpire, by settled standing Rules, . . . and by Men having Authority from the Community, for the execution of those Rules, decides all the differences . . . concerning any matter of right; and punishes . . . offences' (2.87). Thus, it is easy to tell the difference between a political society, in which people are united into one body and have authoritative institutions of law and judicature to appeal to and settle disputes, and the prior natural state from which political society derives, in which each person is judge and executioner (2.87–9). Political society is constituted by the agreement of each person to become a member of a community or '*Body Politick*' in which 'the *Majority* have a Right to act and conclude the rest' (2.95). The majority decide on a constitutional form for the community (monarchy, democracy, etc.) and place political power in the hands of the 'legislative' or law-making body (2.132, 2.134), which places the power to enforce laws in the hands of the executive (2.144–8).

Political communities and governments not only derive from, but also perpetually rest on the abilities of the citizens to judge and act politically. The political relation between governors and governed is a relationship of trust. The members entrust their political power on the condition that the governors will exercise it in accordance with the public good. If the people find that their trustees (either the executive or legislators) abuse the power given to them and 'act contrary to the trust reposed in them', the bond of obligation between governors and governed is forfeited, political power devolves 'into the hands of those that gave it', and they may use it to remove them. 'And thus', Locke emphasizes, 'the *Community* perpetually retains a *Supream Power* of saving themselves from the attempts and designs of any Body, even of their Legislators, whenever they shall be so foolish, or so wicked, as to lay and carry on designs against the Liberties and Properties of the Subject' (2.149). As he explains in more detail in the final chapter, when political power devolves to the people, they exercise it in the form of a revolution to remove their untrustworthy governors, just as they would proceed against lawbreakers prior to the establishment of legislative and executive institutions, and 'the People have a Right to act as Supreme, and continue the Legislative in themselves, or erect a new Form, or under the old form place it in new hands, as they think good' (2.243).

Who has the right to judge when the trust has been forfeited and government dissolved? Locke's answer is that '*The People shall be Judge*' and by this he means '*every Man is Judge* for himself' (2.240–1). Then, the 'Body of the *People*' should execute this judgement by forcefully removing the unjust rulers. If this fails, each person who so judges has the right to act as best one can (2.242–3; cf. 2.168). Thus, the members of a political society always stand ready and able to govern their governors if they abuse the power entrusted to them.

Locke stresses that '*this Doctrine* of a Power in the People' will not lay 'a *ferment* for frequent rebellion' (2.224–30). Even though everyone has a right to resist political authorities on the basis of their judgement that a single violation has been committed, people will not actually engage in a revolutionary contest until oppression touches the majority, or touches only a few but seems to threaten all (2.208–10, 2.230, 2.168). That is, the people are constrained by the same motivational factors that operated in the ad-hoc system of self-government. Although '*Revolutions happen* not upon every little mismanagement in publick affairs', they nevertheless do occur, as a result of the common disposition to remove the yoke of oppression, and so this hypothesis accords with the real world of politics (2.224–5).

The final claim Locke advances is that his account, in addition to being an explanation and justification of resistance to oppression, is also the best means of hindering oppression in the first place. Under any institutionalized form of government, those in power will be tempted in various ways to abuse the power entrusted to them: to develop an interest separate from and in violation of the good of the people (2.209–10, 2.228). This theme is emphasized even more emphatically in *A letter concerning toleration* where he analyses the post-Reformation case of government imposing a uniform religion, and persecuting religious dissenters.[3] The 'properest way to prevent the evil, is to show them the danger and injustice of it': that is, to confront power-holders with a citizenry who know the popular basis of government, who constantly judge the public actions of their trustees, and who are always ready and willing to exercise political power themselves when it is abused (2.226; cf. 228).

II

The distinctive features of Locke's portrayal of political freedom can now be thrown into clear relief by contrasting them with a number of seventeenth-century alternatives. First, the conventional means to check the abuse of institutionalized forms of political power are all found by Locke to be insufficient. The argument, advanced by proponents of mixed and balanced government, that representative institutions, the division of powers, and the rule of law constitute sufficient checks was falsified in practice by the ability of seventeenth-century absolute monarchs to override these limitations (2.107, 2.111–12, 2.163). Further, these institutional arrangements, while important, are not always sufficient to stop an oppressive representative body (2.138, 2.149, 2.221–2). Locke is sceptical of the republican belief that participation in government fosters citizens oriented to the public good and impervious to the temptations of power (2.156, 2.223). He also rejects the claim that as long as citizens are free to appeal to courts and parliaments they will be able to hinder oppression and thus render revolution unnecessary. Locke learned from the unsuccessful attempts by religious Dissenters in the 1660s and 1670s to gain civil and religious liberties by legitimate means that those in power could block the Dissenters' appeals, stigmatize them as

---

[3] John Locke, *A letter concerning toleration*, edited and introduced by James Tully (Indianapolis: Hackett Publishing Company, 1983).

'seditious', and introduce repressive legislation (2.218). In *A letter concerning toleration*, he argues that the separation of church and state, and a clear distinction in law between politics and religion, along with representative institutions and a Bill of Rights, while necessary, are not sufficient to defend a free and tolerant society from oppression. The ultimate guardian is again said to be the ability of the people to judge if their governors are ruling in accordance with the public good and to be ready to remove them if they are not.[4]

Second, Locke's location of political power in the people contrasts sharply with the customary beliefs of his contemporaries. The rebellions of early modern Europe were standardly understood to be non-political acts of self-defence by the people against a ruler who had attacked them. They were not thought of as political acts, because, on the conventional view, political power was never originally in the hands of the people and, consequently, could not devolve back to them. In addition, the 'people' was interpreted as either a single person acting in self-defence or an established representative of the people (usually a parliament or an estate) defending them against an attack by a monarch. Hence, the 'people' was not conceptualized as a whole body or self-organized group acting together politically on their own judgement against monarchs or representatives. Theorists of mixed and balanced government could not claim that the representative bodies, let alone the people, exercised political power in a rebellion without undermining their theory that political power always exists in a mix or balance between monarch and representative bodies. Republicans could not say that the people exercise political judgement and power outside of political institutions because they held that political judgement and power came into being with the establishment of an authoritative political community. And, all these authors agreed that the worst conceivable basis for government would be the judgement of the multitude.

These commonplaces began to appear questionable in the light of the English Civil War. In the latter phase, the people took up arms against their own representatives and they presupposed the right to exercise political power, not just to defend themselves, in trying and executing Charles I and in setting up a new form of government. Either one held to the conventional understanding, and thereby deemed this exercise of popular sovereignty illegitimate, as Kant was

[4] Locke, *A letter concerning toleration*, 52–5.

classically to do, or one reconceptualized the power of the people, and thereby deemed this judicial proceeding legitimate, as Locke did. Moreover, Locke wrote and published the *Two treatises* to justify revolt against the persecution of religious Dissenters during the Restoration. Since the Dissenters were excluded from public office and lacked sufficient support in Parliament he needed to ground the right to judge, initiate revolt and reform government in the people themselves. The extent to which Locke deviated from orthodoxy can be measured by the widespread repudiation of the *Two treatises* in 1690 because it presented an unacceptably radical interpretation of the Glorious Revolution.[5]

III

A contrast with the current debate between liberals and civic humanists can now be used to complete this survey of Locke's understanding of political freedom. Both sides start from the assumption that the foundation of a modern democratic society is the basic structure of post-Reformation institutions of representative government, the rule of law, religious toleration, and civil liberty. Accordingly, the role of the political philosopher, as Rawls typically states, is to explicate or articulate the 'basic intuitive ideas that are embedded in the political institutions of a constitutional democratic regime and the public traditions of their interpretation'.[6] This consists in making explicit the implicit consensus on conceptions of political agency and social co-operation that underlie surface disagreements and accord with the basic institutions. Despite their disagreement on what forms of political agency and co-operation best serve to support and enhance a democratic society, civic humanists are just as concerned to grant priority to political institutions, practices, and communities. Political institutions and public traditions of their interpretation, one might say, are taken to be sovereign.

The leading writers in the debate have not considered Locke's

---

[5] See Julian Franklin, *John Locke and the theory of sovereignty* (Cambridge: Cambridge University Press, 1978); Richard Ashcraft, *Revolutionary politics and Locke's Two treatises of government* (Princeton: Princeton University Press, 1986); Mark Goldie, 'The roots of true whiggism 1688–94', *History of Political Thought*, 1, 2 (1980), 195–236; Mark Goldie, 'The revolution of 1689 and the structure of political argument', *Bulletin of Research in the Humanities*, 83 (1980), 473–564; and chapter 1 above.   [6] Rawls, 'Justice', 225.

opposite hypothesis that political institutions and traditions rest upon the political freedom and popular sovereignty of the people. Instead, they have misinterpreted Locke from within their very different conceptual framework and, as a result, assimilated him to either Hobbes or Benjamin Constant, both of whom share their premise of institutional sovereignty. With Locke's hypothesis elegantly disposed of in this preemptive fashion, there is no reason to test it by actually studying the now 300-year-old tradition of popular sovereignty and the practical roles its proponents may have played in hindering the abuse of institutionalized political power. Rather, the conventional institutional theories, which Locke found insufficient to explain how concentrated political power can be held in check, have been recirculated as the solutions to contemporary problems.

This anti-Lockean consensus can be partly explained by the theoretical sources of the debate. Liberals draw on Kant, who lays it down that the basic structure of law and its agent is sovereign, not the consent of the governed, and can never rightfully be disobeyed.[7] Civic humanists draw on Aristotle, Cicero, Machiavelli, Rousseau, and Hegel, all of whom concur that the necessary precondition of, and limitation on political judgement and action is an established and authoritative political community. Moreover, the assumption that the institutions and practices of modern societies are the *de facto* and *de jure* basis of political thought and action is also accepted by many theorists who do not draw on these sources.

Ever since the Reaction to the French Revolution and the attack on Lockean popular sovereignty by Burke and Bentham, there has been a widespread tendency to take political, social, and economic institutions as foundational and then to ask what forms of freedom are compatible with them. Benjamin Constant, for example, set forth this picture of the relation between freedom and institutions in a form that has become the 'horizon' of modern political thought for many liberal thinkers.[8] Revolution as well has been reconceptualized as a social movement caused by the underlying social and economic institutions of the modern world, rather than as a political action in response to misgovernment. This tendency has served to re-establish the traditional picture of politics that Locke sought to challenge: political

---

[7] John R. Wallach, 'Liberals, communitarians, and the tasks of political theory', *Political Theory*, 15, 4 (November 1987), 581–611, 587–8.

[8] Benjamin Constant, 'The liberty of the ancients compared with that of the moderns', in *Political writings*, ed. Biancamaria Fontana (Cambridge: Cambridge University Press, 1988).

freedom derives from and rests upon the representative and constitutional structures of early modern Europe.

The main theoretical argument against Locke's theory is that the
abilities to judge and act politically are acquired through practice
and practice presupposes and takes place in the context of practices –
political institutions and communities. Therefore, to rest these
institutions on the prior abilities of the people to judge and act
politically is a philosophical mistake as well as a recipe for anarchy
and confusion in practice.

Since Locke wrote extensively on how abilities to judge and act are
acquired by practice in practices, it is difficult to believe that he
overlooked this point when he came to write the *Two treatises*.[9]
Rather, the mistake may lie with his opponents. Their assumption
appears to be that political abilities are acquired in canonical
political institutions: namely, exactly those political institutions
occupied by members whose overlapping consensus of judgements
and actions is said to be authoritative. So, the judgements and actions
of those who are outside these institutions, or are critical of them, will
be, by definition, unreliable and illegitimate. Locke was of course
familiar with this form of argument, used for example by Anglican
royalists against Dissenters, and he devoted most of book 1 of *An essay
concerning human understanding* to exposing its self-validating circular-
ity.[10]

The argument is mistaken because people are able to acquire and
exercise political abilities outside the canonical institutions and
communities. Indeed, they often acquire them through the experience of exclusion from and oppression by these institutions. The
Dissengers' struggle for religious toleration and political enfranchise-
ment, the European women's movements, and Amerindian self-
government are well-known examples of this. Further, according to
Locke, the faculty of judgement, even though it is always developed in
the context of a practice or institution, involves the reflexive ability to
suspend and examine the authoritative traditions of that practice
itself. The mutual relation of conditional trust between citizens and

---

[9] See chapter 6 above and the reply by John Dunn, 'Bright enough for all our purposes: John
Locke's conception of a civilised society', *Notes and records of the Royal Society in London*, 43
(1989), 133–53.

[10] John Locke, *An essay concerning human understanding*, ed. Peter Nidditch (Oxford: Clarendon
Press, 1975), 1.3.20–2; cf. 1.4.22–6. Rorty has carried this form of argument further in 'Thugs
and theorists', *Political Theory* 15, 4 (November 1987), 564–80.

governors turns on this transcendent feature of critical political judgement.[11] Finally, his opponents' argument cannot explain how political institutions are set up or changed. Either they must be taken for granted, as in the current debate, or a mythical legislator is required, as in the republican tradition. Locke's hypothesis, on the other hand, enables a person to conceptualize how the institutions both Locke and his adversaries value were established and continue to be open to change and improvement.

The major pragmatic argument against Locke's theory is that members of modern societies are shaped and constituted by the massive and complex institutions of power and authority. Therefore, from a sociological point of view, their judgements and actions derive from and rest upon these institutions rather than *vice versa*. The absence of revolutions in Europe since 1789 is often said to support this and to falsify the theory of popular sovereignty.

In reply, one might point to the remarkable revolutions that occurred in eastern European countries over the winter of 1989–90. These outbreaks of popular sovereignty were neither predicted by nor did they conform to the social and economic theories of revolution available in the social sciences. The people involved did not have the background representative institutions that are said to be necessary to foster political freedom and judgement. Nor did they have the experience of participating in republican institutions in order to develop civic virtue and discern the common good. Their activity of civil dissent prior to the revolutions was also insufficient to reform their governments. Yet, for all that, their revolts were not simply acts of self-defence. The people claimed to respond to political oppression by governments whom they judged to have forfeited their trust (often in these terms). They proceeded to overthrow their governors, to put them on trial and punish them, and went on to set up new forms of government and new governors, as they thought good.

---

[11] For one way of working out this line of argument, see James Tully, 'Wittgenstein and political philosophy', *Political Theory*, 17, 2 (May 1989), 172–204.

Index

abilities, rights in, 5, 242–61
aboriginal rights, 137–76
absolute monarchy, 35–6, 318
absolutism
  enlightened, 92
  liberty and natural law, 304
  natural freedom theory of, 17–18, 41–2, 44
  and natural law theories, 101–2
  and natural liberty, 287, 288, 289, 290–1
  and political power, 30–1, 37
accusatory system of justice, 21–2, 23, 28, 35
action, 201–25
  and morality, 212–34, 309
agriculture, in the American colonies, 156, 159, 160–6, 168–9
Ailly, Pierre d', 288
Alembert, Jean d', 267
alienation, and political power, 29–32
Almain, Jacques, 288
Althusser, Louis, 98
America
  Amerindian government, 151–5
  justification of Amerindian dispossession in, 4, 86, 142–51, 165–76
  and aboriginal rights, 137–40, 141
Anglican Church, see Church of England
Anti-scepticism (Lee), 185–6
Aquinas, Saint Thomas, 103, 106, 202, 203, 204, 205, 300
  and natural liberty, 288, 289, 291
Argenson, Louis de, 267
Aristotle, 44, 202, 223, 253, 259, 283, 296, 303, 304, 321
armed forces
  Dutch army reforms, 249
  standing armies, 55, 56
Arnauld, Antoine, 308
Ashcraft, Richard, 4, 80, 84, 127, 129, 131, 133, 136

assent, theories of, 183–201, 266
  subversive, 186–8
atheism, 54, 57, 201, 209, 306
atomic warfare, 74, 75
atomism, 206
Atwood, William, 43, 131
automation, 257–60

Babbage, Charles, 257
Bacon, Francis, 204, 207
Bagshawe, Edward, 50
Baldwin, T.R., on Locke and property, 118–22
Barbeyrac, Jean, 109, 111, 115, 121
Barclay, William, 17, 18, 29
  and resistance theory, 41–2
Bayle, Pierre, 9, 197, 208
Beard, Charles, 263
beggars, Locke's proposals for dealing with, 235–6
belief, 183–201
  probable, 194–9
Bellers, John, 247, 249
Bentham, Jeremy, 76, 77, 80, 92, 262, 269, 321
Berlin, Sir Isaiah, 1, 6, 284, 292, 298
Biard, Pierre, 163
Blackstone, Sir William, 108, 170
Blum, Carol, 90
Bohun, Edmund, 16
Bold, Samuel, 192
Boyle, Robert, 183, 202, 203, 204, 205, 206, 213, 238, 308
Braverman, Harry, 123, 254
Buchanan, George, 19, 25, 288
  and resistance theory, 41, 42, 44
Bulkley, Reverend John, 166–7, 168
Burke, Edmund, 76, 271, 321
Burnet, Thomas, 201, 230, 313
Burthogge, Richard, 197, 200

Ideas in context

Edited by Quentin Skinner (general editor), Lorraine Daston, Wolf Lepenies, Richard Rorty and J. B. Schneewind

Forthcoming titles include works by Martin Dzelzainis, Mark Goldie, Noel Malcolm, Roger Mason, James Moore, Nicolai Rubinstein, Quentin Skinner, Martin Warnke and Robert Wokler.

Titles marked with an asterisk are also available in paperback